CACHE LEVEL 3

Diploma in Supporting Teaching and Learning

» Louise Burnham

Orders: please contact Bookpoint Ltd, 130 Park Drive, Milton Park, Abingdon, Oxon OX14 4SE. Telephone: +44 (0)1235 827720. Fax: +44 (0)1235 400401. Email education@bookpoint.co.uk Lines are open from 9 a.m. to 5 p.m., Monday to Saturday, with a 24-hour message answering service. You can also order through our website: www.hoddereducation.co.uk

ISBN: 9781510427259

First published in 2018 by

Hodder Education,

An Hachette UK Company

Carmelite House

50 Victoria Embankment

London EC4Y 0DZ

www.hoddereducation.co.uk

Impression number 3

Year 2019

Illustrations by Aptara Inc.

Typeset in Palatino LT Std Roman 10.5/13.5 pts by Aptara Inc.

Printed in Dubai

A catalogue record for this title is available from the British Library.

Contents

Answers to the 'Check your understanding' questions can be found online at:
www.hoddereducation.co.uk/Product?Product=9781510427259

How to use this book

Key features of the book

Learning outcomes

By the end of this unit you will:

LO1 Understand the structure of education from early years to post-compulsory education

LO2 Understand how schools and colleges are organised in terms of roles and responsibilities

Prepare for what you are going to cover in the unit.

Getting started

What can you remember about your earliest play experiences? How did you feel? What did you enjoy doing?

Activities or discussions to help you to start thinking about the unit topic.

LO1 Understand what is required for competence in your work role

AC 1.1 Describe the duties and responsibilities of your work role

Learning outcomes and assessment criteria are listed in the same order as in the specification to help you to find your way through the text.

Activity

Produce a leaflet for pupils with whom you work explaining the risks they face online and how to reduce them.

Practical tasks to support your learning.

In practice

What is the policy of your setting when taking pupils on off-site visits? How are staff and volunteers given safeguarding advice and guidance?

Real-life situations that show how theory links to practice.

Case study

You are working in a secondary school and some of the Year 10 pupils have come to you and said that they would like to set up a trampoline club.

1 What would you do first?
2 What else would you need to consider?

Scenarios that explore the kinds of issues you may come across and pose questions about how you might resolve them.

Research it

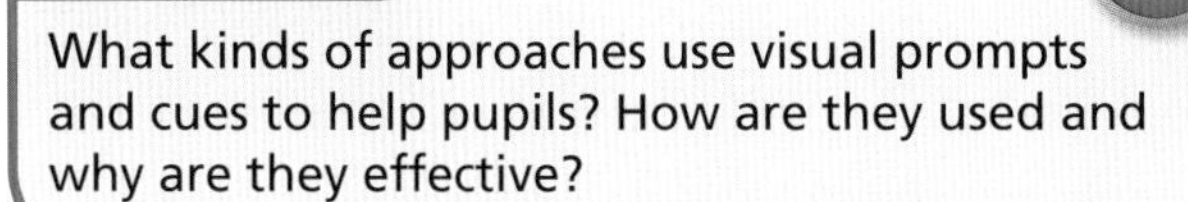

What kinds of approaches use visual prompts and cues to help pupils? How are they used and why are they effective?

Ideas to enable you to explore the topic in more depth.

Tips for best practice: safeguarding

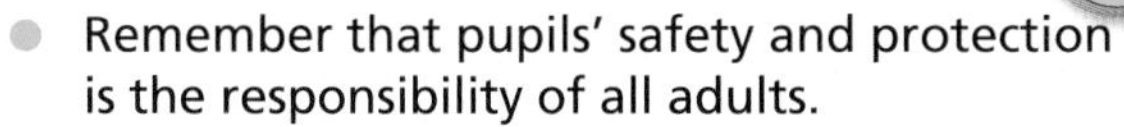

- Remember that pupils' safety and protection is the responsibility of all adults.
- Be clear on your school or college's safeguarding policy.

Guidance for dos and don'ts in a real learning environment.

Stretch and challenge

What can you find out about the relationship between bilingualism and cognitive development?

More challenging scenarios or research ideas.

Class discussion

What kinds of barriers to professional relationships have you faced in your current or previous roles? Discuss with others how these have come about and how you have overcome them.

Questions to prompt debate and discussion.

Key term

Policies and procedures: the principles, rules and guidelines agreed and adopted by the organisation.

A feature to help you to understand the meaning of important terms.

Check your understanding

1 What are the four main areas of development?
2 How do the four areas of development overlap with one another?

Questions at the end of each unit to test your understanding.

Assessment preparation

1 Some of the activities for this unit invite you to write reflective accounts to cover the evidence (LO1, AC 1.1, 1.2, 1.3).
2 For LO2, AC 2.1 and 2.2, unless covered by one of the methods above, you will need to write a list of the different roles and outline their main responsibilities.

Ideas for how to evidence the assessment criteria.

Legislation

- Human Rights Act, Article 2
- UN Convention on the Rights of the Child

A brief summary of the legislation covered in the unit, if applicable.

Read about it

Reference books

Bosanquet, P., Radford, J. and Webster, R. (2016)
The Teaching Assistant's Guide to Effective Interaction: How to Maximise your Practice, Routledge.

Weblinks

www.gov.uk/national-curriculum National Curriculum documents for primary and secondary schools

Suggestions for further reading, websites and useful resources.

Acknowledgements

From the author

I would like to thank Stephen Halder and Imogen Miles from Hodder Education for their support and advice during the writing of this book. I would also like to thank Amy Nicholls, Mogbolahan Koya-Oyagbola, Janet Scott and Janet King at CACHE for their guidance and comments.

As always I would like to acknowledge my colleagues and pupils at Unicorn Primary School in Beckenham, Kent for their support and inspiration.

Dedication

In loving memory of my father, Geoffrey Burnham.

Picture credits

The Publishers would like to thank the following for permission to reproduce copyright material.

p.1 © Mark Bowden/iStockphoto/Getty Images/Thinkstock; p.5 © Monkey Business – Fotolia; p.6 © MBI / Alamy Stock Photo; p.10 © Fairview Primary School; p.14 © 2010 Zero Creatives/photolibrary.com; p.16 © Blend Images / Alamy Stock Photo; p.21 left © BSI Group, right © European Commission; p.22 © Maksym Yemelyanov/stock.adobe.com; p.31 © David Leahy/DigitalVision/Getty Images - UK_Education_DV1183; p.35 © shorrocks/Getty Images; p.48 left © alexsokolov/iStockphoto/Getty Images/Thinkstock, right © ilona75/123RF.com; p.53 © Juice Images / Alamy Stock Photo; p.55 © Monkey Business/stock.adobe.com; p.61 © Rawpixel – Fotolia; p.69 © jovannig/stock.adobe.com; p.73 © karelnoppe/stock.adobe.com; p.74 © oocoskun/stock.adobe.com; p.76 © martinan/123RF.com; p.77 © Ian Miles-Flashpoint Pictures / Alamy Stock Photo; p.78 © JackF/stock.adobe.com; p.79 © Purestock/Thinkstock; p.81 © ehrenberg-bilder/stock.adobe.com; p.95 © pololia/stock.adobe.com; p.97 © Cheam High School; p.98 © Monkey Business/stock.adobe.com; p.100 © Ashgrove Primary School; p.101 © Monkey Business/stock.adobe.com; p.110 © Tyler Olson – Fotolia; p.115 © ALPA PROD/Shutterstock.com; p.123 left © Cultura Creative (RF) / Alamy Stock Photo, right © Blue Jean Images / Alamy Stock Photo; p.127 © lovethephoto / Alamy Stock Photo; p.131 © Blend Images / Alamy Stock Photo; p.147 © Monkey Business/stock.adobe.com; p.149 © Rawpixel.com/stock.adobe.com; p.152 © Westend61 GmbH / Alamy Stock Photo; p.155 © Frank Coenders / Alamy Stock Photo; p.157 © Barry Diomede / Alamy Stock Photo; p.158 © Monkey Business/stock.adobe.com; p.163 © Antonioguillem/stock.adobe.com; p.165 © Image Source / Alamy Stock Photo; p.169 © contrastwerkstatt/stock.adobe.com; p.173 © Hero Images Inc. / Alamy Stock Photo; p.174 © auremar/stock.adobe.com; p.184 © lordn/stock.adobe.com; p.188 © Oksana Kuzmina/stock.adobe.com; p.194 © wonderlandstock / Alamy Stock Photo; p.195 © age fotostock / Alamy Stock Photo; p.203 © Sergey Novikov/stock.adobe.com; p.208 © Angela Hampton Picture Library / Alamy Stock Photo; p.215 © Ian Shaw / Alamy Stock Photo; p.218 © Clare Coe / Alamy Stock Photo; p.220 © BSIP SA / Alamy Stock Photo; p.224 © Hammersmith and Fulham Council; p.230 © Angela Hampton Picture Library / Alamy Stock Photo; p.233 © Blend Images / Alamy Stock Photo; p.236 © Hero Images Inc. / Alamy Stock Photo; p.238 © Picture Partners / Alamy Stock Photo; p.244 © Purestock / Alamy Stock Photo; p.246 © dglimages/stock.adobe.com; p.250 © Galina Barskaya/stock.adobe.com; p.252 © Peter Titmuss / Alamy Stock Photo; p.254 © Monkey Business/stock.adobe.com; p.259 © Ian Allenden / Alamy Stock Photo

1 Schools and colleges as organisations

About this unit

This unit is about preparing you to work in a learning environment, whether this is in a primary, secondary or special school, or in a college. It describes the structure of education and different choices for children and young people from early years to post-16 in all UK Home Nations. The unit also looks at how schools and colleges are organised, and the purpose of key policies and procedures. You will also need to know about the role of different members of staff, as well as some of the external professionals who may come into the school or college to work with pupils.

Learning outcomes

By the end of this unit you will:

LO1 Understand the structure of education from early years to post-compulsory education

LO2 Understand how schools and colleges are organised in terms of roles and responsibilities

LO3 Understand teamwork in schools and colleges

LO4 Understand educational ethos, mission, aims and values

LO5 Understand the purpose of policies and procedures in education

Getting started

Education is something that we all experience, but everyone's experience will be different. Write a list of the different settings you attended, from the earliest stage you remember up until post-16, and discuss with others. How do they differ? What do they have in common?

LO1 Understand the structure of education from early years to post-compulsory education

AC 1.1 Summarise types of early years provision

Early years provision can start from when a child is just a few weeks old. Although not all parents will return straight to work, there is a wide range of settings and provision available for those who wish to do so. Early years provision may be statutory, voluntary or private – in other words, it can be run by local authorities, charity or voluntary organisations, or be privately owned and run for profit. It covers different types of settings – for example, childminders, school- or work-based nurseries and out of school clubs. Childcare settings that are registered to run early years care and education for children will need to follow the Early Years Foundation Stage (EYFS) framework. This is a set of standards that must be followed in order to make sure that children 'learn and develop well and are kept healthy and safe' (EYFS statutory framework). If settings are registered and inspected by Ofsted, they will need to show how they are meeting the quality and standards of provision.

▼ Table 1.1 Types of early years setting

Type of setting	Description	Age of children
Registered childminder	A registered childminder will look after the child in their home and be self-employed. They will need to be registered and inspected by Ofsted, and again offer flexible and individualised care for children. They can look after up to six children between the ages of birth and 8 years, including their own.	0–8 years and above
School-based nursery	A school-based nursery will be attached to an infant or primary school, and will usually be for children who are expected to move on to that school. It will run only in term time. The age at which such settings take children will vary according to the school and type of provision, but may start from 2 years in an independent school. However, a school-based nursery will usually start the year before a child begins full-time education in reception, so will take children aged around 4 years.	Varies, but may be from 2 years
Reception class	A school reception class will start during the year of the child's 5th birthday. Children may start by attending on a half-day basis but will quickly build up to a full day. School-based settings will be registered and inspected by Ofsted.	4–5 years
Children's centre	Children's centres offer a range of different services for children under 5 and their families. They may be located on school sites through extended schools or based in local authority accommodation. These services may vary between different areas but may include health and support for families with young children. They also usually include play centres where parents can attend with their children on any day and time that is available.	0–5 years

Day nursery	A day nursery must be registered and inspected by Ofsted and is usually open all day. There may be different types of provision – for example, private, voluntary and workplace based. Some will have longer hours and will be open during evenings and weekends.	0–5 years
Out of school clubs and play centres	These are clubs that are run for school-age children before and after school and may run during school holidays.	4 years and above
Parent and toddler group	These are drop-in sessions for parents of young children, and are usually run by volunteers and other parents. Parents will have responsibility for their children while they are on site.	0–3 years
Playgroup/ preschool	A playgroup or preschool may be run by parents – or children may be left in the care of staff. If children are left in the care of staff, the preschool must be registered with Ofsted. They are usually run on a voluntary basis during term time and have sessions lasting around three hours.	2–5 years
Workplace nursery	This provides care and education for children at the place where their parents work.	3 months and over
Nanny/home carer	A nanny is a carer who is employed by a child's parents to look after the child in their own home. Nannies will often look after more than one child if needed and are usually very flexible. However, although many do have training, they are not required to have qualifications.	0–5 years and over
Crèche	A crèche will provide interim care for children from time to time while their parents are engaged in a one-off activity such as shopping or sport, usually on the same premises. They are not required to register with Ofsted but can choose to do so.	Varies

Type of provision

Voluntary

This means provision that has been set up and funded by donations and voluntary contributions. It may, for example, be run by a charity or church group in the local community, and parents may have to pay a donation to help cover costs. In some cases parents or carers may stay and supervise their children so that they can socialise with others, but the way in which these operate may vary. If children are left with staff, the setting will need to be registered with and inspected by Ofsted.

Private

This means that parents will need to pay for the provision as it is run privately. This may include settings such as crèche, a workplace nursery, private day nursery or a childminder's home. These settings will need to be registered with and inspected by Ofsted if they are providing regular care and education for children. For example, a childminder will need to be registered and inspected, but a crèche that may just provide care from time to time, does not.

Statutory

This term is used for settings that are government funded as they have to be available by law, such as schools. They will be registered and inspected by Ofsted. They may also be known as 'maintained' settings.

Independent

This term is usually used for independent schools that are not paid for by government or state funding, so parents will be charged for them. Independent schools will still have to follow the EYFS framework and are also inspected by Ofsted.

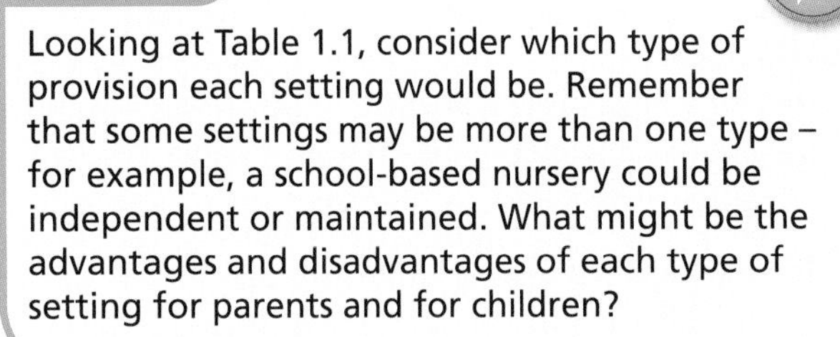

Activity

Looking at Table 1.1, consider which type of provision each setting would be. Remember that some settings may be more than one type – for example, a school-based nursery could be independent or maintained. What might be the advantages and disadvantages of each type of setting for parents and for children?

AC 1.2 Identify key stages of the statutory framework for learning in your UK Home Nation

You will need to know about and be able to describe the key stages of your own statutory framework for learning in your UK Home Nation. This means the way in which the structure of education is broken down by age and stage.

England

In England, the Early Years Foundation Stage (EYFS) framework provides guidance for babies and children from birth to 5 years old. It therefore covers both school nurseries and reception classes. Following the EYFS, the curriculum is split into key stages, as follows:

- Key Stage 1 – Years 1 and 2, between the ages of 5 and 7 years
- Key Stage 2 – Years 3 to 6, between the ages of 7 and 11 years
- Key Stage 3 – Years 7 to 9, between the ages of 11 and 14 years
- Key Stage 4 – Years 10 and 11, between the ages of 14 and 16 years.

Wales

The curriculum is split by a Foundation Phase for pupils from 3 to 7 years, replacing and incorporating Key Stage 1. The rest of the key stages remain the same as for England.

Northern Ireland

In Northern Ireland, Primary 1 and 2 are ages 4 to 6 and are part of the Foundation Stage. In addition:

- Key Stage 1 covers Primary 3 and 4, and ages 6–8
- Key Stage 2 covers Primary 5, 6 and 7, and ages 8–11
- Key Stage 3 covers Years 8 to 10, and ages 11–14
- Key Stage 4 covers Years 11 and 12, and ages 14–16.

Scotland

- P1 (Early Level) is the equivalent to reception in England, ages 4–5
- P2–P4 (First Level) runs from ages 6–8
- P5–P7 (Second Level) runs from ages 8–11
- S1–S3 (Third/Fourth Level) runs from ages 11–14
- S4–S5 (Senior Phase) runs from ages 14–16.

> **Activity**
>
> Write an account, in your own words, of the structure of education and statutory framework for learning including the Foundation Stage in your UK Home Nation, or what you use if you are in an international school. You can then use this account as evidence to cover AC 1.1 and 1.2.

Other

In Gibraltar and most international schools, key stages are the same as in England.

AC 1.3 Explain post-16 options for young people and adults

The options for young people in the UK post-16 will also vary according to their Home Nation. This may involve staying at school or transferring to a further education college to study A levels, undertake an apprenticeship or study towards a full-time vocational programme.

England

In England, young people born after 1 September 1997 must stay in education and training until they are 18. This may involve staying at school or transferring to a further education college to study A levels or other qualifications such as HNDs, or going into an apprenticeship or traineeship. These are designed to combine on-the-job training with continuing study, and also give young people a chance to get into the workplace and earn money. These courses can be applied for while pupils are still in school.

In addition, the International Baccalaureate (IB) for pupils from 16–19 years old is offered by increasing numbers of independent and state schools in the UK, as well as to students in international schools. It leads to the IB Diploma, which is recognised by many universities.

Wales

In Wales, if pupils are 16 before the end of the summer holidays of that academic year, they can leave school on the last Friday in June. As well as making the decision whether to continue to study A levels in a school or college, or study towards

▲ Figure 1.1 Do you know the options available post-16 in your UK Home Nation?

an apprenticeship of a full-time vocational area of learning, young people in Wales are able to apply for a job without training.

Northern Ireland

In Northern Ireland, if pupils are 16 during the academic year (1 September to 1 July) they will be able to leave school after 30 June. If they are 16 between 2 July and 31 August they will not be able to leave school until 30 June the following academic year. Pupils can stay on at school, go to sixth-form college, do a training course or apprenticeship or go into employment.

Scotland

In Scotland, if pupils are 16 between 1 March and 30 September, they can leave school after 31 May of that academic year. If they are 16 between 1 October and the end of February they can leave at the beginning of the Christmas holidays in that academic year. S6 (Senior Phase) runs from ages 16–18 and is non-compulsory (A levels and SCE Highers), and young people are also offered a place in training between their 16th and 20th birthdays if they are not in education.

> **In practice**
>
> Outline the options for post-16 pupils in your UK Home Nation. If you have been involved in supporting or advising young people in this age group as to their choices, write a reflective account stating how you have set out the options available to them.

LO2 Understand how schools and colleges are organised in terms of roles and responsibilities

AC 2.1 Explain the role held by: governors, senior management team, other statutory roles (e.g. SENCo), teachers/tutors, support staff

All school and college staff will be organised into roles and responsibilities and will have job descriptions outlining what these are. You should know about and understand the roles of governors and key members of staff in your school or college. This is because you should know about how your role fits in to the overall organisation, as well as who to approach or ask for advice where needed.

Governors

All state schools and colleges in England, Wales and Northern Ireland must have a governing body or board who meet as a whole at least three times a year. Many independent schools will also elect to have governing bodies, although this is not statutory. The role of governors is to discuss the running and strategic management of the organisation as well as to support the work of the principal or head teacher. They will also monitor the progress of the school or college, and set objectives and targets that form part of its Development Plan. They may be involved in appointing new staff, meeting parents, reviewing

▲ Figure 1.2 How much do you know about the role of a governor?

exclusions, managing budgets, and deciding on priorities for the school or college.

As well as meeting as a full group, there will also be smaller governing body committees. These may include finance, staffing, facilities, curriculum and others. There will usually be between ten and twenty elected governors depending on the size and organisation of the setting and they will be from different groups:

- **Parent governors** – these will be present or past parents of children or young people in the school or college
- **Staff governors** – these will be members of staff. The head teacher will automatically be one of these, but does not have to attend. Their number should include one teacher and one member of support staff
- **Co-opted governors** – these governors will be members of the local community. They will usually have a skill set that is helpful to the running of the organisation – for example, a background in finance or personnel management
- **Authority governors** – these governors are nominated by the local authority
- **Foundation, partnership and sponsor governors** – these are governors who are representatives of sponsors of the organisation.

Governors are unpaid, although they may claim expenses. They are likely to be offered training and support through their local authority, government or other organisations.

In practice

Find out what you can about the governing body of your setting. How big is it? What are the different committees and how regularly do they meet? Is this information easy to find, and are roles within the governing body clear to staff and parents?

Senior management team (SMT)

The members of the senior management team of a school or college will work together very closely to monitor and discuss a range of issues, as well as the day-to-day running of the setting. They will also closely monitor teaching and learning, and staff development. The SMT will be made up of the head teacher or principal, deputy and other more experienced managers within the organisation. Schools and colleges may structure their management responsibilities in different ways depending on the size of the organisation but there are likely to be curriculum/department, programme area, year group leaders or key stage co-ordinators within the team. The special educational needs co-ordinator (SENCo) may also be a member of the SMT.

Other statutory roles (e.g. SENCo)

As well as a head teacher and deputy or assistant head teachers, schools will need to have a SENCo who will oversee and implement the special educational needs (SEN) policy. The SENCo will also:

- support the identification and monitor the progress of pupils who have special educational needs or disabilities and ensure that they have access to the support they need to access the curriculum
- provide guidance to teachers and support staff in order to implement Education, Health and Care (EHC) plans
- meet with pupils, parents, teachers, tutors, and professionals who are external to the setting in order to support the needs of these pupils
- keep records of SEN pupils up to date and confidential
- work closely with the head teacher and the special educational needs governor.

A further education (FE) college does not have to have a SENCo but will need to have a named person to ensure that students with SEN are supported and that this is regularly reviewed. Colleges will need to follow the Special Educational Needs and Disability (SEND) Code of Practice and allow such students to attend if they are named on their EHC plan.

For more on supporting pupils with SEND, see Unit 14, page 218.

In addition, primary schools will also need to have an early years co-ordinator to oversee the Early Years Foundation Stage (EYFS) and to monitor pupil progress with senior leaders.

Teachers/tutors

The main role of all teachers and tutors is to plan and deliver lessons based on the needs of all pupils and carry out assessment and evaluation. They will also have responsibility for:

- keeping records of learner progress and needs
- promoting equality, diversity and inclusion within the setting
- working within school or college policies and procedures
- contributing to the work of the school or college team
- contributing to the wider work of the school or college (school or college fairs, productions, community cohesion)
- ensuring the health and safety of pupils at all times
- communicating with parents and discussing pupil progress
- other specialist responsibilities, such as curriculum leadership or management roles.

In the FE sector, as well as teachers and tutors there may also be individuals who perform 'associate' teacher roles (Associate Teacher Learning and Skills, or ATLS, status). This is usually if they are working towards a full teaching qualification so they will have fewer responsibilities than a teacher or tutor.

Activity

Find out about and write a reflective account describing the support staff roles discussed here and any more in your setting. If you can find job descriptions easily, you might prefer to highlight and write about these, and use them for your portfolio as a work product.

Case study

Andy has been working as a support assistant in a special school for four months. He was told at interview that he would be given a job description when he started but has not heard any more about it.

1. Should Andy say anything? If so, to whom?
2. Give reasons for your answer.

Support staff roles

There is now a wide range of support staff in schools and colleges who sustain and enhance the work of the setting. Their roles will all differ as they offer a range of support to teaching staff:

- office/administration staff and business managers
- learning support and teaching assistants
- site staff such as caretakers
- specialist staff such as computer technicians.

AC 2.2 Identify external professionals who may work in education

Although you may not work with external professionals as part of your role, you should know about them and what they do. The roles of some of these external professionals are discussed elsewhere in the book – where this is the case you will find a unit reference and page number.

Educational psychologist – see Unit 5, Table 5.6, page 92.

Speech and language therapist – see Unit 5, Table 5.6, page 92.

School nurse – see Unit 5, Table 5.6, page 92.

Tips for best practice: understanding schools and colleges

- Be clear on your own type of school or college.
- Make sure you know about the key members of staff in your organisation and who is in the senior management team.
- Read about the work of the governors and the current priorities for development.
- Find out how your school or college is supported externally by other professionals and organisations.

Home schools and colleges liaison officer

This role involves working with parents and carers to ensure that pupils maintain regular attendance in the setting. At some schools and colleges they will be part of the staff, however, local authorities may also provide this support through their education welfare service.

Child and adolescent mental health advisor

The role of these advisors, usually within CAMHS (Child and Adolescent Mental Health Service) is to work with children and young people, as well as their parents, through the assessment process and to ensure that they are given access to the services they need. These may include specialist support such as counselling, cognitive behavioural therapy (CBT), child psychotherapy, child and adolescent psychiatrists and family therapy.

SENCo – see AC 2.1, page 6.

PANCO

The role of the physical activity and nutrition co-ordinator (PANCO) has been developed by early years professionals for those working with young children. Their role is to work in a similar way to the SENCo, and to promote health and well-being in young children.

Social worker – see Unit 5, Table 5.6, page 92.

Research it

Can you find out about any other external professionals who may come into schools and colleges to support the work of pupils? Write a brief description of each and of what they do.

LO3 Understand teamwork in schools and colleges

AC 3.1 List characteristics of effective teamwork

When you are working in a school or a college, as well as being a member of staff you will be part of different teams. These may be year group teams, support staff teams, subject or department-based teams, and so on. You may also meet with external professionals to discuss the progress of an individual pupil. These different teams will meet from time to time to discuss how you are working together to meet the needs of pupils. In order to work together effectively, a team will need to have a number of characteristics.

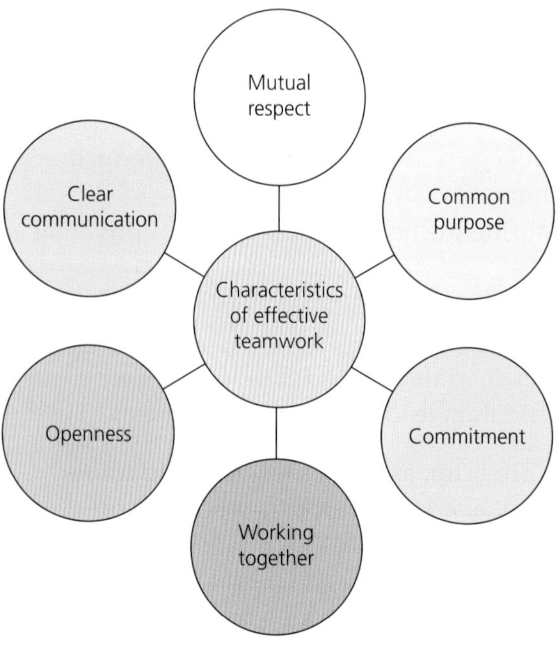

▲ Figure 1.3 Characteristics of effective teamwork

Activity

Look at the different teams in which you work at your school or college. Using the subheadings below to guide you, list examples of the ways they demonstrate the characteristics of effective teamwork. You can then use this for your portfolio.

Mutual respect

Members of the team should show respect to one another and value the contributions of their colleagues. In this way they will be able to work more collaboratively towards team objectives.

Common purpose

All team members should have a common purpose and shared vision so that each member knows what they want to achieve as a group.

Commitment

It is important that each person in the team is committed and motivated towards the work of the team.

Working together

It is important that the team members work together and that the group agenda is more important than that of the individual.

Openness

This means openness with one another so that any issues can be resolved. It is also about being open to change within the team as well as the organisation.

Clear communication

This is vital in any team (see AC 3.2 below).

AC 3.2 Explain the role of communication in establishing professional relationships for effective teamwork

Communication is essential to effective teamwork and it is important that there are frequent opportunities for members of the team to discuss day-to-day issues that will come up. In a busy school or college environment, it is easy to forget to pass on information, or for it to go to some people and not to others through informal channels. This can cause problems for the effectiveness of the team and also issues between individuals if people think they have been missed out. For teamwork to be effective, there should be regular meetings and formal opportunities to discuss ongoing items.

Stretch and challenge

Individuals will all have their own ideas and ways of working, and however well groups of people work together, there will be times when a dispute or disagreement threatens the stability of the team. Investigate different ways of dealing with team conflict to find out how the team can turn this into an opportunity for growth and development.

Clear communication between members of the team will also make the team more efficient and team relationships more professional. If meetings are regular and result in action points for team members, this will provide a structure as well as a record of what has been agreed, and will ensure that all team members have an opportunity to contribute. In this way, the team can ensure that things are dealt with as they arise and each member will know that their contribution is valued.

You should remember that communication is not only verbal, there will also be letters, emails and other written methods you will need to check and respond to regularly. Important information may be sent using these methods and require a response, usually as soon as possible. Acknowledging the importance of a prompt reply is another way of showing that you are professional.

See Unit 4, LO5, page 63, for more advice on effective communication.

LO4 Understand educational ethos, mission, aims and values

AC 4.1 Explain how the ethos, mission, aims and values of an educational setting may be reflected in working practices

You will need to know about these terms as they may be on your school or college website and on other literature such as the prospectus. They may overlap slightly with one another and appear together or under joint headings.

Ethos

This is the 'spirit' of the organisation and its value system. It should be agreed by all staff and governors, and may depend on the type of school or college – for example, a parochial or faith school may have a more spiritual element to its ethos. It is likely to state that the organisation will support pupils to fulfil their potential in all areas. A positive school or college ethos is very important as it will have an impact on many areas such as behaviour management, pupil achievement and the ways in which staff and pupils support one another.

Mission

This means the statement outlining what your place of work sets out to do. For example, some colleges might have a mission that sets out to foster 'inspirational learning for all' or 'to inspire outstanding learners to have outstanding futures'.

In practice

Without looking at your school or college website, what do you know about the ethos of your setting? Talk in groups about whether you are able to define what it is about your setting that determines its ethos and how it influences your working practice.

School Aims

To provide opportunities within a broad and balanced curriculum so that each child can achieve success and can fulfil his or her potential.

To develop rounded individuals socially, emotionally, spiritually, physically and creatively.

To value independence and enable our pupils to become responsible citizens and lifelong learners.

To provide a welcoming, safe and stimulating environment where everyone is listened to and respected.

To encourage and enable the continuous professional development of staff, ensuring effective communication between all.

To display a commitment towards making Fairview a sustainable school, actively focusing on a wide range of environmental issues.

To nurture strong partnerships and positive relationships with parents, carers and the wider community.

To recognise and celebrate success in all aspects of school life.

Vision Statement

We will strive to make our school a place where staff, governors and parents work actively together to ensure children receive a rich, inspiring, dynamic and engaging education enabling each child to become a lifelong learner, aspiring to high standards of achievement in all areas of their life.

Mission Statement

We aim to attain our vision by providing inspiring teaching within a supportive learning environment which empowers children to achieve.

▲ Figure 1.4 What is meant by the aims of a setting?

Class discussion

Look at one another's ethos, mission, aims and values, and discuss them. Have you as a staff been involved in their development? Your tutor will tell you if you can use this discussion as evidence for your portfolio.

Aims

The aims of the setting are what it sets out to achieve – for example, 'to create a happy and stable environment in which pupils are able to achieve their best'. They will usually be set by the head teacher, staff and governors and are often displayed on the website, prospectus and other areas of the school or college.

Values

These should be the things that bring the school or college together. They may be listed or encompassed in a motto or belief system – for example, respecting one another, achievement for all, celebrating diversity, inspiring ideas, and so on. They may also be closely tied in with personal, social, health and economic (PSHE) education and citizenship in the setting.

These should all be reflected in the working practices of staff and communicated to all those who have contact with the school or college. It should be clear to all visitors to the setting that the environment is inclusive – that staff have good relationships with pupils based on trust and respect.

AC 4.2 Identify ethos, mission, aims and values of your workplace

You should be able to find out about the ethos, mission, aims and values of your workplace easily as it is important that settings communicate them to parents, staff and pupils. They should also be reflected in the way the school or college is run and in the day-to-day practice of all who work there.

In practice

Find out about the ethos, mission, aims and values of your workplace through looking at your website and the literature available. Alternatively, you can use your prospectus if they are listed and highlight and annotate it to show you know what it means and how it impacts on your practice. You will then be able to use this for your portfolio as evidence for this assessment criterion.

LO5 Understand the purpose of policies and procedures in education

AC 5.1 Identify the policies and procedures schools and colleges have relating to: staff; pupil welfare; teaching and learning; equality, diversity and inclusion; health, safety and security

All educational establishments, similar to other organisations, are required to have **policies and procedures** in place. These are to ensure that all those involved in running day-to-day aspects of the setting have clear guidelines from which to work, and that everyone knows what these are and where to refer to them. They are also useful to have when speaking to parents and carers, and when making decisions about the way in which the setting is run.

Each school or college will have a number of policies and procedures relating to different areas, and many of them are a statutory requirement. You are likely to be able to find them on your school or college website. For the purposes of this unit, you will need to know about those relating to the headings listed in Table 1.2 on the next page. Bear in mind that the titles of the policies may differ slightly from those listed.

Key term

Policies and procedures: the principles, rules and guidelines agreed and adopted by the organisation.

▼ Table 1.2 Relevant policies and procedures by area

Area	Relevant policies and procedures
Staff	• Performance management/teacher appraisal policy • DBS checks for all staff, and records of this • Procedures for dealing with allegations of abuse against staff • Pay policy • Confidentiality policy • Grievance policy • Whistleblowing policy • Data protection policy • Records of courses attended and qualifications obtained
Pupil welfare	• Safeguarding/child protection policy • Health and safety policy, including school/college and residential trips • Online safety policy • Anti-bullying policy • Drugs awareness policy • Data protection policy • Mobile phone and social media policy • Sickness and medication/first aid policy • Supporting pupils with medical conditions • Special educational needs policy • Annual report/information on SEN • Confidentiality policy • PSHE policy • Sex education policy • Behaviour/code of conduct policy • Attendance and punctuality policy
Teaching and learning	• Teaching and learning policy • Early years policy • Sixth form policy • Learner commitment policy • Special educational needs policy • Planning and assessment policy • Homework policy • Marking policy • Curriculum policies for different subject areas (e.g. mathematics) • Enrichment policy • School or college development plan
Equality, diversity and inclusion	• Inclusion policy • Equal opportunities policy • Special educational needs policy • Gifted and talented pupils policy • Disability and access policy • Accessibility plan
Health, safety and security	• Health and safety policy • Lockdown policy • First aid policy • Risk assessment policy • Premises management documents • Records of accidents and contagious illnesses

A list of statutory policies and procedures required by education legislation and which schools/colleges are required to have them can be found on the www.gov.uk website – search for 'Statutory policies for schools'.

AC 5.2 Explain how policies and procedures contribute to quality in education

Policies and procedures contribute to quality in education as they provide a clear framework from which the school or college community can function. They will need to be reviewed regularly (around every two or three years) by staff and governors. This gives everyone the opportunity to look closely at working practices, and to think about whether the policies are still relevant as they are or need to be updated. Each set of policies and procedures will contribute to quality in education in a distinct way, as described below.

Staff

Recruitment and the way in which staffing is monitored in the setting will influence the quality of pupils' education due to the checks and regular performance appraisals that are carried out. As well as recruitment procedures to ensure that qualifications, experience and curriculum knowledge of all staff is valid and up to date, all staff will need to have regular appraisals of their practice and be aware of school or college procedures. It is also important that new staff are given a job description and an induction into the working practices of the organisation so that they are clear about their responsibilities.

Activity

Find out about the different policies that your school or college has for each of the groups in the left-hand column of Table 1.2: staff; pupil welfare; teaching and learning; equality, diversity and inclusion; health, safety and security.

Pupil welfare

Research shows that pupils will not be able to learn if they are in situations that are abusive or dangerous, whether this is within or outside the setting, and whether it has occurred once or is ongoing. Policies for child protection and safeguarding, e-learning and e-safety, bullying, and so on, will contribute to ensuring that pupils know what to do if they find themselves in these situations. Staff will also need to be familiar with these policies so that they can support pupils where needed if their advice is sought.

Teaching and learning

Teaching and learning policies will have an impact on the way in which schools and colleges manage the quality of their curriculum provision and evaluate pupil progress. Regularly looking at policies such as marking, homework, special educational needs and inclusion, as well as different subject areas, will influence the ways in which pupils are supported in their learning as part of the curriculum. In addition, policies such as those for enrichment will also contribute to the quality of pupil education. This is because they focus more on the development of wider skills and opportunities that may not be available within the school or college curriculum. These may be through activities such as:

- **Forest School**
- transition activities such as discussions and working with teachers or tutors from their next class, college or school
- cookery, sport, creative or language clubs
- activities that develop links with the local community
- volunteering activities.

Key term

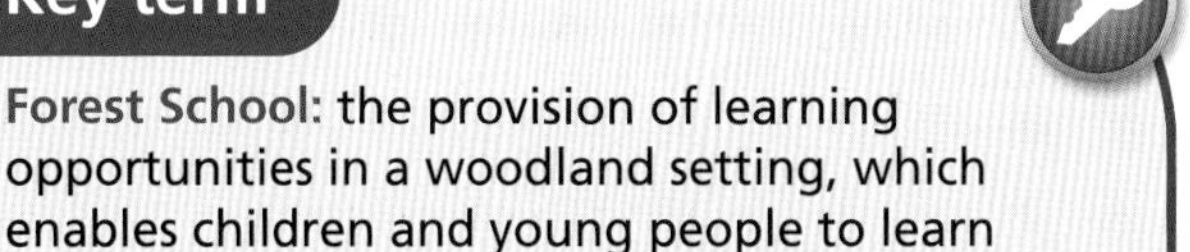

Forest School: the provision of learning opportunities in a woodland setting, which enables children and young people to learn through experiences in the natural environment.

▲ Figure 1.5 What does your school or college offer pupils as part of the wider curriculum?

In practice

Thinking about your own workplace, write a reflective account outlining the ways in which your setting enriches the learning experiences of children and young people through the activities it offers.

These kinds of activities will also contribute to raising pupil self-confidence and self-esteem, which in turn enables pupils to achieve more.

For more on additional activities that may be offered by your school or college, see Unit 16.

Equality, diversity and inclusion

Along with current legislation, these policies and procedures contribute to quality in education as they ensure that all pupils are given equal access to the curriculum and wider life of the school or college. All groups should be valued and able to reach their full academic potential through being supported in an environment of mutual respect. Educational organisations will need to ensure that they do not discriminate in any way towards any group of pupils or staff, and that they guide pupils in becoming tolerant and accepting members of a diverse society where differences are recognised and celebrated.

Activity

Looking at your policies for equality, diversity and inclusion, consider their impact on the day-to-day running of the school or college. How do they influence what happens in the classroom, on school visits and in the wider curriculum?

Health, safety and security

All pupils, whatever their age, need to feel safe and secure in the setting before they are able to learn – it is a key factor affecting learning. The setting will need to show that it promotes a safe and healthy learning environment and a healthy lifestyle through its policies and procedures. Pupils should also be encouraged to think about health and fitness, and to consider the effect of diet and exercise upon the body. The way in which settings care for those who are ill and for pupils with medical conditions is also important.

Check your understanding

1 What do you understand by the term 'early years provision'? Name three types of early years settings.
2 What age would a child be if they were just starting Key Stage 3?
3 What are the post-16 options for pupils in your own UK Home Nation or international school?
4 Outline the roles of the SENCo and PANCO.
5 What would you say are the characteristics of effective teamwork?
6 What is meant by the ethos of a workplace and how would this be reflected in working practices?
7 What is meant by the aims and values of an educational setting and how are these communicated to staff, parents and pupils?
8 What kinds of policies would schools or colleges have that relate to pupil welfare? Which of these do you need to know about?
9 Are any polices statutory? Which might these be?
10 Name three ways in which school or college policies and procedures might contribute to quality in education.

Assessment preparation

This is a knowledge-only unit, which means that you will need to show your knowledge and understanding through methods of assessment such as reflective accounts, assignments, observed professional discussions or questioning by your assessor.

1. Some of the activities for this unit invite you to write reflective accounts to cover the evidence (LO1, AC 1.1, 1.2, 1.3).
2. For LO2, AC 2.1 and 2.2, unless covered by one of the methods above, you will need to write a list of the different roles and outline their main responsibilities.
3. For LO3, evidence for AC 3.1 is covered by the activity on page 9. For AC 3.2 you will need to write a reflective account explaining the role of communication in establishing professional relationships.
4. For LO4, AC 4.1, check with your tutor, if you have carried out the classroom discussion, to see whether you can use this as evidence. For AC 4.2, use the 'In practice' activity on page 11.
5. For LO5, create a policy list (AC 5.1) for your setting for the five areas given in Table 1.2, page 12 (staff; pupil welfare; teaching and learning; equality, diversity and inclusion; health, safety and security). Make sure you use those of your setting. You will then need to say how the policies and procedures for each group contribute to quality in education (AC 5.2).

Legislation

The legislation and statutory guidance relevant to this unit is mainly that which affects schools and colleges themselves. Key legislation that affects them is as follows:

- Data Protection Act (this will be changing to GDPR – General Data Protection Regulation – in May 2018)
- UN Convention on the Rights of the Child 1991
- Freedom of Information Act 2000
- Education Act 2002
- Education and Inspections Act 2006
- Every Child Matters 2003
- Children Act 2004/2006
- Human Rights Act 1998
- Equality Act 2010
- Special Educational Needs Code of Practice 2015
- For special educational needs – Children and Families Act 2014 Part 3 – Children and Young People in England with Special Educational Needs or Disabilities
- Special Educational Needs and Disability Regulations 2014.

Read about it

Weblinks

www.careersforyoungpeople.co.uk Careers for Young People – information on post-16 options for the UK

www.gov.uk Government website – information about the role of school and college governors

www.gov.uk Search for 'education, training and skills' for more information on schools and colleges

www.gov.uk Search for 'statutory policies for schools (DfE, 2014)'

www.gov.uk/government/uploads/system/uploads/attachment_data/file/596629/EYFS_STATUTORY_FRAMEWORK_2017.pdf

EYFS Statutory Guidance

2 Support health and safety in the learning environment

About this unit

This unit will give you the knowledge, understanding and skills required to support children and young people's health and safety in the learning environment and when you are taking pupils off-site. It requires you to demonstrate competence in recognising and dealing with hazards, as well as understanding how to support children and young people in being able to recognise and manage risk for themselves. You will need to know the appropriate responses you should take in cases of incidents, illness, accidents and emergencies according to the policies and procedures of your school or college. This includes knowing about your own role in the administration of medication and how this is managed in your setting.

Learning outcomes

By the end of this unit you will:

LO1 Understand how to plan and provide environments that support children and young people's health and safety

LO2 Understand how to recognise and manage risks to health, safety and security in a learning environment or during off-site visits

LO3 Understand how to support children and young people to assess and manage risk for themselves

LO4 Understand appropriate responses to accidents, incidents, emergencies and illness in the learning environment and during off-site visits

LO5 Understand your role in assisting in the administration of medication

Getting started

In groups, discuss your understanding of what is meant by health and safety in the learning environment. You can use different headings if this helps.

According to British law, all employees are required to:

- take reasonable care of their own health and safety and that of others who may be affected by what they do at work
- co-operate with their employers on health and safety matters
- carry out their work in accordance with training and instructions; and
- inform the employer of any work situation representing a serious and immediate danger, so that remedial action may be taken.

In addition, teachers and other staff in schools have a common law duty to act as any prudent parent would do when in charge of pupils.

Source: *Health and safety: advice on legal duties and powers. For local authorities, school leaders, school staff and governing bodies*, DfE, February 2014

LO1 Understand how to plan and provide environments that support children and young people's health and safety

AC 1.1 Identify legislation in relation to health and safety in a learning environment

You will need to know about the main legislation that exists in relation to health and safety that affects those who work in schools and colleges:

- Health and Safety at Work etc. Act 1974
- Management of Health and Safety at Work Regulations 1999
- Workplace (Health, Safety and Welfare) Regulations 1992
- RIDDOR – Reporting of Injuries, Diseases and Dangerous Occurrences Regulations 2013
- Management and Storage of Medicines – Children and Families Act 2014 Section 100.

Although you do not need to know these in detail, you should be able to say how they affect what you do in your workplace.

Health and Safety at Work etc. Act 1974

This is key legislation that affects the management of health and safety in all organisations and work settings. Under the Health and Safety at Work etc. Act, all those who work in schools or colleges will have responsibilities for health and safety, which include:

- reporting hazards
- following the policies and procedures of the setting for health and safety
- using safety equipment where needed
- ensuring all materials, equipment and resources are safe
- not harming themselves or others by their actions.

Management of Health and Safety at Work Regulations 1999

This was introduced as an amendment to the above Act. Among other additions, it places more responsibility on employers to carry out regular risk assessments and to ensure that all staff have health and safety training.

Workplace (Health, Safety and Welfare) Regulations 1992

This guidance covers requirements for basic health, safety and welfare, including regulations for cleanliness, ventilation, temperature, lighting, room dimensions and other environmental facilities.

RIDDOR – Reporting of Injuries, Diseases and Dangerous Occurrences Regulations 2013

This Act places a duty on employers to report any serious accidents, diseases or dangerous occurrences.

Management and Storage of Medicines – Children and Families Act 2014 Section 100

This places a duty on governing bodies of schools and colleges to make arrangements for supporting pupils with medical conditions. Staff will need to be trained to administer medicines, and policies should be in place for ensuring that they are stored safely.

See also LO5, page 27, for more on the management and administration of medication.

Research it

Choose two of the pieces of legislation from the previous page and find out more about them so that you can make a presentation to others in your group. If you make notes on others' presentations as well as keeping your own, you can use this as evidence for your portfolio.

AC 1.2 Describe the factors to take into account when planning healthy and safe indoor and outdoor environments

In your role supporting teaching and learning, you will need to know how to plan and provide learning environments that support children and young people's health and safety. All adults who work with children and young people need to have an awareness of health and safety issues, particularly when planning for, setting up and carrying out activities with children and young people. Before you start a learning activity, you should always ensure that the learning environment is safe and that you have checked it for any **hazards** so that you and the pupils can focus on what you are doing.

You will need to think about a number of different factors when you are planning learning environments for children and young people, whether these are indoors or outdoors. These factors will need to include:

- the individual needs, age and abilities of the children and young people
- specific **risks** to individuals such as pregnancy and sensory impairments
- the needs of carers, where relevant
- the function and purpose of environments
- the duty of care
- desired outcomes for the children and young people
- lines of responsibility and accountability.

Key terms

Hazard: something in the environment that could cause harm.

Risk: the chance, whether high or low, that someone could be harmed by a hazard.

The individual needs, age and abilities of the children and young people

As well as knowing the details of the learning activity you will be working on, you will need to show an awareness about the pupils you will be working with so that you can plan effectively. Younger children, for example, will be more likely to need support in recognising and acknowledging risk, and you may need to talk this through with them, particularly if you are carrying out activities that are more hazardous. You should also take into account pupil behaviour, which can potentially pose a risk if it is unchecked.

You may also be working with individuals who need support in looking out for risks due to their abilities or specific needs, and it may benefit them for you to talk through what you are going to be doing with them in advance. For example, saying things like 'Let's make sure your chairs are pushed in so that we don't trip anyone over' or 'I think we should pull the blinds down so that it's not too bright for you while you are working.' In this way you will be reminding them about safety just through providing a commentary on what you are doing.

Case study

Saskia is preparing to carry out a cooking activity with groups of Year 2 children. She has been asked to work with four children at a time using a portable oven in a corridor area outside the classroom, and will be making and icing cakes with them for a school cake sale.

1. What kinds of hazards will there be in the setting up and carrying out of the activity?
2. How should Saskia introduce the activity with regards to health and safety, bearing in mind the age of the children (6–7 years)?

Specific risks to individuals such as pregnancy and sensory impairments

You will need to be mindful of any specific risks that exist owing to the individuals with whom you are working – for example, if they are pregnant, have special educational needs or disabilities, or a sensory impairment.

▼ Table 2.1 Factors to consider when planning safe learning environments

Specific risk	What to be aware of
Pregnancy	• The individual will need to avoid any activities that may put themselves or their unborn baby at risk. • Be careful when you are planning any food tasting or cooking activities and avoid soft cheese, raw eggs, milk or pâté, which can carry *Listeria* and other bacteria that are potentially harmful to the unborn baby. • Contact with animals is a potential hazard due to infections that they can carry. This is particularly true of some farm animals, so check before going on any trips or visits. If you have animals in the learning environment it is safer if others clean them out and change their bedding. • Always plan for and observe good hygiene and ensure that everyone washes their hands after carrying out any activities that pose a potential risk.
Sensory impairment	• **Visual impairment:** these pupils may not be as aware of risks in the environment so will need you to be mindful of this when you are planning learning activities. Make sure access to the activity is clear and that you have provided materials they can find and use easily. Plan for them to be close to you or to another individual who can support them if they need it. If they need specific materials or resources to support their learning, you must also find out about and provide these. • **Hearing impairment:** these pupils may need to have equipment or access to sign language so that they are able to participate effectively. You may need to wear a microphone or other radio aid to support this, or if you have a student who wears a hearing aid, ensure that they are able to hear you before you start. • **Dyspraxia**, sometimes known as a sensory processing disorder, affects an individual's co-ordination and movement skills. It will be harder for these pupils to concentrate and follow instructions as well as carry out physical activities. You will need to be aware that these may be challenging for them and they may need more time or support to complete their work.
Special educational needs and disabilities (SEND)	When planning healthy and safe learning environments for pupils who have special educational needs and disabilities, you will need to have been informed about these needs so that you can take them into account. For example, if pupils have: • **physical needs**, they may need more space or access for wheelchairs or other equipment, or they may need adult support to ensure that there are no barriers to their taking part in the activity • **cognition and learning needs**, they may have less awareness of hazards in the environment, so you should ensure that you have talked about potential hazards in advance and remind them during the activity if necessary • **social and emotional needs**, these needs may mean that pupils behave in a way that could be unsafe to themselves or others – you may need to plan for fewer pupils in a group or have another plan ready; they may also need reassurance and ongoing support while working with others during the activity • **communication and language needs**, you will need to ensure that pupils have understood the nature of any hazards before you start the lesson, and that they have any communication aids that are needed.

The needs of carers, where relevant

If pupils have carers with them, you should ensure that there will be provision made for them, both in the space they need and any additional resources or time they may need to support pupils.

The function and purpose of environments

It is important that the learning environment, whether indoor or outdoor, is organised with safety in mind so that risks are minimised. Issues such as tidiness, space to work, access to materials and resources, and suitability for the activity being organised should all be considered when planning. Pupils will also be affected by aspects of their environment such as temperature or lighting. Make sure as much as possible when you are planning activities that you take the physical environment into account to ensure that pupils are comfortable and able to focus on the activity. This is particularly relevant where curriculum subjects carry an element of risk – for example, science subjects, art, design and technology, or physical education (PE).

The duty of care

All school and college staff have a duty of care towards keeping pupils safe and free from harm. The Management of Health and Safety at Work Regulations 1999 outline what employers should do to meet their overall duty of care. This includes having clear policies and procedures in place as well as giving staff appropriate training and undertaking **risk assessments**. As a member of staff, you should do your best to ensure that you apply your training, judgement and professional experience. If you do this, your duty of care requirements will have been met.

Key term

Risk assessment: this is a check for potential risks so that measures may be put in place to control them.

Desired outcomes for the children and young people

The learning environment should lend itself as much as possible to meeting the desired outcomes of the activity. For example, if the outside learning environment is a more appropriate place to meet learning outcomes, it is important to use this. You also need to ensure that the learning environment is set up in a way that maximises opportunities to learn and minimises risk or distraction.

Lines of responsibility and accountability

It is important that you know who in your setting is responsible for health, safety and security – you should be clear about who you need to go to in an emergency, or how to report and record any incidents. Their name is likely to be displayed in your setting on a health and safety poster and should also be in your health and safety policy. This should contain up-to-date information and you should check to make sure that you know where it is and have read it – this is your responsibility.

AC 1.3 Explain how health and safety is monitored and maintained in the learning environment

Your school or college will have a facilities or site manager who is likely to be responsible for checking the indoor and outdoor environment routinely on a daily basis to ensure that there are no obvious hazards that have gone unnoticed. There will also be other safety routines and measures in place so that they can be kept up to date by others with any changes as they occur:

- a general check first thing in the morning to look at security and outdoor areas before pupils and staff come onto the site
- a maintenance book so that staff can report any issues or hazards as they occur
- regular evacuation procedures so that everyone knows what to do in case of emergency
- there should be a way of contacting them quickly in an emergency, such as a pager, if needed.

This person will also be responsible for ensuring that safety checks are made regularly on any fire, electrical or other equipment that requires it. Safety equipment should carry a symbol such as the BSI Kitemark or CE (Conformité Européenne) symbol to show that it meets accepted standards of the British Safety Institute or demonstrates 'European conformity'.

Pupil behaviour is also an important aspect of safety, and all schools and colleges should have safety education as part of the agenda so that staff and pupils are reminded regularly about the importance of safety, particularly if it is closely linked to the subject they are working on. Your school's behaviour policy should also give information about ways in which adults should manage challenging behaviour when safety is an issue.

▲ Figure 2.1 Check equipment for dates of any inspections and look for recognised safety standard marks

Stretch and challenge

Find out who is responsible for health and safety in your setting and devise a set of questions to ask them about their role and responsibilities. These may include questions on day-to-day management, risk assessment, security, staff training and awareness, and safety checks on equipment. You should then ask them about each area. Do any of their answers surprise you?

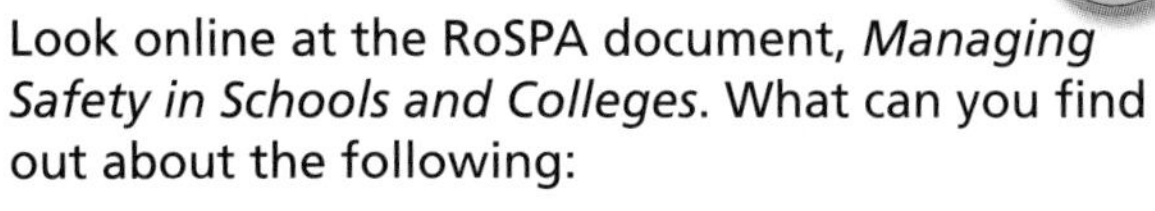

Activity

Look online at the RoSPA document, *Managing Safety in Schools and Colleges*. What can you find out about the following:

- health and safety audits
- training for schools and colleges
- preparing for Ofsted?

The document can be found here: www.rospa.com/rospaweb/docs/advice-services/school-college-safety/managing-safety-schools-colleges.pdf

LO2 Understand how to recognise and manage risks to health, safety and security in a learning environment or during off-site visits

AC 2.1 Demonstrate how to identify potential risks and hazards for: the learning environment; off-site activity

In order to locate potential health and safety hazards within and outside the work setting, you will need to be consciously aware of what may happen at any time. If you are first on the scene you should make it safe if you can and/or inform those responsible for dealing with them so that nobody is put at risk.

The learning environment

When thinking about the learning environment, remember that potential risks and hazards may take a number of different forms, which may be:

- physical
- security
- fire
- food safety
- personal safety.

Physical

These types of risks and hazards will be the ones you might come across in the general environment, such as coats being left on the floor and causing a trip hazard or broken glass around a litter bin. They will also include issues such as materials and equipment being unchecked and safety equipment not being used appropriately. Where possible you should act on them yourself to avoid others being put at risk. If you are unable to act on them yourself, for example in cases of broken furniture or faulty equipment, you should make sure that you are aware of and follow school or college policy so that others are not put in danger. This may mean moving or labelling the item as faulty, and reporting in a maintenance book or through email.

Activity

Fill in the following table, identifying what action you would take for each of the hazards in the environment listed.

Type of hazard	Action you would take
Wet floor in corridor	
Fox mess in playground	
Broken equipment or resources	
Unsafe storage, e.g. cupboard too full	
Insufficient adult supervision for number of children	
Dangerous pupil behaviour	
Untidy and disorganised learning environment	
Medicines not locked away	
Students smoking on-site	
Pupils not using correct safety equipment	
An outside gate broken or left open	
An aggressive parent on-site	
No staff on reception desk	

Security

These kinds of hazards can be to do with unidentified people gaining access to the site or young children being able to leave it. Look out for gaps in fences or hedges and gates being left open. There are likely to be security cameras on-site, and staff will be given entry codes, which should not be written down or given to others. All access points will need to be monitored to ensure that the premises are secure. You should always be vigilant, particularly at the beginning and end of the day, and if you see anyone who is unfamiliar or not wearing a visitors' badge, you should challenge them by asking if you can help them. All staff and volunteers will have to complete a DBS check to ensure that they are suitable to work with children and young people. (For more on the DBS check, see Unit 3, page 38.) Security risks can also be caused by incidents outside the setting such as civil disturbance, a terrorist incident or a fire in the vicinity. In these types of situations schools and colleges may operate a lockdown policy, meaning that all staff and pupils are brought into buildings and doors are locked.

Fire

Smoking is unlikely to be permitted anywhere on-site and can cause a fire hazard if it takes place anywhere close by. Use of candles or other exposed flames should be avoided. In the case of cooking, safety equipment such as fire blankets should be on hand to use if needed. Fire extinguishers will also need to be checked regularly to ensure that they are not faulty and dates of these checks should be displayed on the equipment. All staff should be aware of the different types of fire extinguishers and the types of fires they should be used for.

Figure 2.2 Do you know what kinds of fires each of these fire extinguishers can be used for?

Food safety

You will need to be well prepared when you are carrying out cooking or food technology activities, and always demonstrate good practice. When cooking with children and young people, you should talk to them about potential risks so that you help to develop their own awareness. Make sure you are a good role model, observe correct hygiene procedures and safe use of equipment. There are specialised qualifications for best practice in food handling and preparation.

Personal safety

Staff should make pupils aware of the need for personal safety and take care when they are carrying out activities that have a higher level of risk, ensuring they make use of safety equipment where needed. These may include working at height and using a ladder when needed, or taking care while lifting heavy items and doing this correctly. Personal Protective Equipment or PPE should be available where needed to protect employees and ensure that hazards are limited. These may be, for example, safety goggles, earplugs, high visibility clothing and other equipment. For more on PPE and when it should be used, see **www.hse.gov.uk/toolbox/ppe.htm**. You should also ensure you are vigilant at all times in the setting for your own personal safety, particularly if you are working alone or are in an isolated part of the setting away from other staff.

See Unit 16 for information on risk–benefit assessments (RBAs).

▼ Table 2.2 Dealing with hazards in the work setting

Hazard	How to manage
Electrical items	All electrical items that are used in the setting will need to be checked regularly by a qualified electrician and if this is done they should not be hazardous. However, you should always look over electrical appliances carefully before using them and encourage pupils to do the same. You should not bring in your own electrical items from home to use with students as these will not have been tested.
Chemicals	Any hazardous chemicals that are purchased, stored, used or disposed of in schools and colleges should be locked away in cupboards when they are not being used, in order to limit danger to pupils or staff. These may be cleaning materials or other chemicals that are used in subject-based lessons. It is important to keep records of these chemicals, and that there is restricted access to them and they can be accounted for. If you work with chemicals as part of your role you will need to know about your setting's guidelines and the lines of responsibility. For more information on storage of chemicals in schools you can find this through COSHH* on the Health and Safety Executive (HSE) website.
Work equipment	All equipment used in schools and colleges should be checked regularly, but if you find any faulty or unsafe equipment you should remove and report it straight away. Make sure you know how to correctly use any equipment if you have been asked to do so. Guidance and ideas about the use of equipment in schools and colleges, particularly those used in science and D&T-based activities, may be found on the two CLEAPPS** websites.
Protective equipment	Always use, and ensure others are using, any protective equipment that is provided to minimise risk during learning activities. Think particularly about PE and sport, cooking, science and D&T activities.

* COSHH (Control of Substances Hazardous to Health) Regulations 2016, **www.hse.gov.uk/coshh/**
** CLEAPSS (Consortium of Local Education Authorities for the Provision of Science Services for primary and secondary schools), **www.cleapss.org.uk** (click on 'Primary' and 'Secondary science' in the menu on the left)

Off-site activity

When you go on trips and visits outside the setting, the person who is responsible for the trip will need to complete a risk assessment, which will outline any potential hazards and help to comply with health and safety law. They will usually need to organise a pre-visit to the centre and carry out a 'dry run' of what pupils will be doing so that everything has been covered. The site will need to have been checked for suitable toilet facilities as well as somewhere safe for pupils to eat and drink. Where relevant to the age of the pupils, adult to pupil ratios will need to be observed in line with statutory requirements. All adults who are going on the trip will then need to read and sign this document so that they know and understand what to do if any of the risks or hazards should occur, and be aware of their own responsibilities. The kinds of questions they will need to ask are:

- What activities will pupils be doing when on the visit?
- What are the potential hazards and how likely are they to occur?
- What safety measures are in place to manage them?
- What should the responsible adult do in case of emergency?
- Who is the first aider on the trip?

If pupils go on regular trips to the same venue, such as swimming or Forest School activities, or college students are going into the workplace, they may use the same risk assessment but should check it regularly to ensure that all aspects are still relevant and up to date.

If you have dealt with hazards when you have been off-site with pupils you may be able to write about how you did this as a reflective account, or ask a responsible adult to write a witness testimony to say that you managed the hazard appropriately.

The Health and Safety Executive (HSE) has produced a useful guide entitled Five Steps to Risk Assessment, which is a helpful document for employers. It is available at **www.rospa.com/rospaweb/docs/campaigns-fundraising/hse-five-steps-to-risk-assessment.pdf.**

Research it

Using the HSE website (www.hse.gov.uk), find out how the appropriate member of staff should report an incident or illness.

What can you find out about the BSI (British Standards Institution) Kitemark and what it is used for?

In practice

Next time you are asked to go on an off-site visit, ask the organiser if you can carry out the risk assessment with them.

- Does anything surprise you about the potential risks that are highlighted?
- Why is it important to go through risk assessments prior to going on trips with pupils?

Tips for best practice: managing risks and hazards in the setting

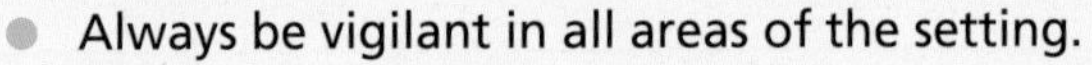

- Always be vigilant in all areas of the setting.
- Report any concerns straight away and make the area safe if possible.
- Use and store all equipment safely and check regularly.
- Keep up to date with any health and safety training.
- Challenge any unidentified people in the setting.
- Make sure pupils are using any protective equipment provided.
- Make sure you are fully prepared before going on trips and visits.
- Always follow the setting's procedures when dealing with incidents and accidents.
- Use PPE where necessary.

LO3 Understand how to support children and young people to assess and manage risk for themselves

AC 3.1 Explain why it is important to take a balanced approach to risk management

While schools and colleges need to carry out the correct health and safety procedures and ensure that children and young people are not put in any unnecessary danger, we still need to support them in assessing risks in the environment for themselves. Taking a **balanced approach** to risk management is important because children and young people will inevitably be exposed to a certain amount of risk in their lives. They should be taught to weigh up and decide for themselves whether a situation is potentially dangerous – adults should not make every decision for them as this will put them at a disadvantage as they grow up.

See Unit 16, LO2, page 249, for more on understanding your own role in relation to the requirements of play and leisure activities.

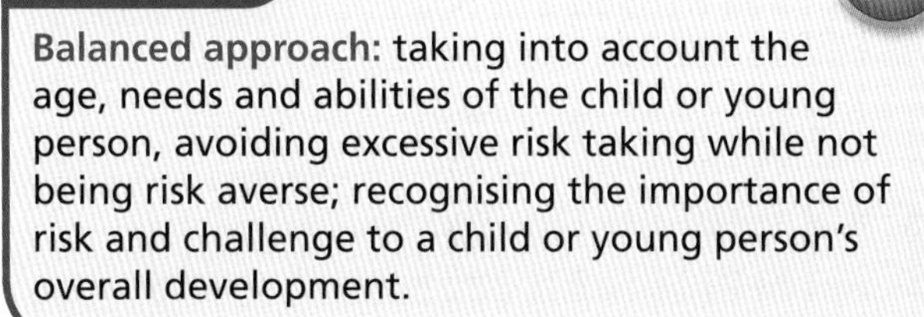

Key term

Balanced approach: taking into account the age, needs and abilities of the child or young person, avoiding excessive risk taking while not being risk averse; recognising the importance of risk and challenge to a child or young person's overall development.

Activity

You are responsible for ensuring that children and young people are kept safe at all times. You are also responsible for supporting and encouraging their ability to understand risk for themselves. Discuss how you think practitioners might do this in the following age ranges:

- 5–7 years
- 8–13 years
- 14–19 years.

AC 3.2 Explain the dilemma between the rights and choices of children and young people, and health and safety requirements

Health and safety requirements mean that adults are responsible and will need to do whatever they can to keep the environment safe and free from hazards. Bear in mind that a hazard is usually something that a child or young person can see, but a risk may be something they cannot. If a balanced approach is taken, children and young people will be able to develop their independence and confidence in managing hazardous situations, and exercise their own rights and choices. Staff will need to talk to children and young people about the reasons for taking particular courses of action and weighing up the risks before acting in certain situations. As they grow older, pupils should also consider and discuss the impact of their actions on those around them.

Class discussion

Consider and discuss the level of risk awareness of the children and young people with whom you work, and how often risk is mentioned and discussed. Do you think that this this appropriate to the age and abilities of the pupils?

Case study

Paul is working alongside teaching staff on a foundation degree sports coaching course in college. As the students are older, he assumes that they will be risk aware so does not mention basic safety rules when he takes the groups out for training sessions; it has not been mentioned to him by tutors either.

1. Why is it important to be clear about health and safety issues in this instance?
2. What would be the best way of maintaining a balanced approach so that students have their own rights and choices?

AC 3.3 Reflect on your practice of supporting children and young people to assess and manage risk

For this assessment criterion, you will need to be able to reflect on ways in which you have supported children and young people to assess and manage risk in different learning environments. Where possible, you should choose different age ranges, abilities and environments so that you can show the different ways in which you do this.

> **Activity**
>
> Read the following scenarios:
>
> - sending a group of Year 2 children onto the playground at break time
> - preparing to work with a group of Year 10 pupils on a chemistry activity
> - going on a visit to a local museum by bus with Year 4 pupils
> - working with an 18-year-old special needs student on a food preparation activity
> - acting as referee for a Year 9 rugby match.
>
> In which of these situations would it be beneficial to speak to the pupils about the risks beforehand?

LO4 Understand appropriate responses to accidents, incidents, emergencies and illness in the learning environment and during off-site visits

AC 4.1 Explain the policies and procedures of the learning environment in response to accidents, incidents, emergencies and illness

Your setting's health and safety policy is an important document, and all adults in the setting will need to be aware of it as well as their own roles and responsibilities. Whether you are a member of staff or a volunteer, you will have responsibilities for making sure that the children and young people in your care are looked after appropriately in case of sickness or emergency. If you are first on the scene of an accident, you should send for help immediately.

You will need to know the identity of the first aiders in your setting – there should be several on-site at any time and their names may be displayed in different locations. When pupils go off-site on visits and trips, there should always be a first aider in the accompanying staff and all adults should know who this is. It is important that all first aiders attend regular training to keep up to date.

According to RIDDOR legislation, all serious workplace accidents and dangerous occurrences, as well as notifiable diseases, must be reported. Guidelines for how settings should do this may be found on the HSE website at **www.hse.gov.uk**.

The different accident and emergency situations you may need to respond to are detailed in Table 2.3.

> **Activity**
>
> Using Table 2.3 as a guide, find out about your own setting's policies and procedures in response to each kind of event. You will then be able to use this towards your portfolio.

AC 4.2 Explain the correct procedures for recording and reporting accidents, incidents, injuries, signs of illness and other emergencies

You will need to make sure that you are aware of the correct procedures for recording and reporting any accidents or other emergencies, so that you are able to follow your setting's policy when necessary.

Make sure that you know what to do in the event of an emergency, and remember that all incidents will initially need to be recorded by staff who were present at the time using the

▼ Table 2.3 Accidents, incidents, emergencies and illnesses which must be recorded

Event	Description
Accidents	These include accidents to children, young people or adults. They may range from relatively minor cuts or playground accidents to those that are more severe and likely to require first aid.
Incidents	Possible incidents may include: • bomb scares and off-site evacuation – it is essential that all pupils and staff are aware of the setting's emergency procedures in these situations so that they can move safely out of the building and off-site if necessary • strangers on the premises – the policy should detail what staff should do if they notice a stranger on-site; if you are unsure what to do, ask another member of staff immediately • weapon incidents – if a weapon is being used to threaten staff and/or pupils, your first concern should be to your own and others' safety • extreme weather conditions – these may include heavy snowfall or extreme hot weather which can affect and restrict individuals' ability to work.
Emergencies	These may include fire, missing pupils, life-threatening allergic reactions, evacuations and breaches of security in the setting. Fire and evacuation drills should take place regularly – at least once a term. If you are a new member of staff, make sure that you find out this information as soon as you can so that you know what to do in case of an emergency.
Illness	These include recognising signs of illness such as fever and rashes, and taking appropriate action in these situations. In some cases, illness can come on rapidly and staff should be prepared and able to act quickly. Always make sure you speak to a first aider if you have any concerns.

correct documentation; in this way the setting will be covered by having as much information as possible on the incident. The format may vary between settings, but the setting will have established reporting and recording methods. If the accident or injury is severe, this will also need to be reported to the HSE so that it is aware of it.

Illnesses may need to be reported to local authorities so that these can be monitored in case of local outbreaks. These are called notifiable diseases; a list of them may be found at: **www.gov.uk/guidance/notifiable-diseases-and-causative-organisms-how-to-report**.

In practice

If you do not know already, find out about your school or college's policy on recording and reporting any incidents, and ask to see the documentation that is used.

LO5 Understand your role in assisting in the administration of medication

AC 5.1 Outline the organisational policies and procedures for the management of the administration of medication

For this learning outcome, you will need to find out about and outline the policy of your school or college for administering medication. This may be part of your school's health and safety policy or in a policy of its own. In particular, you will need to know about the following aspects.

Legislation around storing and administering medication

Section 100 of the Children and Families Act 2014 states that governing bodies must support pupils at their school with medical conditions. It is important that the medication is stored only in its original container, which in the case of prescribed medications should show the name of the child or young person and the required dose.

The child or young person must know where their medicine is stored and who has the key, particularly in the case of emergency medicines such as asthma inhalers and EpiPens, to enable them to be accessed quickly.

Consent and record keeping

Although schools and colleges are not legally required to administer medicines, any prescription medication that parents and carers ask the setting to administer to children under 16 will need to come with clear instructions and have consent forms signed by them in advance. The setting should then keep records to show when and how much medication has been given. You must not administer any medicines to children and young people unless these consent forms have been signed. Older children or young people may be given responsibility for their own medication, although it should still be kept locked up until needed.

Medication/individual care plans

These are plans for pupils who are on long-term medication that needs to be administered regularly when they are in the setting. It may be for health conditions such as epilepsy or a condition such as diabetes, which requires the administration of insulin. The plans will be drawn up and used by the school or college, parents and healthcare professionals so that all of their needs are considered. As part of their individual plan, there may be specific instructions for the administration of medication so that it is clear what their needs are and how any medication should be administered. If a pupil also has a special educational need or disability, this should be mentioned in their individual care plan and linked to their statement or EHC (Education, Health and Care) plan. The plan should be reviewed annually.

The DfE has produced a document entitled *Supporting Pupils at School with Medical Conditions* (2015). It provides valuable guidance for head teachers, parents, pupils and staff. It can be found here: **www.gov.uk/government/uploads/system/uploads/attachment_data/file/484418/supporting-pupils-at-school-with-medical-conditions.pdf.**

> **Research it**
>
> Refer to the DfE document above. What does this document say about the roles and responsibilities of governing bodies, head teachers, teachers and other staff in administering medicines (see pages 7–14 of the document)?

Risk assessment

The setting may draw up specific risk assessments for administering medication, particularly with regard to off-site visits, but this will depend on organisational policy.

Infection control

Children and young people should be sent home from the setting if they are suffering from a condition or illness that is infectious so that it is not passed on to others. The term 'infection control' usually applies to the kinds of precautions the setting needs to take to avoid the spread of infection, usually if clearing up a spillage of blood or other body fluids, or while putting dressings on wounds. If administering medicines using needles, staff should ensure that they follow hygiene procedures and that sharps are disposed of appropriately and according to policy.

The Public Health Agency has produced a document called *Guidance on infection control in schools and other childcare settings* (2017). It can be found here: **www.publichealth.hscni.net/sites/default/files/Guidance_on_infection_control_in%20schools_poster.pdf.** What responsibilities does your setting have regarding infectious diseases?

AC 5.2 Describe your responsibilities and accountabilities in relation to the administration of medication

You may have a role within the organisation as a first aider or person who is able to administer medication. If you do, you should be able to outline your own responsibilities and describe the steps you would need to go through in each situation. You may also be able to provide witness testimonies from those you have worked with to demonstrate your competence in doing this. If you do not have any responsibilities for administering medicines yourself, you may still need to remind pupils to go to the appropriate person at a set time, or ensure that those who are responsible for their own medication have taken it.

Accountability in the event of any legal action around the administering of medication or related issue will be with the employer rather than with the employee, and insurances such as employers' liability insurance should be up to date. This is one of the reasons that accurate record keeping by staff is so important.

Activity

Write a reflective account detailing your own responsibilities when dealing with medication, giving examples from your own practice where possible. You will then be able to use this for your portfolio.

Check your understanding

1. Name four health and safety factors you should think about when you are planning to carry out learning activities with children and young people.
2. What kinds of measures do settings need to put in place to ensure that health and safety is monitored and maintained?
3. Explain what you understand by the term 'risk assessment'.
4. Why is it important to plan carefully for school trips?
5. Name four hazards you might come across in a school or college, and say how you would deal with them.
6. What does a balanced approach to risk management mean?
7. What should staff do when faced with an emergency situation such as an accident, and immediately afterwards?
8. How should you respond if you come across an unidentified visitor in your setting?
9. What is an appropriate response to finding several younger pupils with similar signs of illness – for example, a rash and fever?
10. Can all members of staff administer medication to pupils where needed? Give reasons for your answer.

Assessment preparation

This is a knowledge-only unit, which means that it can be assessed with methods of evidence from outside the workplace. However, on a setting visit you should aim to show your assessor safety items such as fire extinguishers and fire exits, along with any potential risks or hazards in the setting. You should also locate the accident book and explain how it is used, along with first aid procedures and your responsibilities for administering medication. This will help you to cover more evidence for your portfolio.

In addition, you can use the following:

1. Write a report for the governors in your school or college, describing the kinds of factors staff should take in to account when they are planning healthy and safe learning environments (indoor or outdoor). This will need to take into account the factors in the unit guidance. Explain how health and safety is monitored and maintained in your setting, and how staff and pupils are made aware of it and encouraged to stay safe (LO1, AC 1.2, 1.3). You can use the 'Research it' feature on page 18 as evidence for AC 1.1.
2. Go on a health and safety walk in your school or college, and see if you can identify potential hazards. Record these and describe how you should deal with them. You should think about the following types of hazards: physical, security, fire, food safety, personal safety (LO2, AC 2.1).
3. Use the classroom discussion suggested for LO3 to cover the assessment criteria in the specification. If you contribute to the discussion and it is recorded by your assessor, you will be able to use this as evidence (LO3, AC 3.1, 3.2, 3.3).
4. Write a reflective account or have a professional discussion outlining the policies and procedures of your school or college for managing accidents, incidents, illness and emergencies (LO4, AC 4.1, 4.2). Do the same for policies and procedures for the administration of medication, including your own responsibilities and accountabilities (LO5, AC 5.1, 5.2).

Legislation

- Health and Safety at Work etc. Act 1974: www.hse.gov.uk/legislation/hswa.htm
- Management of Health and Safety at Work Regulations 1999: www.hse.gov.uk/pubns/hsc13.pdf
- Workplace (Health, Safety and Welfare) Regulations 1992: www.hse.gov.uk/pUbns/priced/l24.pdf
- RIDDOR – Reporting of Injuries, Diseases and Dangerous Occurrences Regulations 2013: www.hse.gov.uk/riddor/
- Management and Storage of Medicines – Children and Families Act 2014 Section 100: www.gov.uk/government/uploads/system/uploads/attachment_data/file/638267/supporting-pupils-at-school-with-medical-conditions.pdf

See AC 1.1, page 17 for more detail on legislation.

Read about it

Weblinks

www.gov.uk Offers a number of helpful online documents and other reading material to support schools and colleges in managing health and safety issues

The following organisations produce material and resources to support health and safety in schools and colleges, which are available on their websites:

www.rospa.com Royal Society for the Prevention of Accidents (RoSPA)

RoSPA also produces a helpful guide, *Managing Safety in Schools and Colleges* (November 2012), which can be downloaded from its website.

www.hse.gov.uk Health and Safety Executive (HSE)

www.cleapss.org.uk CLEAPSS (Consortium of Local Education Authorities for the Provision of Science Services for primary and secondary schools); provides advice on health and safety

The following link is helpful for supporting pupils with medical conditions as it links to other resources and further reading: **www.gov.uk/government/publications/supporting-pupils-at-school-with-medical-conditions--3/supporting-pupils-with-medical-conditions-links-to-other-useful-resources--2**

For guidance on infection control in schools and other childcare settings, see: **www.greatsampford.essex.sch.uk/sites/default/files/Guidance%20on%20Infection%20Control%20in%20Schools%202016.pdf**

The booklet *Guidance on First Aid for Schools* also gives useful information about health, safety and first aid: **www.gov.uk/government/uploads/system/uploads/attachment_data/file/306370/guidance_on_first_aid_for_schools.pdf**

3 Understand how to safeguard children and young people

About this unit

This unit provides the knowledge and understanding required to support the safeguarding of children and young people. You will need to show how legislation is reflected through the policies and procedures followed at your school or college. This in turn will keep children and young people safe and promote their welfare and well-being. This includes preventative measures such as making children and young people aware of the importance of their own safety and in particular of staying safe online. You should also be aware of the steps you should take if you have concerns about a child or young person, and the importance of partnerships with other organisations in order to support safeguarding.

Learning outcomes

By the end of this unit you will:

LO1 Understand legislation, guidelines, policies and procedures for safeguarding children and young people

LO2 Understand how to work in partnership with other organisations to safeguard children and young people

LO3 Understand the need to ensure children and young people's safety and protection in the learning environment

LO4 Understand how to respond to evidence or concerns that a child or young person has been abused or harmed

LO5 Understand how to work with children and young people to support their well-being

Getting started

What do you understand the term 'safeguarding' to mean?

LO1 Understand legislation, guidelines, policies and procedures for safeguarding children and young people

AC 1.1 Outline current legislation, guidelines, policies and procedures within UK Home Nations affecting the safeguarding of children and young people

By law, all organisations working with children and young people up to the age of 18 need to have guidelines, policies and procedures to make sure that they are protected and kept safe from harm. Legislation exists in all UK Home Nations to support the way in which schools and colleges manage **safeguarding** in the learning environment and while on off-site visits.

According to the DfE guidance, *Working Together to Safeguard Children* (2015), safeguarding involves four separate strands:

1 protecting children from maltreatment
2 preventing impairment of children's health or development
3 ensuring that children grow up in circumstances consistent with the provision of safe and effective care
4 taking action to enable all children to have the best outcomes.

As a member of school or college staff, you should be aware of the key legislation that exists within your own UK Home Nation. This means, as well as UK schools and colleges within England, Northern Ireland, Scotland and Wales, international schools will also need to take note of this legislation. It is important to know that the safeguarding and welfare of children and young people is the responsibility of everyone in the school or college who comes into contact with them, including volunteers and students on work placement.

There are a number of Acts of legislation you should know about and be aware of within your UK Home Nation: safeguarding and child protection legislation is updated regularly and you should have regular safeguarding training from your school or college to incorporate this so that all staff are aware of it. Safeguarding legislation and systems will also differ slightly in each of the UK Home Nations although all exist to keep children safe from harm. International schools will also need to compare the legislation in their own country with that of the UK.

Key term

Safeguarding: action taken to promote the welfare of children and protect them from harm (NSPCC, 2018).

Legislation, guidelines, policy and procedures: all nations

The following Acts of legislation affect all nations.

Human Rights Act 1998

This legislation was made UK law to incorporate the rights of individuals, which are contained in the European Convention on Human Rights 1950, although at that time children were hardly included in the Convention. It is relevant to safeguarding because it sets out the entitlements of all individuals, whatever their status. The articles most relevant to safeguarding children and young people are:

- Article 3 – Freedom from torture, inhuman and degrading treatment. This is for the protection of children's rights and is so that the state can take action to prevent abusive treatment from occurring.
- Article 8 – The right to respect for private and family life. This article states that everyone should have a right to family life and that public authorities should remove children only if they are in danger of harm.

United Nations Convention on the Rights of the Child 1989

This international treaty sets out a series of 54 articles that outline the rights and freedoms to which all children should be entitled. It came into UK law in 1992 and covers all aspects of a child's life. Several of the articles are relevant to safeguarding, however Article 19 – protection from violence, abuse and neglect – states that 'governments must do all they can to ensure that children are protected from all forms of violence, abuse, neglect and bad treatment by their parents or anyone else who looks after them'.

Help Children Achieve More (previously known as Every Child Matters)

This guidance was produced in 2010 as an amendment to the Every Child Matters agenda. Under it, the government aims to improve outcomes for children under five strands, whatever their circumstances:

1. be healthy
2. stay safe
3. enjoy and achieve
4. make a positive contribution
5. achieve economic well-being.

All schools and colleges have a statutory duty to protect the children and young people in their care. They must have the following in place by law:

- a child protection policy and procedures
- a designated member of staff with responsibility for safeguarding
- safe recruitment processes for all, including volunteers.

Legislation, guidelines, policies and procedures: England and Wales

The following Acts of legislation affect schools and colleges in England and Wales.

Children Act 1989/2004

The Children Act 1989 outlines the responsibilities of parents and all those who work with children and young people. It includes two specific sections that focus on safeguarding:

1. Section 17 – this states that services must be put in place by local authorities to 'safeguard and promote the welfare of children within their area who are in need'.
2. Section 47 – this states that the local authority has a duty to investigate instances where 'they have reasonable cause to suspect that a child is suffering, or likely to suffer, significant harm'.

The Act was amended in 2004 to reinforce the message that all organisations that work with children and young people have a duty to help safeguard and promote the welfare of children, and created the post of Children's Commissioner for England.

Counter-Terrorism and Security Act 2015

This Act contains powers to help the UK respond to the threat of terrorism. It is relevant to safeguarding as it aims to prevent children and young people being radicalised or drawn into terrorist acts. Under the Act, schools and colleges have a legal duty to prevent young people from being drawn into terrorism.

Prevent Duty and Fundamental British Values 2015

This guidance refers to the Counter-Terrorism and Security Act 2015 and can be found here: **www.gov.uk/government/uploads/system/uploads/attachment_data/file/445977/3799_Revised_Prevent_Duty_Guidance__England_Wales_V2-Interactive.pdf**.

The statutory document that schools and colleges should refer to, *Keeping Children Safe in Education* (published September 2016), is available at: **www.gov.uk/government/uploads/system/uploads/attachment_data/file/550511/Keeping_children_safe_in_education.pdf**.

It outlines the key areas all staff should be aware of and their specific legal duties. It should be read alongside the document *Working Together to Safeguard Children* (published March 2015), which

Activity

What can you find out about Prevent? Read the sector-specific guidance, and paragraphs 57–74 in particular, to look at how it affects schools.

is a guide to the way in which agencies should work together. You can find this here: **www.gov.uk/government/uploads/system/uploads/attachment_data/file/592101/Working_Together_to_Safeguard_Children_20170213.pdf**.

Care Act 2014

This Act is designed to protect vulnerable adults and those who need safeguarding protection. Adults at risk include those who are in community care due to mental or other disabilities, age, or illness, and those who are unable to take care of themselves. Find out more at: **www.england.nhs.uk/wp-content/uploads/2017/02/adult-pocket-guide.pdf**.

Legislation, guidelines, policies and procedures: Scotland

Described below is the main legislation affecting schools and colleges in Scotland.

Children (Scotland) Act 1995

This Act sets out the framework for the child protection system in Scotland, including parental rights and responsibilities as well as the powers that public authorities have in cases of concern.

Protection of Vulnerable Groups (Scotland) Act 2007

This Act outlines the measures that should be taken to stop unsuitable adults from working with children.

Children and Young People (Scotland) Act 2014

This Act aims to put children's rights at the centre of all services in the public sector.

National Guidance for Child Protection in Scotland 2014

This is the key safeguarding guidance for anyone who works with children and young people in Scotland. It provides general as well as specific advice to support professionals and ensure they work together. Find it here: **www.gov.scot/Resource/0045/00450733.pdf**.

Getting it Right for Every Child

This guidance reinforces the Children and Young People (Scotland) Act 2014, and aims to shape all policy, practice and legislation affecting children and young people and their families.

Adult Support and Protection (Scotland) Act 2007

This Act deals with protection of vulnerable adults from harm.

Legislation, guidelines, policies and procedures: Northern Ireland

Described below is the main legislation affecting schools and colleges in Northern Ireland.

The Children (Northern Ireland) Order 1995

This is the legislative framework for the child protection system in Northern Ireland, and includes parental rights and responsibilities as well as the powers that public authorities have in cases of concern.

Addressing Bullying in Schools Act (Northern Ireland) 2016

This Act outlines the duties of governors in grant-aided schools.

Children's Services Co-operation Act (Northern Ireland) 2015

This Act sets out the need for agencies to work together to support the well-being of children and young people.

Safeguarding Board Act (Northern Ireland) 2011 (SBNI)

This Act sets out the law for the creation of a Safeguarding Board for Northern Ireland.

Our Children and Young People – Our Pledge: A Ten-Year Strategy for Children and Young People in Northern Ireland 2006–2016

This ten-year plan sets out the way in which children and young people in Northern Ireland should be respected and kept safe.

Guidance to Safeguarding Board for Northern Ireland (SBNI)

This provides guidance and sets out the way in which member agencies should work together.

Legislation and guidance relevant to safeguarding in all UK Home Nations

There is a detailed and easy-to-use guide on the NSPCC website that sets out all legislation and guidance that is relevant to safeguarding in all UK Home Nations. Find it here: **www.nspcc.org.uk/preventing-abuse/child-protection-system**.

For the roles and responsibilities of different organisations regarding safeguarding, see AC 2.4 on page 36.

Research it

Look up the legislation and guidance for your UK Home Nation or that of your own country. As you work through this unit, consider how this affects your work with children and young people in your school or college. If you are working in an international school, compare and contrast current UK legislation guidelines with those of your own country.

LO2 Understand how to work in partnership with other organisations to safeguard children and young people

AC 2.1 Explain the need to safeguard children and young people

All adults who work with children and young people have a responsibility and obligation to protect their welfare and safety. This is important because children have a right to be kept safe and free from harm, as outlined in the United Nations Convention on the Rights of the Child (see page 33). Safeguarding means protecting children and young people from all types of abuse and bullying, including that which happens online.

AC 2.2 Explain the impact of a child or young person-centred approach

When working with children and young people, all professionals who are involved will need to work together to ensure that the needs of the child or young person are at the centre of any decisions that are made. When discussing their needs,

Class discussion

Have a discussion about what you think your role is when safeguarding the children and young people you work with. In which ways should you do this?

▲ Figure 3.1 How will a child- or young person-centred approach help children and young people in the context of safeguarding?

there should be a child- or young person-centred approach that puts these at the heart of what happens to them. It is important that the child or young person's wishes, needs and feelings should be taken into account and they should be involved in any decisions that are made about them. In this way, they will feel that they have some say in what is happening, and have a voice and some influence.

AC 2.3 Explain what is meant by partnership working in the context of safeguarding

Schools, colleges, agencies and other partners will also need to work together in the context of safeguarding to ensure that there is a 'joined up' approach to meeting the needs of children and young people. The different organisations may draw up an information sharing agreement (ISA) to set out the kind of information that may need to be shared. The safety and welfare of children and young people depends on this, as information will

Activity

Find a copy of your setting's safeguarding policy. How does your school or college make sure that it adopts a child- or young person-centred approach when working with outside agencies on any safeguarding concerns? Find out the name of the person responsible for safeguarding in your school or college.

need to be shared effectively at the earliest possible stage. For example, if there are concerns about a child or young person's unsociable behaviour, there may be a meeting between the child and family, police, social services and the school or college to discuss the way forward. In cases of serious abuse, a lack of information sharing between agencies and other organisations has contributed to deaths and serious injuries in children.

AC 2.4 Describe the roles and responsibilities of the different organisations that may be involved when a child or young person has been abused or harmed

If a child or young person has been the victim of harm or abuse, a number of different services may be involved:

- the school or college
- health services
- social services
- police/probation and Youth Offending Team (YOT)
- charities (for example NSPCC, Save the Children, Child Exploitation Online Protection Centre (CEOP), Barnardo's, The Children's Society)
- psychology service
- local authority
- GP/health visitor.

The school or college

The school is responsible for developing children and young people's awareness of what is acceptable behaviour. This may be both in themselves and in others, whether online or face to face, so that they know and understand when abuse may be happening and how to report it. Schools and colleges should be vigilant for signs of abuse and refer any concerns they have. They will also need to monitor and keep records of what has happened so that they can share information with others. Schools and colleges should read the statutory guidance *Keeping Children Safe in Education* (2015), which outlines how they should fulfil their duties under the law.

Health services

Different health professionals may be involved in discussion about a child's well-being. These may be GPs, health visitors, Children and Adolescent Mental Health Services (CAMHS), or emergency services who have had to deal with injuries that they suspect may be non-accidental. Health services may be asked to examine children and young people or to write reports, or give evidence in court if a crime has been committed.

Social services

Social services have a key role in safeguarding children and young people who may be in need. Their responsibilities are usually focused on what should be done where concerns have been raised about a child or young person. In cases where children are referred to social services, social workers are obliged to acknowledge and decide on a course of action within one working day.

Police/probation and Youth Offending Team (YOT)

Police and probation officers should be aware of situations in which children and young people may be at risk and act on them if needed – for example, in cases of domestic violence where children or young people may be at risk of harm, or where they have been victims of crime. The police have a responsibility to share information with others in order to ensure the protection of children. They also have emergency powers where needed to enter premises and remove a child or young person if they are likely to suffer harm, although this decision will usually be made by a court over a longer period. The probation service, which works with offenders while they are returning to the community, is also in a position to identify when children and young people may be at risk of harm or exposure to criminal behaviour. In this situation it should develop a supervision plan that includes planned interventions for the protection of children and young people. It may also work with the local Youth Offending Team, which is a local authority initiative to prevent young people aged 10–17 from offending and re-offending where they are considered to be at risk of this.

Charities (NSPCC, Save the Children, Child Exploitation Online Protection Centre (CEOP), Barnardo's, The Children's Society)

Charities that work with children and young people have a number of responsibilities regarding safeguarding. These include making sure that children and young people who benefit from or come into contact with them are not put at any risk of harm. Charities must take steps to show that they are:

- protecting children from maltreatment
- preventing impairment of children's health and development
- ensuring that children grow up in circumstances consistent with the provision of safe and effective care; and
- taking action to enable all children to have the best outcomes.

Source: *Policy paper: safeguarding children and young people*, Charity Commission, July 2014

Keeping Children Safe: www.keepingchildrensafe.org.uk

Keeping Children Safe is a global network that aims to keep vulnerable children safe from abuse. They have produced a document entitled 'Child safeguarding standards and how to implement them', to assist organisations in meeting their responsibilities when safeguarding children. You can find it here: **www.keepingchildrensafe.org.uk/sites/default/files/resource-uploads/KCS_STANDARDS_2014.pdf**.

Psychology service

The psychology service may work with parents who are suffering from ill health, mental health issues or learning difficulties, and will need to consider the potential impact of this on any children or young people in the family. It may become aware of domestic violence issues, controlling behaviour or cases where children or young people bring perceived 'shame' on their families or break cultural expectations. It may also work with children or young people who are vulnerable, and need to make special provision to ensure that they are not at any risk from the adults. In any of these cases, psychologists will need to report concerns immediately to their designated Child Protection Officer or LSCB (see below).

Local authority

The local authority is responsible for safeguarding co-ordination locally. This is known as the LSCB (Local Safeguarding Children Board) and its role is to ensure that all organisations work together to protect children. The local authority should also have a dedicated officer or team of people whose role is to manage allegations against people who work with children.

Research it

To find out more about the duties and responsibilities of different organisations, see: **www.gov.uk/government/uploads/system/uploads/attachment_data/file/592101/Working_Together_to_Safeguard_Children_20170213.pdf** (published March 2015).

Using this document, find out about the following and how agencies work together in each case: initial child protection conferences; developing a child protection plan; child protection review conferences.

LO3 Understand the need to ensure children and young people's safety and protection in the learning environment

AC 3.1 Explain why we need to ensure children and young people are protected from harm in the learning environment

Children and young people must be protected from harm while they are in the care of their school or college. Employers must make sure that the adults who look after children and young people are suitable to do this and that they have had the relevant checks before they are able to work with them. This is done through applying to the

Disclosure and Barring Service (DBS) to ensure that they have not had any criminal convictions that may affect their ability to work with pupils.

Children and young people's protection and welfare is paramount while they are in the care of school or college staff, and all staff have a responsibility to ensure that they are kept safe and free from harm. This may be for health and safety reasons (see Unit 2) or in the context of safeguarding.

If you suspect that a child or young person in your care is in any danger of harm, you and your colleagues will be responsible for acting on it and removing them from danger. If you suspect or find out that another member of staff is abusing a child or young person, you are responsible for reporting it. This is known as **whistleblowing**.

Key term

Disclosure and Barring Service (DBS): all adults who work with children and young people will need to apply through this service, which will check their background and suitability to work with children.

Whistleblower: a person who reveals any type of information within an organisation that may be illegal or unethical, or that should not be happening.

Case study

Rania has recently started working as an Individual Support Assistant in a secondary school. She is working with Amara in Year 7, who has significant learning difficulties. Rania has noticed that Amara regularly seems distressed after coming back from lunch, when she is cared for by another adult so that Rania can have a break.

1. Does Rania have any cause for concern?
2. Should she say anything and, if so, to whom?

Stretch and challenge

What more can you find out about whistleblowing? Is it different in the private and public sectors? Why is this?

AC 3.2 Identify the risks and possible consequences for children and young people of being online and using digital mobile devices

For children and young people who have grown up with the internet it is a way of life. It is a very effective way of finding out information and of learning about the world, and also offers a very quick and effective way to communicate. However, due to increased use of the internet in recent years, and the fact that many children and young people now have access to a phone, computer or tablet, it is all the more important that adults talk to them about how to keep safe online. As children start to use technology independently, they may make assumptions that everyone they talk to online is telling the truth. Very young children can have social networking accounts and see it as a way of being more 'grown up', but may not be worldly enough to understand the dangers. As adults we need to be able to talk to them about why it is not always safe to go online. Many primary and secondary schools now have e-safety awareness talks for both parents and pupils although these usually take place separately. Colleges may be less likely to do this with older students, although they may offer support and advice if it is sought. Schools and colleges should be able to give advice and support both to children and young people and their parents about keeping safe online and about the risks they may face.

Risks and possible consequences of children being online

Grooming through befriending people they do not know

This can be dangerous, particularly if the new 'friend' asks them to send photos of themselves, give out personal details or wants to meet them. There have been cases of grooming and abuse where children or young people have gone to meet people that have not been as they expected.

Increased chance of bullying and abuse

Children and young people are often bullied and abused online as the bully is not seen and is therefore more confident about saying things that may be very cruel.

Buying online

As young people start to buy items or services online, they are more at risk as they may not always consider the fact that they need to pay for them. There is a risk of them paying to look at violent or pornographic materials. There may also be security aspects such as safe use of passwords and making sure they do not give out too much personal information.

Banking and financial scams and identity theft

As children and young people are likely to have personal email addresses, they may be the victims of 'phishing' or other financial scams in which they are asked to click on links that may involve them giving out personal information to fraudsters, which can then be used for criminal activity.

Exposure to inappropriate or illegal material or views

Children are at increased risk of viewing material that is pornographic or violent, that might incite intolerance or hate, or that is not appropriate for their age. They may also view material that is illegal.

Viewing misleading information

Children and young people are more vulnerable to this as they are more likely to believe what they read – whether this is 'fake news', people asking for help or financial assistance, or those looking to radicalise others.

Online gaming and gambling

This can seem innocent but can very quickly become addictive. As no money seems to change hands and financial details are linked to accounts, gambling can appear to be similar to other games that children and young people can access online but it is possible to run up large debts.

Social networking

There are a number of risks to children and young people from social networking. These include:

- posting too much personal information and risking identity theft
- sharing photos that they may not want everyone to see
- being vulnerable to bullying or abuse from peers or predatory adults
- reduced time for other forms of socialisation or physical activity.

Sleep deprivation

Children and young people can become addicted to being online and as a result may suffer from sleep deprivation. This may become evident while they are in school or college, and may distract or prevent them from studying.

Activity

Find out about different ways in which your school or college highlights e-safety to pupils. How regularly does this happen? Are there other talks or information that are available to parents?

AC 3.3 Describe ways of reducing risk to children and young people from: social networking; internet use

As well as making sure schools and colleges have e-safety and online safety as a regular part of their agendas, they have other responsibilities to ensure that any computers that are used on the premises have appropriate safety measures in place. While they are on the premises and using school or college computers, children and young people's use of the internet will be protected by the systems and firewalls that are in place for blocking inappropriate websites and materials. While these are usually very effective, it is sometimes possible for inappropriate material to be accessed. If staff are working with pupils on a classroom-based activity where they are asked to research using the internet, they will need to monitor what is being accessed by pupils to ensure that it is appropriate while on-site.

While using personal equipment such as smartphones, tablets and personal computers, children and young people will be much more vulnerable to risks. This is less likely to take place on school or college premises, although many pupils will have access to phones. The main steps that can be taken, apart from regular e-safety talks and raising awareness on a regular basis, should include:

- keeping e-safety on the agenda through talking about it
- talking to parents, and making them aware of parental controls and other settings that they can use on home networks
- making sure pupils manage their settings correctly so that social networking accounts are kept private and others do not have access to their details
- ensuring pupils talk regularly to their parents about what they do online.

The UK Council for Child Internet Safety (UKCCIS) was established in 2008 to keep children safe online through organisations working together. You can find out more information about it here: **www.gov.uk/government/groups/uk-council-for-child-internet-safety-ukccis**

Activity

Produce a leaflet for pupils with whom you work explaining the risks they face online and how to reduce them.

AC 3.4 Explain how support staff can take steps to protect themselves within their everyday practice in the learning environment and during off-site activities

You should be aware of the importance of protecting yourself in the context of safeguarding so that you are not susceptible to accusations of abuse. For example, when in the learning environment or on off-site visits, you should not be left alone with children or young people unless absolutely necessary and should always take steps to avoid this. This is because there have been cases where allegations have been made by parents, children and young people, colleagues or employees against adults, which have later been found to be untrue. This may happen for a number of reasons:

- others in the setting have seen something happen that they have mistaken for abuse
- children may make wrongful accusations because they misunderstand something that has happened, or they have been abused somewhere else
- parents may make accusations if their child has told them about something that has happened, if they are unhappy with the school or college for some reason, or if they are covering up abuse at home
- people may have different ideas about what they deem to be 'appropriate' contact with a child or young person.

In some cases lone working may be unavoidable – for example, if you have been asked to work with a small group of children away from the classroom or if another adult has to leave the room suddenly. In some schools or colleges there may be rules around leaving one adult alone with a child or young person. However, if the situation is unavoidable you should:

- make sure doors are left open where possible so that others can see in to the room
- if you know the situation is going to arise, ask colleagues to check in on you
- be aware of your own actions and make sure you do not do anything that could be misinterpreted as abuse
- be aware of physical contact and think about your dress code. Ladies should avoid wearing a low necked top or skirts that are too short as these are not professional in a school or college environment when you are working closely with learners. Physical contact is sometimes unavoidable, particularly with very young children, as they will often instigate holding hands or hug an adult, however, make sure if you can that others are around and always make sure your hands are visible.

You should also be sensible with your own social networking and personal information – do not 'friend' older children or make your information accessible to them as this might be misinterpreted in some way. Your role should always be seen as a member of staff to a student and should not be over-friendly.

Off-site visits

When you go on residential trips or off-site visits, the surroundings and situations will be different for both staff and pupils. Children and young people who are staying away from home may need reassurance and support but this should be given to pupils as a staff rather than individually. Make sure that you are with others if you need to go into dormitories or bathrooms, and keep doors open at all times if you need to go in for any reason. You should also remember not to use personal recording equipment such as cameras or phones to take photographs of children and young people during school trips – always use those that are provided by the school or college. In this way, you will also protect yourself as you will not have photographs of children on your phone.

In practice

What is the policy of your setting when taking pupils on off-site visits? How are staff and volunteers given safeguarding advice and guidance?

LO4 Understand how to respond to evidence or concerns that a child or young person has been abused or harmed

We all have a responsibility for the safety and welfare of children and young people in our care. Sadly they can be victims of abuse and harm, in many cases from those people who should be caring from them. Children and young people with special educational needs and disabilities may be particularly vulnerable. You will need to know how to respond and what to do if you have any concerns about a child or young person.

1 in 14 children have been physically abused; in the case of disabled children this is three times more likely.

1 in 20 have been sexually abused, 90 per cent by a known person. Around a third have been abused by another child or young person.

1 in 10 have suffered from neglect. It is the most common reason for taking action in cases of child protection.

1 in 14 have experienced emotional abuse. It is the second most common reason for a child protection plan.

Source: *Child abuse and neglect in the UK today*, 2011, Radford, L. et al. London: NSPCC.

AC 4.1 Explain child protection within the wider context of safeguarding children and young people

'Child protection' is the term generally given to protecting children and young people and to keeping them safe.

'Safeguarding' is a wider term, which incorporates the policies and procedures that organisations have in place to prevent harm to children and young people. These kinds of policies are shown in Table 3.1 below.

▼ Table 3.1 Policies and procedures for child protection

Policy	Action
Having a named Child Protection Officer	All organisations that are responsible for children and young people should have a designated Child Protection Officer with clear responsibilities.
Ensuring all staff have regular safeguarding training	It is a legal requirement to ensure that staff are kept up to date with safeguarding issues. This training should be revised on a regular basis.
Having a clear process for reporting concerns, and ensuring all staff are aware of it	The safeguarding policy should outline what staff should do if they have any concerns about a child or young person in the setting.
Having clear recruitment, selection and vetting procedures	All staff and volunteers who have contact with children should be checked through the DBS (Disclosure and Barring Service) and these checks should be updated regularly.
Having clear guidance on confidentiality and information sharing	All members of staff and those volunteers who deal with sensitive information should read and understand the organisation's confidentiality policy.
Having an up-to-date child protection and safeguarding policy	These policies should be revised regularly and staff should sign them to show that they are aware of their responsibilities.

AC 4.2, 4.3 Identify different types of abuse and bullying, and outline the possible signs, symptoms, indicators and behaviours that may cause concern in the context of safeguarding

There are many different types of abuse and bullying of which you should be aware and will need to look out for in order to protect children and young people. They may occur in isolation or the child or young person may be the victim of more than one form of abuse.

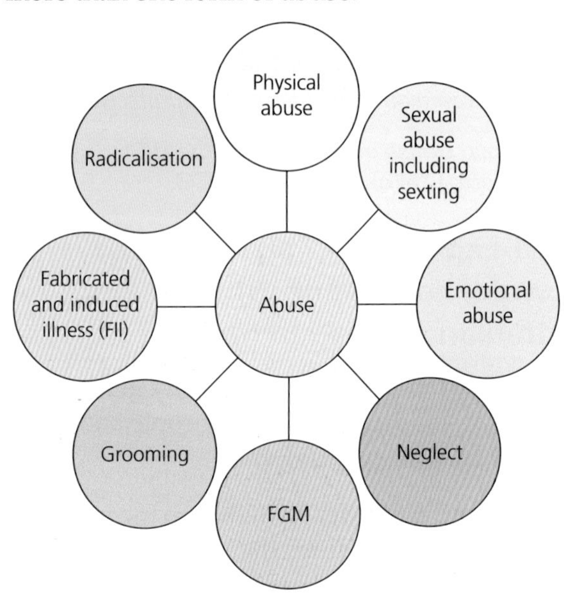

▲ Figure 3.2 Types of abuse

Physical abuse

Physical abuse occurs when a child or young person is subjected to being physically hurt or injured in any way. You should look out for:

- excessive bruising, cuts or burns, or any unexplained marks, particularly if you notice them on a regular basis
- behavioural signs such as the child flinching when they are approached
- reluctance to change for PE or sports activities in case marks are seen
- withdrawn or depressed behaviour
- increased aggression
- fear of parents being notified regarding things that happen in school or college
- truancy, running away from home or going missing.

Sexual abuse, including sexting

This is when a child or young person is forced or persuaded into sexual activity by others. It includes both physical and non-physical contact, which may be forcing the victim to look at pornographic material or sending sexual photographs or messages via text.

Indicators may include:

- child becoming withdrawn or easily upset
- self-harming behaviour
- eating disorders
- sexualised behaviour
- language or comments that are inappropriate for their age
- being anxious if others go near their phone.

Emotional abuse

This form of abuse usually happens over a prolonged period and affects a child or young person's emotional development. Emotional abuse occurs when a person is regularly and repeatedly made to feel worthless, unloved or frightened. Emotional abuse may happen in isolation but can also accompany other types of abuse.

Signs may include:

- a delay in emotional or other areas of development
- speech delays and disorders
- self-harming behaviour
- low self-esteem
- emotional reactions
- abuse of drugs or alcohol
- truancy, running away from home or going missing
- difficulty in making friends.

Neglect

Neglect can be described as a persistent lack of care from those people who have responsibility for looking after the child or young person. It may include insufficient food, inadequate clothing or living space, and a lack of medical care or emotional support when needed. This can impact on the child or young person's physical and emotional development and, depending on the

Class discussion

Consider the following:

- If a Key Stage 1 child came in to school every day saying they were hungry, what would you do?
- Rob is 12 and has frequent long periods of absence. Discuss any necessary actions you think the school should take in this instance.
- Maria is in Year 6 and is very tall for her age. You have noticed that she is regularly being met after school by a much older boy who you have not seen before. She has started to wear make-up and jewellery to school and to act in a much more confident way. Should you be concerned?

extent of the neglect, their ability to make friends. Look out for:

- poor hygiene
- inadequate, dirty or inappropriate clothing
- hunger
- untreated health problems
- frequent illnesses or time away from school or college.

FGM (female genital mutilation)

FGM is the partial or total removal of all of the external female genitalia for non-medical reasons. It is sometimes called female circumcision or cutting, and is recognised as a violation of human rights. FGM originates from communities in Africa, the Middle East and Asia, where it is carried out for cultural and religious reasons, and usually happens when a girl is between infancy and puberty. Girls may be taken abroad for this procedure, particularly in the summer holidays when they have longer to recover. It is extremely painful and traumatic for the child, and can cause emotional problems and anxiety throughout their life.

Signs may include:

- child being taken out of school for long periods for holidays
- reluctance to participate in physical activity
- withdrawn or clingy behaviour.

Case study

Ross is working as an assistant in a Year 1 class that has a high number of children from ethnic minority countries. He has noticed that Ndiaye, a girl whose parents had taken her back to their home country in Senegal for an extended half-term break, seems very weepy and clingy towards staff in the school since they have come back. She has not participated in PE since she came back as her mother has sent a letter to say that she cannot 'due to medical reasons'. After a few weeks, Ross is becoming concerned about Ndiaye's welfare.

1. What should Ross do in this situation?
2. Why is it important that he acts upon his concerns?

Grooming

This can take place online or in person and involves adults building up the trust of a child or young person with the intention of abusing that trust at a later stage through sexual abuse or exploitation. Grooming can involve someone known to the child or young person and may be carried out over a long period of time. Victims may be given presents or cash, or taken on holidays and made to feel special. Those who groom younger children online can often claim to be younger than they are or post photographs that are inaccurate and misleading, to entice victims to come and meet them. In some cases the child or young person may not be aware that they are being abused and just think that they have a boyfriend or girlfriend that is older than them.

Fabricated and induced illness (FII)

This is quite a rare form of abuse and takes place when an adult (usually the child's mother) makes up, exaggerates or brings on symptoms of illness in their child. It is also known as Munchausen syndrome by proxy. In this situation, the adult may say that the child or young person is showing symptoms of illness when they are not, or exaggerate symptoms that they may have, usually due to a personality disorder in themselves. They may also attempt to bring on symptoms of illness in the child or young person in other ways, such as food poisoning.

Research it

In Rochdale in 2012, 12 men were convicted of taking part in a sex abuse ring that involved a number of underage vulnerable teenage girls. The men involved were all well-respected members of their community.

Find out what you can about how the perpetrators used grooming to encourage the situation to develop.

What kinds of signs of grooming might the girls have been demonstrating?

What actions should have been taken in order to avoid this from happening?

Radicalisation

This has become a serious issue in recent times, and involves an individual or group being coerced into a set of extreme political, social or religious aspirations. It may take place over a long period of time or can happen reasonably quickly.

Those who may have been radicalised show signs of:

- becoming more argumentative and angry
- not listening to another's point of view or being willing to discuss it with them
- spending much more time online and showing increased secrecy
- expressing sympathy for more extremist views.

The DfE has a helpline so that school staff can raise concerns about extremism direct: 020 7340 7264. You can also email: **counter.extremism@education.gov.uk**.

The Prevent duty

The Prevent duty is non-statutory advice from the DfE to support a range of organisations that are public facing. It falls within the Counter-Terrorism and Security Act 2015 to prevent individuals from being drawn into terrorism. Schools are likely to provide training for staff on Prevent so that they can identify children who may be at risk, and the local authority may also have a Prevent lead who can provide support if you are in a Prevent priority area. You can find and download the guidance here: **www.gov.uk/government/uploads/system/uploads/attachment_data/file/439598/prevent-duty-departmental-advice-v6.pdf**.

Bullying

Bullying is also seen as a type of abuse as it involves being hostile towards another person or group of people. The signs of bullying may be difficult to see unless it is witnessed, but withdrawn and quiet behaviour may be an indicator and children should always be encouraged to seek help from an adult if they are affected. Sustained bullying can seriously affect the children and young people who are the victims and cause long-term damage. Figure 3.3 shows the different types of bullying.

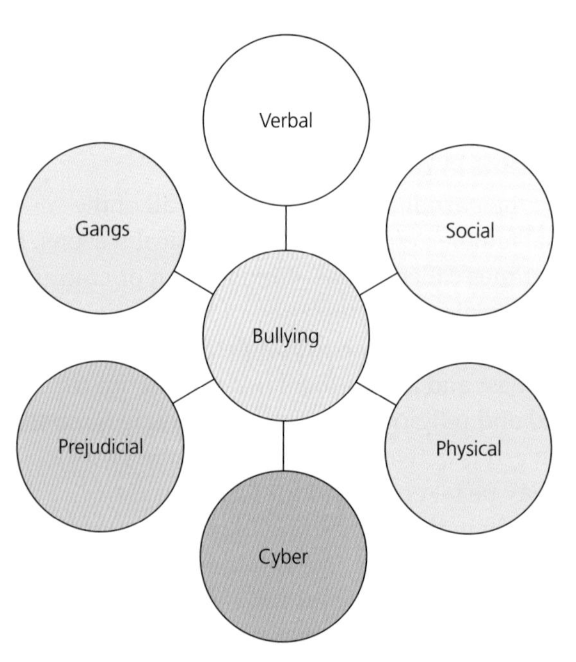

▲ Figure 3.3 Types of bullying

Tips for best practice: safeguarding pupils

- Remember that pupils' safety and protection is the responsibility of all adults.
- Be clear on your school or college's safeguarding policy.
- Ensure you always act on your concerns straight away.
- Be mindful of safeguarding issues at all times, for example e-safety, unfamiliar adults, off-site risks.
- If pupils confide in you, *always* take them seriously.

Verbal

This is the oldest form of abuse. It involves name-calling, spreading rumours, teasing and other ways of verbally bullying an individual or group.

Social

This form of bullying takes place when a group picks on an individual and singles them out, or leaves them out of social activities, while encouraging others to do the same. Social bulling can often take place in schools or colleges where children and young people start to form groups. They may spread rumours about the victim, embarrass them or look for ways of discriminating against them. Social bullying can be very damaging and can sometimes be seen as a criminal offence.

Physical

Physical bullying may take the form of hitting, kicking, punching, pushing or using other means of physical or threatening behaviour against another individual.

Cyber

This is when bullying takes place online or through text messaging, and can include emotional, racist or sexual forms of abuse as well as online stalking.

Prejudicial

Prejudicial bullying takes place when an individual or group are targeted because of their view or identity. They may be bullied emotionally, verbally, physically or through cyber-bullying because of their religion, sexual orientation, skin colour, race or gender.

Gangs

This is similar to social bullying in that groups of people single out an individual or group and pick on them in different ways, sometimes using violence.

Stretch and challenge

The NSPCC website (nspcc.org.uk) offers a range of help and support with different forms of abuse. Find out what you can about the different areas of support that it provides. It also produces a leaflet for children and young people that identifies both the types of abuse, and the help that is available and how to access it.

AC 4.4 Describe the actions to take if a child or young person alleges harm or abuse in line with policies and procedures of your setting

As a member of support staff in a school or college, working regularly with children and young people in small groups or on a one-to-one basis, you may build close relationships with them. As a result of this, you may be the person that a child or young person goes to for advice or help if they need someone to talk to. If a child or young person in your school or college alleges harm or abuse, you will need to ensure that it is reported through the correct channels, and in keeping with your setting's policies and procedures. You will need to act carefully and avoid overreacting to what they tell you, while providing reassurance. The NSPCC outlines a series of steps you should take, as shown in Figure 3.4 on the next page.

If a child discloses abuse, you should:

Listen carefully to the child. Avoid expressing your own views on the matter. A reaction of shock or disbelief could cause the child to 'shut down', retract or stop talking.

Let them know they've done the right thing. Reassurance can make a big impact on the child, who may have been keeping the abuse secret.

Tell them it's not their fault. Abuse is never the child's fault and they need to know this.

Say you believe them. A child could keep abuse secret in fear that they won't be believed. They've told you because they want help and trust you'll be the person to believe them and help them.

Don't talk to the alleged abuser. Confronting the alleged abuser about what the child has told you could make the situation a lot worse for the child.

Explain what you'll do next. If age appropriate, explain to the child that you'll need to report the abuse to someone who will be able to help.

Don't delay reporting the abuse. The sooner the abuse is reported after the child discloses the better. Report as soon as possible so details are fresh in your mind and action can be taken quickly.

Source: NSPCC

▲ Figure 3.4 What should you say to a child or young person who speaks out about abuse?

It is important that, if a child confides in you but has not told anyone else, you must ensure that you tell them that you will have to tell other people so that they can be helped. Report straight away to your organisation's Child Protection Officer.

The following guidance is also useful: **www.gov.uk/government/publications/what-to-do-if-youre-worried-a-child-is-being-abused--2.**

AC 4.5 Explain the rights that children, young people and their carers have in situations where harm or abuse is suspected or alleged

Children and young people

Since the introduction of the European Convention on Human Rights 1950, which barely mentioned the rights of children and young people, a number of conventions and laws have been introduced that take both their needs and views into consideration in cases of suspected or alleged abuse:

- Protection from violence, abuse and neglect (Article 19: United Nations Convention on the Rights of the Child 1989).
- Respect for the views of the child and the right to be heard and taken seriously (Article 12: United Nations Convention on the Rights of the Child 1989).
- Human Rights Act 1998 (Article 3: Freedom from torture, inhuman and degrading treatment). This is for the protection of children's rights and is so that the state can take action to prevent abusive treatment from occurring.
- The Children Act 1989 (England and Wales) legislates that children's welfare and developmental needs are met. This includes the need to be protected from harm.

These rights and laws have evolved over time and have affected the way in which consultations and hearings take place concerning the child or young person so that they are included and consulted throughout.

Parents and carers

Parents and carers will also have rights in cases of child abuse. Parents have a right to be informed about what is being said, and to contribute their own views and opinions. However, in all cases, if the child or young person is or has been suffering significant harm while under their care, parents or carers' rights will be removed.

In this case, the rights of the child or young person will come first.

AC 4.6 Explain how serious case reviews inform practice

Serious case review (SCR)

A serious case review (SCR), as it is known in England, has different names in other parts of the UK:

- Wales – child practice review (CPR)
- Northern Ireland – case management review (CMR)
- Scotland – significant case review (SCR).

In all cases, inquiries and reviews will take place when a child or young person has been significantly injured or has died due to abuse or neglect. Sadly these cases do occur and investigations will need to be made as to what happened and how practice can be improved in the future. The findings of these reviews will be summarised and shared with all agencies and with the public (although names of children and young people will not be given) so that lessons can be learned.

Individual UK Home Nations will have their own statutory guidance for carrying out these reviews, although in all cases a final report will outline what has happened and what needs to happen to prevent it from recurring.

Activity

Find out about a SCR that has occurred in your UK Home Nation in the last 12 months. What are the lessons that have been learned and how might these affect future practice? If you are in an international centre, compare and contrast UK practice with that in your own country.

LO5 Understand how to work with children and young people to support their well-being

All adults working with children and young people will need to be able to support their well-being so that they are kept safe from harm. This involves developing their confidence and awareness so that they are able to protect themselves in different situations, as well as starting to judge things that are safe and unsafe. They will need to be aware of what is happening around them and to be able to make decisions for themselves.

AC 5.1 Describe ways support staff can work with children and young people to build self-confidence and self-esteem

Children and young people's self-confidence and self-esteem are important when it comes to safety and safeguarding as these are closely linked to the way in which they relate to others. Self-confidence and self-esteem can be high or low, and this will affect the way in which we perceive ourselves throughout our lives. Individuals will have high, or positive, self-esteem when they feel valued, and low, or negative, self-esteem when they do not. Children and young people who experience a range of different activities and who have positive relationships with others will be able to develop their communication skills; this will in turn affect their self-confidence and self-esteem. If children are limited in what they do and have fewer social opportunities, their communication skills and self-esteem may be affected, particularly if they have a tendency to be shy.

Children and young people will need to be confident enough to talk to adults about something that may be happening to them, either inside or outside school or college. If they have a poor self-image, they may be less likely to think that someone will be interested in what they are saying or concerned about helping them.
You can support children and young people's

▲ Figure 3.5 Why is it important that we listen to children and value what they say?

self-confidence and self-esteem as well as empowering them by:

- making sure you listen to them and valuing what they say
- giving them plenty of praise and encouragement
- celebrating their differences as well as their similarities
- giving them opportunities to be independent.

AC 5.2 Describe the role of support staff in recognising the signs of mental heath concerns in children and young people

Evidence suggests that mental health issues in children and young people have risen compared to 30 years ago. According to the Mental Health Foundation, around 1 in 10 children and young people are affected by a mental health problem and, of these, 70 per cent do not receive appropriate support.

While adults affected by mental health issues may have more ability to understand what is happening and seek support, children and young people are more vulnerable and, if their problems are not resolved, it is likely that they will have long-term problems that will continue into adulthood. In addition, anxiety-related problems such as depression, self-harming and suicidal feelings are increasing in children and young people.

▲ Figure 3.6 Do you know what to do if you suspect a child or young person has mental health issues?

As adults in schools and colleges, we are all responsible for making sure that children and young people are kept safe. In your role as a member of support staff, you may spend more time than teachers and other staff in talking to individual children or small groups. You should be aware of the need to identify those children and young people who are more vulnerable to mental health issues so that the school or college can offer support. Key events and risk factors that make children and young people more likely to experience problems are:

- having a parent who has a drug, alcohol or mental health problem
- having parents who are separating or separated
- bereavement or trauma
- psychological causes
- being bullied or abused
- being discriminated against
- living in care
- living in poverty
- having a long-term physical illness or disability
- being a carer and taking on adult responsibilities
- domestic violence in a home situation
- puberty.

Of these, the Young Minds charity reported that children living in care are the most likely to have behavioural or emotional problems, with a statistic of 72 per cent experiencing these in 2008.

AC 5.3 Identify the signs of possible mental health concerns in children and young people

A young person with mental health issues may try to hide the signs that there is something wrong, so staff will need to be more vigilant and look out for them. Depending on the individual, signs may be harder to identify in some children and young people than in others. There are some signs of possible mental health concerns that you should be aware of so that you can look out for them. These are described in the following paragraphs.

Eating disorders

These usually take the form of anorexia or bulimia, and can occur at any time although are more likely to start during the teenage years. They are more common in girls but are increasingly also affecting boys. It is important to note that eating disorders are caused by a complex combination of factors and are unlikely to be about being thin but are more about relieving stress and stressful situations. Warning signs may include missing meals, regularly talking about what they have or have not eaten, claiming that they are fat when they are not, or saying that they have already eaten when asked about meals.

Self-harm

According to the Mental Health Foundation, between 1 in 12 and 1 in 15 people self-harm. Remember that self-harming does not just mean cutting or scratching, but can also include hurting themselves in other ways, such as burning, overdosing or poisoning, or pulling out hair. Children and young people who self-harm may be good at hiding it, but as well as unexplained cuts and bruises on arms and legs look out for pupils who keep themselves covered at all times, particularly in warm weather, and signs of low self-esteem such as saying they are not good enough.

Changes in mood or personality and reluctance to communicate

Although there can be many reasons for children and young people to have a change in mood or be reluctant to communicate, be aware and ready to speak about your concerns if this goes on over time and particularly if it happens alongside other possible indicators of mental health issues.

Anxiety-related problems such as panic attacks or phobias

These can occur at any time and can be very debilitating for the individual. If you are aware that a child or young person regularly has panic attacks or other anxious reactions, you should speak to other staff about how to support them.

These kinds of behaviours are a reaction against something that is happening in the child or young person's life, and can happen if they are having difficulties in dealing with emotions. If you are concerned about a pupil either because of their behaviour or due to something they have said to you, make sure you speak to a more senior member of staff, ideally the person with responsibility for safeguarding, so that your concerns can be recorded. If a pupil confides in you, you must tell them that you are unable to keep secrets but that you can help them by telling others and making them aware that there are ways of seeking help.

In practice

Do you know what to do if you have concerns about a pupil? Find out about the procedures in your own setting and what you should do in this situation.

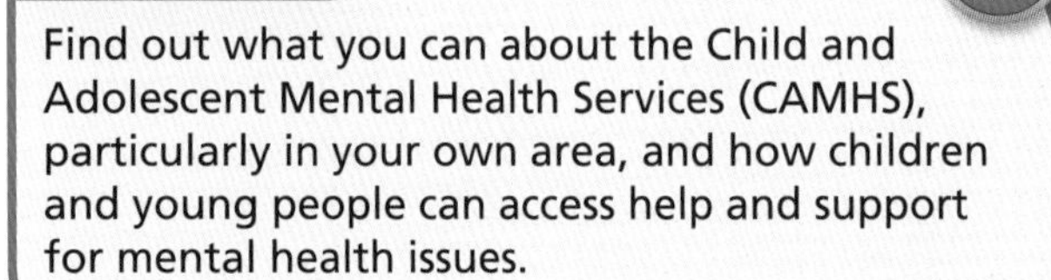

Research it

Find out what you can about the Child and Adolescent Mental Health Services (CAMHS), particularly in your own area, and how children and young people can access help and support for mental health issues.

AC 5.4 Explain the need to work with children and young people to enable them to develop emotional resilience and mental well-being

Although this will not be practical in all situations and some may need more targeted help, children and young people can be taught specific strategies to protect themselves when suffering from mental health issues and stressful situations. They can be taught to develop emotional **resilience** and coping strategies to enable them to manage and deal with situations that threaten them. Adults should therefore support them in finding ways of developing emotional resilience and mental well-being so that they can do this. According to Action for Children, the children's charity, the ability to develop emotional resilience is linked to positive outcomes in later life; the kinds of strategies and interventions that should be used with children and young people, however, are dependent on their age and stage of development.

Key term

Resilience: the ability to recover from difficulties.

Research it

Using the booklet produced by Action for Children, which you can download here: www.actionforchildren.org.uk/media/3420/resilience_in_children_in_young_people.pdf, find out more about specific intervention strategies for promoting resilience that can be used with the pupils with whom you work.

Check your understanding

1. Why do you need to be aware of safeguarding legislation in your UK Home Nation? What else do you need to be aware of?
2. Define safeguarding and give two reasons why it is important.
3. What is a child- or young person-centred approach, and why is it used?
4. Why is it important for you to be aware of how to protect yourself when thinking about safeguarding?
5. What is e-safety and what kinds of risks are there for children and young people when online?

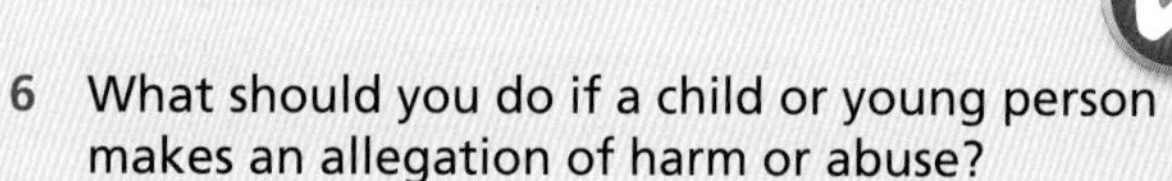

6. What should you do if a child or young person makes an allegation of harm or abuse?
7. What is the difference between safeguarding and child protection?
8. What is a serious case review?
9. Why is it important that children and young people learn to protect themselves when making decisions about their safety?
10. Outline the role of support staff in recognising the signs of mental health concerns in children and young people.

Assessment preparation

This is a long knowledge-only unit and you will need to use different forms of evidence where you can to show that you know and understand the learning outcomes covered. Your assessor may give you assignments or other means of collecting evidence for this unit, or you can use those listed below.

1. For LO1 you can use the 'Research it' feature on page 35 (LO1, AC 1.1).
2. LO2 deals with the need to work in partnership with other organisations. Write a reflective account explaining why professionals need to work together in order to safeguard children and young people, and include the importance of being child- or young-person centred. You will then need to describe the roles and responsibilities of the organisations that may be involved when a child has been abused or harmed. Make sure you use your own words (LO2, AC 2.1, 2.2, 2.3, 2.4).
3. For LO3, prepare a presentation to use with other schools or colleges about the importance of protecting children and young people from harm in the context of safeguarding. This should include risks that may occur both in the learning environment and online, as well as ways in which these may be reduced. You should also explain how staff can protect themselves when carrying out their role in the learning environment and during off-site visits (LO3, AC 3.1, 3.2, 3.3, 3.4).
4. For LO4, write a reflective account to explain child protection within the wider context of safeguarding, and outline the different types of abuse and bullying (LO4, AC 4.1 and 4.2). For AC 4.3 and 4.4, create a fact sheet of signs and indicators that may cause concern and the actions that should be taken within the context of your own setting. For AC 4.5 and 4.6 you can have a professional discussion with others, which can be recorded by your assessor and used as evidence (LO4, AC 4.5, 4.6).
5. For LO5, create an information pack for support staff in your school or college about mental well-being. Describe ways of building self-confidence and self-esteem, and look at the role of support staff in identifying and recognising the signs of mental health concerns. Give examples of how staff can work with pupils to enable them to develop emotional resilience and mental well-being.

Legislation

The legislation relevant to safeguarding is mainly listed in LO1 in this unit.

Read about it

Weblinks

www.nspcc.org.uk The NSPCC works to keep all children safe and protect them from abuse and cruelty; its website offers a range of support for different forms of abuse, such as FGM and bullying

www.nhs.uk/NHSEngland/AboutNHSservices/sexual-health-services/Documents/List%20of%20FGM%20Clinics%20Mar%2014%20FINAL.pdf Download a list of NHS FGM clinics, where you can go for support and advice, here; FGM help and support is also offered through the NSPCC by emailing **fgmhelp@nspcc.org.uk**

www.safekids.co.uk This site offers safety advice on a range of topics, including the internet, food safety, fire safety, etc.

www.childlawadvice.org.uk This organisation provides information on legal matters regarding child law in England; the website contains separate sections on family law, education, attending court and other matters

www.gov.uk/government/uploads/system/uploads/attachment_data/file/591903/CSE_Guidance_Core_Document_13.02.2017.pdf The document, *Child Sexual Exploitation* (DfE, February 2017) provides advice and guidance for practitioners who are working with children and young people

www.mentalhealth.org.uk/a-to-z/c/children-and-young-people The Mental Health Foundation offers support and advice for those working with children and young people

https://my.rcn.org.uk/__data/assets/pdf_file/0003/596451/RCNguidance_CYPmental_health_WEB.pdf The Royal College of Nursing document, *Mental Health in Children and Young People: An RCN Toolkit for Nurses Who Are Not Mental Health Specialists (2014)*, can be downloaded here

www.counselling-directory.org.uk/young-people-stats.html Key statistics about children and young people

www.mind.org.uk Support for mental health in young people

www.actionforchildren.org.uk/media/3420/resilience_in_children_in_young_people.pdf NCH – The children's charity, *Literature Review: Resilience in Children and Young People*

www.england.nhs.uk/wp-content/uploads/2017/02/adult-pocket-guide.pdf NHS document on safeguarding vulnerable adults

www.gov.uk/government/groups/uk-council-for-child-internet-safety-ukccis The UK Council for Child Internet Safety (UKCCIS)

4 Develop professional relationships with children, young people and adults

About this unit

In this unit, you will explore how you work with adults and children and young people in your school or college, and develop professional relationships with them. It will give you the knowledge and understanding to show your competence in developing effective communication and professional relationships with others. You will need to think about issues around confidentiality and data protection as well as the legislation that protects the disclosure of information. On a practical level, you will also need to be able to demonstrate how you support those around you through the way in which you interact and build relationships. Learning outcomes 3–7 will need to be assessed in the workplace so that your assessor can see you demonstrating how you do this.

Learning outcomes

By the end of this unit you will:

LO1 Understand the principles of developing positive relationships with children, young people and adults

LO2 Understand legislation, policies and procedures for confidentiality and sharing information, including data protection

LO3 Be able to develop professional relationships with children and young people

LO4 Be able to communicate with children and young people

LO5 Be able to develop professional relationships with adults

LO6 Be able to support children and young people in developing relationships

LO7 Be able to support inclusion and inclusive practices in work with children and young people

Getting started

Think about two people (adults or children) with whom you have a positive relationship. Think particularly about:

- how often you speak to them
- what you have in common
- how you show interest in what is happening to them.

Why do you think your relationship with them is a positive one?

LO1 Understand the principles of developing positive relationships with children, young people and adults

AC 1.1 Explain why effective communication is beneficial in developing positive relationships with children, young people and adults

What is effective communication? Before we think about why it is beneficial, we should make sure we know what it means.

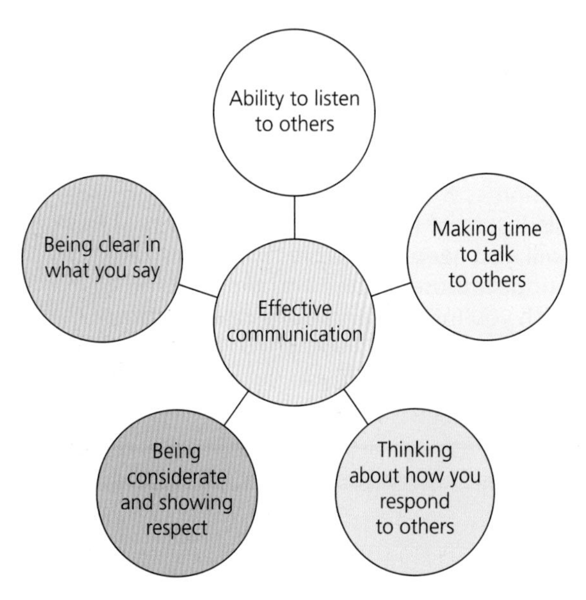

▲ Figure 4.1 What is effective communication?

Ability to listen to others

Many of us appear to listen to others but are really thinking about what we are going to say next. Take time to think about how much you can remember about what people are saying to you rather than just thinking about your own responses.

Making time to talk to others

Sometimes colleagues or children and young people will just need some time to talk through an issue or will need advice. Make sure you offer this, particularly if you are specifically asked for support.

Thinking about how you respond

Show a genuine interest in what people are saying to you through your responses and body language. This can be difficult if your day is busy or if they say something you are not interested in; make sure you consider how your response will look to them.

Being considerate and showing respect

Check that you are considerate in your responses and take account of any cultural differences that may affect how others interact with you.

Being clear in what you say

Make sure you are very clear, particularly if you are speaking to someone who has communication needs or speaks another language.

Effective communication

Effective communication is important. This is true in any profession, and in your role supporting teaching and learning you will need to communicate effectively with both children and young people, and also with adults.

Children and young people need us to act as a role model for them. They will still be developing their own communication skills and will need to see those around them showing how effective these are so that they can work and play together co-operatively. The development of communication skills will also affect other areas – for example, their social and emotional development. This will help them to develop positive relationships both with their peers and adults, and also with those from other backgrounds and cultures.

For more on areas of development and how they are interlinked, see Unit 5.

▲ Figure 4.2 Why is effective communication an important part of your work with others?

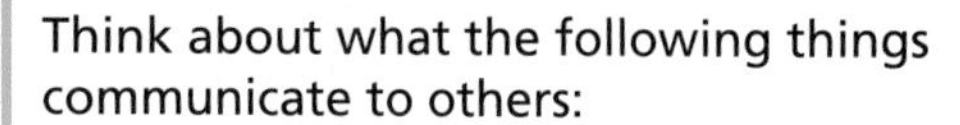

Activity

Think about what the following things communicate to others:

- the way we dress and how we look
- how long it takes to reply to an email or text
- being late to a meeting
- giving eye contact when speaking
- whether or not we shake hands in a formal situation.

What are the reasons for this? Are they professional, social or cultural?

Adults should be able to communicate with one another in a way that is open and professional. This applies to colleagues, parents and other professionals with whom you may come into contact as part of your role. You will need to be able to support others in a number of different ways.

For more on developing professional relationships with adults see LO5, page 63.

For more on developing professional relationships with children and young people see LO3, page 59.

If we have positive relationships with children, young people and adults, we are far more likely to want to interact and share things with them, and this in turn will make support within the school or college beneficial to all, from staff and parents to children and young people.

Unit 12 deals with supporting children and young people's speech, language and communication.

AC 1.2 Explain how different social, professional and cultural backgrounds may affect relationships and the way people communicate

The context of social and professional relationships will affect the way in which people communicate with one another because different situations will require it. For example, if you are meeting friends informally, the language and vocabulary you use, and the way in which you behave and communicate, will be different from when you are in a work situation; if you are writing a work email it will be different from an email to friends. You are likely to do this without thinking about it. However, in some situations you will need to have more of an awareness that people from different backgrounds or cultures may approach things in a different way. This may be in spoken communication but can also include written or non-verbal forms. Remember that those from other cultures may not respond in the same way that you do.

AC 1.3 Describe ways the practitioner can build and maintain professional relationships with children, young people and adults

When building and maintaining professional relationships with colleagues, parents or pupils, the most important factor is effective communication. Always treat others with respect and be polite in your dealings with them, even if they do not act in the same way towards you. You will need to be approachable yourself while bearing in mind that the way in which you communicate with these different groups will vary.

Here are the key points to remember:

- **The context of the relationship** – whether this is adult to child, colleague to colleague or staff to parent, you should ensure that the relationship is a professional one. With children or young people and their parents, remember that you should maintain that relationship. You can be friendly but do not try to be friends.

- **Always be approachable** – you should always be approachable because you will want others to feel that they can communicate with you. Take time to have informal chats with people and ask about them, and share a smile or a joke.
- **Follow up on what you have said you will** – this is important as others will be relying on you to carry out actions. These may be mentioned informally or within meetings but you should make note of them so that you are seen by others as a reliable member of staff.
- **Be interested in what others have to say and remember things that are important to them** – a good way of being interested in others is to ask them about things that are happening to them – for example, asking how their house move went or about their child's first day at secondary school.
- **Do not gossip or talk about other people in a negative way** – people will find it hard to see you as a professional if you talk about others negatively. Always try to remain positive in your relationships and be mindful that this is important.

AC 1.4 Explain how barriers to professional relationships can be overcome

Barriers to professional relationships can take different forms. They can range from simply not getting on with someone and having disagreements or professional differences, to having cultural or communication differences that affect the relationship. Barriers may be short or long term and you will need to be aware of them so that you can try to overcome them where possible. In this way you will be able to support the needs of children and young people more effectively.

Types of barriers may be:

- **Communication differences** – these may be with colleagues who have a sensory or speech, language and communication impairment, or with those who speak English as an additional language.
- **Emotional difficulties** – these may be due to something that is happening in the person's life at the time, or something that has come up during the working day. Emotions such as being angry, tired or upset can make it difficult for people to communicate effectively and focus on what they are doing professionally.
- **Cultural differences** – cultural differences can sometimes cause issues with communication if the other party is not aware of them.
- **Different values and ideas** – you may be working with a colleague or parent who has a different way of seeing things from the school or college.
- **Breakdown of relationships** – from time to time, professional relationships may break down due to poor communication or a difference of opinion.
- **Lack of communication** – if a colleague or parent has not been given information about a particular issue, this may cause problems in the relationship.

See AC 7.2, page 69, which deals with identifying barriers to children and young people's participation.

Activity

Look at the examples of barriers above and think about whether each of them is short or long term. Give examples of how you might overcome each one so that you can use this activity towards your portfolio.

Class discussion

What kinds of barriers to professional relationships have you faced in your current or previous roles? Discuss with others how these have come about and how you have overcome them.

Tips for best practice: developing positive relationships

- Communicate in a positive way with others.
- Act as a good role model to pupils in your relationships.
- Take time to listen to what others have to say.
- Follow up on issues that count.
- Maintain your professionalism.
- Be polite and respectful.
- Be sympathetic to the situations of others.
- Work to overcome any barriers.

LO2 Understand legislation, policies and procedures for confidentiality and sharing information, including data protection

AC 2.1 Summarise the main points of legislation and procedures covering confidentiality, data protection and the disclosure of information

When you are working within an organisation such as a school or college you will need to know about UK legislation, and the procedures of your setting regarding **confidentiality** and **data protection**. This is because there are legal requirements around these that will affect what you are able to communicate to others and how you keep safe any information you may have. The main legislation you should know about includes that described below.

Data Protection Act 1998

The Data Protection Act 1998* concerns the way in which organisations keep and use information that they hold on file. Personal information should be shared with others only if:

- it is necessary for the purpose for which it is being shared
- they have a need for it
- it is accurate and up to date
- it is shared securely and in a timely fashion
- it is not kept for longer than necessary for the original purpose.

> **Key terms**
>
> **Confidentiality:** the importance of keeping information private.
>
> **Data protection:** making sure that data is shared only with those who need to know it.

* Replaced by the GDPR (General Data Protection Regulation) in May 2018.

Schools and colleges must have regard to this Act due to the amount of data they hold on pupils and staff. As well as personal information on all individuals, this will include anything that is relevant to the welfare and educational needs of the child or young person, such as:

- any medical reports or information
- records of special educational needs or disabilities (meetings, diagnosis, professional advice)
- records from social services
- records of achievement
- records from previous schools.

The General Data Protection Regulation (GDPR), in force from May 2018, has been adopted into EU law. Although the UK is leaving the European Union, the GDPR is also likely to be enshrined into UK law. The GDPR strengthens the rights of the individual concerning data which is held about them and also gives the authorities the power to fine organisations that do not comply.

Records will usually be kept on file and computer in the school or college, and those who have access to them will need to be aware of confidentiality requirements. If any information needs to be passed on to others – for example, other professionals outside the learning environment – parents or carers may need to complete a consent form to authorise this. If you are working with an individual child or young person, you should also think carefully about how much you talk to others and not take any records or files off the premises. In this way you will ensure that they do not go astray.

Research it

What more can you find out about the GDPR and how it affects schools and colleges? How does it differ from the Data Protection Act?

Case study

Sasha works in a secondary school as an individual support assistant with Simeon, who has global learning delay. Simeon will shortly be transferring to another school as his mum has a new job. One of the other mums in the year seems to regularly question Sasha about her role and what is 'wrong' with Simeon. On the day that Simeon leaves the school, she says to Sasha that she will be able to tell her all about him now as he won't be in the school any more.

1. What should Sasha say to the mum who is asking the question?
2. Should she do anything else and if so, what?

Activity

Find out whether your school or college has a confidentiality policy. If so, what are outlined as the requirements for staff?

The Human Rights Act 1998

This legislation did not include new rights for individuals but incorporated the European Convention on Human Rights into UK law. The Act has particular relevance for confidentiality under Article 8, which is the Right to Respect for Private and Family Life. It includes:

- the right to respect for private life
- the right to respect for family life
- the right to respect for one's home
- the right to respect for correspondence.

Any information that is held on individuals will need to be held confidentially and securely as failure to do this may interfere with these rights. They can be interfered with only by the state for specific legitimate reasons.

See AC 2.3, right, which deals with situations when confidentiality protocols must be breached.

AC 2.2 Explain the need to reassure children, young people and adults of the confidentiality of shared information and the limits of this

If you are in a position in which you need to collect information or share it with others, you may need to reassure those who are directly involved of the fact that it is confidential. They should be told that legal requirements around information sharing will mean that individuals will not be able to disclose anything personal in other situations. In most cases, parents and carers would be informed or asked to sign a consent form, unless there is a legal reason or a child or young person is at risk of harm or abuse. It is important that professionals are able to share anything that is in the best interests of the child or young person.

AC 2.3 Discuss situations when confidentiality protocols must be breached

There are few circumstances when confidentiality protocols must be breached.

The Data Protection Act 1998 states that information may be shared if this is in 'vital interest'. In other words, in situations where a child or young person is at risk of serious harm or distress, or in a life-threatening situation, information may need to be shared with others. It is unlikely that you would be the one to make a decision on this, but you may be asked to share information for this reason.

The Human Rights Act 1998 states that for a 'legitimate social aim', confidentiality laws may be breached. A legitimate social aim may be:

- in cases of national security
- for the protection of public safety
- for protection of health or morals
- for prevention of crime or disorder
- for protection of the economic well-being of the country
- for protection of the rights and freedoms of others.

Case study

Susie is working in a primary school as a teaching assistant between two Key Stage 2 classes. She spends more time in Year 3, where she works in the mornings to support literacy and numeracy. Kayleigh, one of the Year 3 children, confides in Susie that she is being collected by her uncle that night but that she does not like spending time with him, and that he is 'creepy' and 'always wants to sit next to me'. She tells you that he regularly spends time staying with her family at the moment as he has recently split up from his wife.

1 Should Susie be concerned? If so, should she say something and to whom?
2 What should Susie say to Kayleigh?

The public body will have to weigh up the public interest necessity of breaching Article 8 against the rights of the individual. In some cases, if the child or young person is old enough to make a judgement, and if they do not wish for information to be shared with their family, their own human rights will outweigh the rights of the family.

You may also need to share information with others if a child or young person confides in you about something that has happened to them. This may occur in cases of suspected child abuse or where they are at risk of harm. In this situation, you would need to tell the child or young person that you will help them but are unable to keep this to yourself for safeguarding reasons.

LO3 Be able to develop professional relationships with children and young people

AC 3.1 Show how to establish rapport and respectful, trusting relationships with children and young people

When you are building relationships in any context, the relationship with the other person will be dependent on having trust and being comfortable in their company. This will lead to more effective communication and knowing each other better. With children and young people,

▲ Figure 4.3 Do you remember to use these when establishing and maintaining relationships with pupils?

although this is very important, they will also need to know that the relationship is one of teacher to pupil. Remember also that although you need to get along with pupils in order to support them, you should not try to 'befriend' them, or be overly familiar in the school or college context. This is true with children and young people of any age and is because it then becomes difficult for you to show authority and set boundaries for behaviour.

Showing respect

Always remember to be courteous and to show respect to children and young people if you expect them to do the same for you. You should acknowledge their views and show that you are taking the time to know their name and listen to them.

Being considerate

You should show empathy to the feelings of others, especially if you know that they have other things on their mind or are having a bad day.

Actively listening

You should show that you have time to actively listen to pupils and to respond to what they are saying. When you are working with them, show that you are interested through your responses and body language, and value what they say.

Communicating effectively and using questions to clarify understanding

You should make sure that you are clear when you are communicating with children and young people. Remember to give eye contact and speak slowly, and if you are giving instructions ensure that they have understood what you are saying by questioning them about it.

Summarising and confirming key points

You should go over and check with pupils by summarising key points so that you can be sure they know and understand them.

Remembering important issues

This means that you should try to remember what children and young people have told you about the things that are important to them – for example, if something was worrying them or if they are excited about something that is coming up. In this way you will be showing an interest in their lives and developing your relationship with them.

Showing a non-judgemental attitude towards differences

Cultural or religious differences, or differences in accents and dialects, should be celebrated and pupils should not be judged if they are 'different' from the majority.

Avoiding making assumptions or stereotyping

Take care, especially with younger children, that you do not make assumptions about what they know or have understood. Always go back and check that they are happy with what has been said. You should also ensure that you do not stereotype pupils in any way – for example, 'I'll ask the boys if they would like to enter trials for the football at lunchtime.'

Giving attention to all

You should make sure you give equal amounts of attention to the children and young people you are working with if possible (see also AC 3.3, page 61).

Maintaining authority and following through on actions

This is very important if you want to have effective relationships with pupils – they need to know and understand boundaries for behaviour.

Activity

Which of the following should you NOT do with children and young people?

- Befriend them on social media.
- Chat to them about what you have done over the weekend.
- Tell them that you will not tell the teacher if they misbehave when they are with you.
- Threaten them with unrealistic rewards or punishments that you will not be able to carry out.
- Share jokes with them.
- Socialise with them outside the school or college.

Similarly, you should always follow up on what you have said you will do, as this will ensure that they know that they are not idle threats.

AC 3.2 Show how to support children and young people in making choices for themselves

You will need to be able to show children and young people the importance of making choices for themselves in a variety of contexts. This is because they should not grow up to be reliant on adults to make decisions for them; this will put them at a disadvantage and make it harder for them to develop initiative and problem-solving skills. If you are working one to one with a child or young person with special educational needs, remember to step back and let them take some ownership of decisions which they need to make. It is good practice to allow children to start to make decisions from an early age within the guidelines and boundaries of the school so that they have opportunities to develop some control over their decision making. Examples of this might be:

- giving young children choices over play and leisure activities
- whole classes deciding on class rules or charters for behaviour
- pupils being involved in school councils and decision making
- children and young people being encouraged to vote on different matters within the school or college

Tips for best practice: working with a group of pupils

- Find out as much as you can about the group before you start, and separate any individuals who may not work well together.
- Find out about any specific needs of pupils and sit close to any that need particular support.
- Make sure you set ground rules with the group at the start.
- Be very clear on what you have to do with the group and make sure that they know too.
- Encourage all pupils to put their ideas forward.
- Make sure you take particular note of any quieter or more reticent pupils and try to 'draw them out'.

▲ Figure 4.4 What opportunities do pupils in your school or college have to make decisions and work things out for themselves?

- older pupils being encouraged to debate and see issues from one another's point of view
- older pupils and college students running interest groups.

AC 3.3 Give attention to individual children and young people in a way that is fair to them and the group as a whole

When you are communicating with children and young people, whether supporting their teaching and learning or in other situations, you will often be doing so as part of a group. Due to dynamics and the needs of the group, it can be difficult to balance your attention, particularly if you have one or two individuals who tend to take over: ensuring that you give attention to all individuals can be difficult, particularly in a larger group. If you are working with children or young people with specific needs, the teacher or tutor should have taken this into account as they may need more adult support. However, with all groups, make sure you speak to them before you start about your expectations so that everyone is clear.

Class discussion

Discuss with others how they manage their attention when working with a group of pupils.

Are there any additional ideas you could use to help you?

LO4 Be able to communicate with children and young people

AC 4.1 Use different forms of communication to meet the needs of children and young people

You will need to be able to show that you can use different forms of communication so that you can meet the needs of the pupils with whom you work. A pupil who has communication and interaction needs, for example, may need you to enhance what you are saying through the use of sign or body language. All of the forms listed here are important aspects of the communication process. You should think carefully about the needs of the pupils with whom you work and the way in which you use different forms of language to add to what you want to say.

These may be:

- spoken language (see Unit 12, AC 4.2, page 198)
- play
- body language
- sign language (see Unit 12, LO2, page 190)
- written communication.

Play is an effective means of communicating with young children or those with special educational needs. You may use it as a tool to encourage them to communicate through finding an activity that they particularly enjoy.

Body language can be used on its own to communicate quickly with others if you are unable to make yourself heard or if you do not want to disturb a lesson – for example, if you catch someone's eye. You can use it to communicate a number of different things across a room if you use it on its own. You can also use it to add meaning to what you are saying – for example, if you are working with a pupil or adult who may not pick up on what you are saying if you are using spoken language.

Case study

Rowan is 7 and has social and communication needs as he is on the autistic spectrum. He does not interact a great deal with his peers and prefers to work on computers in the classroom. However he is very interested in trains and can tell you all about them when you get him on his subject. You have been asked to work on some speaking and listening activities with Rowan and are keen to use trains as a tool to help you to break the ice.

1. How might you go about doing this?
2. Why might this be a way of helping to engage Rowan in speaking and listening with others?

Activity

Think about how you might convey the following using just body language:

- Well done!
- You shouldn't be doing that now.
- Stop talking.
- This doesn't taste good.
- I'm not sure.
- He's outside.

Written communication is an effective way to pass information quickly to another person, whether this is handwritten or through email or another medium. You may use written communication if you are working with a pupil who is unable to use speech or who finds it easier to communicate in this way.

See Unit 12, LO2, page 190, which covers the role of support staff when supporting speech, language and communication development in the learning environment.

AC 4.2 Demonstrate how to adapt communication with children and young people for: the age and stage of development of the child or young person; the context of the communication; communication differences

See Unit 12, LO2, page 190, where you will find these points covered in detail.

AC 4.3 Respond to learners' use of home language and local accents and dialects in a manner that values cultural diversity and reinforces positive self-images

See Unit 13, LO2, page 209, for more on understanding how to support bilingual learners.

It is important that, wherever possible, staff in the setting respond positively to learners' use of **home languages** or local dialects, so that they are encouraged to communicate. If these are not seen in a positive way, it may make children and young people lose confidence and feel excluded from the life of the school.

Key term

Home language: the language or languages that are spoken in the home environment.

Case study

Mark has recently started at a secondary school in London where you are working as an individual support assistant to another pupil. His family have had to move down from Newcastle because of his father's job. Mark is a quiet pupil who is taking a long time to settle; you have noticed that some of the other pupils are laughing at Mark's accent and this is making him even more withdrawn.

1 Should you say anything in this situation? If so, to whom?
2 Why is it important not to ignore what is happening?

LO5 Be able to develop professional relationships with adults

AC 5.1 Demonstrate how to establish rapport and professional relationships with adults using techniques to promote mutual trust and understanding

When you are working in a school or college to support teaching and learning, you will part of a wider team of adults. Those with whom you work may be colleagues and members of your internal team, but they can also be external to the setting.

It is important that you communicate effectively with them so that you can support children and young people through professional relationships that promote mutual trust and understanding.

Colleagues

You may be part of several different teams within your school or college: by year group, by curriculum area, by key stage, by department or by role. You are likely to be closest to members of this 'colleagues team' as you will see them the most and so have the greatest opportunity to develop your relationships with them. You should be supportive through ensuring that information is passed quickly and ensuring that you look for opportunities to help, whether this is practical or in other ways.

In practice

Think about the different school or college 'teams' you may be included in as part of your role. What opportunities are there for you to get together as a group, exchange information and talk through any issues?

Parents/carers

You may have limited contact with parents and carers due to your role, and communication may be limited to written forms of communication. If so, you should ensure that these are accessible to parents – for example, if they speak English as an additional language. However, if you work with younger children, or support pupils with special educational needs or disabilities, you may have discussions with them each day about their child. Remember that although you may develop friendships with parents and carers your relationship should always be a professional one.

Noticeboards, websites, blogs and newsletters are also a good way of encouraging parents to communicate and interact with the school.

Volunteers

Volunteers may work in your learning environment for different reasons – either to support teaching and learning in the school or college, as teaching students, or as parents or other volunteers who wish to help. You may be asked to mentor those who are working in the same role as yourself, or you may experience working with student teachers or other volunteers. Remember that volunteers will need you to help, by passing on information where they need it, particularly if they are not in the school or college every day. Also, remember to be sociable – everyone is busy but volunteers can often be excluded from conversations in busy staff rooms or communal areas.

Class discussion

Discuss with others in your group the different people with whom you come into contact – how effective are the professional relationships that people have?

Governors

Governors may not be seen regularly but you should get to know them and find out their names as they will do a lot to support your school or college. There may be photographs of your governors in the entrance hall or staff room, which detail their responsibilities or committees. If you are a support staff governor, try to ensure that others are aware of who governors are and what they do for the school or college.

Outside professionals

These will be individuals who come in to the school or college discuss issues that concern children or young people. They are likely to be health professionals or others who work with children or young people with special educational needs and disabilities.

External stakeholders/visitors

These will be people who have an interest in the school or college but are not directly part of it. They may be concerned with a group of academies or federations that the school is part of, or they may be a social care organisation or agency that arranges work placements for students. It is important to have good relationships with external stakeholders as they may have considerable impact on what happens as well as being able to hold the school or college to account – for example, Ofsted, DfE, Society for Education and Training and BIS (Business, Innovation and Skills) officials.

You will need to consider the same techniques of developing trust and rapport in relationships with adults as with children and young people, particularly the ones discussed on pages 59–60. To recap, these are:

- showing respect
- being considerate
- actively listening
- communicating effectively and using questions to check understanding
- summarising and confirming key points
- remembering important issues
- showing a non-judgemental attitude towards differences
- avoiding making assumptions about what they know, or stereotyping.

In practice

Looking at the techniques in the list above, think of some examples of how you have used them as part of your role. You can use the examples on pages 59–60 to help you.

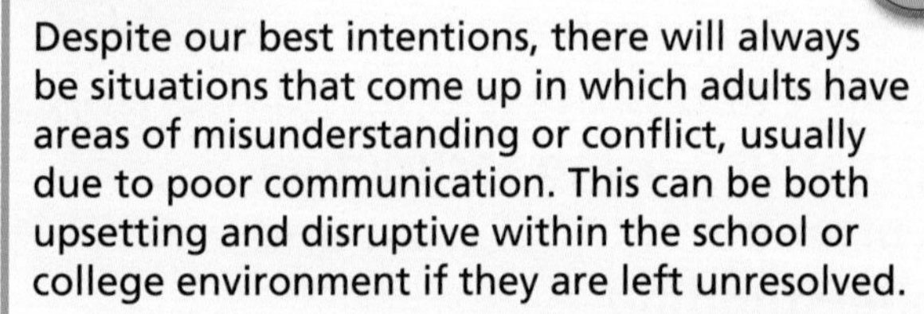

Activity

Despite our best intentions, there will always be situations that come up in which adults have areas of misunderstanding or conflict, usually due to poor communication. This can be both upsetting and disruptive within the school or college environment if they are left unresolved.

Look at the following and think about how each situation might be worked out:

- an experienced teaching assistant with a newly qualified teacher, neither of whom thinks the other likes them; they spend as little time as possible together
- a student who misses classes regularly and has emailed you to say they want to pull out of the course
- a member of staff who seems very disorganised, has a messy learning environment and is always late for meetings; other staff often talk about her and she has started to be teased because of it
- an anxious parent who avoids appointments although she needs to come into school to discuss her child's behaviour; when approached by staff she says that she is busy and can be written to.

AC 5.2 Demonstrate how to adapt communication with adults for: cultural and social differences; the context of the communication; communication differences

We life in a diverse society that enriches all our lives and it is good for children and young people to see adults who are working together. As communication is a key part of developing professional relationships with others, you will need to think about how to adapt your method of communication if needed in different contexts so that that the person with whom you are communicating has access to it. You should always think about others' perception of what you have said and be aware of the need to change the way you communicate if needed.

Cultural and social differences

Cultural and social differences exist due to the nature of society, and individuals' life experiences will be formed around them. Although differences will exist, they should enhance rather than limit communication between adults. These differences may be based on:

- **Age** – this can cause issues with communication, because different age groups may use different vocabulary to communicate, or assume that the other person is aware what they mean when it may be outside their experience due to their peer group. If you are older and the other person is younger, for example, you may need to ask them to clarify what they have said.
- **Sense of humour** – although this is important in a school or college setting, be careful when using humour as sometimes it is not transferable between different social groups or cultures. Be aware that what you say can sometimes be misinterpreted.
- **Opinion** – differences in opinion may cause division and barriers to communication but in a professional context you should be able to agree to disagree if necessary.
- **Sex** – if there are social differences here – for example, if a child or young person has parents who are in a same-sex marriage – it may mean that you would need to think about how you address the couple.
- **Economic status** – all individuals should be treated in the same way, whatever their economic status. If they have difficulties in coming to the setting or if communication is difficult, you should speak to others about how you can help to ensure that you can communicate with them.
- **Cognitive ability** – if you are communicating with individuals of a different cognitive ability you may need to adapt your vocabulary so that what you are saying is clear to them.
- **Language, religion, race or culture** – if you are aware that the language or culture of the individual you are speaking to may cause problems with communication, you should seek advice from other staff in the school about how this usually takes place. There may be translators or other staff available who are able to speak the language and support communication. You should also be aware of the differences that another culture can make. These may be clear straight away – for example, if there is a language barrier – however, even if you do speak the same language, for example, as an American or Australian, there are cultural differences that you may find surprising. Be careful not to stereotype or discriminate for any reason because of this. Different cultures may not always be apparent, but the meaning of what you are saying may be altered by a slight difference.

Activity

Find out how many different home languages are spoken in your school or college. This information should be available through your school or college office. Are you surprised by the results?

The context of the communication

This means that you will need to think about adapting your communication skills according to the situation – for example, whether this is formal or informal, written or verbal. Make sure you take account of both who the communication is with and what it is about.

Activity

Think about the following contexts:

- a staff meeting about the curriculum
- a conversation with a parent who is very disappointed that their Year 2 child has lost a coat
- creating a newsletter for your school or department
- writing an email to an external professional about a forthcoming meeting
- writing on lesson plans that you share with teachers and tutors.

How and why might you need to adapt your method of communication? What considerations would you need to have in each case?

Communication differences

You may find that there are differences in the way you communicate with others, which may create barriers to effective communication. You will need to think about how you come across to others and adapt your communication skills accordingly.

Sensory impairment

This means that either you or the person you are communicating with has an impairment with their vision or hearing. In this situation it is possible that you or they are likely to need sensory aids. For the hearing impaired, these may be a hearing loop or hearing aid, or support with communication through signing. For the visually impaired, notes of meetings may need to be read or provided in another format. You should also remember that those with a sensory impairment are less likely to pick up on some of the subtleties of communication such as body language or facial expressions as they will be concentrating on the spoken word. If you have, or if you are communicating with a person who has a sensory impairment, particularly if you have a formal meeting, make sure that you are prepared and have the required aids or support with you.

Speech, language or communication impairment

You may not be aware that adults with whom you are communicating have a speech, language or communication impairment as they may not have told you. This can mean that there are misunderstandings due to being unable to communicate effectively or due to information being only partially understood. If you always ensure that you speak clearly and check the understanding of the other person, misunderstandings will be reduced. However, your school or college should be able to offer support if you need to work with another adult who has a communication impairment.

Emotional state

This may be positive or negative, but either can influence the extent to which you are able to listen to others and communicate effectively. Although it is difficult, you should try not to let what is happening in your own life influence the way you come across to others or let your own mood dictate how you react to what others say. Similarly, if you find that another person with whom you are speaking is in an emotional state, it may be better not to discuss any important issues but first to make sure that they are OK and support them if necessary; you may need to delay your conversation until they have recovered.

For more on cognitive ability and language and cultural differences, plus how these may affect communication, see page 65.

LO6 Be able to support children and young people in developing relationships

AC 6.1 Use ways of helping children and young people to understand the value of positive relationships with others

As well as showing children and young people the benefits of positive relationships through your own practice, you should also work with your school or college to ensure that they see its importance and value. This should happen over time as they pass through the school or college, and work with one another in different contexts, listening to one another's views and ideas. School pupils of all ages will also have subject-based lessons around

Activity

Consider the ways in which you work with your school or college to support children and young people in understanding the value and importance of developing positive relationships with others. Give examples of some of the ways in which you have done this.

relationships through their work in PSHE (personal, social, health and economic) education, and primary children may also use circle time as a way of talking through issues as they occur. Colleges may focus on the impact of positive relationships through life skills courses and pastoral care.

AC 6.2 Show how to be an effective role model in your relationships with children and young people

Always remember in your own relationships with children and young people that you are a role model, and they will look to you as an adult to show them how to behave and communicate with others. It is important that we show children and young people how we get along with one another in a positive way – if we show respect to others and value what they say, they are more likely to do the same. It will also mean that we are more likely to communicate effectively with one another if our relationships are good.

In practice

Think about all the different people you communicate with on a busy day. How do you ensure that you provide an effective role model to children and young people?

AC 6.3 Demonstrate ways of encouraging and supporting children and young people to: understand and respect other people's individuality; deal with conflict for themselves; respect the feelings and points of view of others

Understand and respect other people's individuality

The learning environment should be a place in which all children and young people feel that they are accepted and valued, whatever their individual personalities, backgrounds or needs. In some ways this is easier with smaller children as they can be more accepting, whereas teenagers can find it more difficult to stand up for what they think or to celebrate the fact that they are different, as they often like to be the same as their peers and are reluctant to stand out. It is up to us as adults to encourage pupils to learn to value and enjoy the fact that we are not all the same.

Tips for best practice: developing professional relationships with adults and children/young people

- Always ensure that you find out how individuals like to be addressed – write it down if necessary to help you to remember – for example, Ms Rathour, Doctor Dymock, or different given names for children or young people. Remember that parents do not always have the same surname as each other, or as their child.
- Invite people to contribute to discussions and conversations, and take account of all points of view.
- Use any communication aids or support if needed.
- Use questioning to check understanding if there is any ambiguity.
- Do not make assumptions or stereotype individuals.
- Be a good role model for children and young people in your professional relationships with others.
- Summarise key points at the end of important conversations.

Deal with conflict for themselves, and respect the feelings and points of view of others

As we encourage pupils to be individuals, there are likely to be situations in which they have disagreements and areas of conflict with their peers. Adults will need to support children and young people in developing ways of managing their emotions as well as being able to articulate how they are feeling. Discussions and debates can be an effective forum for doing this, particularly for older children and young people, as they will be encouraged to think about the points of view of others. They will also need to learn to think about the way in which their actions impact on others. It can be helpful to use tools such as restorative justice to enable them to see others' points of view. They may then be able to talk though and resolve conflict for themselves rather than by reacting in a negative way.

LO7 Be able to support inclusion and inclusive practices in work with children and young people

AC 7.1 Explain what is meant by inclusion and inclusive practices

The term **inclusion** refers to the process of identifying, understanding and breaking down barriers to participation and belonging in society. In the school or college context, it means that all children and young people, whatever their needs, should be given the same rights, access and opportunities to participation and learning. Inclusion is closely linked to equal opportunities, and schools and colleges will have policies around this.

The term 'inclusive practice' means that all children and young people should be involved and have full access to the curriculum, and no pupil or group of pupils should be discriminated against. Staff will need to be aware that some children and young people may be more vulnerable to this.

Groups that are more vulnerable to discrimination include those who are in a minority, such as pupils and staff from minority ethnic and faith groups, those who speak English as an additional language, those who have special educational needs or disabilities, travellers, asylum seekers, gifted and talented pupils, and excluded pupils. All groups should be accepted and celebrated in society, and schools and colleges should be the starting point for learning about and promoting diversity and inclusion.

Key term

Inclusion: the right for all children and young people to participate fully in the curriculum.

Research it

Find out what you can about restorative justice and how it has been used successfully to resolve conflict situations in different workplaces and situations.

In practice

How does your school or college celebrate diversity and challenge inequalities? Give examples of ways in which they can ensure that all staff, parents and pupils are valued and respected as part of the school or college community.

Activity

Find a copy of your school or college's policies on inclusion, equality and diversity. In what ways does the school or college outline how it will ensure that all individuals are treated fairly and with respect?

Stretch and challenge

Find out about the Disability and Discrimination Acts 1995 and 2005 and the Equality Act 2010. As a result of these Acts, what changes have had to be made for schools and colleges and to which UK Home Nations do they apply?

AC 7.2 Identify barriers to children and young people's participation

Despite positive changes in the law, barriers may still exist that can limit children and young people's full participation in education. These may be:

- physical barriers
- organisational barriers
- barriers caused by people's attitudes.

Physical barriers

These tend to be caused by a problem with equipment, resources or access, which means that the child or young person is unable to fully participate in what others are doing. If they have special educational needs or a disability, they may need to have adaptations made or specific equipment to help them to access the curriculum. There may also be physical barriers in the school or college if it was built before the Disability Discrimination Act, as it was not a legal requirement before this for schools and colleges to have facilities for pupils with disabilities. These would include ramps, handrails, lifts and disabled toilets. In this situation, the school would need to make sure that the environment is adapted for the needs of the pupil.

Organisational barriers

These are barriers that are caused by issues within the setting. They are likely to arise because there are insufficient processes and policies in place for the school or college to include all pupils effectively.

▲ Figure 4.5 How can you actively show that you value diversity and inclusion within your work setting?

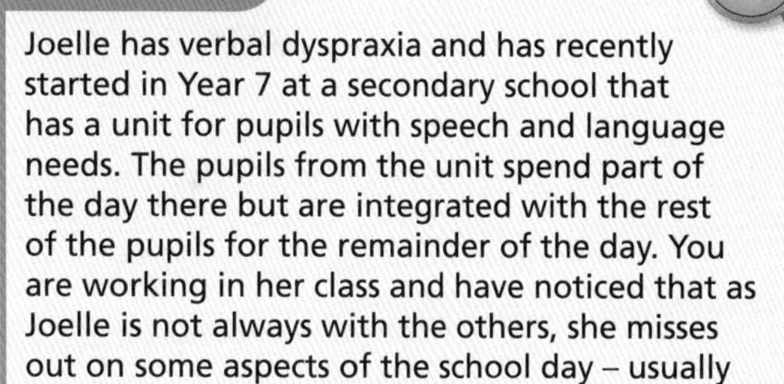

Case study

Joelle has verbal dyspraxia and has recently started in Year 7 at a secondary school that has a unit for pupils with speech and language needs. The pupils from the unit spend part of the day there but are integrated with the rest of the pupils for the remainder of the day. You are working in her class and have noticed that as Joelle is not always with the others, she misses out on some aspects of the school day – usually notices, assemblies and class time.

1. What effect do you think this would have on Joelle?
2. Is there anything you could do to help and, if so, what?
3. Is this an example of inclusion?

Barriers caused by attitudes

These kinds of barriers are caused by the attitudes of others who are part of the school or college community. They may discriminate against pupils or others without realising it due to their own beliefs, which differ from those of the school or college. Examples of this may be parents, governors or staff who are possibly unaware that their views are not consistent with those of the setting and make negative comments about others. Unhelpful attitudes can also be in the form of low expectations of pupils who have special educational needs and disabilities; this can be damaging if it means that these pupils are not given opportunities to fulfil their potential.

AC 7.3 Demonstrate ways of supporting inclusion and inclusive practices in your work with children and young people

You should be able to show that you are committed to equality, inclusion and inclusive practices through your work with children and young people, and also with adults with whom you come into contact in your setting. You can do this in a number of ways, as described on the next page.

▲ Figure 4.6 How can you support inclusion?

Having positive relationships with all

You should demonstrate positive relationships with all individuals and never show preferential treatment to children or young people.

Having a working knowledge of your inclusion policy

It is important that you are familiar with your organisation's inclusion policy so that you are able to follow it. For your qualification it will help if you can highlight key points and show this to your assessor so that they can see that you have understood them.

Respecting and valuing others

It should be clear from your interactions with both staff and pupils that you respect and value individuality. Diversity should be embraced, and all children and young people should have experiences that reflect this.

Acting as a role model to pupils

You should always show children and young people that you are an inclusive practitioner through the way in which you relate to others.

Challenging discriminatory practice

If you hear about discrimination in your workplace, or if you see it taking place, you should always challenge or act upon it to prevent further incidents.

For more on inclusion and supporting pupils who have special educational needs and disabilities, see Unit 14.

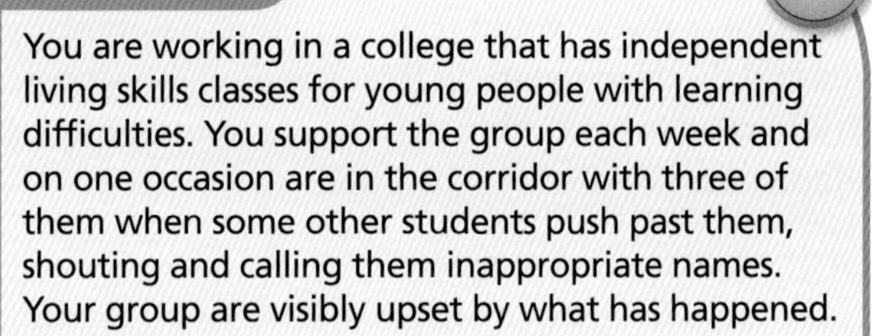

Case study

You are working in a college that has independent living skills classes for young people with learning difficulties. You support the group each week and on one occasion are in the corridor with three of them when some other students push past them, shouting and calling them inappropriate names. Your group are visibly upset by what has happened.

1 What should you do here?
2 Why is it important that you do not ignore the incident?

Check your understanding

1 Give three reasons why it is important to have effective communication skills in your role.
2 How might a child or young person's social or cultural background affect the way in which they communicate with others?
3 Why do you need to be aware of legislation surrounding data protection?
4 In which of the following situations would you need to share confidential information with others?
   - When there is a case of suspected child abuse.
   - When pupils transfer to another school or college.
   - When you are working with a new member of staff.
   - When a child or young person is in danger of harm.
5 How can you ensure that you establish positive relationships with others?
6 What different forms of communication might you use when working with children and young people?
7 Give three reasons why you may need to adapt your communication with children and young people or adults to meet their needs.
8 Why is it important that adults provide effective role models to children and young people when forming relationships?
9 How can we support children and young people to understand and respect one another's individuality and points of view?
10 What is the meaning of the term 'inclusive practice'? How will this affect your work with children and young people?

Assessment preparation

In order to gather the majority of evidence for this unit, your assessor will need to see you in a professional environment demonstrating the skills in the learning outcomes and assessment criteria. When your assessor visits, you should plan to be in different situations in which you are communicating effectively both with adults and with children and young people.

The first part of this unit (LO1 and LO2) is knowledge based and outlines the importance of effective communication and positive relationships, as well as key legislation. This will need to be assessed through assignments or reflective accounts, or through questioning or professional discussions that are witnessed by your assessor. In order to cover these assessment criteria you may like to use the assignments below.

1 Create a confidentiality booklet for new members of staff at your setting, which details the main points of legislation and school or college procedures that cover confidentiality. You will need to explain how to reassure children, young people and adults about when information must remain confidential and justify when it should not, with reasons (LO2, AC 2.1, 2.2, 2.3).
2 Explain why effective communication is important in developing positive relationships with others and give examples of the factors that would influence this. Have a professional discussion in groups with your assessor present about different social, cultural and professional backgrounds, how they may affect the way in which people communicate and how to overcome barriers that may occur (LO1, AC 1.1, 1.2, 1.3, 1.4).
3 Write a reflective account about inclusion and inclusive practice, and what it means in the school or college setting. Identify any barriers to inclusion that you have come across or that might arise in the workplace. Give examples from your own setting of how inclusion has worked effectively and how you have been involved (LO7, AC 7.1, 7.2).

Legislation

- Data Protection Act 1998 (this will be changing to General Data Protection Regulation in May 2018). Although this is an EU directive it is likely to be converted to British law.
- Human Rights Act 1998
- Equality Act 2010

For full details, see AC 2.1, page 57.

Read about it

Weblinks

https://set.et-foundation.co.uk/about-us/our-mission/ Society for Education and Training – professional organisation for practitoners working in the post-16 training system

www.circle-time.co.uk Jenny Mosley's website and books have many ideas for circle time activities

www.pshe-association.org.uk PSHE curriculum – there is plenty available online to support the teaching of PSHE; try this PSHE Association website as a starting point

restorativejustice.org.uk The Restorative Justice Council (RJC) promotes quality restorative practice for everyone

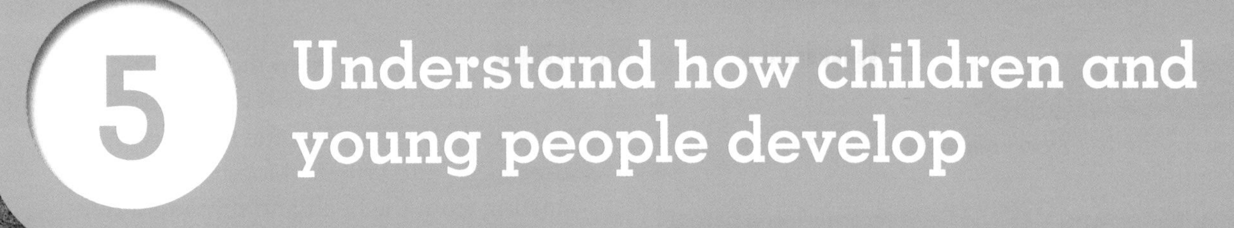

5 Understand how children and young people develop

About this unit

When you are working with children and young people it is very important that you know about and understand how they grow and develop so that you will be able to meet their needs and support them more effectively. This knowledge-based unit requires you to know about and understand the different areas of development for children and young people from birth to 19 years. It includes factors that affect the way in which they develop, as well as the rate and sequence of their development. You will need to look at different theoretical perspectives that underpin the development of children and young people in different areas of their development, and how these might influence your practice. This unit will also explore the actions that should be taken by professionals in schools and colleges if children and young people's development is not following the expected pattern.

Learning outcomes

By the end of this unit you will:

LO1 Understand the expected pattern of development for children and young people from birth to 19 years

LO2 Understand the factors that influence children and young people's development and how these affect practice

LO3 Understand how to monitor children and young people's development and interventions that should take place if this is not following the expected pattern

Getting started

Discuss the following learners with others in your group:

- a learner who is 15 and has a recently lost a parent
- a learner aged 7 who has just arrived in the school or college from another country.

Do you think that the development of either of these learners will be affected by their situation? Give reasons for your answer.

LO1 Understand the expected pattern of development for children and young people from birth to 19 years

AC 1.1 Describe milestones in children's holistic development from birth to 19 years

Childhood is a rapid period of growth and development, which varies between individuals. Some parts of it will be very memorable to us, such as learning to read or to ride a bike. Our individual development is affected by our own experiences and the many different things that happen in our lives. You will need to know about the different aspects of child development and the way in which children progress from birth, as well as the different factors that may affect this. This unit will look at what these factors might be, and how children and young people may be affected at different stages of their development.

Development is closely linked to **growth**, as it is the process by which children and young people mature in different areas. The aspects of development are usually broken down into four main areas and we will look at each of these more closely; however, you should remember that human development also comprises three basic principles:

Key terms

Development: advancement towards maturity.

Growth: the process of increasing in size.

1. Development starts from the head and works its way down. A baby will gain control over the muscles in their neck in the first few months after birth, and will develop this strength starting from the head and moving down towards the base of the spine and central nervous system. It will later start to develop outwards towards the hands and feet so that movements will become more complex.
2. Although the sequence or order of development will stay the same, the rate or speed at which it happens will vary from child to child.
3. The skills that children are learning are linked together and will often overlap – for example, learning to play a musical instrument will require co-ordination as well as cognitive skills and self-expression; communication and language skills will need to develop so that children can learn to talk about their feelings and control their emotions through social and emotional development.

▲ Figure 5.1 How are different areas of a child's development connected to one another?

Stretch and challenge

Find out more about the cephalocaudal **pattern of development**.

Development should also be looked at in a **holistic** way – that is, as part of the whole child or young person.

Key terms

Pattern of development: the sequence (order) and the rate (time frame) in which development occurs.

Holistic: believing that the parts of something are interconnected and looking at the whole as well as the parts.

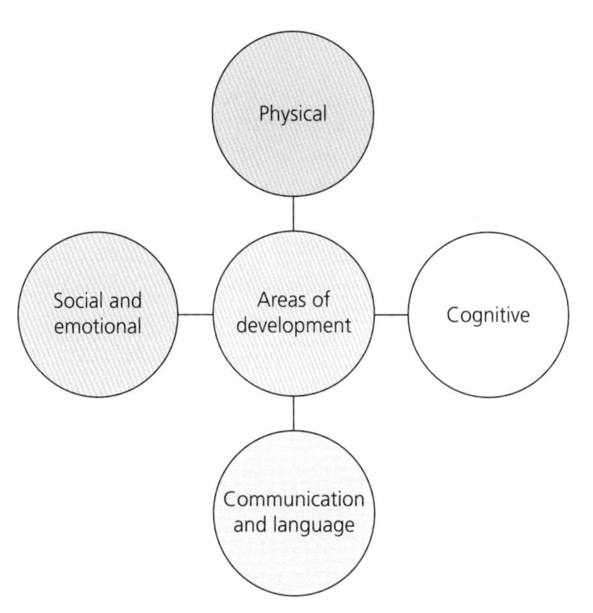

▲ Figure 5.2 Areas of development

Physical development

The rate of a child or young person's physical development is the most outwardly visible indicator. It is about the way that children grow and learn movement through developing control and co-ordination of their body and muscles. It is divided into two areas:

1. Fine motor skills – these skills are needed to hold and handle smaller objects, and to control this by using hands and fingers – for example, holding a pencil or being able to do up a zip.
2. Gross and locomotive motor skills – these types of skills are needed to control and develop the movement of large limbs, and to allow the body to balance and move. They are needed for throwing and catching a ball, jumping and skipping, riding a bike, and so on.

Children and young people will also need to develop perceptual skills, which are needed to be able to judge distance and space between objects in relation to their size.

Birth to 3 years

Infants and children go through a period of rapid physical development from birth to 3 years. This can be divided further so that progress can be seen more clearly, as shown in Table 5.1.

▼ Table 5.1 The stages of physical development

Age	Stage of physical development
0–6 months	At this stage, physical development will be based on primitive reflexes that originate in the lower areas of the brain and are not a learned response. These will stay in place for the first few months after birth and will stimulate the nerve growth that is needed before the conscious brain takes over. By around 3 months, babies will start to show some control over their hands and try to reach for objects, or their feet when on their back. They will be able to lift and turn their head if they hear a sound.
6–12 months	Babies of this age will have control over their head and be able to roll over. They may start to sit without support, and to shuffle or crawl and pull themselves up to a standing position. As they continue to gain control over their arms and hands, they will start to pick things up and put them in their mouths. They are likely to look for things that have been dropped and deliberately repeat this action.
1–2 years	Children will start to be able to feed themselves with a spoon and use their hands to grasp a crayon or an object. They will be gaining more strength in their body and are starting to walk unsteadily but will be developing their confidence. They may attempt to crawl or bump up and down stairs.
2–3 years	Between 2 and 3 years, children will start to use their increased levels of control and strength to practise new skills such as throwing, kicking and running. They will have more control over their fine motor skills and be able to turn pages in a book and make marks on a piece of paper. They may start to use a preferred hand for these kinds of activities.

3–7 years

Children between the ages of 3 and 7 will be developing co-ordination and confidence in their physical skills. They will be refining their control over fine motor skills such as drawing, cutting, threading, completing puzzles, and using a zip or buttons. They will also have more confidence and stamina in their gross motor skills such as walking upstairs, running and hopping, riding a bicycle and using play equipment.

7–12 years

Children of this age will continue to develop in these areas and may have a preference in one area, such as sport or dance, which will mean that they practise and develop more in this area. They will also have developed their fine motor skills and can show great control and co-ordination, for example, when using movements such as those needed for playing a musical instrument. Puberty may start in some children towards the end of this stage, particularly in girls in their last year or two of primary school, when they may grow and develop rapidly.

▲ Figure 5.3 What kind of skills are developed when learning to play an instrument?

Stretch and challenge

Research the following reflexes in a newborn and their significance: sucking, rooting, Moro, grasping. How do they affect development?

What more can you find out about the development of reflexes and their influence on development?

12–16 years

This is the start of adolescence and another time of rapid physical change for both boys and girls. There may be a wide variation in physical development between these ages as the age and rate of puberty will vary. While some girls are almost at their full height between the ages of 13 and 15, with boys this may be slightly later, and they will still be developing strength and co-ordination.

16–19 years

The young person will continue to grow and develop so that, by the age of 19, they will be close to their full physical adult maturity.

Cognitive development

Cognitive or intellectual development involves the construction of pathways and thought processes within the brain. It is about the way in which the child or young person learns to think and to process information from the earliest stages – they will need to use their memory and skills and to make connections between experiences. Cognitive development is also closely linked to the learning of language as it is another aspect of brain development.

The brain changes dramatically within the first two years after birth; it actually triples in size during this time. **Neural pathways** are formed and connections made through the development of signals within the brain. The child's experiences and emotions will cause the brain to respond and develop processes that will strengthen over time as the child becomes more proficient.

Research it

This is a period of rapid change. Research the following stages in a child's cognitive development and find out what you can about them: 0–6 months; 6–12 months; 1–2 years; 2–3 years.

Key term

Neural pathway: a developed path in the brain that is formed by repeated experiences.

Stretch and challenge

Research has shown that periods of stress can affect both physical and brain development in babies and young children due to the release of a hormone called cortisol. Find out about the causes of this and its long-term effects.

In practice

- If you are working with children between 3 and 7 years old, practise simple games that help to develop their memory skills, such as matching pairs, I spy or Kim's game.
- Outline three other ways in which you can support children's cognitive development at this age.

▲ Figure 5.4 How does reading support the development of cognitive skills?

3–7 years

Children will be finding out more about the world around them, although their memory and concentration skills will still be developing. They will be starting to use and understand symbols, for example, when learning to read and write, and be able to do simple sorting. They will be developing independence and learning about their own identity.

7–12 years

Children of this age will be developing fluency in learning to read, write and use numbers. Their problem solving and use of abstract skills will be becoming more developed, and they will be starting to have their own ideas in preferred areas and subjects. They will still be trying out new activities and learning about themselves.

12–16 years

The young person will be developing their responsibilities and starting to focus on subjects that they enjoy so that they can make choices for later study. They will be more motivated in these areas of strength and will tend to lack confidence in areas they find more challenging.

16–19 years

The brain starts to reach maturity, and young people of this age will be continuing to develop capabilities and strengths in their chosen subjects. They will be looking forward to adulthood and making choices that will impact on their future pathways.

Communication and language development

This aspect of development enables us to interpret what others are saying, as well as be able to respond appropriately. Children and young people need to learn how to make sense of language as well as facial expressions and body language, and to develop the way in which they communicate with others. This area of development also includes reading and writing skills as these are another aspect of communication and language.

Birth to 3 years

Although very young babies will not be able to speak until around 1 year, they will be starting to learn the basics of communication from an early age. They will start to recognise faces from around 2 weeks and be able to respond to familiar voices. Until around 1 year, babies will be listening to speech and will start to communicate by smiling, crying and cooing. By around 9 months, they will be starting to babble and later to reproduce words. Between 1 and 2 years, children will be starting to use words in isolation or possibly putting two words together such as 'my cup' or 'daddy gone'. Between 2 and 3 years, vocabulary will increase more rapidly and they will be able to use simple sentences.

Research it

What is the average number of words a child can speak at the following ages: 1 year; 18 months; 2 years; 30 months; 3 years?

Case study

Maggie is working as a teaching assistant in a reception class. She has been asked to carry out a simple speech and language test with all the pupils in the class to check on their communication and language skills as they come into school. This involves their listening skills as well as their expressive language skills.

1. What do you think are the advantages and disadvantages of these kinds of tests?
2. How might they be used by the school once it has the results?

3–7 years

Children will be able to speak in sentences, although some aspects of their language may still be immature at this age. They will be starting to understand and use some of the nuances of gestures and body language. As they grow older they will ask increasing amounts of questions about their world.

7–12 years

Children will be fluent and will be developing their capacity for learning, as well as being able to reason and explain more abstract ideas. They will use more complex sentences and use tenses correctly.

12–19 years

Children and young people will be fluent speakers of their home language, although their vocabulary will continue to develop and mature. Their communication and language skills will enable them to read and write effectively in the same way as adults. Young people of this age may sometimes have their own jargon or words that they use when communicating with their peers.

▲ Figure 5.5 Why is communication and language such an important aspect of development?

For more on supporting speech, language and communication, see Unit 12.

Social and emotional development

This area of development is concerned with the experience and management of emotions and feelings, and how children and young people learn to control them. It is also about the way in which they start to relate to other people and develop relationships with them.

Birth to 3 years

Children of this age will be starting to develop attachments with those closest to them. They will be very dependent on these attachments and will become upset if they are away from familiar adults. By around 2 years, children will become frustrated if they do not get their own way immediately and will find it difficult to share with others.

3–7 years

Children's social skills will be developing, they will be starting to have preferred friends, and to be able to share and take turns. They will usually understand the need to wait for their needs to be met and start to recognise why we have rules. Children of this age will look to adults for approval and will respond well to being given responsibilities, as this will help them to develop independence skills.

Research it

Find out what you can about the terms emotional intelligence and theory of mind. How will having these skills help children and young people to develop friendships and empathise with others?

▲ Figure 5.6 What skills do children and young people need to have in order to be able to form attachments?

7–12 years

This phase of social and emotional development is more steady and settled, and children will have a wide circle of friends although close friendships are likely to be with those of the same sex. They will be developing a greater understanding of why others may behave as they do.

12–16 years

As children enter adolescence, they will experience a range of emotions as their bodies change and they start to become adults. They can be vulnerable as in some cases they will look older than they are, and will enjoy the feeling of maturity, although they will not have the experience to be able to deal with some of the expectations that this brings. They will still need adult support and guidance as they negotiate some of the more challenging aspects of growing up.

16–19 years

Young people of this age are entering adulthood and finding their place in the world. They will still need to have some guidance as they develop their experience and grow in emotional maturity and emotional intelligence.

Case study

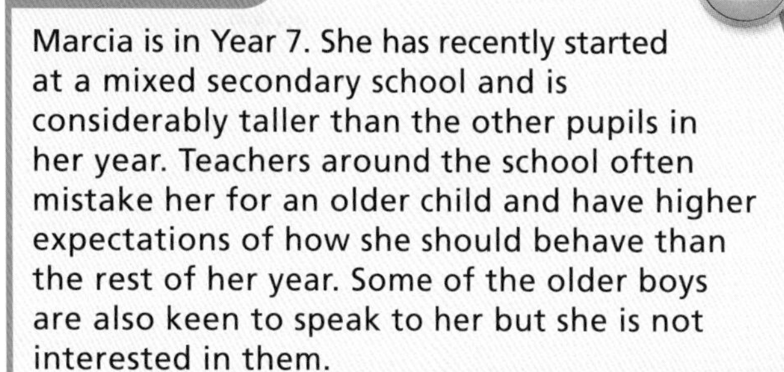

Marcia is in Year 7. She has recently started at a mixed secondary school and is considerably taller than the other pupils in her year. Teachers around the school often mistake her for an older child and have higher expectations of how she should behave than the rest of her year. Some of the older boys are also keen to speak to her but she is not interested in them.

1 How might these two things affect Marcia?
2 Is there anything that staff can do to help her?

While each child will follow the same sequence or stages of development, it is important to remember that the age and rate at which they reach these will differ, as each child is individual. The ages given here offer an approximate idea of when children may be able to achieve different milestones, but these will vary. As children grow older and develop aptitudes and talents for different things, they may also overtake their peers in different areas. You should be aware that each child or young person, for a number of reasons, may develop slightly differently, and that the milestones given are a guide to, or an average of, when these stages may occur.

For more on factors influencing children and young people's development, see LO2 below.

LO2 Understand the factors that influence children and young people's development and how these affect practice

As well as looking at the rate and sequence of development, the way in which children and young people grow and develop will be influenced by many different factors, due to the environment and background in which they are growing up; some of these will be biological and some of them external. They will also be influenced by their genes and other hereditary factors that are passed on by their parents. This is sometimes known as the 'nature vs nurture' debate. You will need to know about these influences and how pupils may be affected by them so that you can best support their learning and development.

AC 2.1 Explain how children and young people's development is influenced by a range of biological factors

Biological factors will be those over which the child or young person has no control but that influence different areas of their development. They may be visible to others but in some cases they will not and you may not know about them until you ask. In your role as a member of support staff you should be sensitive to this, as pupils may find different areas challenging or be affected by them in different ways.

Biological factors will include:

- health conditions or disabilities
- congenital conditions, i.e. present at birth
- gender.

Health conditions or disabilities

There are a number of health conditions and disabilities that may affect the development of a child or young person. These may range from conditions such as asthma or attention deficit hyperactivity disorder (ADHD) to more severe conditions such as childhood cancers or physical disabilities. These conditions will not just affect their physical development but also their social and emotional development as the activities in which they take part are likely to be restricted to some extent. Depending on their age and level of realisation, as well as the attitudes of others, they may feel excluded – for example, on the playground or in the sports hall – if they are unable to do the same things as other children. The extent to which this will affect development will depend on the condition itself and how pupils see themselves.

See Unit 12, AC 1.4, page 189, to find out how difficulties in this area will impact on overall development.

See also Unit 14, which deals with how to support children and young people with special educational needs and disabilities in the learning environment.

Congenital conditions

A congenital condition is one that exists at birth and has been caused by a defect in the development of the foetus. This may be for genetic reasons or due to an abnormality in the chromosomes. As with health conditions, congenital conditions may affect all areas of a child or young person's development, depending on the extent of the condition itself.

Gender

Remarks are often made about the fact that boys and girls will grow and develop physically at different rates, or that they are 'wired' differently. This occurs in different areas of development and at different ages and stages. These changes are not only physical, but also neurological (occurring in the brain) and this can affect children and young people's development, motivation and academic achievement. This should in turn affect the way

In practice

Have you worked with children or young people who have been affected by health or congenital conditions or disabilities? Has this affected their development in any way and, if so, how?

Activity

Look at the list of health and congenital conditions below. Consider how they might affect different areas of a child or young person's development and how you might best support them:

- diabetes
- epilepsy
- muscular dystrophy
- cleft palate
- Down syndrome.

that we approach teaching and learning. There are a number of ongoing studies on gender differences that have looked at rates of development across the areas of physical, cognitive and language development – the three aspects that are most affected.

For more on boys' and girls' learning see Unit 7, page 117.

Physical development

Boys and girls will grow at a slightly different pace from one another, and girls will usually develop and mature physically more quickly. The rate of hormone production is also higher at different ages and stages of development, but particularly around puberty, and this can affect behaviour in boys and girls.

The average age for puberty is 11 for girls and 13 for boys, although every individual is different so some may reach puberty a while before this and some a while after. As a result of these broad differences, many girls will reach puberty before their male peers, towards the end of primary school. Hormonal changes will also give girls a head start in the development of the prefrontal cortex of the brain, which is the part responsible for rational thinking.

▲ Figure 5.7 How does their sex impact on the development of boys and girls?

Cognitive and language development

There has been much neurological research about the differences between the male and female brain, and this is still continuing. Brain structure, size and rate of development, sometimes in different parts of the brain, tend to differ slightly between boys and girls. As brains' sizes and shapes are physically different, they also tend towards different characteristics, although there will always be other influences on learning, and we should take care not to stereotype – whether the structural differences affect learning or vice versa is still a topic for debate. From an early age, girls seem to have an advantage with language development due to the structure of the brain. They usually talk earlier and have larger vocabularies, and will often outperform boys in the areas of reading and writing. This is because the left hemisphere of the brain, which controls producing and interpreting language, develops before the right in girls. In boys, the right hemisphere will develop first and this controls spatial abilities and visual imagery. Boys will therefore have more of a tendency to need speech and language support in the early stages of development, but this will even out over time.

Case study

Thomas and Lucy are twins. They are 12 months old and the health visitor is about to carry out their one-year check. They are a similar height and weight. However, Thomas is able to walk and is 'cruising' around furniture by holding on to it. He is keen to climb the stairs and is very adventurous physically. Lucy does not seem interested in doing these things but has started to say a few words, and responds to nursery rhymes and songs by clapping alongside an adult.

1. Do you think that these differences in development have anything to do with the fact that Thomas and Lucy are a different sex?
2. Why is it important not to stereotype when talking about children's development?

In practice

Look at four children or young people of the same age in your own learning environment. They should be a mixture of boys and girls. Observe them in different situations and look at their stage of development in the following areas:

- physical development
- social and emotional development
- communication and language development.

What do you notice? How do they compare?

Stretch and challenge

What can you find out about the differences in neurological development between boys and girls? Find out what you can about the gender debate and put together your own argument, making sure you use evidence to back it up.

AC 2.2 Explain how children and young people's development is influenced by a range of external factors

External factors affecting a child or young person's development will centre around their circumstances and family background. While some of these factors may be positive, others will be negative or affect their health and development. You will need to be alert to any changes in behaviour so that you can give help and support where needed.

External factors will include those described in Figure 5.8.

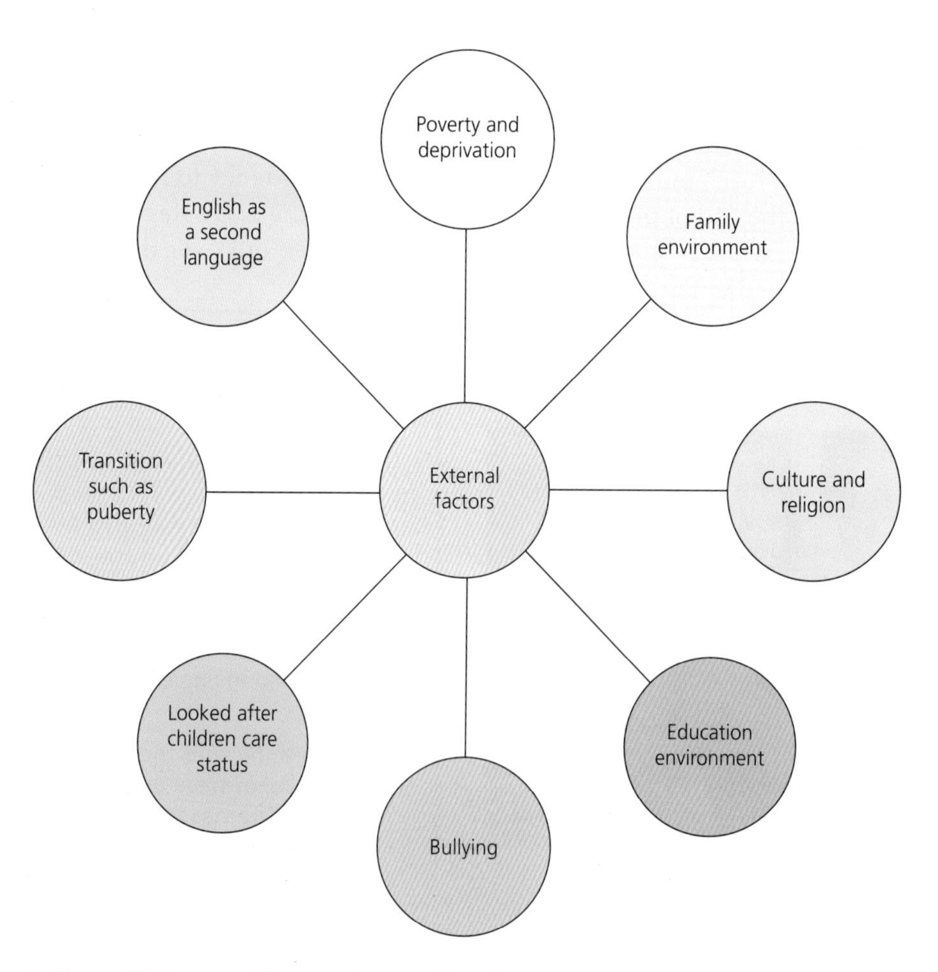

▲ Figure 5.8 External factors that could influence development

Poverty and deprivation

This may influence all areas of development as the child or young person may be undernourished and hungry, and so find it hard to concentrate. This will affect their ability in the learning environment as they will not be as focused on what they are doing, so will suffer academically. Physically they may be affected by lack of food or by being cold if they are not kept warm enough at home in winter. Emotional and social development will also be affected as they may notice what others have and possibly feel left out or excluded because they do not have the same things as their peers.

Family environment

This can cover aspects such as housing, overcrowding, refugee or newly arrived status, domestic violence, substance/alcohol abuse, young carer, divorce and bereavement.

▼ Table 5.2 The effects of negative domestic situations on a child or young person's development

Domestic situation	Effect on development
Housing or overcrowding issues	The child or young person may be living in a situation where their housing needs are causing a stressful situation, for example, if they are overcrowded or awaiting permanent accommodation. This will be difficult emotionally for them as the family will feel unsettled, as well as physical issues such as less sleep due to overcrowding and noise.
Refugee/newly arrived status	This situation may be hugely difficult for children and young people and there may be several factors to consider. They will have had to leave their home, perhaps in a hurry, and suffered the trauma of this along with losing personal belongings. They may have suffered bereavements or lost contact with family members, and not know or understand the cause. Journeys may have been hazardous and frightening for them. If they are newly arrived with no knowledge of the language or culture, they will be very unsettled and confused. One of these factors alone would cause them to have emotional anxieties and would impact on their development. The effects will be life long and they will need plenty of reassurance, love and support.
Domestic violence	It is very important that children and young people feel safe and protected in their home environment. Domestic violence will affect their right to being protected from harm. Those who are growing up in an environment of domestic abuse or violence may suffer long-term physical, psychological and emotional effects. This is because they will be permanently anxious and worried about when the next incident will occur. They may also feel that they need to try to protect the parent or carer who is the victim, and feel guilty or blame themselves if they are unable to. The stress caused by this situation is likely to affect their emotional and physical development, and have a number of other effects including aggressive or attention-seeking behaviour, depression, eating disorders, withdrawal, lack of ability to concentrate, lack of sleep and a reduced immune system.
Substance/alcohol abuse	If the child or young person has a family member who abuses drugs or alcohol, they will be subjected to sudden changes in mood and behaviour from that person. They may think that this is their fault, and be frightened or left on their own if that person is addicted, and may not have regular meals or be cared for appropriately. This is likely to affect all areas of their development, from physical to cognitive, as they are unlikely to be able to concentrate at school or college.
Young carer	A young carer who looks after a parent is likely to be preoccupied with their needs; this will affect their emotional development. They will also be tired and in need of both emotional and practical support to help them to manage their responsibilities.

Domestic situation	Effect on development
Divorce	This may affect a child or young person's social or emotional development due to changes that will take place in their day-to-day life; however, the impact can be more from the parents' behaviour and attitudes towards one another than from the divorce itself. Children and young people may be anxious about what will happen, or blame themselves for their parents' separation. If they have to move home or school there may also be behavioural issues depending on their age and understanding of what is happening.
Bereavement	The effects of bereavement will depend on the relationship of the child or young person to the deceased, but it will be an emotional reaction and affect emotional development to a greater or lesser degree, sometimes causing regression. It may be someone close, a friend or family member, or a much-loved pet, and this will affect the length of time that the child is grieving. Depending on the age of the child or young person the impact and reaction may be different – younger children may be visibly upset and emotional, whereas teenagers may be withdrawn and reluctant to talk. The death of a parent will affect children and young people the most – their behaviour may be affected and they may become withdrawn or angry, or find it difficult to sleep. The long-term effects of this will also have a greater and longer-lasting effect on their emotional development.

Culture and religion

Our culture or religion is an important part of who we are, and children and young people will be connected to their culture or religion through their community. Their sense of belonging and feeling valued will be a positive aspect of this. If they have good relationships and experiences through their culture, and enjoy positive connections with others in this way, they are more likely to have a deeper sense of their own identity and where they belong. These secure feelings will have a positive impact on their social and emotional development. If they feel excluded, however, and are unable to relate to others in their community, for whatever reason, this may have a damaging effect on their feeling of self-worth and sense of belonging.

Education environment such as exclusion or a school or college in special measures

A child or young person who is excluded from school, either for a fixed period or permanently, may also be excluded from friendships or bullied by peers. Their emotional development and behaviour may be affected both by this and the exclusion itself. As their education has been disrupted, they will also have gaps in their knowledge and understanding, which will be a further reason to feel excluded by others. A school or college in special measures is likely to be a stressful environment for staff, governors and pupils as there will be termly inspections until the leadership and management of the school improves, along with pupils' personal development, behaviour and welfare alongside teaching and learning.

Class discussion

Discuss in groups the consequences of young people in particular becoming excluded or detached from their culture or religion within the community. What could be the wider impact? How can communities try to prevent this from happening?

Bullying

This is very likely to damage a child or young person's emotional and physical health. Many cases of bullying now take place online as bullies are able to hide behind a computer. Bullying can cause the victim to have low self-esteem and depression, and can have long-term effects that can be devastating – for example, having difficulty in forming trusting relationships. It may also affect their sleep patterns or appetite due to anxiety, and there may also be physical injuries. For bullies themselves there are also likely to be issues that have caused this behaviour and, if left unresolved, can make them more likely to drop out of school or college.

Looked after children care status

A child is referred to as 'looked after' if they are under local authority care for more than 24 hours. Reasons for this may be that they have been removed from danger, they are the subject of a full care or permanence order, they are in a secure children's home or young offender's institution, or they are unaccompanied and seeking asylum. A looked after child may be living in one of the following situations:

- in a residential children's home
- with foster parents
- with their own parents but under social services supervision
- in another residential setting.

Owing to their status, children who are 'looked after' are at greater risk than other children of being kept healthy and safe. This is because they may have had a traumatic or unsettled background that is likely to have affected their social and emotional development – they may find it difficult to form strong and positive relationships with adults. They are 'looked after' until they are returned home, adopted or reach 18 years.

As someone who is in close contact with the child or young person, you may be one of the first to notice if there is a change in their behaviour that could be caused by one of these factors. However, you may also be working in an environment in which children and young people are at risk due to a number of them. You should always speak to others if you are anxious about their well-being or suspect that something may be wrong.

Case study

Sam is working in a college in a deprived inner-city area. She works with 16–18 year olds, some of whom have been in social care or are living with foster parents. Some of the backgrounds of the young people are said to be 'chaotic', and there are many social issues in the area such as drug and alcohol abuse, as well as housing shortages.

Sam and her colleagues regularly deal with issues such as student absences and challenging behaviour, however, she is particularly concerned about one of the girls in her group who has recently become much quieter and less involved with what they are doing in class. She has started to remove herself from the group and is not interested in what they are doing. Sam is concerned that she will not be attending the college for much longer.

1 How would you approach this situation?
2 Why is it important that Sam does something?

Transitions such as puberty

Transitions (see page 86 for definition) occur at different stages of our lives. For children and young people, the way in which these are managed may affect their emotional development. Puberty will have physical as well as psychological and emotional effects due to an increase in hormone activity as their bodies take on adult characteristics.

What other transitions may affect the development of children and young people?

For more on transitions and their impact, see Unit 15.

▼ Table 5.3 Some of the effects of puberty

Effects of puberty	Impact on development
Physical changes	These changes will have the most impact on development. For those who grow and develop more quickly or slowly than others there may be issues with fitting in with their peers as they become self-conscious about their changing bodies. Girls and boys become more body aware and may feel pressure to lose weight or develop muscles.
Emotional changes	Children's moods and interests will be affected and they may suffer from mood changes and lack of self-esteem due to their rapidly changing hormones. They may also spend more time on their own as they start to become independent from their parents and develop their own identity. They are likely to start to question parental views and decisions more, and may rebel or challenge society in different ways.

Effects of puberty	Impact on development
Changes to sleep patterns	As body rhythms are regulated by hormones, a young person's sleep pattern is likely to change and make them more likely to be awake late in the evening and need to sleep longer in the morning. This can impact on their mood as well as their ability to concentrate, and can cause frustration as well as tension between the young person and their parents.
Social changes	As young people's bodies start to change, they will begin to experience different social experiences and interests, which may be influenced by sexual arousal as well as peer pressure. They may be treated in a different way by others and find that they are more popular if they mature more rapidly.
Neurological changes	Changes will still be taking place in the brain during adolescence and this means that teenagers' cognitive skills will still be developing and maturing. They will not have the maturity to make informed and balanced decisions, and may act hastily without thinking of the consequences. It may also be more difficult for them to regulate their emotions and control their feelings.

Key term

Transition: a period of change.

Activity

Make a list of the different types of transitions that children and young people will experience to the age of 19. Draw up tables similar to those above highlighting the effects and impact of each to show how these transitions might affect different areas of their development. You will also be able to use this as evidence in Unit 16 for AC 1.2.

English as a second language

This will affect different areas of development but most specifically that of communication and language, as bilingual children will tend to have a smaller vocabulary in each language. It will also affect social development as the child or young person's ability to communicate with their peers may be affected for a short time due to the restrictions this may bring. However, research and studies on bilingualism have shown that the benefits of bilingualism tend to outweigh the disadvantages, and the way development is affected is overall a positive one.

There are two types of bilingual acquisition; simultaneous and sequential.

Simultaneous acquisition

This is when a child is raised bilingually from birth and learns both languages together – for example, if one parent is English and the other is French. In this case the child's language will pass through the same stages of development as a monolingual child, although they may start to speak slightly later.

Sequential acquisition

This is when a child is introduced to a second language after being fluent in the first. This may happen if they start school in the UK after speaking only their home language, or if they immigrate and need to learn a new language.

▼ Table 5.4 Bilingualism and development

Benefits of bilingualism for development	Negative effects
Bilingualism enhances children's linguistic development through the superior development of linguistic structure (metalinguistic awareness).	Slightly later at learning to speak, although this will still be within the expected age range.
Children who are learning to read in two languages show no reduction in progress, and in the cases of two languages that share a system, such as English and Spanish, they will show greater progress.	Reduced vocabulary in each language.
Bilingual children between the ages of 4 and 8 show a large advantage in problem-solving activities over monolingual children and a greater ability to concentrate without distractions.	

For more on communication and language development, see Unit 12.

For more on supporting bilingual children and young people, see Unit 13.

Stretch and challenge

What can you find out about the relationship between bilingualism and cognitive development?

AC 2.3 Explain how theories of development and educational frameworks influence current practice

Academics have, over the years, put different ideas and theories together about how children learn, and the way in which the brain develops through childhood and beyond. These have influenced the way that we think about children's learning and the 'nature vs nurture' debate, and many have an impact in classrooms today.

▼ Table 5.5 Theories of development throughout history

Theory of development	Description
Cognitive (e.g. Piaget, 1896–1980)	Piaget was a psychologist who believed that children's cognitive development was based on the construction and progression of ideas. In other words, as knowledge is built up, children will pass through different stages, each of which is based on the one before. These are: • **the sensorimotor stage (0–2 years)*** – to move on from this stage, a child will need to learn about object permanence; this means that an item still exists, even when it is not visible • **the preoperational stage (2–7 years)*** – this is the ability to think using symbols such as letters and numbers • **the concrete operational stage (7–11 years)*** – at the end of this stage, children will be able to work things out mentally rather than physically trying them • **the formal operational stage (11 years to adult)*** – at the end of this stage, which not all individuals reach, individuals will start to be able to think about abstract ideas. According to Piaget, children will also need to work through activities and discover things for themselves as an active learner, rather than be taught them directly. The process of learning is more important; we still base teaching and learning on this today. ** These are average ages; Piaget did not claim that the stages were age dependent.*
Psychoanalytic (e.g. Freud, 1856–1939)	Freud was a psychoanalyst who developed a theory about personality development based on three parts of the subconscious mind: the id, the ego and the superego. These three structures will conflict with one another as the individual grows up. • The **id** is based on our instincts and needs, and seeks pleasure for its own sake – for example, through eating, sleeping or having sex. • The **ego** is driven by knowledge of reality and will rationalise with the id about how it achieves its basic needs, for example, through the use of delaying what we want. • The **superego** is based on the development of morality and conscience. It seeks to judge our behaviour through the use of guilt and our knowledge of right and wrong. Freud's ideas help us to understand the relationship between a child's subconscious and their actions – for example, if they deny doing something when they have done it.

Theory of development	Description
Humanist (e.g. Maslow, 1908–1970)	Abraham Maslow was an American psychologist who believed that humans set out to meet certain needs in themselves and this is what motivates their development. These will start with the most basic psychological needs of food, shelter and sleep, and then move on through safety, belonging and esteem until they reach the last, which is known as self-actualisation or meeting one's own individual potential. Maslow believed that those who achieved self-actualisation share similar personality traits, which represent a high level of health and functioning. Maslow's theory helps us to recognise that children and young people will need an environment that is conducive to learning and meets their basic needs so that they can achieve their potential.
Social learning (e.g. Bandura, 1925–present)	Bandura believes that children learn and develop by watching those around them and copying what they do. He believes that humans will remember, reproduce and copy those things that are socially meaningful, and that learning takes place when the observer watches not only what happens but also the consequences of what happens. Bandura's ideas influence our ideas about role modelling and social behaviour when we are with children and young people, as they are likely to observe the behaviour of those around them.
Operant conditioning (e.g. Skinner, 1904–1990)	This type of learning is based on an idea that was based on Skinner's studies of animal and human behaviour. Operant conditioning means that individuals will remember things that lead to a successful outcome and this will make them more likely to repeat them. He carried out research that gave reinforcement when the subjects were given a positive response. This also worked when they were given a negative response as it made the subjects less likely to repeat the action. When children are learning, they are more likely to want to be involved if their efforts are acknowledged and praise is given.
Behaviourist or classical conditioning (e.g. Watson, 1878–1958)	John B. Watson's ideas were based on the thought that we are all born with the same capacity for learning and that we can be taught to behave in a particular way. His ideas were similar to those of Skinner as he agreed that we learn responses in particular situations and will associate behaviour will a particular stimulus. For example, he famously carried out an experiment in which he frightened a baby by making a loud noise each time the baby saw an animal. In due course the baby was frightened by the animal, even if the noise was not being made. Watson's studies have some bearing on our current practice through looking at the importance of the environment and taking its influences into account.

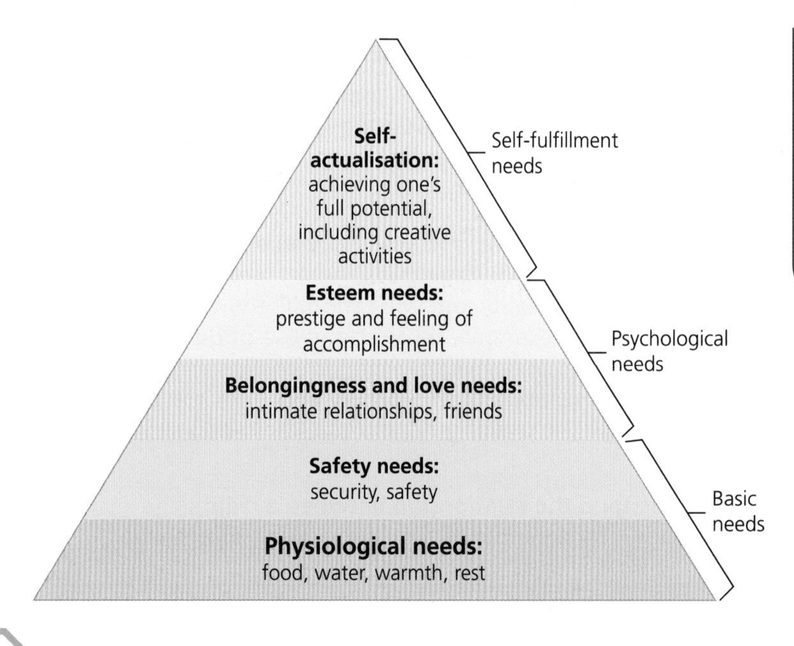

Figure 5.9 Maslow's hierarchy of needs. Why is it important that we consider different theoretical approaches when thinking about children's learning?

In practice

How do you think these theories of development influence the work you do with children and young people? Write a reflective account, giving examples from your own experience, and use this for your portfolio.

LO3 Understand how to monitor children and young people's development and the interventions that should take place if this is not following the expected pattern

AC 3.1 Explain how to monitor children and young people's development using different methods

As educators, we need to monitor and assess children and young people so that we can ensure that they are making progress towards expected developmental milestones. We do this all the time in a variety of different ways.

Assessment frameworks

These exist to support practitioners in making judgements about a child or young person at different stages to ensure their health, welfare and development. They may be related to the curriculum and education, or to health and social issues. The assessment triangle sets out to show how this may be identified.

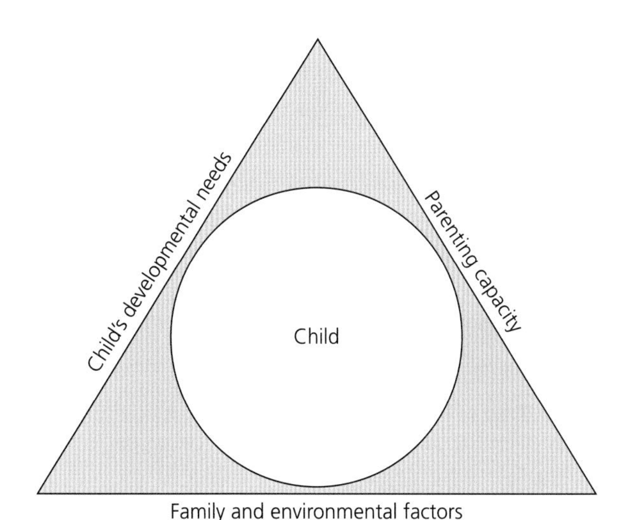

▲ Figure 5.10 How might the assessment triangle support the way in which we think about children's developmental progress?

Early Intervention Frameworks and forms of assessment are used by all those who work with children and families in England and Wales to support early identification where there may be areas of concern in any aspect of a child or young person's development. In many areas this early help pathway is known as the **Common Assessment Framework,** or CAF. This multi-agency approach looks at the child's education and learning as well as parental care, environmental issues, and housing and financial considerations, and provides a structured and holistic approach to forming and reviewing planning to support their needs and the needs of the family. If your setting has concerns about a child or young person and wishes to complete a CAF form, it will first need to check with parents or carers, who must give their consent. Depending on the age and level of understanding of the child or young person, they will also need to be involved in the process. A CAF may be used for any child or young person from before birth until age 19, or beyond if they have a learning difficulty or disability.

In Northern Ireland this is known as **UNOCINI (Understanding the Needs of Children in Northern Ireland)** and it has three assessment areas:

1 the needs of the child or young person
2 the capacity of their parents or carers to meet these needs
3 wider family and environmental factors that impact on parental capacity and children's needs.

Through looking at assessing these three areas through the eyes of different professionals, the framework aims to support the child or young person and their family circumstances, with a view to improving outcomes.

In Scotland, the framework used is known as the **National Practice Model**. It is used to assess the needs of the child or young person and sits within a wider model known as GIRFEC (Getting it right for every child). In a similar way to the other systems, it aims to involve practitioners from all services in order to plan how to move forward in the best interests of the child or young person.

Curriculum assessment frameworks are used to assess children and young people's academic development. For example, at the end of Key Stage 1 and 2 they will set out the expected curriculum levels that children are working towards in English (reading and writing), mathematics and science. The frameworks will outline what pupils should be able to do so that teachers can determine whether they are working at, above or below this level.

Observations

These are used both formally and informally to check on a child's development, particularly in the early and primary school years. When you carry out observations to support teaching and learning, you will be building up a picture of the child or young person so that you can work alongside the teacher to meet their needs more effectively. You may be a participant observer, in other words doing an activity with the child or young person, or you may be sitting apart from them to observe what they are doing.

Formal observations are used regularly, particularly in the early years, to establish how the child is progressing in each area of learning and development. There are different types of formal observations that will follow various formats:

- **Event/time samples** – these are used to check on how regularly a pupil displays a particular behaviour or activity over a period of time. The observer would need to be away from the subject so that they are not involved in the activity themselves, and do not interrupt or change the course of what is happening.
- **Checklists** – these are simply to tick off what a pupil can do; the focus in this situation will be whether or not they are able to do it rather than the process.
- **Anecdotal** – these are a brief description of an incident or activity where it would be useful to have a record to pass on to others. It will contain information on what happened, where and when, and what was said and/or done by the pupil. They are usually written down after the incident.
- **Free description or running record** – these allow us to write everything down, usually during a timed period. During a free description the observer will usually focus on how the pupil responds to the activity and what is said to others, as well as their behaviour. As they are usually quite detailed, the period of observation is likely to be short, around 5–10 minutes.
- **Structured description** – this type of observation will usually follow a series of headings for a particular focus. These headings will enable an observer to note down only specific things such as how regularly a pupil participates in a group activity and what takes place.

Research it

Find a copy of your local authority CAF, or the assessment framework in your own UK Home Nation, and the guidance surrounding it, and note down the process that would need to be followed as well as who would be responsible for initiating the process in your school or college.

In practice

Carry out an observation on a pupil after discussion with your class teacher or tutor to decide how it will be useful. Use one of the observation types above and outline why you have chosen it in this situation.

Informal observations are those that you carry out simply by working with pupils and talking to them about what they are doing on a regular basis. These kinds of observations may or may not be recorded, and you may simply chat to the teacher afterwards about what you have observed so that they also have the information.

Activity

Using a table such as the one below, consider the advantages and disadvantages of each type of observation.

Type of observation	Advantages	Disadvantages
Event/time sample		
Checklist		
Anecdotal		
Free description		
Structured description		
Informal		

For more on observations, see Unit 7, LO4, page 123.

Standard measurements

Standard measurements are often used by health professionals to check on a child or young person's rate of growth, and to ensure that they are following the expected pattern of development. They are most likely to be used to measure physical development.

Information from parents/carers

We will need to speak to the parents and carers of children and young people regularly while they are in education. This helps us to find out more about how events in their home environment may be affecting them and how we can work together to support them. They may also be able to offer information that can help us to understand why they are behaving or reacting in a particular way.

Information from colleagues

It is very helpful to speak to colleagues to find out more about pupils' development, and we can gather information quickly and easily through talking to them. For example, at the end of an academic year, before moving to another class or tutor group, it is helpful to discuss their progress and any issues that may have come up over the course of the year, so that we are prepared when they come into our own class. Informal conversations can also help us to find out information that can be useful in supporting our understanding.

AC 3.2 Identify how other professionals and different types of interventions can promote positive outcomes for children and young people where development is not following the expected pattern

If a child or young person's development is not following the expected pattern, you will need to discuss the best course of action with parents, carers and other professionals. In your school or college this might be your class teacher or the SENCo (special educational needs co-ordinator). They will be able to speak to parents so that they can refer pupils for further assessment to others who work outside the school or college. You are likely to need evidence of your concerns so should be able to back them up through observations, curriculum assessments or other information you have gathered on the child or young person.

Following their assessments, these professionals may use or recommend different types of interventions so that children and young people will be able to meet their potential. Some of these may be school or college based, while others will be external.

Other professionals could include those listed in Table 5.6 on the next page.

▼ Table 5.6 Professionals that work with children and young people to support their development

Type of professional	Role	Possible intervention
Social worker	A social worker may be called upon if there are concerns about a child or young person's welfare or social needs. This may have been reflected through their behaviour, attendance or something they have said that causes concern. Social workers may provide counselling services to pupils or support families where needed if there are concerns around welfare, attendance or safeguarding, so that outcomes for pupils can be improved.	• Access to external services • Resources
Speech and language therapist (SLT or SALT)	A speech and language therapist may work with children and young people for blocks of therapy at any stage if they are causing concerns with their speech, language and communication development. They will also work closely with other health and education professionals, as well as parents, to support the needs of the child or young person. Some schools may have a speech and language unit attached. For more on supporting pupils with speech and language needs see Unit 12.	• Activities • Assistive technology
Psychologist	Children and young people may be referred to an educational psychologist if they are in need of support or assessment due to possible learning difficulties or emotional problems. The psychologist will carry out an assessment in school or college, and then interview the child or young person and their parents and teachers. They may also work in partnership with other professionals so that they can devise interventions and programmes that will best meet the needs of the child or young person.	• Resources • Coping strategies • Activities • Access to external services
Psychiatrist	A child and adolescent psychiatrist will work with children and young people up to 18 years.	• Coping strategies
Youth justice worker	A youth justice worker will help and support children and young people who offend or who are at risk of doing so. They will need to do this through counselling, and work with other external services as well as families to develop intervention plans and deliver programmes of support and treatment.	• Access to external services • Resources
Physiotherapist/ occupational therapist	A physiotherapist will work with children and young people where they have a physical disability or a difficulty with movement that requires professional support or treatment. They will work with families to plan and deliver treatment that involves physical exercise and programmes that will need to be carried out at home and school.	• Adaptations to the environment • Activities • Resources • Assistive technology
Nurse specialist	A nurse specialist or school nurse will come in to work with children and young people of all ages in schools and colleges. They will usually be based elsewhere, for example, in a GP surgery or a local health centre. Nurses will be there to monitor pupils' health and carry out assessments and immunisations, starting in the first year of school. They will also support families where needed if children's development is not following the expected pattern, or if they need advice about childhood conditions and illnesses such as asthma or diabetes. School nurses are also there to support children and young people in making lifestyle choices that support positive outcomes and enable them to reach their potential, for example, through stop smoking programmes, healthy eating advice, and drink and drug awareness.	• Resources • Access to external services

Type of professional	Role	Possible intervention
Additional learning support (school or college based)	Additional learning support may be given where children or young people need focused intervention to enable them to meet their potential outcomes. Support assistants will work with parents, SENCos and other professionals to deliver specific teaching and learning programmes.	• Resources • Coping strategies • Activities
Health visitor	Health visitors will monitor children's development, particularly in the early months and years and after birth. They will support families and provide advice as well as having a role in the safeguarding and protection of children.	• Access to external services

Activity

Using Table 5.6, think about how each intervention might be used to support children and young people where their development is not following the expected pattern, giving examples.

Tips for best practice: monitoring the development of children and young people

- Speak to teachers and other professionals if you have any concerns about a child or young person's development, whether physical, intellectual, emotional or social.
- Be able to back up what you are saying with evidence, for example, through dated observations.
- Make sure you are aware of the role of others in monitoring pupils' development and carrying out assessments.

Check your understanding

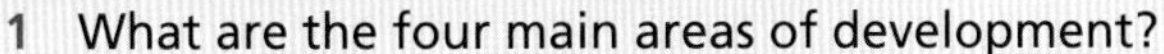

1. What are the four main areas of development?
2. How do the four areas of development overlap with one another?
3. How many words does the average 3 year old have?
4. What is meant by 'nature vs nurture' when talking about child development?
5. Define 'sequence of development' and 'rate of development', and explain the difference.
6. Name two biological and three external factors that may influence the development of children and young people.
7. Which learning theory was developed by Abraham Maslow and how does this influence practice today?
8. Describe two ways in which you might monitor children and young people's development.
9. What other professionals might be involved if a child or young person's development is not following the expected pattern?
10. What type of intervention might be used if a pupil is causing concerns with their speech and language development?

Assessment preparation

This knowledge-only unit requires you to explain, compare and identify different aspects of children's and young people's development through writing about them. This means that you will need to use evidence methods such as reflective accounts, assignments, and some of the activities in this unit to help you to pass it. Your tutor may also use questioning or a test environment to check your knowledge.

Alternatively you may choose to use some of the questions below, depending on how much evidence you have already gathered.

1. Several areas of development are discussed here, from birth to 19 years. In your own words, write about them separately, detailing the sequence and rate of each and explaining the difference between them (LO1, AC 1.1).
2. Create a table showing how biological factors and external factors influence the development of children and young people (LO2, AC 2.1, 2.2). You can use the 'In practice' feature at AC 2.3 for your portfolio.
3. Write about how your school or college promotes positive outcomes for children and young people. Show how different interventions made by other professionals, as well as those in-house, can help support children and young people to achieve their potential (LO3, AC 3.1, 3.2).

Legislation

There is no legislation for this unit.

Read about it

Reference books

Abbott, R. (2015) *Child Development and the Brain: An Introduction*, Policy Press.

Bialstok, E. (2010) *Bilingualism in Development – Language, Literacy and Cognition*, Cambridge University Press.

Gurian, M. (2010) *Boys and Girls Learn Differently! A Guide for Teachers and Parents*, Jossey Bass.

Meggitt, C. (2012) *Child Development, an Illustrated Guide: Birth to 19 Years*, Pearson.

Noble, C. and Bradford, W. (2000) *Getting It Right for Boys and Girls*, Routledge.

Weblinks

www.cruse.org.uk Cruse – bereavement support

www.kidscape.org.uk Kidscape – bullying support

www.naswdc.org NASWDC – National Association of Social Workers

www.refuge.org.uk Refuge – help for domestic violence

www.talktofrank.com/contact-frank FRANK – drugs advice

www.youngminds.org.uk Young Minds – bereavement support

6 Support positive behaviour in children and young people

About this unit

To complete this unit, you will need to show how you promote positive behaviour in your school or college. This means that you will need to have a clear understanding of the policies and procedures you should follow when managing behaviour in the learning environment and in the wider setting as part of a whole school or college approach. You should know about the way in which you should promote positive behaviour and also the sanctions and strategies you will need to use in the event of challenging or inappropriate behaviour.

Learning outcomes

By the end of this unit you will:

LO1 Understand policies and procedures for promoting children and young people's positive behaviour in a learning environment

LO2 Be able to promote positive behaviour

LO3 Be able to manage behaviour that challenges in a learning environment

Getting started

Discuss with others in your group the way in which your school or college manages both positive and inappropriate behaviour. Are you aware of the kinds of sanctions that are available to you? Are students clear about the expectations of the school or college, and do they know how good or poor behaviour will be dealt with? Are you allowed to use restraint in extreme cases? Make your own list of anything you think you will need to find out in order to complete this unit.

LO1 Understand policies and procedures for promoting children and young people's positive behaviour in a learning environment

AC 1.1 Summarise policies and procedures relevant to promoting children and young people's positive behaviour

Your school or college will need to have set **policies and procedures** for managing the behaviour of children and young people. This will be achieved through policies and procedures such as those described below.

Behaviour policy

If you have not seen it already, look up your school or college's behaviour policy. This may be on its website or in your staff room, but it should be freely available so that all staff are able to consistently apply strategies and **sanctions** to manage behaviour.

Key terms

Policies and procedures: these will be the methods that staff in your school or college agree to use when managing behaviour. All staff should know and be aware of them and all students should know the expectations of the setting.

Sanctions: these set out the consequences of what will happen if the rules are broken.

Code of conduct

This spells out your setting's expectations for behaviour and should be clear to all students, whatever their age. It should be displayed on the walls of the setting and students should be regularly reminded of it so that the expectations for behaviour are clear. Schools and colleges will usually use positive language to remind students about the code of conduct rather than negative – for example, 'Show respect for others', rather than 'Don't be unkind.'

Rewards and sanctions

Your school or college should set out the kinds of rewards that are used to encourage positive behaviour, and the sanctions that are used as consequences for inappropriate behaviour. For example, the reward system may be a team or house point for older students or a sticker chart for younger ones. Sanctions should be clear to students so that they know what will happen if they break the code of conduct.

Dealing with conflict and inappropriate behaviour

Make sure you know exactly what you should do in cases of conflict or inappropriate behaviour. The kinds of sanctions you use should be set out in the behaviour policy so that all adults in a position of responsibility can apply them and are prepared when faced with conflict or inappropriate behaviour.

Anti-bullying

There is likely to be an anti-bullying policy, which may be part of the behaviour policy or set out on its own. It should outline the procedures the setting has for managing any incidents of bullying. This includes cyber-bullying, which can be devastating to students and can take place through mobile phones, social media and other online groups.

For more on how to deal with bullying, see Unit 3, pages 44–5.

Student code of conduct

The student code of conduct indicates expectations of behaviour. Students are expected to:

- contribute to a well-ordered learning environment by:
  - working to the best of their ability in lessons and on homework tasks
  - ensuring that all work is submitted punctually
  - being properly equipped for school
- show respect for others by:
  - being polite and courteous to each other and refraining from bullying, fighting and name-calling
  - being polite, courteous and honest with staff and listening to and carrying out instructions
- act in a responsible manner by:
  - doing nothing to endanger a healthy, safe and secure environment
  - ensuring forbidden items are not brought to school
  - keeping the school buildings and grounds clean and tidy
  - moving about in a quiet and orderly manner
  - avoiding areas which are deemed out of bounds
  - conducting fire drills in silence
- ensure the best possible attendance and punctuality
- promote a positive image of the school by:
  - taking a pride in their appearance, being smartly and correctly dressed for any school activity and when travelling to and from school
  - behaving in a sensible and courteous manner when travelling to and from school
  - being polite and courteous to visitors

▲ Figure 6.1 Why is it important for all students to be clear on the expectations of the setting?

Attendance

This policy will need to show how the school or college views attendance, and is likely to emphasise its importance. Attendance will be monitored and if parents regularly take their children out of school or college, particularly for holidays, it is likely to be noted and possible fines issued. Where students have high attendance this may be acknowledged and rewarded.

> **In practice**
>
> For each of the headings in AC 1.1, find out about your setting's policies and procedures, and write a clear summary for each as a reflective account. You will then be able to use this for your portfolio.

AC 1.2 Explain effective practice in relation to behaviour management

Charlie Taylor, a former government advisor on behaviour in schools, produced a checklist in 2011 on how to manage behaviour effectively. In it, he produced a set of simple guidelines for teachers and head teachers to ensure that all staff and students are clear on the behaviour that is and is not acceptable. He cited in particular the importance of consistency when managing behaviour, as this makes children less likely to push the boundaries.

Key principles for head teachers to help improve school behaviour:

- Ensure absolute clarity about the expected standard of students' behaviour.
- Ensure that behaviour policy is clearly understood by all staff, parents and students.
- Display school rules clearly in classes and around the building. Staff and students should know what they are.
- Display the tariff of sanctions and rewards in each class.
- Have a system in place for ensuring that children never miss out on sanctions or rewards.

Behaviour checklist for teaching staff:

- Know the names and roles of any adults in class.
- Meet and greet students when they come into the classroom.
- Display rules in the class – and ensure that the students and staff know what they are.
- Display the tariff of sanctions in class.
- Have a system in place to follow through with all sanctions.
- Display the tariff of rewards in class.
- Have a system in place to follow through with all rewards.
- Have a visual timetable on the wall.
- Follow the school behaviour policy.

Source: *Getting the simple things right: Charlie Taylor's behaviour checklists*, DfE, 2011

School and college policies and procedures are important when considering effective practice, and all staff, students and parents should be aware of them and where to find them. The setting should regularly review policies for behaviour as well as other areas, and it is the responsibility of all staff to be up to date, to know exactly how to apply boundaries and rules and why it is important. In addition, all staff should have equal status in the setting and this should be reinforced by the senior management or leadership team so that students give them the same respect.

▲ Figure 6.2 Are you clear about the way in which behaviour should be managed in your setting?

Class discussion

Look at the following list. Discuss in groups whether all of the staff below should be equally aware of the behaviour policies and be able to apply sanctions where needed to manage the behaviour of children and young people in your school or college.

- Teaching staff
- Support staff
- Office staff
- Midday/lunchtime supervisors
- ICT technicians
- Caretaker/facilities manager/maintenance workers
- Play leaders
- Staff at breakfast/after-school clubs/extended school provision
- Cleaning staff
- Governors

Case study

Mirella is a midday supervisor at a secondary school; she has been working there for several months but does not really feel part of the school – she comes in, does her job and goes home each day. She has been given a copy of the behaviour policy but does not feel that the staff work together to implement sanctions and as a consequence behaviour in the school is poor.

On one particular lunchtime she notices some children throwing litter on the field and calls over to them to pick it up and put it in the bin. A girl calls out to her, 'Why should I? You are just a dinner lady!'

1 Why is it important that Mirella sees this through and makes the girl pick up the litter?
2 What else should Mirella do, and why?

LO2 Be able to promote positive behaviour

AC 2.1 Review expectations in relation to behaviour when working with others

Although it is very important for all staff to know the policies and procedures of the setting for

Research it

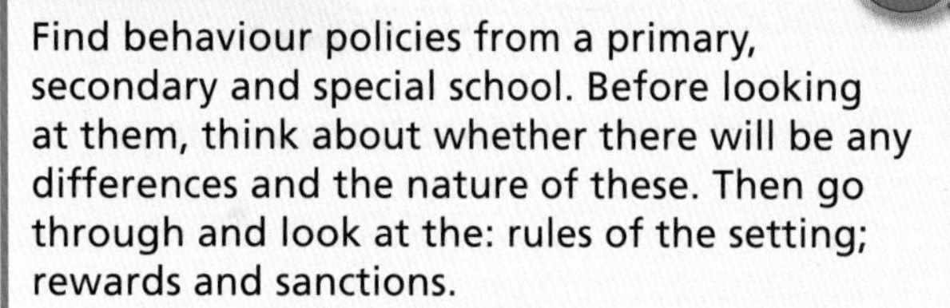

Find behaviour policies from a primary, secondary and special school. Before looking at them, think about whether there will be any differences and the nature of these. Then go through and look at the: rules of the setting; rewards and sanctions.

Are there many differences? Why might this be?

promoting positive behaviour, it is important that these are reviewed regularly and that all staff, including volunteers, are aware of them. School or college staff, alongside senior management, may decide to change the rules from time to time, as well as their policies for rewards and sanctions. There may be meetings or discussions in which behaviour policies are reviewed once every year or two years, to make sure they are still up to date and relevant, or additional information may be added as and when it is necessary.

Reviews of expectations may also occur at the beginning of a new year or term, as a whole school or college or as a class or group, so that everyone knows what is expected and can remember. If you are working with new colleagues or have started in a new setting, you will need to make sure you know what is required of you.

When you are starting to work with a group of children or young people, whether the group is large or small, you should always review expectations for behaviour before you start. One way of doing this is by agreeing ground rules with them. This is a good starting point as it ensures that everyone is clear on the expectations of the group. It can also be helpful for students to devise these themselves so that they have more ownership of the rules and will be more likely to remember them. It is also particularly helpful if you will be working with the group for several sessions. The time spent doing this is worthwhile as it gives students the opportunity to think about their behaviour and the potential impact it has on other people; sanctions should also be discussed so that they know what will happen if the rules are broken.

School behaviour policy

Aims of our positive behaviour policy

This policy exists to provide a framework for supporting the aims of the school and ensuring the happiness and learning of every individual in our community. It will do this through:

- encouraging a calm, purposeful and happy atmosphere within school
- helping our children develop into caring and thoughtful individuals who respect and value the feelings, opinions, beliefs, property and differences of others
- encouraging increasing independence and self-discipline so that each child learns to accept responsibility for their own behaviour
- a consistent approach to behaviour throughout the school with parental cooperation and involvement
- helping our children develop appropriate self-esteem
- encouraging our pupils to co-operate with one another and with the adults in school
- helping to create a positive, stimulating learning environment where positive attitudes and behaviour are encouraged and rewarded
- helping to work alongside parents to encourage our children to develop socially, academically, orally and spiritually in preparation for a positive role in society
- ensuring that everyone is clear about their role when managing a pupil's behaviour
- making the children aware of unacceptable behaviour
- allowing all children equal opportunities to learn
- allowing all adults in school equal opportunities to fulfill their role
- rewarding and encouraging positive behaviour
- using sanctions where appropriate in accordance with this policy
- developing skills necessary to resolve conflict and differences of opinion with sensitivity.

Encouraging positive behaviour

We support positive behaviour and a positive environment through:

- a consistent approach by the whole school community
- monitoring pupil attendance and taking swift action where necessary
- developing the voice of the child through, for example, the school and class councils
- appreciating and following the agreed code of conduct
- encouraging our children to see themselves as part of a whole school community and recognising their responsibility within this
- developing the skills of cooperation and discussion
- encouraging everyone to take pride in the school environment
- having a positive and consistent approach to playtimes and lunchtimes
- creating a stimulating classroom environment
- providing a clear and positive learning experience fairly and consistently
- offering a broad and balanced curriculum that is well planned, prepared and stimulating
- ensuring that the curriculum issues concerning organisation, methods of teaching and learning, content and differentiation are addressed.

▲ Figure 6.3 Have you read your setting's behaviour management policy?

In practice

The next time you take a small group for a learning activity, start by talking to them about the rules that are in place in their learning environment and ask them why rules are important. Tell them that you are going to set out some ground rules for the work that they will be doing so that they are clear what is acceptable.

▲ Figure 6.4 Why are shared ground rules more likely to make students think about the impact of their behaviour?

The reasons that shared ground rules are important are:

- students have a shared responsibility for their behaviour
- everyone knows what is expected
- they have thought about and know why each rule is in place
- they encourage students to listen to and have respect for one another
- if they behave in a negative way, they can be reminded that they devised the rules.

AC 2.2 Explain strategies for promoting positive behaviour according to the policies and procedures of the setting

As well as setting out ground rules with students, there are some other ways in which you can promote positive behaviour in your setting (see Table 6.1).

▼ Table 6.1 Promoting positive behaviours

Strategy	Effect
By using active listening	Actively listening to students shows them that you value what they say and are taking time to think about their point of view. In this way you can build positive relationships with them. When managing behaviour, it helps students to know that you can talk through issues as they arise and build their trust.
By giving regular positive feedback	Noticing when students are trying hard to manage their behaviour is a powerful reinforcer. It shows that you are aware that they are making an effort. It also gives the students positive attention.
By being consistent when addressing behaviour	Consistency between adults is very important, so that children and young people are clear about expectations. Use the preferred method of promoting positive behaviour, which is approved by your setting – for example, verbal praise, a behaviour chart, or giving privileges to older children.
By being a positive role model	This is significant as it shows that you recognise the importance of positive behaviour. It is difficult to ask students to do something you are not doing yourself.
For more on this, see AC 2.3, on being an effective role model.	

Giving students responsibilities within the setting is also a positive way of giving them attention. It also helps to raise their self-esteem and make them feel good about themselves, and can avoid the need to gain attention in a negative way.

Make sure you take time to think about how you react when dealing with the behaviour of children and young people. Try to behave in a way that will have a positive effect on what they do, and think about the way in which your own behaviour influences them. Your responses need to be realistic, consistent and supportive:

- **Realistic** – targets and expectations of behaviour should be realistic for the age and ability of the student or group. For example, you should not ask 5 year olds to sit still and listen to an adult for a long period of time as they will find this very difficult at this age (see also AC 2.3) These kinds of expectations will mean that students become disheartened and stop trying to meet them.
- **Consistent** – you should make sure that you are consistent in what you ask of students. For example, if you allow them to do something one day and not the next, this will send a mixed message to them and they will not be clear on what is expected. You should also be consistent with other staff and in line with the policies of the school or college so that all adults give students the same message.
- **Supportive** – this means that you should encourage students wherever possible to develop positive behaviour. Regular incidence of poor behaviour is often a reaction to something that is happening in their lives. You can be supportive to students in a number of ways:
  - by asking them how they are and listening to them
  - by talking to them about issues that are important to them
  - by developing behaviour targets and reviewing them with the students and other staff
  - by praising and rewarding positive behaviour, and noticing when they are trying hard.

In practice

Think about the way in which you manage behaviour in your setting. Using the three headings 'Realistic', 'Consistent' and 'Supportive', note down how you demonstrate this support in your day-to-day practice.

AC 2.3 Use effective role model behaviour for the standards of behaviour expected of children, young people and adults within the learning environment

Being an effective role model is something you will need to consider in different contexts when you work with children and young people. They will watch adults and should observe them showing the same behaviour that they are being asked to demonstrate. Adults should not be asking children and young people to conform to a set of rules when they are not able to do it themselves – this is also true of how we act and how we treat other people.

The way in which we treat others (parents, students and staff)

Being kind, considerate and remembering what is important to others will show children and young people the foundations of how to build positive relationships.

Having positive relationships with others

Adults should show students positive relationships through their interactions with others – this is because others will look at how we interact. Positive relationships are crucial if we want to engage with students and improve motivation. It will also develop their trust and make them more likely to speak to adults about any issues if they arise, and also develop their sense of belonging.

Having good manners

You should always show good manners and professionalism when speaking to others, even if you are having a bad day yourself. Having good manners is an extension of showing respect. Being rude or aggressive does not help anyone to be productive, it is demotivating and can cause stress as others may feel unwelcome or sense a lack of trust. Politeness and kindness can make a real difference to the way others feel and in particular how they respond to you.

▲ Figure 6.5 Do you model the behaviour you expect from children and young people?

The way we communicate (make eye contact, speak calmly, show we are interested)

Always remain calm when speaking to others, and try not to raise your voice – noise levels often escalate if staff use higher volume than is needed as students will do the same.

See also Unit 12 for more on supporting children and young people's speech, language and communication.

Being on time for school/lessons

Adults need to show that they take their responsibilities seriously and that they expect students to do the same. Being late gives others the impression that you do not attach importance to what you are doing.

Dressing smartly

This is important, particularly if we are asking students to wear a uniform smartly – for example, keeping a top button done up, wearing a tie or making sure their hair is a particular length. Your clothes and appearance should be suitable for working in a school or college environment – this also communicates to students that you are a professional.

Acting responsibly – having own duties to perform daily or picking up litter

Students will need to be given responsibilities from an early age so that they start to understand the importance of being trustworthy; this in turn will make them feel positive in themselves as they are making a contribution to their environment.

Case study

Alan, an individual support assistant, is sitting in a whole school assembly with his secondary tutor group. As the children come into the hall, he is talking to one of the teachers about something that happened earlier. The head teacher has put some music on and is indicating to students that they should be quiet.

1 What should Alan be doing?
2 Why is it important that he is a good role model to students?

Tips for best practice: promoting positive behaviour

- Take time to establish ground rules with students.
- Be clear on the policies of the setting.
- Be consistent, realistic and clear in your expectations.
- Recognise and praise positive behaviour, and act fairly.
- Be a good role model for the behaviour you expect to see.

LO3 Be able to manage behaviour that challenges in a learning environment

It is likely that you will need to manage disruption and behaviour that challenges in your position as a member of support staff; this is part of your role and should be something you are able to do confidently.

Types of **behaviour that challenges** may be:

- verbal abuse – towards yourself, a colleague or another student
- physical abuse – towards yourself, a colleague or another student
- behaviour that is destructive to the child or young person
- behaviour that is illegal.

AC 3.1 Demonstrate strategies to minimise disruption in a teaching and learning environment

As well as promoting positive behaviour and knowing your setting's policies, you will unfortunately need to be prepared for disruption caused by poor behaviour and know exactly what to do when it occurs. You should do this at the first sign of any disruption, either to teaching or learning, or to the activity that is taking place. The kinds of strategies you may need to use could be:

- keep the focus on the main cause of the disruption
- make the behaviour wrong, not the student
- ensure students know that they have the choice
- always remain calm and never shout at a student
- act as you have said you will
- catch them being good and give a positive comment
- develop relationships by knowing student names and giving eye contact.

Key term

Behaviour that challenges: behaviour that conflicts with the accepted values and beliefs of the setting.

Keep the focus on the main cause of the disruption

Don't allow yourself to be diverted by students who have been asked not to do something, such as deliberately tripping another student over. For example, a child or young person might say, 'But he did it to me first' or 'But I haven't done anything!' to make themselves feel better. Make sure you repeat back calmly what you have asked the student to do so that you do not get drawn into another, separate conversation and are able to keep the focus on what you have asked them.

Make the behaviour wrong, not the student

Choose your language carefully – for example, say 'That wasn't a very sensible choice' rather than, 'You aren't very sensible.' This means that the student will not start to see themselves as the problem or think that they are unable to change. Always try to follow up afterwards if you can see that a student is trying to make a more sensible choice.

Ensure students know that they have the choice

This means giving them responsibility for their behaviour. Remember to use this word – for example, 'I have asked you to line up twice and you have chosen not to. This means that you will miss two minutes of playtime.' In this way they are aware that the consequences of the wrong choice have been their decision. We should also use the word 'choice' when talking about positive behaviour – giving students choice also gives them confidence along with responsibility.

Always remain calm and never shout at a student

Make sure you are not reactive when managing behaviour – students can see this as a way of gaining attention. Sometimes being silent and waiting for them to stop behaving in a negative way can be very effective.

Act as you have said you will

Make sure you follow through with what you have said so that students know you will follow up on the choice they have made. You should be fair and consistent in what you say to students. In this way they will know that the boundaries and rules you have established with them are not negotiable.

Catch them being good and give a positive comment

This is important as giving a positive comment as soon as possible after a misdemeanour will boost the student's self-esteem and show that you notice good as well as poor behaviour.

Develop relationships by knowing student names and giving eye contact

You should always develop your relationships with students in a positive way – for example, by learning their names, greeting them and saying goodbye, and by smiling and using positive comments where you can, even if they do not respond to you straight away. Through showing that you value them you will start to develop positive relationships, which can form the basis of trust and co-operation.

> **Class discussion**
>
> Have you been involved in a situation in which you have had to manage disruption in the teaching and learning environment? Discuss with others what happened and how the situation was resolved.

AC 3.2 Use policies and procedures to manage behaviour that challenges

Behaviour that challenges may include:

- verbal abuse (e.g. racist comments, threats, bullying others)
- physical abuse (such as assault of others, damaging property)
- behaviour that is destructive to the child/young person
- behaviour that is illegal.

You will need to be able to use the policies and procedures of your school or college to manage behaviour that challenges. It is important that you apply the rules and boundaries of the setting both consistently and fairly, by being fair to students and explaining reasons when using any sanctions. Make sure you know WHY you are acting to manage the behaviour according to the setting's policy and be ready to tell the student why you are taking these measures. 'Because I said so' or 'Because I am in charge' are not legitimate reasons. This is because they should understand they have had the choice about whether or not to behave appropriately and that the sanctions have been applied because they made an inappropriate choice. If students are not clear on this, they are more likely to test the boundaries with different

Case study

Dan, who is 8 and has attention deficit hyperactivity disorder (ADHD) and Tourette's syndrome, has been causing some disruption in class and calling out abuse to other students. Instead of applying a graduated response, which is what is in the class charter, the class teacher has asked you to take him out of class as soon as he starts misbehaving, to 'cool off'.

1 Why might the teacher have done this?
2 What message does it send to Dan?
3 Is there anything you can do in this situation?

adults in the setting. In addition, if you only threaten to use sanctions, or do not act quickly when there are incidents of poor behaviour, students will quickly learn that you do not mean what you say. This will then influence how they behave around you going forward.

The age and ability of the child or young person will also influence the types of sanctions that are appropriate and the scale with which they are applied. This is because they are unlikely to respond to sanctions that they do not understand or that are seen as 'babyish'. Many primary schools have systems such as cards, which are given out for each incident of unacceptable behaviour, and if several are given in one day they may then miss part or all of playtime. If their behaviour is more disruptive or challenging, they may go straight to a senior member of staff. Secondary or college students may be given verbal warnings, followed by classroom-based detentions and later after-school detentions and/or be sent to a senior member of staff.

Where sanctions for poor behaviour are given to students with special educational needs, their level of understanding must be taken into account so that they know why sanctions are being applied. Students who have needs in the area of social and emotional development may find this particularly challenging, as they may not pick up on social signals or understand the way in which others behave, or react with frustration. You may need to explain reasons for others' behaviour to them, and go through why their own behaviour is not appropriate.

In practice

What scale of sanctions is used in your school or college for managing behaviour that challenges? Are all students aware of them? Should the same sanctions always be used for all students?

There may also be times when you need to go straight to senior management or act decisively yourself to minimise risk to others – for example, in cases of physical abuse. The kinds of strategies you could use to quickly minimise behaviour that challenges may be:

- remove student from situation, or others from student
- speak with authority and act decisively
- go straight to a member of the senior management/leadership team, or send for them if needed.

Remove student from situation, or others from student

If behaviour is challenging or disruptive, and where there is a possibility of doing this, it may be in the best interests of all to remove the student from the situation. It will help to give time out to the student to 'cool off' and will also allow any other student who are involved to be separated from them.

Speak with authority and act decisively

When you are managing behaviour, it is important to always speak to students in a way that shows you mean it. This is because if there is any doubt about your authority, students are more likely to question it.

Go straight to a member of the senior management/leadership team, or send for them if needed

In some extreme cases this may be necessary, particularly if a student or colleague is in danger.

AC 3.3 Provide support for colleagues in relation to behaviour that challenges

You may need to provide support for colleagues who are dealing with inappropriate or challenging behaviour in your setting. This may be for several reasons:

- the behaviour of the child or young person is regularly difficult to manage
- the child or young person has suddenly become very disruptive
- the behaviour of the child or young person is causing physical danger to others
- your colleague needs another adult to reinforce what they are saying and back them up.

If the situation is ongoing, there are likely to be meetings so that staff can be prepared, and there is likely to be an EHC (Education, Health and Care) plan put in place that will set out what help will be implemented, how this will be done and how regularly it will be reviewed. The child or young person will also be involved in setting manageable targets so that they are involved in any decisions that are made and can also put their views forward.

If the situation is not typical, or there is a specific incident that needs to be dealt with quickly, you may need to act swiftly in order to avoid danger to the student or others. In this situation, further help will also need to be sought and you should do this through sending another student or sounding an alarm, depending on the policy of your school or college. You may need to remove the student from the situation in order to prevent further disruption or potential harm to others. If the situation has escalated quickly, this may need to be pointed out to the child or young person so that they can see the consequences of their behaviour.

AC 3.4 Explain referral processes in line with policies and procedures for behaviour that challenges

The sorts of behaviour or discipline problems that should be referred to others are those that:

- present danger to themselves, you or others
- are regularly disruptive to other students' learning
- do not respond to the school or college's behaviour management strategies
- are a cause for concern.

These kinds of behaviour problems will need to have additional support and strategies from those given to others. If the issues are ongoing and you have tried a number of different strategies, your first source of advice will be your school or college SENCo. They may come and observe the child or young person in class, or give you additional strategies to help manage their behaviour. They will also be able to refer you to other professionals external to the school or college if additional strategies have been tried.

At the first signs that there may be a problem, it may be helpful for you and other staff to keep an incident log so that you have dates and can remember exactly what has happened and how it was dealt with. It may also be helpful to note if there are any triggers or situations that spark this behaviour. This is because your SENCo, and later others, are likely to ask you for as much information as you can provide. It is also helpful to have specific evidence over time as it may be needed at a later date.

Outside the school or college, your SENCo may refer the child or young person for support from an educational psychologist or CAMHS (Child and Adolescent Mental Health Services), so that they can have a specialist assessment. Parental approval will need to be given for this to take place, and staff and parents will then be given ongoing advice and support so that strategies and help can be provided.

Stretch and challenge

Using the following weblink and others you can find, find out about CAMHS and the support it provides for children and young people in your area. How are children and young people referred in your setting?

www.nhs.uk/NHSEngland/AboutNHSservices/mental-health-services-explained/Pages/about-childrens-mental-health-services.aspx

Tips for best practice: managing behaviour that challenges

- Make sure you act straight away if the behaviour is severe, so that you can avoid further disruption.
- If necessary/possible, remove the child or young person from the situation and speak to them calmly.
- Send for help from another adult straight away.
- Keep a record of any inappropriate behaviour that is ongoing and does not respond to behaviour management strategies.
- Make sure your SENCo is aware of any incidents of challenging behaviour and keep a record of when it occurs.

Check your understanding

1. Name three policies or procedures that are important when promoting positive behaviour in a school or college.
2. Why is it important that all staff understand and follow the school or college's behaviour management policy?
3. What is meant by the term 'ground rules' and why are they effective?
4. What kinds of strategies might you use in order to promote positive behaviour in your setting?
5. Why is being a good role model so important when you are around children and young people?
6. How can you manage behaviour that challenges effectively and minimise any disruption?
7. How would you define behaviour that challenges?
8. Name three ways in which you can support colleagues when dealing with behaviour that challenges.
9. How would you refer behaviour problems to others and in what order?

Assessment preparation

This unit requires you to be able to promote positive behaviour in your setting, as well as know what to do when you are faced with challenging or inappropriate behaviour. You can have a face-to-face discussion with your assessor to show that you are familiar with the policies and procedures of your own setting, or you may be asked to carry out an assignment in which you outline these. Alternatively, you can complete the 'In practice' exercise in AC 1.1, which asks you to summarise them. If you extend this to explain why it is important that staff are consistent and fair in applying boundaries and rules for behaviour, you will have also covered AC 1.2.

The second and third learning outcomes will need to be observed by your assessor or a witness so that it is clear that you can show how you manage behaviour.

Legislation

Although there is no specific legislation around behaviour, there is statutory guidance as schools do have legal responsibilities around behaviour and attendance. The guidance has been published by the government in order to support staff and help them to maintain good behaviour in schools. Colleges are not specifically listed here although they are bound by the same legislation. They are listed on the **www.gov.uk** website under several different areas:

- Policy Paper – 2010 to 2015 government policy: school behaviour and attendance
- Behaviour and discipline in schools – Guidance for head teachers and staff (2013, updated 2016)
- Behaviour and discipline in schools – Statutory guidance for governing bodies (2013, updated 2015)
- School discipline and exclusions – Exclusion from maintained schools, academies and student referral units in England: Statutory guidance for those with legal responsibilities in relation to exclusions (September 2017)
- Use of reasonable force in schools – Advice for head teachers, staff and governing bodies (July 2013).

Read about it

Reference books

DfE (2011) *Getting the Simple Things Right: Charlie Taylor's Behaviour Checklists*, DfE.

Weblinks

www.gov.uk/government/publications/use-of-reasonable-force-in-schools

www.gov.uk/government/publications/searching-screening-and-confiscation

www.gov.uk/government/publications/school-exclusion

www.gov.uk/government/publications/keeping-children-safe-in-education--2

https://youngminds.org.uk/find-help/your-guide-to-support/guide-to-camhs/ Your guide to CAMHS: a beginner's guide to the NHS's Child and Adolescent Mental Health Services (CAMHS) for young people and parents

www.educationsupportpartnership.org.uk/sites/default/files/resources/ed_support_managing_pupil_behaviour_0.pdf Managing Pupil Behaviour (Education Support Partnership)

7 Support children and young people during learning activities

About this unit

This important unit is about the way in which you support learners before, during and after learning activities. You will need to be able to show that you have the knowledge, understanding and skills to do this in different learning environments both in the setting and when on trips and excursions. When supporting learners, you will need to show that you use a variety of strategies to ensure that you meet their needs effectively. You will also need to demonstrate how you work with teachers and other staff to enable learners' learning, through working closely with them in advance and through feeding back to them following learning activities. Finally, you should be able to show how you contribute to the evaluation of learning activities through feeding back to teachers and reflecting on your own practice.

Learning outcomes

By the end of this unit you will:

LO1 Be able to contribute to planning learning activities

LO2 Be able to prepare for learning activities

LO3 Be able to support learning activities

LO4 Be able to observe and report on learner participation and progress

LO5 Be able to contribute to the evaluation of learning activities

Getting started

Write down what you know about the role of the teaching assistant when supporting the teaching and learning process. Think about all stages of the process, from planning and carrying out activities to evaluating learning and assessing your own part in what happened. Keep this activity and look at it again when you have completed the unit.

LO1 Be able to contribute to planning learning activities

For more about the roles of teachers and support staff see Unit 1, page 7.

AC 1.1 Explain how support staff may contribute to the planning, delivery and review of learning activities to support teaching and learning

Teaching assistants, support assistants, and individual or learning support assistants play an important role in the planning, delivery and review of learning activities. They will know the needs and abilities of learners so can share ideas with teachers and tutors and contribute to the planning process. It is important to know that planning, delivery and review follow a cycle that feeds in to the teaching and learning process so that the needs of individual learners can be met.

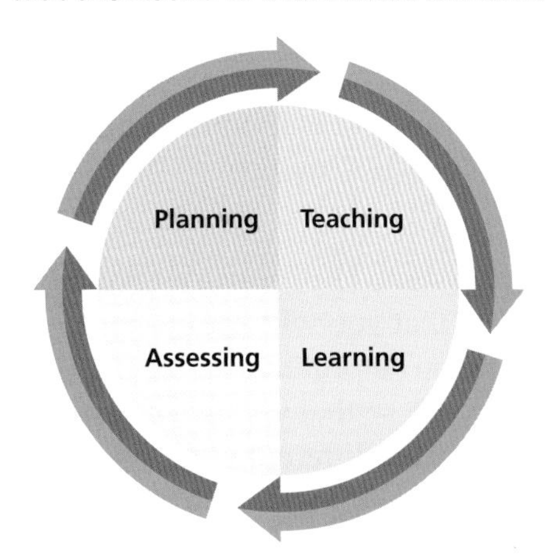

▲ Figure 7.1 What do you know about the teaching and learning cycle?

Key terms

Long-term planning/schemes of work: this is usually planning for the year or for the duration of a college course, or for a specific unit through the identification of lesson content in relation to a syllabus.

Medium-term planning: this will be planning for the term or half term and will usually be split into weeks.

Short-term planning: this will be detailed weekly or daily planning, which includes learning objectives and assessment.

Long-term plans and schemes of work will usually be completed well in advance and may even be continued, with some amendments, year on year. Depending on your level of experience, you are most likely to be involved in the **medium- and short-term planning** of learning activities with teachers or tutors. This may take place on a formal basis with time set aside each week to plan together, or through informal discussions and conversations both before and after the activity takes place. You will need to know about the way in which planning takes place so that you can contribute and make constructive suggestions.

Class discussion

How much opportunity do you have in your school or college to discuss plans with teachers? What effect does this have on your role when supporting learners?

Activity

What do you know about the way in which different teachers or tutors in your school or college plan? Are planning formats the same or different between different age groups? What can you find out about an age group that you do not support?

Science Medium Term Planning

YEAR: 6 | Teacher: Mrs B | Support staff for first 30 mins of session: Mrs L | Term: 2 | Topic Title: Reversible and Irreversible Changes/Changing Circuits | Time: Tuesday 1.30-3.30

WEEK	LEARNING OBJECTIVES	LEARNING ACTIVITY	Evaluation/Next steps
1 5/01/18	To recognise that mixing materials with water can cause them to change and that some changes are reversible.	• Start with quick quiz on work done last term. • Revise work done last term on dissolving and go over important vocabulary – solution, suspension, evaporation. • Go through homework from end of last term and think about what happened to the solutions on the windowsill and write up. • Important to recognise that dissolving is only one type of change. Is it reversible or irreversible? Ask pupils to assess their learning from last term with support from Mrs L. • Ask what they would do to separate a) salt and b) sand from water. Introduce the word 'reversible' to describe the changes. Show interactive BBC clip as a refresher. • Carry out investigation using plaster of Paris, some cement, cornflour, salt, flour, powder paint, baking powder, Andrews Salts/water and observe what happens. Mix them up and then try to separate them. • If they finish this try to think of some of their own which are reversible/irreversible.	• Kelly very good with quiz and especially definition of forces. • Mia did not give good example of food chain. • Josh remembered photosynthesis. • Alex not clear on how to get a solid back from a liquid. • All seemed to understand reversible/irreversible. • Adam/Elijah absent.
2 12/01/18	To recognise that heating materials can cause them to change and new materials to be formed.	• Remind students about last week and ask them to check back over their work after marking, particularly the write up of the investigation. Mrs L to support/note down any issues. • Put a series of objects on each table – egg, chocolate, water, wood, wax, paper, popcorn one at a time and ask children to answer questions on whiteboards about what will happen when they are heated. • Show photos and discuss fact that irreversible changes <u>often</u> caused by heating. • Move on to discuss what happens when you mix things together to cook them – what is this change? Discuss difference between physical and chemical changes – physical can be reversed, chemical cannot and a new substance can be made. • Complete test base questions, no time to do last week. • Talk about their ideas and ask them to suggest materials that are changed by cooling and decide whether these changes are reversible or irreversible. Make sure to distinguish the difference between burning and heating. • Discuss the kinds of materials and watch video on reversible and irreversible changes at end of lesson (15 mins).	All very impressed by video and understood concept of an irreversible change.

▲ Figure 7.2 What plans are shown in advance and how do you contribute?

AC 1.2 Use knowledge of children and young people to contribute to planning and offer constructive suggestions for your role

Planning alongside teachers and tutors is beneficial for everyone – learners, teachers and assistants. As members of staff who work regularly with learners, you will each know about their individual needs and be able to discuss the best approach to learning activities in order to meet them effectively. In some cases you may know more about the learners than the teachers do, particularly if you are an individual support assistant or work with them each day. It is important to share your knowledge of how individual children and young people learn with teaching staff so that plans are personalised to provide appropriate strategies.

Learner needs

If you support an individual learner who has special educational needs or a disability this is particularly important as you will know about the way in which they learn best; however, this is also true for other learners. It is vital for learners that learning is relevant to them and that they are actively involved as this will help to keep them motivated and engaged in activities.

Learner interests

If you work with the same learners on a regular basis, it is also likely that you will know about their interests. It can be helpful to take this knowledge into account so that you can make your own suggestions for different ways you can use this so that they might be more engaged in their learning. However, you may not always be able to incorporate this into your work with learners.

Case study

Read the following scenarios.

Sam in Year 2 has dyslexia and is very reluctant to participate in activities that relate to literacy. He is interested in learning and speaks with confidence but finds it very difficult to write his ideas down. The planned activity is mainly asking learners to write answers to a series of grammatical questions but there is no differentiation for Sam.

Allegra and Myra in Year 5 do not work well together in your experience. There have been a few incidents in which they have had to be separated as learning becomes interrupted when they sit together. You have been asked to work with them and two other learners on some maths problem-solving activities although you will also be working with others in the group.

You have been asked to work with a group of Year 11 learners in French to carry out an activity in several different stages. You know the group well and realise that, due to their needs, this will take much longer than one session to complete.

1 What should you do in each situation?
2 How could you speak to teachers in a way that does not undermine what they have said but ensures that learners get maximum learning opportunities in each case?

Your own strengths and areas of knowledge or ability

You may have a particular strength or area of ability that can be utilised by teaching staff in order to support teaching and learning. For example, if you know that you are particularly creative and enjoy carrying out these activities with learners, you may have some specific ideas which you know will work or have tried before, which can be incorporated into the plan. Similarly, if you lack confidence in a subject area that is included in the plan, feel that you would not be able to support it effectively, or you need more information in order to do so, you should raise your concerns at the planning stage.

In practice

Using a plan you have contributed to with the teacher or tutor, annotate it to show how you have contributed to the planning process as well as being part of the evaluation following the activity. Show how your knowledge of the learners has enabled you to make constructive suggestions and look at what went well, along with what could be improved next time. This can contribute to your evidence for this assessment criterion as a work product.

LO2 Be able to prepare for learning activities

AC 2.1 Select and prepare the resources required for the planned learning activities

Resources to support learning activities include:

- materials
- equipment
- books and other written materials.

Another reason that it is helpful to plan alongside teachers and tutors is that you will know in advance about the kinds of resources that are needed. If you wait until just before the activity you may be unable to find them, others may be using them, or if they are consumable materials you may find that they need to be ordered.

Your school or college will have a number of resources as well as teaching and learning materials that staff will have access to in order to support learning activities. These will be items that are available within the classroom as well as those that may be stored in other areas of the building. The kinds of materials, resources and equipment you might need could be:

- subject-specific equipment, for example, for science or maths
- resources for creative subjects such as art or design technology
- written materials
- outdoor equipment, for example, for PE or Forest School, or items for school trips
- general classroom items and consumables
- artefacts that may be used for a topic
- computers or computer-based resources or technical equipment.

Any resources that are needed for the session should be listed on the lesson plan so that you can prepare effectively for the session in advance. If the plan is not clear, or you are not familiar with a particular piece of equipment or resource you have been asked to use, always tell the teacher or tutor as you may need specific training or some time to learn to use it.

You should also keep an eye on replenishing more general classroom resources and materials, for example, sharpening pencils or making sure that there are enough supplies of paper or new exercise books to hand so that they are accessible when needed.

AC 2.2 Explain the objectives, content and intended outcomes of learning activities

Before carrying out learning activities with learners, you should make sure that you know the learning objectives, content and intended outcomes for each session from the teacher. Learning objectives need to be very clear so that the success of learners can be measured against them. Learners will also need to be told about objectives at the start of the session. In this way they will be able to identify what they are learning and start to assess their own progress. Teachers may use Bloom's Taxonomy in order to help them to pitch activities that are appropriate for learners at different levels of learning.

Bloom's Taxonomy was developed in 1956 to classify a series of intellectual skills. At the lowest level, it asks learners to simply recall and remember facts. This is gradually built up to the processes of analysing, evaluating and creating something new based on what they have learned. As you can see from Table 7.1 on page 115, the kinds of verbs that can be used at each stage will help us to devise suitable objectives.

See Unit 10, AC 2.1, page 160, for more on supporting assessment for learning.

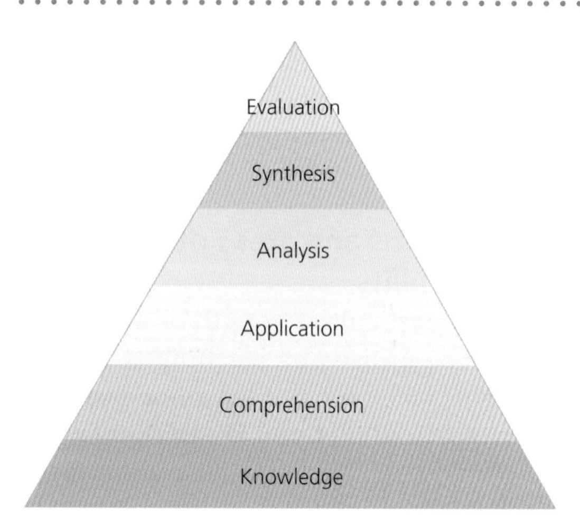

▲ Figure 7.3 How does Bloom's Taxonomy help us to create learning objectives?

Activity

Find out more about Bloom's Taxonomy and why it is a useful tool in pinpointing aspects of learning. Can you find any examples of where it is used in your own classroom?

Stretch and challenge

Find out about the work of Geoff Petty and some of the examples he gives on his Teaching Today website at http://geoffpetty.com/for-team-leaders/downloads/. You will find a download of Bloom's Taxonomy there and activities showing how it can be applied to the classroom.

When you are observed working with learners, you should be able to talk the learning objectives through with them before the session. Alternatively, if you do not have time to do this before the observation, you should be able to give them a plan for the session, which includes objectives, content and outcomes you have highlighted and annotated showing that you know what they are.

AC 2.3 Develop and adapt resources to meet the needs of learners

You may need to develop and adapt resources in order to meet the needs of the learners you are supporting. Developing your own may be basic – for example, cut up and laminated resources that can be reused, or a bank of resources you have accumulated over time to help support learners with specific needs such as dyslexia. In some cases you may be able to adapt resources as you use them – for example, if learners are not able to operate equipment or resources without support.

▲ Figure 7.4 Have you been able to develop learning resources to meet learners' needs?

LO3 Be able to support learning activities

AC 3.1 Select and demonstrate learning support strategies to meet the needs of learners

You will need to demonstrate that you are able to use a wide range of learning support strategies while also meeting the needs of the learners with whom you are working. The strategies you use will depend on the situation and the responses of the learners, but you should show an awareness of their needs and how best to meet them.

Creating a positive learning environment

All adults who are responsible for teaching and learning should have positive expectations of learners and encourage them to take a shared responsibility for the learning and wider environment as a whole. Teachers and assistants should ensure that the environment (both indoor and outdoor) is welcoming and organised so that resources and equipment are easy to find. There should be clearly labelled displays as well as classroom rules or a charter that learners have signed, which outlines rights and responsibilities in a way that is appropriate for the age of the learners.

▼ Table 7.1 Examples of some 'active' verbs that are appropriate for use when devising learning objectives

Type of learning	Active verbs
Knowledge (remembering)	Tell, identify, label, reproduce, recall, list, match, memorise, outline, reorganise, arrange, define, describe, record, relate, repeat, name, order, select, state, say
Comprehension (understanding)	Clarify, discuss, summarise, classify, sketch, translate, distinguish, explain, express, generalise, give examples of, identify, indicate, find, predict, recognise, review, select
Application (applying)	Translate, use, apply, choose, demonstrate, dramatise, employ, illustrate, interpret, intervene, manipulate, modify, practise, relate, solve, criticise, examine
Analysis (analysing)	Calculate, compare, contrast, analyse, examine, inspect, distinguish, investigate, debate, appraise, outline, question, discriminate, relate, differentiate, test
Synthesis (or evaluating)	Assemble, categorise, rewrite, collect, construct, design, devise, elaborate, formulate, modify, compose, plan, arrange, propose, rearrange, revise, set up, start, summarise, tell, write, develop
Evaluation (or creating)	Argue, value, justify, compare, appraise, create, discriminate, revise, evaluate, interpret, judge, predict, conclude, rate, assess, relate, score, select

Our class charter

We have the right to:

- feel safe
- be ourselves
- make friends
- learn and play in a happy environment.

We have a responsibility to:

- keep our learning environment and school tidy
- look after equipment
- be kind to one another
- try our best with our work and our behaviour.

▲ Figure 7.5 What examples have you seen of a class charter?

When working with individuals or groups it is important to role model positive approaches to teaching and learning. Make sure you show through your own expectations that you are aware of the importance of a positive environment and encourage learners to be responsible for maintaining it.

Activity

Write a reflective account listing different ways in which you can create a positive learning environment in your own setting. If you have created specific areas or displays in your setting, describe these and say how they have enhanced the environment for learners.

Managing behaviour

At the start of teaching and learning sessions, you will need to set ground rules so that learners are clear on your expectations and know the boundaries for behaviour. Always acknowledge and praise when learners are doing the right thing and making good choices so that good behaviour is recognised. It is also important that you act immediately to manage behaviour that challenges so that learners know this is not acceptable. In cases where behaviour is causing disruption to the learning of others in the group you should refer to the teacher or remove the learner from the group.

See Unit 6 for more on supporting children and young people's positive behaviour.

Encouraging group cohesion and collaborative learning

Where learners are working together in a group on a task that requires them to collaborate, you may need to keep them on task. Some personalities may find it difficult to listen to or acknowledge the ideas of others, while others may prefer to let others take over rather than put their own ideas forward. You should ensure that everyone is given the opportunity to contribute and be part of the process.

Case study

Penny is working on a maths activity with a small group that includes Nicolas, who she knows is gifted and talented. After they have been working on the task for a time, she can see that Nicolas has shown that he has met the learning objective and is working through the remaining questions quickly. Although he has not finished all of them, she decides to give him an extension activity.

1. Do you think that Penny has done the right thing in giving Nicolas another activity before the task is complete?
2. Is there anything else that she could do if she senses he is becoming restless?

Responding to learners' needs appropriately

As you work with learners regularly you will get to know them and be aware of their needs. These may be that they lack confidence in their own abilities, have special educational needs, are bilingual, are gifted and talented, or have other issues going on in their lives that mean they need more reassurance from adults. You should be able to show how you respond to these through the way in which you encourage and support them.

See also AC 3.3, page 120, on supporting the inclusion of all learners.

Acknowledging effective teaching and learning approaches for boys and girls

There are a number of different theories about teaching and learning approaches for boys and girls. While some say that their brains are different, and have male and female characteristics, others state that these come about because of the way in which they are nurtured and develop. When it comes to teaching and learning, if there is a wide range of activities and an approach that is accessible to all, this is the most important thing, whether they are boys, girls or LGBT.

We should be careful not to stereotype boys and girls, as all learners are individuals and will learn in their own way.

Class discussion

Look at the following general characteristics of the minds of boys and girls, which have been put forward by some researchers.

- Girls lack confidence in their own abilities/ boys are more confident.
- Boys have higher-developed spatial skills.
- Boys are more impulsive and need to move more.
- Girls are more able to multitask as they can make quicker transitions between activities/ boys lateralise their thinking.
- Girls have better language skills and more empathy.

Are these statements true in your experience? Can these help us in the classroom? If there are neurological differences, should we plan teaching and learning to accommodate them?

Also see Unit 5, which deals with understanding how children and young people develop.

Translating or explaining words and phrases

When you are supporting learners you may need to remind them of, translate or explain words and phrases that have been used by teachers, particularly if learners are very young or their first language is not English. Make sure that key vocabulary is accessible to them so that they are able to refer to it, and ensure that the meaning of any new words is clear to them.

Reminding learners of teaching points made by the teacher

As learners work through activities, you may need to remind them of learning objectives or teaching points, to keep them on task.

Questioning learners effectively

Questioning learners effectively is one of the most important ways in which we can support learners and to take their learning forward. After extensive research carried out by the Institute of Education between 2003 and 2009,* it was flagged up as an area of concern for those who support teaching

*DISS (Deployment and Impact of Support Staff) Project; EDTA Effective Deployment of Teaching Assistants Project. See also Bosanquet et al. (2016).

and learning in classrooms. This was because they found that, although teaching assistants spent more time talking to learners, they had not had sufficient training in how to open up talk and question learners effectively. A subsequent project by the Institute focused on interactions and questioning of learners as one of the areas that could be developed. It cited types of talk that are helpful, as well as those that are not. An example given is that of **dialogic talk** (Alexander, 2005).

Some talk is less helpful in supporting learning as it closes it down; this has been referred to as the IRF (initiation/response/feedback) pattern. An example of this is as follows:

Initiation: This would be a question posed by an adult – for example, 'Does anyone know the date of the Battle of Hastings?'

Response: This would be the learner's response – '1068'

Feedback: This is the feedback then given to the learner – 'No, it was in 1066.'

The IRF model closes down learning, and does not provide any further opportunities to take the learner forward. Dialogic talk, on the other hand, gives both the learner and the adult the opportunity to have a discussion, as in the following example:

Adult: 'What do you think it would have been like for William's men when they landed in England?'

Learner: 'They would have been curious about seeing a different land, and wanting to fight.'

Adult: 'There is a place called Battle in Sussex where you can visit the site of the battle itself and look at a museum. We can find out more about it if you like.'

Key term

Dialogic talk: using talk to clarify and explain ideas as part of the teaching and learning process.

In practice

Observe the ways in which teachers question learners when you are in class. Can you find examples of dialogic talk? How does it support the teaching and learning process?

Scaffolding learning

Scaffolding is a term used to describe a strategy that supports the learner through structuring their learning to reach a specific goal. Developed by Wood, Bruner and Ross in the 1970s, scaffolding was based on the idea that learners could be supported to reach the next stage in their learning through guidance and encouragement. It is important not to change the task itself but to break it down into smaller steps and to observe learners carefully as they complete each one. The purpose of scaffolding is that we are creating opportunities to develop learner independence. Adults should intervene only if they are unable to work through any difficulties on their own. The scaffolding framework pictured here has been developed by Paula Bosanquet, Julie Radford and Rob Webster to support learners with special educational needs in avoiding what they call 'learned helplessness' – in other words, becoming over-reliant on adults. The ultimate goal is to give the least amount of help that you can.

- **Self-scaffolding:** this involves observing the learner, and allowing them time to consider and tackle the task themselves.
- **Prompting:** this stage involves giving encouragement or questioning learners with prompts such as 'What is the first thing you need to do?'

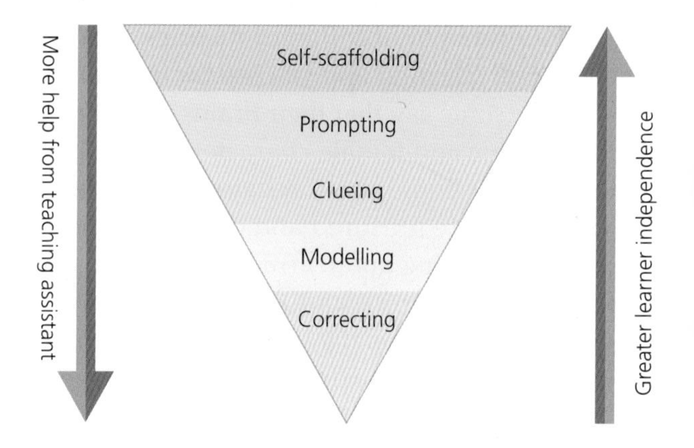

▲ Figure 7.6 How can you ensure that you encourage maximum learner independence during learning activities? Source: Bosanquet et al. (2016)

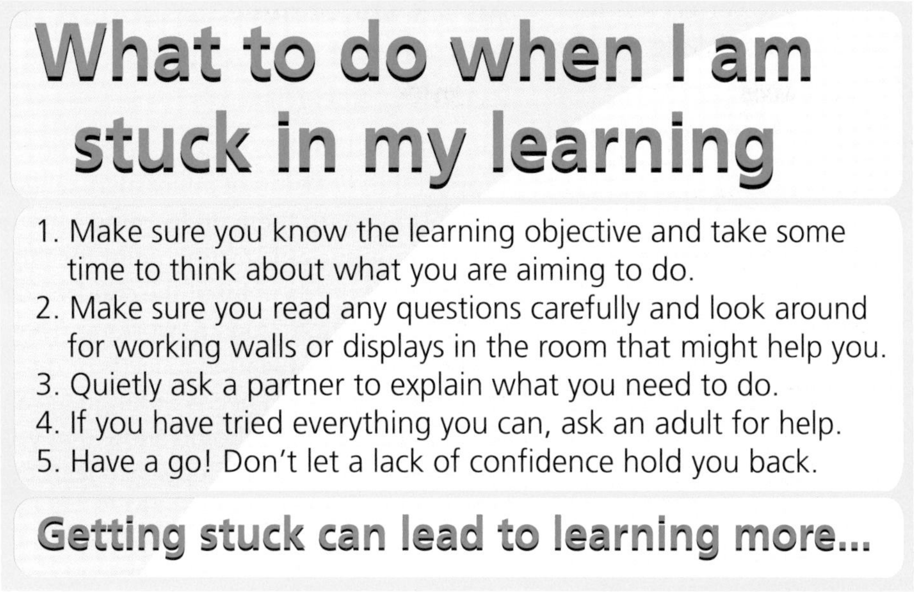

What to do when I am stuck in my learning

1. Make sure you know the learning objective and take some time to think about what you are aiming to do.
2. Make sure you read any questions carefully and look around for working walls or displays in the room that might help you.
3. Quietly ask a partner to explain what you need to do.
4. If you have tried everything you can, ask an adult for help.
5. Have a go! Don't let a lack of confidence hold you back.

Getting stuck can lead to learning more...

▲ Figure 7.7 Do learners in your class know how to proceed when they don't know what to do?

- **Clueing:** this might involve giving a small clue to learners so that they are able to move forward in their learning.
- **Modelling:** if learners are learning a new skill, they may need to have it modelled for them by the adult. They can then watch and attempt to do it themselves.
- **Correcting:** this is where adults give the answer. It should be avoided as it does not require any independent thinking.

Research it

Find out more about scaffolding and how you can use it to support learner learning. Look in particular at the work of Vygotsky as well as that of Wood, Bruner and Ross (1976).

Stretch and challenge

What do you know about learning theories? Use the internet to research the theories of Piaget, Kolb and Bruner. How might these theories fit in with the process of scaffolding?

Keeping the responsibility for learning with the learner and developing their independent learning skills

Learners need to learn that the responsibility for learning is theirs and that adults are not there to do the work for them or to give them the answers. Ensure that there are opportunities for learners to find things out for themselves and develop their independence rather than asking an adult – for example, through the use of scaffolding (as discussed). Always allow learners the opportunity to do this; you can give them a checklist of approaches to take when they don't know what to do – for example, check that they have done everything they can, look for clues in the learning environment, ask a friend.

Modelling correct use of language and vocabulary

When you are speaking with learners, particularly younger learners or those who speak English as an additional language, you will need to model the correct use of language or vocabulary; this is because they may not always use it correctly. If they make an error, the best way to correct it is to repeat back what they have said, modelling the correct use of language.

Ensuring learners understand the learning tasks

At the start of any activity, it can be helpful to ask the learners to tell you what they are required to do so that you can ensure they understand the task and the objectives. This may be a strategy to use with learners that you know have not been listening, or with those who may have difficulties in their understanding.

Helping learners to use resources relevant to the learning activity

You may need to support learners in using resources for the activity, particularly if they have not used them before or are unsure what to do.

Modifying or adapting activities

From time to time you may need to change or modify an activity to ensure that learners are able to stay on task. More able learners may complete tasks quickly and need an extension activity, while those who need more support may need you to simplify the activity by going back a few steps so that it is more achievable for them.

AC 3.2 Show how to work in partnership with others to support learning activities

In order to support teaching and learning effectively, you will need to work in partnership with other members of your team. If you are supporting learners with special educational needs or disabilities you may also work in partnership with external professionals. As well as teachers in the school or college these may be the SENCo, senior managers and other support staff who may share ideas and strategies with you as well as information about learners with whom you are working. You should be able to outline their roles and why it is important to work closely with them in order to support learning activities.

For more information on the roles of internal and external professionals, see Unit 1.

AC 3.3 Show how to support the inclusion of all learners involved in learning activities

You will need to show your assessor how you support the inclusion of all learners when you are working with them on learning activities. The most important starting point for this is to be aware of the needs of all of the children or young people with whom you are working. These may relate to special educational needs or disabilities, social and emotional needs or language and communication. You should show that you are prepared for and can include each learner who is involved in the learning activity.

For more on understanding how to support children and young people with special educational needs and disabilities in the learning environment, look at Unit 14; see Unit 13 for information on how to support bilingual learners; and Unit 12, which deals with supporting children and young people's speech, language and communication.

AC 3.4 Explain barriers when supporting learning activities and how to overcome these

You are likely to face barriers to the learning process during your work with children and young people. Although these are unavoidable, you should be adaptable enough to be able to deal with them or know what to do so that interruptions to teaching and learning are minimised. Barriers when supporting learning activities may take different forms but will relate to five main areas, as described below.

1. The learning activities

There may be a number of different barriers concerning learning activities.

- **Learning objectives may be unclear or unachievable for the learner:** you will need to know what to do when objectives are not clear or learners are not able to meet them. If you are unable to speak to the teacher, you may need to adapt the activity or go back several steps in order to help them to achieve.

- **An activity you are working on may be too difficult or too easy for the learner:** in this situation you will need to adapt the learning activity (see pages 115 and 120 for more on this).
- **You may not have enough information from the teacher:** you will need to go back and speak to the teacher so that you are able to support the task effectively. If this is not possible because they are teaching, you will need to wait until they are able to speak to you.
- **You may be unable to understand the task yourself:** if learning outcomes are unclear or too complex, it is important that you speak to the teacher immediately. You will not be able to support the learning of children and young people unless you are absolutely clear on the task yourself.

2. The learning resources

Learning resources should enhance what you are doing with learners, however, you may find that they can be a barrier to the support you are giving children and young people. This can be for the following reasons.

- **You may have insufficient time to prepare resources for what you have been asked to do:** everyone is busy in schools and colleges and it is possible that you may be given plans and activities at the last minute. While you should do what you can, if there really is not enough time to prepare resources for the activity, you will need to prioritise those that are essential and those that you may be able to do without.
- **You may be unfamiliar with the resources you have been asked to use:** if you have time, find out more about the resources by asking other staff or working out what to do yourself. It is important that you know what to do before starting your work with learners as otherwise you will lose learning time.
- **You may not know where to find the resources you need or they may be in use by others:** this can be an issue, particularly if you do not have time to look for them. You should speak to the teacher and try to adapt the activity if you can, or ask learners to help you if resources need to be found.

3. The learning environment

Barriers within the learning environment are likely to relate to the following.

- **Noise levels:** there may be too much noise coming from other learners who are working in the room, which will act as a distraction to those with whom you are working. There may also be noise coming from outside the room or building that is causing learners to comment or lose focus. If this is the case you may need to move to another area outside the room if necessary or speak to the teacher about the noise level.
- **Light or temperature:** if the learning environment is too hot or cold for learners to work, or if there is insufficient or too much light, you should adjust blinds or heating so that they are comfortable and can think about their learning.
- **Space to work:** you may find that you are unable to find a suitable space in which to work with a group, or that the space you have been given is too small for the learners to remain focused on the activity. You should also ensure that there is space for any equipment or resources you have been asked to use.

4. The learners' assessment

If you or learners are unclear about objectives, or if you are unable to assess learner learning for any reason, you should always speak to teachers. You should as a minimum requirement be able to talk about how each learner has responded to the activity, even if you have not had time to carry out assessment for learning with learners.

To find out more about supporting assessment for learning, read Unit 10.

5. The learner

Learners will for the most part want to achieve at learning activities, however, there may be barriers preventing this which may include the following.

- **Behaviour of others:** if others in the group are behaving inappropriately, it is important to intervene straight away. Praise good behaviour and ensure that you remove any learners from the group if they continue to interrupt.

See Unit 6 for more on supporting children and young people's positive behaviour.

- **Lack of concentration:** learners may not be able to concentrate and may need you to remind them to keep focused on the task.
- **Range of learning needs:** it may be difficult for you to support learning if you have a large group who may place different demands on you due to their needs. If the group is too large, or you are unable to support every learner, you will need to speak to the teacher.
- **Learners' confidence:** sometimes learners will lack confidence in their own ability and this may affect their ability to 'have a go' at some activities. You may need to give encouragement or break the learning down into smaller steps so that they are able to achieve learning objectives.

There will also be other issues that will affect the ability of children and young people to focus on the learning activity. You should be aware that you may not have been told about these kinds of issues, or that parents or carers may not have told the school or college. These might include the following.

- **Home environment:** domestic problems are likely to preoccupy the child or young person, and mean that they find it difficult to concentrate. These may relate to a marriage breakdown, addicts within the family, bereavement or a number of other issues. If you have concerns about a child or young person, you should always speak to someone in your organisation who may have more information and be able to help.
- **Basic needs:** these may be lack of sleep, food, worries about housing or other needs that many of us take for granted. A child or young person who is affected by these kinds of issues may well struggle to concentrate on their work.
- **Emotional issues:** emotional issues, such as bullying, trauma or abuse, are likely to cause long-term issues that will affect many aspects of a child or young person's life. It is important that adults know about them so that they are able to offer support.

If you have any concerns about a learner due to their behaviour – for example, if this changes or they become withdrawn – you should always speak to their teachers to find out if there are concerns about them. If not, you should outline your own observations so that the information is passed on.

See Unit 3 for more information about understanding how to safeguard children and young people, and Unit 14, which discusses mental health issues.

Tips for best practice: supporting learning activities

- Make sure you are clear on what you need to do and know the learning objective.
- Take time to be prepared and familiarise yourself with resources.
- Make sure the learning environment is comfortable for learners and conducive to learning.
- Ensure you know the names of learners and as much as possible about each of them.
- Include all learners in the activity, and consider their needs and interests.
- Check that learners understand any specific vocabulary or terminology used.
- Use positive praise and encouragement.
- Keep the responsibility for learning with the learner.
- Effectively question learners and scaffold learner learning.
- Encourage them to 'have a go' and ensure they know what to do if they get stuck.
- Adapt any work or resources if necessary.
- Use assessment for learning where possible so that learners can evaluate their progress.
- Talk to the teacher about any problems with learning or behaviour.
- Evaluate learning activities and feed back to teachers on learner progress.

Activity

Abraham Maslow was a psychologist who worked during the 1950s and studied the different needs humans have that enable them to achieve their full potential. Look again at his hierarchy of needs pyramid (Unit 5, Figure 5.9, page 88), and find out about these.

- How might Maslow's ideas help us to understand learners' ability to focus on their learning?
- Is an awareness all we need to have or is there more that we can do to support learners?

AC 3.5 Show how to support learning in different environments, indoor and outdoor

You will need to be able to show how you support learning in both indoor and outdoor environments. If your assessor is able to see you in only one of these, you should be able to provide evidence to show how you have worked in the other. It is likely that most of your work will take place indoors, but you may support sports lessons outdoors, be involved in Forest School, or go on educational trips or journeys.

LO4 Be able to observe and report on learner participation and progress

AC 4.1 Assess learner development, participation and progress

While you are working with learners, you will need to be able to assess what they are doing so that you are able to feed back effectively to teachers. As well as monitoring their responses and looking at how they participate during the activity, it is also important to be able to look at their progress towards the learning objectives. You will need to be able to say whether you have supported them through scaffolding or questioning, or whether they have been able to work through the activity independently. If appropriate for the age of the learners, you should also mention how much you have used peer and self-assessment to check on learners' learning.

▲ Figure 7.8 What opportunities do you have to support teaching and learning in an outdoor learning environment?

See Unit 10 for more on supporting assessment for learning.

AC 4.2 Use required methods and materials to record observations and feed back to others on learner development, participation and progress

When you are supporting learning activities, you will need to use the methods that have been outlined by teachers or tutors to record your observations on learner development, participation and progress. These may be through feedback sheets, notes on lesson plans, or verbally. You will need to make sure that you comment in particular on any learners who have found the activity very straightforward and have completed it quickly as well as those who have found it challenging, and reasons for this. If planning has been done well and is the activity pitched at the correct level, most learners should have been able to complete the task successfully.

▲ Figure 7.9 How often are you required to carry out observations?

You may also be asked to complete more structured observations by teachers or others such as outside professionals if there are specific things that need to be checked or assessed. These may be reported immediately after the activity or at a later date, for example, in a meeting. In this situation you will need to use the format that has been specified. Usually, if you are working with learners these are known as participant observations, as learners' learning may be influenced by having an adult present. However, there are other types of observations in which adults only report on what has happened and are seated away from the activity. These types of observations may be:

- **Checklists or tick sheets:** a straightforward list where the observer ticks through a list showing what the learner has been able to do.
- **Event samples:** these are used if we need to know how regularly a learner demonstrates a particular behaviour or activity.
- **Filming:** this is a means of ensuring that nothing is missed, although it can be an intrusive method of observation.
- **Anecdotal records:** these are simple and contain a brief description, usually of a single incident that has occurred, giving details of what happened, when, where and what was said. They are usually written after the event.
- **Photographs or audio recording:** these can also help us to feed back to teachers, particularly if learners' work has been practical or outdoors.
- **Structured description:** this method means that your observation will be focused around a series of headings that will guide you on the content of what needs to be observed.
- **Free description or running records:** these consist of a detailed account of everything that happens over a set period of time. It usually works best when observing an individual learner and requires you to detail everything you have seen.

LO5 Be able to contribute to the evaluation of learning activities

AC 5.1 Show how to contribute to the evaluation of learning activities

As mentioned at the start of the unit, evaluation is an important part of the teaching and learning process – all those who are involved will need to be part of this. For those who support teaching and learning, this will be through the way in which you feed back both to learners and teachers. In order to evaluate, you will need to consider the learning objectives, and whether the learners have been able to achieve or partially achieve them. You should also think about their level of engagement in the activity – they may have been unable to meet the objectives but have been enthusiastic and tried throughout, so you should record or feed this information back somewhere. This information may be recorded on a straightforward grid or table, which has a space for each learner.

AC 5.2 Use the outcomes of observations and assessments to: provide feedback to learners on their progress, provide the teacher with constructive feedback on the learning activities

Providing feedback to learners

Both during and after learning activities, it is important to provide feedback to the learners on the progress they are making. This can take the form of praise while they are working, as well as encouraging them to focus on what they are doing or to think about their next steps. If they are using assessment for learning, you can talk to them about the peer and self-assessment that has taken place. You may also like to discuss progress towards individual targets they may have. When providing feedback to learners, be specific. Rather than just saying, 'Well done' following an activity, try 'Well done, you have really listened and are going through all the steps we discussed at the beginning.' In this way they will be sure about exactly what they are doing correctly.

Providing feedback to teachers

Although it is difficult to find time to give constructive feedback to teachers, it is a crucial part of teaching and learning, and it is important that it takes place. If there is not time during the day, you may be able to talk on the phone or give them written feedback so that they can use the information to help plan for follow-up activities. If the activity has not gone well because learners have not responded positively and you know the reason for this, you will need to tell teachers if you can.

Where you have provided more formal written observations, you should not need to give as much feedback to teachers as a lot of what is needed will be detailed in the observation.

AC 5.3 Reflect on your practice in supporting learning activities

You should always take time out to reflect on your own practice and the way in which you responded to learners and how they responded to you. This is important as it is a way of evaluating what you do and considering the way in which you approach your role. You should remember that everyone who works with children and young people will find that some activities work better than others and that we do not have control over all variables. However, through thinking about what has happened we may be able to learn from our experiences and develop our practice.

When reflecting on your practice, you should think about:

- What went well and not so well? What were the reasons for this? (Consider the appropriateness of the activity, your own input, learner behaviour, resourcing, levels of engagement.)
- Were resources appropriate and effective?
- Did learners meet the objectives? Were they clear? Were there opportunities for assessment for learning?
- What might you change if you did the activity again? (Consider timings, seating plans, combinations of personalities, resources, number of learners.)

See Unit 11 on engaging in personal and professional development.

Class discussion

How do you provide feedback to teachers in your setting? Do you find it effective? Talk to others in your group about the way in which you do this and share ideas.

Check your understanding

1. How might a support assistant contribute to the planning and review of learning activities?
2. Why is it important to know the needs and interests of the learners you are supporting?
3. How do the following help you to prepare for learning activities?
   - Learning objectives
   - Lesson plans
4. Give examples of five different support strategies you may need to use in order to meet the needs of learners.
5. Why might you need to adapt resources to meet the needs of learners?
6. Name three barriers you might face when supporting learning and say how you would overcome them.
7. Explain how you would assess learner development, participation and progress during learning activities.
8. What methods of observation might you use for the following?
   - Persistent poor behaviour
   - To check that a learner has met a series of learning requirements
   - To write up an incident that has occurred earlier in the day
9. Why is it important to evaluate learning activities and to whom should you provide the feedback?
10. How does reflection on your own contribution affect the process?

Assessment preparation

The guidance states that this unit will need to be assessed in the workplace by your assessor. You will need to be able to demonstrate your skills through the way in which you support and encourage learners in your own setting. In order to get the most from your observation you will need to plan it carefully to maximise what your assessor can see to cover this unit.

Make sure that you:

1. Plan some time for a teacher or tutor, with whom you regularly work, to speak to your assessor to cover any areas they are unable to see and talk to them about how you contribute and add your own ideas to planning (AC 1.1, 1.2). They may also be able to outline how you work in partnership with others (AC 3.2).
2. Give your assessor a copy of the plan before the session, and talk to them about the needs of the learners.
3. Get out the resources and materials you will need while your assessor is present and adapt any if necessary to meet learners' needs; if you are unable to do this on the day, show some examples of resources you have created or adapted previously to meet learner needs (AC 2.1, 2.3).
4. Talk to learners about the objectives and content of the lesson (AC 2.2).
5. Support learning using different support strategies in order to meet learner needs and demonstrating inclusion; provide feedback to learners (AC 3.1, 3.3, 3.5).
6. Assess and record learner progress by annotating plans or using other required methods so that you can feed back to teachers (AC 4.1, 4.2).
7. Discuss with your assessor how you overcame any barriers during the session, and how you evaluate learning activities and reflect on your own practice when supporting teaching and learning (AC 3.4, 5.1, 5.2, 5.3).

Your assessor is likely to question you or the teacher about any areas that have not been covered during their time in school, or ask them to provide a witness testimony.

Legislation

There is no legislation for this unit.

Read about it

Reference books

Bosanquet, P., Radford, J. and Webster, R. (2016) *The Teaching Assistant's Guide to Effective Interaction: How to Maximise your Practice*, Routledge.

Nasen (2014) *Effective Adult Support: A Quick Guide to Maximising the Impact of Teaching Assistants and Other Adults Who Support Teachers*, Nasen.

Petty, G. (2014) *Teaching Today*, Oxford University Press.

Vygotsky, L.S. (1978) *Mind in Society: The Development of Higher Psychological Processes*, Harvard University Press.

Wood, D., Bruner, J. and Ross, G. (1976) *The role of tutoring in problem solving.* Journal of Child Psychology and Child Psychiatry, 17, 89–100.

Smith, L.T. (2017) *Meet Maslow: How Understanding the Priorities of Those Around Us Can Lead To Harmony And Improvement.*

Gershon, M. (2015) *How to use Bloom's Taxonomy in the Classroom: The Complete Guide.*

Weblinks

www.gov.uk/national-curriculum National Curriculum documents for primary and secondary schools

8 Support English and maths skills

About this unit

This unit will give you the knowledge, skills and understanding to provide assistance in English and maths when supporting teaching and learning. This means not only helping with English and maths in these specific subject areas but also helping learners with the demands of literacy and numeracy across all subjects in the curriculum. You will need to be able to work with teachers and tutors to ensure that you know the needs of the pupils as well as the requirements of the activities you are required to support. You will also need to use other opportunities that arise to reinforce learning in these subjects and to support the development of English and maths skills.

Learning outcomes

By the end of this unit you will:

LO1 Be able to identify learner needs for English and maths support

LO2 Be able to provide English support to help learners access teaching and learning

LO3 Be able to provide maths support to help learners access teaching and learning

Getting started

Discuss with others the way in which you support English and maths during day-to-day activities. Remember that this will not always be during literacy and numeracy sessions but throughout the timetable.

LO1 Be able to identify learner needs for English and maths support

AC 1.1 Collate information about learners': English and maths skills; learning targets; English and maths support needs

In order to provide evidence for this unit, you will need to show your assessor how you support English and maths in a range of contexts across the curriculum. However, before you can do this you will need to be able to identify their needs for English and maths support. As you speak to teachers and tutors and get to know pupils, you will find out about their needs and abilities in each area. If you are supporting pupils during learning activities, you should also be able to gain additional information about learners' English and maths skills, learning targets, and English and maths support needs.

Pupils' English and maths skills

This is about pupils' level of competence in English and maths. Being able to read, write and use numbers competently will help them in many ways, not only during their education but throughout their lives. In order to collate information about their skills you will need to speak to them, work with other staff and look at previous work, as well as their levels and records of achievement.

Pupils' learning targets

Most pupils will have specific targets in English and maths that they will need to bear in mind when working on learning activities.

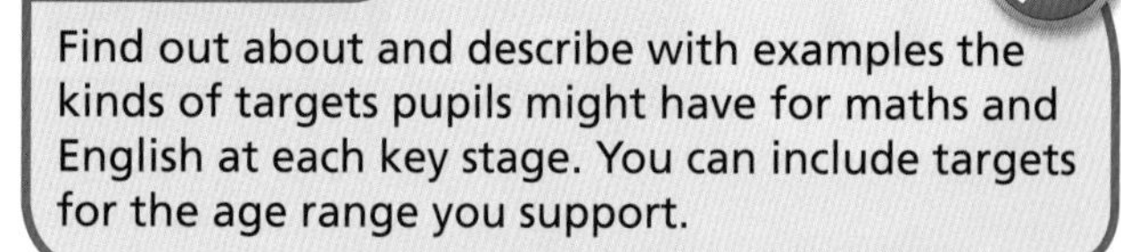

Research it

Find out about and describe with examples the kinds of targets pupils might have for maths and English at each key stage. You can include targets for the age range you support.

In practice

Make sure you are fully aware of the maths and English skills, support needs and learning targets of the pupils you support so that you have these to hand when you are working with them. You can choose a group you support and record these yourself, or use working documents from your everyday practice to show to your assessor.

Pupils' learning targets will be linked closely to assessment for learning so that they know what they are working towards and can assess themselves against this; older pupils may set their own targets, which will give them more ownership over their learning. It is important when setting targets that these are clear and achievable, and can develop pupils' confidence to help them to progress. Their targets should be recorded somewhere so that they are to hand when pupils are working – for example, in the front of an exercise book or folder.

Pupils' English and maths support needs

Teachers should be able to talk to you about pupils' support needs in maths and English. For example, they may need specific help in the area of calculations if they are learning a new way of working in maths, or need support when problem solving.

AC 1.2 Identify and explain: the teaching and learning objectives of a planned activity; the English and maths demands of learning activities

Look at Unit 7, which has more on supporting children and young people during learning activities.

The teaching and learning objectives of a planned activity

In addition to knowing pupils' maths and English skills, and their targets for these subjects, you will also need to be aware of the teaching and learning objectives of each planned activity that you work on with them. Learning objectives are important for several reasons:

- they will specifically state what pupils should be able to do at the end of the activity
- pupils will be able to tell you what they are learning and why
- they help pupils to stay on track with what they need to focus on during the activity
- you and they will be able to assess their learning at the end of the session
- they help us to think about pupils' next steps for learning.

Teachers should ensure that objectives are outlined at the start of each lesson, and you should also make sure that pupils are aware of them when you start an activity with them. Teaching and learning objectives will usually be recorded along with the date on pupils' work at the start of the activity, although it is not helpful to spend a long time making pupils write them if they find this difficult as it is not an effective use of learning time.

Case study

Rosa has been asked to work with a group of Year 7 pupils on a maths activity using basic algebra. The objective has been outlined by the teacher at the start of the lesson and it is clearly shown on the smartboard: 'I can solve simple linear equations using an appropriate method.' Rosa starts to look at the equations with the children and they are working through them with some support, but she does not mention the learning objective at any point during the activity or at the end.

1. Why might the activity be less successful than it could be?
2. Give two reasons for the importance of starting by talking about the objective with the pupils.

Research has shown that pupils are more motivated when they know why they are doing something and can see the steps they need to take to achieve it; awareness of learning objectives helps them to do this. It is also helpful to refer back to teaching and learning objectives at different stages during the lesson and relate our questioning to them.

The English and maths demands of learning activities

In addition to knowing the teaching and learning objectives of the activities you are supporting, you should be aware of any English and maths demands when supporting other subjects – this is one of the reasons why it is important to be able to see plans in advance. For example, if you are supporting pupils during a science investigation they will need to write a plan describing what they will do and predict what will happen, as well as outline how they will carry it out. This will mean that they are using the skills and knowledge learned in English lessons, such as spelling, punctuation and grammar. They may also need to collect data or use calculations as part of the investigation and will therefore also be using maths skills. It is helpful if you can 'link the learning', for example, if you have been looking at the use of modal verbs in English you can tie this in with the write-up of the science investigation. Vocabulary that is part of the topic may be displayed and pupils should be encouraged to look at and use it, as well as dictionaries or other reference books or websites. You should check whether pupils are permitted to use calculators if they need to carry out calculations.

Activity

Think about some of the subjects you support apart from English and maths. How have the skills learned in these subjects been incorporated into what pupils are learning in others? Give as many examples as you can and then discuss with your group.

Science investigation and experiment

My experiment is about:

My prediction

I think this will happen:

This is because:

My variables

The variable I am going to change:

The variables that I might measure:

The variables I am going to keep the same:

▲ Figure 8.1 Do you think in advance about the English and maths demands of learning activities in other subjects?

LO2 Be able to provide English support to help learners access teaching and learning

AC 2.1 Use knowledge of the individual needs of learners to provide English support

You will need to use the knowledge you have obtained about the needs of learners to help you to provide effective support in English. This means making sure that you have this information to hand when you are working with pupils so that you are able to do this more effectively. You should also use whatever opportunities you can to develop pupils' skills in speaking and listening, reading and writing, particularly if you know that these are areas in which they need additional support.

For more on supporting children and young people during learning activities and in their speech, language and communication needs, see Units 7 and 12.

Provide opportunities for learners to engage in conversation, discussion and questioning, prompting shy or reticent learners to contribute

If you know that you are working with children and young people who find it more difficult to put their thoughts and ideas forward due to shyness or communication needs, you may need to prompt and encourage them to participate. You can do this in different ways:

- through additional questioning during the teaching and learning process
- by asking them to work with talk partners in order to share ideas, particularly if they are more anxious about contributing when they are working in larger groups
- by praising and encouraging them when they try hard or do well during a discussion
- by prompting them to speak out in class if you know that they have an effective answer prepared.

Use language and vocabulary that is appropriate to learners' level of understanding and development

This is important as learners may 'switch off' from learning quite quickly and become distracted if adults around them are using language or vocabulary that it is difficult for them to understand. If you know the individual needs of pupils you are more likely to know who these pupils will be. You should check with learners if they appear unsure or if the teacher is using new or unfamiliar vocabulary or sentence structures, as you will be in a position to clarify meaning. You should also bear this in mind if you are working with children or young people who speak English as an additional language.

Introduce learners to new words and language structures to help extend their vocabulary and structural command of the language

As part of the teaching and learning process, it is helpful to introduce learners to new words and language structures. This can be done in a fun way, for example, a 'word of the week' with younger pupils that they need to learn, perhaps with spellings, or word challenges for older pupils so that they have to go and find out meanings of unfamiliar words and use them. In addition, when working on new topics or subjects there should be opportunities for learners to discuss the new vocabulary they will need to know.

Help pupils to interpret and follow oral and written instructions

You should work with children and young people to ensure that they can understand both oral and written instructions at the start of a learning activity. Sometimes this can be harder for pupils who have communication and language needs or find it more difficult to process information. Instructions can be challenging for them to work out, particularly if several are given in succession. When working with groups of pupils, a good starting point is often to ask them to tell you what they know so far about the topic. If they have written instructions, for example on a sheet or in a textbook, ask one member of the group to read these out – this will give others in the group the opportunity to ask questions if they are unsure.

Help pupils to select and use appropriate resources, for example, personal dictionaries

When you are supporting teaching and learning, it is important to encourage learners to be independent and select appropriate resources if needed, wherever they can, rather than asking adults to tell them what to do. Some children and young people have a tendency to ask for adult support instead of attempting to find resources or displays to help them in the learning environment. Using dictionaries can assist them with spelling as well as looking up the meaning of individual words.

▲ Figure 8.2 How do you encourage pupils to select and use appropriate resources when carrying out learning activities?

Adapt or differentiate learning materials

If you are working with pupils that you know will need more help, or with those who complete work quickly, you may need to adapt or further differentiate the materials you are using. This may take different forms but can be as simple as reducing the amount of work they need to complete or by extending their learning by asking them to devise some questions of their own to ask others on the topic. In cases of pupils with SEN and disabilities, you may need to adapt materials in order for them to access the curriculum, for example, using large print for visually impaired pupils.

Explain words and phrases used by the teacher

For information on this, see Unit 7, page 117.

Act as a scribe while the teacher is talking with the class

If you are working with pupils who have additional needs, or are unable to take notes quickly when others are doing so, you may need to support them by acting as a scribe. This means noting down important points for them so that they are able to refer to them later.

Prepare pupils for lessons by, for example, reading the relevant chapter of a book in advance with them

This may help if you know that any of the pupils you are working with need more time or a quieter moment in order to process information. It may give them more confidence to know in advance of the lesson what the class or group will be reading so that they can think about it.

Activity

Using the headings above, write a reflective account of occasions on which you have used your knowledge of learners to support them in different ways. You may then be able to use this as evidence alongside your assessor's observation to cover any gaps. You will not be able to use this to cover every heading, since as much as possible must be seen by your assessor.

AC 2.2 Use opportunities to support the development of learners' English skills

Many of the lessons and learning activities you support will use the skills of reading and writing as well as speaking and listening. For children and young people to develop these **English skills**, they will need adult support and guidance as well as regular practice. Opportunities to do this will occur throughout learning activities as well as at other times of day, and you will need to look out for them so that you can encourage and support learners.

Developing learners' reading skills

It is crucial that children share books with adults as often as possible, particularly in the early stages of reading and during the primary school years. This is because reading is at the heart of children's learning. As they start to be able to read for themselves, it is important that you make regular opportunities for doing this. There are a number of different opportunities you can use to support reading development.

- Dedicated reading time with an individual pupil gives you time to spend with them talking about the book. As many opportunities as possible should be given to this. When pupils read to you, it may help to use the checklist in 'Tips for best practice', particularly with younger or less confident children.

Key term

English skills: reading, writing, speaking/talking and listening.

Tips for best practice: hearing children read

- Make sure you and the child are comfortable.
- Ensure that the child is holding the book, not you. They will be doing the reading. Encourage them to point to each word as they read, as they will sometimes lose their place.
- Encourage children to use pictures to try to find clues as to what a word says (picture cues). **Never** cover pictures up to try to 'catch them out'.
- Ask the child to use the initial sound of a word (phonic cues) to have a guess at a word that makes sense.
- Encourage children to make substitutions that make sense in context for words if they are unable to decode them (context cues).
- If they are able readers, don't correct any mistakes too quickly. Give them time to realise that what they have read doesn't make sense and allow them to correct themselves. Always encourage children to question the sense of their reading, to re-read and to self-correct. When they reach an unknown word, encourage them to use picture cues, phonic cues and context cues as above. If they still have no idea, please just tell them the word.
- If children make mistakes, ask them whether the word makes sense, or ask them to look again, rather than saying 'that's wrong'.
- Encourage them to 'word build' simple words if they have enough sounds to do this.
- Always use plenty of praise and encouragement in order to build children's confidence.
- Talk to the child about what they are reading – encourage them to predict at different stages – for example, before you start, look at the cover and ask 'What do you think this book will be about? Why do you think that?' As you read, ask them about what the different characters might be thinking or feeling and why. Ask them to retell the main points of the story, talk about any jokes or funny bits and discuss any interesting facts, remembering to use open questions. This is important because some children are able to decode words but are unable to talk about what they have read.

- You may also hear groups of children read during shared reading or guided reading sessions. During shared reading, adults will revisit the text several times with the group and build on what pupils know. In shared reading, young children can also work with older pupils and this can be a very effective motivator.
- Guided reading is more effective with slightly older children who are developing their fluency and understanding. Adults will work with a group of children who are around the same level of reading rather than one individual child. These sessions are useful for developing pupils' vocabulary and understanding as they focus on comprehension skills and rely on pupils' increasing independence, reading around the text and looking at areas such as inference.
- Look at displays and other print in the environment with pupils, and encourage them talk about what they are reading. Make sure you use opportunities to do this as part of your daily practice so that you can build on what children know about the process as well as demonstrating to them how useful reading is.
- Role-model reading, for example, during quiet reading times. Talk to pupils about the kinds of things you read in different formats, whether these are books, websites, newspapers or magazines. It is important for children and young people to see and hear about adults around them using their reading skills too.

Developing learners' writing skills

Learning to write is a complex process. In order to be successful, children will need to know what they want to say, be able to apply their skills of phonics, spelling, punctuation and grammar, and then be able to physically form the letters. They will therefore need to remember and apply a wide range of different skills. Although there will be specific lessons dedicated to creative writing, and to spelling, handwriting, punctuation and grammar, it will help learners if you talk about these skills during other lessons so that they are not only seen as useful in 'English' classes but an important part of the whole curriculum.

- Draw attention to the formation of letters in contexts other than handwriting sessions.
- Use other opportunities and encourage pupils to talk about spellings such as through the use of mnemonics, dictionaries and displays.
- Remind pupils about teaching points from English lessons if you can see an opportunity to relate them to other written work – for example, if you know pupils have been thinking about the use of punctuation when writing a list and you see that they are writing a list during a geography lesson.
- Encourage pupils to read back what they have written to check for meaning when they are working in different contexts.
- Notice their progress and relate their written work to writing targets if you can – for example, 'Well done Jack, your target is to make sure you use capital letters correctly and you have done so well with this piece of writing.'

As there are so many things to remember when writing, do not use every opportunity you come across to point out errors as it is easy for learners to become disheartened, particularly if they find writing a challenge. Choose one or two that are the most important.

Developing learners' speaking/talking and listening skills

For information on this, look at Unit 12, which deals with supporting children and young people's speech, language and communication.

There will be many opportunities during the day for you to support the development of learners' communication skills. Remember that you are a role model for the way in which children and young people learn to communicate with others, so making sure that you are interested in what they have to say and spend time talking to them is very important. Depending on the needs of the children and young people you support, you may also need to use other means of communication, for example, Makaton or visual cues.

- Encourage individual pupils to put forward their own ideas as much as possible rather than relying on others, particularly those who are quieter.
- Use open questions so that children and young people have the opportunity to extend their answers rather than using 'yes' or 'no'.
- Make sure you use other forms of communication to show your interest, for example, getting down to their level if necessary, making eye contact and using body language, showing them that you are listening.
- Allow children thinking time and do not give them the answers during learning activities. Prompt them if needed or use additional questioning rather than telling them what you think.
- Role-model good speaking and listening skills, and show good manners, for example not allowing children to interrupt one another.

AC 2.3 Use a range of strategies for supporting learners to develop reading and writing and communication skills

Depending on your role within the classroom and the age range of pupils you support, you should be able to use a variety of strategies to help them to develop their English skills, both in the subject itself and in others. Teachers may point you towards specific programmes and materials if you need to work on focused literacy interventions, however, many of the following strategies will be available to you as part of your daily practice and can be used to support pupils' reading, writing and communication skills.

Targeted prompts and feedback to develop the use of independent reading and writing strategies

The kinds of prompts and feedback you give pupils will depend on their learning needs, but will help them to develop their independence when learning to read and write. Targeted prompts may be visual, spoken or written, and may depend on the situation. For example, a pupil who regularly rushes when reading aloud, and tends to miss out parts of the text, may have 'I will slow down when reading' as a target and need a verbal reminder from an adult at the start of the reading activity. They may also have the target recorded on a bookmark so that they see it when they open their book.

Encouraging pupils to engage in talk, discussion and oral rehearsal before completing reading and writing tasks

You may have more time than teachers to work with individual pupils and groups on reading and writing tasks. This is helpful for many reasons, but you may have the opportunity to talk about and 'rehearse' with them what they are going to say before carrying them out. You may find it helpful to suggest this to pupils who lack confidence and need to practise what they would like to say, and who need to be very clear about this before attempting to write.

Facilitating the participation of individuals or small groups in shared reading and writing activities

When working on shared reading and writing activities with groups, you will need to ensure that some of the more reticent pupils are involved in them. This is because some pupils have a tendency to 'take over' or are more confident than others. You can do this by telling each learner that they will be able to contribute and that everyone will be given the opportunity to do so. You may also need to question pupils carefully or scaffold what they are doing to ensure that they take part.

For more on this, see Unit 7, which deals with supporting children and young people during learning activities.

Using phonics to help learners understand the sound and spelling system, and to read and spell accurately

All pupils will be taught the use of phonics when learning to read and write, and you may need to remind or encourage them to do this when carrying out learning activities. Phonics encourages the use of 'sounding out', or hearing the sounds within words, and children will be taught to name the different phonemes as well as diagraphs and trigraphs, and to use these terms. You should ensure that you know the different terms that are used to describe different aspects of the phonics system. The phonics system is used throughout Key Stages 1 and 2 and beyond to support the development of reading and writing.

Phoneme

Phonemes are the smallest unit of sound. They do not necessarily correspond to individual letters of the alphabet. There are 44 phonemes in English although there will be some regional variation in this due to accents and dialects in different areas. These are put together in order to form words. Individual phonemes are listed in Table 8.1 on the next page.

Grapheme

This is the way in which we write a phoneme. A grapheme can be formed from one letter, two letters (for example, 'ch'), three letters (for example, 'igh') or four letters (for example, 'ough').

Diagraph

This is a grapheme that has two letters but makes one sound. These can also be known as vowel diagraphs and consonant diagraphs, depending on how they are formed – for example, 'ai' (vowel) or 'ck' (consonant). See Table 8.2 on the next page.

Trigraph

This is a grapheme that has three letters but makes one sound.

▼ Table 8.1 Individual phonemes

	Phoneme	Grapheme	Examples
	(speech sound)	**(letters or groups that show the spellings for individual phonemes)**	
	Consonant sounds		
1	b	b, bb	bag, cobble
2	d	d, dd, ed	dig, add, aged
3	f	f, ph	fan, phone
4	g	g, gg	go, egg
5	h	h	hot
6	j	j, g, ge, dge	jet, cage, barge, judge
7	k	c, k, ck, ch, cc, que	cat, kitten, duck, school, occur, antique, cheque
8	l	l, ll	leg, bell
9	m	m, mm, mb	mad, hammer, lamb
10	n	n, nn, kn, gn	no, dinner, knee, gnome
11	p	p, pp	pie, apple
12	r	r, rr, wr	run, marry, write
13	s	s, se, ss, c, ce, sc	sun, mouse, dress, city, ice, science
14	t	t, tt, ed	top, letter, stopped
15	v	v, ve	vet, give
16	w	w	wet, win, swim
17	y	y, i	yes, onion
18	z	z, zz, ze, s, se, x	zip, fizz, sneeze, laser, is, was, please, xylophone

Source: Adapted from *Orchestrating Success in Reading* (Reithaug, 2002)

▼ Table 8.2 Diagraphs

	Phoneme	Grapheme	Examples
	Consonant diagraphs		
19	th (not voiced)	th	thumb, thank, thin
20	th (voiced)	th	the, then, feather
21	ng	ng, n	sang, monkey, sink
22	sh	sh, ss, ch, ti, ci	shop, passion, chef, potion, special
23	ch	ch, tch	cheek, etch
24	zh	ge, s	garage, measure, division
25	wh	wh	what, when, where, why

Source: Adapted from *Orchestrating Success in Reading* (Reithaug, 2002)

Diphthong

A diphthong is a sound formed by combining two vowels, for example, in the words coin and cloud.

Blending

This is the process of hearing and saying the individual sounds in a word and then being able to blend them together, for example, in the word 'c-a-t'.

Segmenting

This is the process of being able to break a whole word up into the phonemes that form it.

Note

Staff will need to work closely to ensure that they pronounce or enunciate phonemes in the same way. For example, when enunciating the sounds 's' or 'm' it is 'ssssss' or 'mmmmm' rather than 'suh' or 'em'. This is important because pupils will not be able to blend the sounds together to form words if they pronounce phonemes incorrectly.

Research it

If you use phonics regularly in your practice, make sure you are aware of the correct pronunciation for their use. Find out about the system your school uses and go through the list of pronunciations with a colleague so that you can be sure.

▼ Table 8.3 Vowel sounds

	Phoneme	Grapheme	Examples
	Short vowel sounds		
26	a	a, au	man, laugh
27	e	e, ea	led, bread
28	i	i	pin
29	o	o, a, au, aw, ough	cot, want, haul, draw, bought
30	u	u, o	up, ton
	Long vowel sounds		
31	a	a, a_e, ay, ai, ey, ei	bacon, tray, say, gain, they, eight
32	e	e, e_e, ea, ee, ey, ie, y	me, these, heat, sheet, key, brief, baby
33	i	i, i_e, igh, y, ie	rind, side, fight, try, lie
34	o	o, o_e, oa, ou, ow	no, rote, coat, soul, crow
35	u	u, u_e, ew	human, fuse, dew, drew
	Other vowel sounds		
36	oo	oo, u, oul	look, put, would
37	oo	oo, u, u_e	moon, truth, mule
	Vowel diphthongs		
38	ow	ow, ou, ou_e	bow, shout, mouse
39	oy	oi, oy	coin, boy
	Vowel sounds influenced by 'r'		
40	ar	ar	bar
41	ar	air, ear, are	air, chair, fair, lair, bear, care
42	ir	irr, ere, eer	mirror, here, cheer
43	or	or, ore, oor	for, core, door
44	ur	ur, ir, er, ear, or, ar	burn, first, fern, heard, work, dollar

Source: Adapted from *Orchestrating Success in Reading* (Reithaug, 2002)

Use of specific support strategies, e.g. paired reading, writing frames

Specific support strategies are helpful for pupils who need help in that area, for example, the structure of a writing frame to remind them how to set out a piece of work. Paired reading is a strategy in which pupils read aloud to each other – usually, one less fluent reader is paired with a more fluent reader. It may also be used with readers of the same ability who have read the book before and can support each other. Paired reading can also be a useful system if older pupils come to read with younger ones. You may use other specific support strategies in order to support pupils to develop their literacy skills.

Use of specific support programmes, e.g. graded reading books, differentiated computer-based learning programmes, additional literacy support programmes

Pupils may benefit from the use of specific support programmes and interventions to help with the development of reading and writing. These should be supplied or directed by teachers so that you can implement their use, but it is not the responsibility of assistants to find them.

Stretch and challenge

Investigate the different types of literacy support programmes that are available for use in schools. You can include those that are used as a boost as well as those for pupils with specific learning needs such as dyslexia.

AC 2.4 Show how to work with children and young people in ways that encourage self-esteem and confidence in relation to English skills

The development of reading, writing and speaking and listening skills will support the self-esteem and confidence of learners in many ways; they have benefits that will be felt on a daily basis. Simply communicating with others, for example, will enhance a child or young person's self-esteem and be self-perpetuating as it enables them to express their own thoughts and feelings, and to develop relationships with others.

See Unit 12, AC 1.3, page 187, for more about how communication skills affect social and emotional development.

Development of reading skills

As children and young people learn to read, they will be gaining access to a range of other skills, as well as improving their confidence. The process of reading gives them the opportunity to develop in other areas too and is closely linked to the development of writing skills.

Development of writing skills

In order to develop pupils' confidence when they are writing, it is important to ensure that any targets are achievable for them, as it is very easy for their confidence to be damaged. For example, a

▼ Table 8.4 The benefits of reading

To develop skills of phonemic awareness, decoding, word recognition, prediction, comprehension and fluency	These are the skills that children need to develop when they are learning to read. The more children are able to practise using their reading skills, the more they will consolidate them and so build their confidence; this will also help with their writing.
To widen their vocabulary	Reading with children will develop their vocabulary, as they will be exposed to more new words. Being with an adult will enable them to ask about meaning straight away. Children may also be able to guess meanings due to the words being in context. Alternatively, adults can point out words that may be challenging for pupils to understand.
To develop relationships	Reading encourages children and young people to spend time with older children and adults, whether these are family members or staff in school. This time helps to develop relationships and gives the child time out – it will also encourage them to develop confidence.

To learn more about the world and develop curiosity	Both fiction and non-fiction books can help children to learn about the world through talking about events or stories. They can learn about things they have not experienced or seen for themselves, and discuss people, places and events. They will also ask questions about this and the knowledge will give them confidence when talking to others.
To improve concentration	Reading helps children to improve their concentration skills. They will need to be able to sit quietly and think about what they are doing: the more they practise, the longer they will be able to do this.
To develop empathy and understand others	As children read about characters in stories they will be able to talk about feelings and put themselves in the position of another person.
To provide enjoyment and encourage them to become lifetime independent readers	Reading should be seen as something that is done for pleasure. Regular practice with reading will make it part of the norm for children and young people and not something that 'has to be done for school'. As they grow in fluency and confidence they should be encouraged to read books that interest and engage them.
To develop imagination	Reading stories with young children encourages their imagination by helping the developing brain to form mental pictures. This will entice them to think about a range of situations and scenarios, and make them more confident in doing this, particularly when writing themselves.

child who is not confident when writing will need adults around them to encourage and support them and look at their progress using small steps so that they do not feel overwhelmed by what they are being asked to do.

Case study

Damien is a bilingual child in Year 1 who is at an international school. He finds writing a challenge as he confuses the sounds in English words with those in French. He also tries hard to be neat with his work but finds this very difficult as he is left-handed. Damien has a set of targets at the front of his writing folder, which are the same as for the others in his group. They include:

- I can form lower-case letters correctly
- I can use the suffixes s, es, ed, er and ing in my writing
- I can spell all words in the Year 1 spelling list accurately
- I can use my knowledge of phonemes to help with my spelling.

Although Damien is making progress, he regularly becomes upset when writing and says that he 'can't do it'.

1. How could you help Damien and develop his confidence when writing?
2. Why is it important that you talk both to him and to teachers about his progress?

Development of communication skills

See Unit 12, LO4, page 198, for ways in which you can create confidence and self-esteem in relation to pupils' communication skills.

LO3 Be able to provide maths support to help learners access teaching and learning

AC 3.1 Use knowledge of the individual needs of learners to provide maths support

In a similar way to supporting English, you will need to use the knowledge which you have obtained about the needs of learners to help you to provide effective **maths support**, both in terms of the subject and across the curriculum. This means making sure that you have this information to hand when you are working with pupils. You should also use whatever

Key term

Maths support: support given to pupils to help them meet the numeracy demands of the wider curriculum.

opportunities you can to develop their skills in the use of number, measures, understanding shape, and gathering and using information, particularly if you know that these are areas in which they need additional support. An important thing to remember when working on maths activities is that pupils' knowledge and use of language is also a key factor to their understanding of concepts. This is therefore particularly relevant if you are working with pupils who have communication and interaction needs, or those who speak English as an additional language.

Clarifying the learning task and helping pupils understand the mathematical aspect or content of the task

When starting to work on activities where maths is involved, particularly those in which pupils are less confident, you should first go back and check their understanding of what they have been asked to do. They may not realise that there is maths content, particularly if the activity is being delivered through a different subject. Pupils who have less confidence or who are aware that they find new concepts difficult may also be less likely to speak out in front of the class about problems with their understanding. You should go back and talk to them about the learning objectives as well as exactly what they are being asked to do, to ensure that they have understood the mathematical aspect.

Helping pupils to draw on their previous mathematical learning and experiences to encourage their active involvement in the learning activity

When working with individuals and groups on activities that may involve maths, it is helpful to discuss with them exactly what they have been asked to do. This gives them more thinking time as well as checking that they understand the links to maths. You should also encourage them to use what they know during the learning process, for example, discussing with them that they may be able to use their tables to work out simple problems. An effective strategy following the activity is also to ask students to share their working out so that they can see different methods of working and how others have used their previous knowledge.

Explaining words and phrases used by the teacher

This may be particularly important when using mathematical vocabulary and language, as children and young people may not necessarily understand terms that may seem obvious to adults. For example, 'record your findings on a table' or 'create a block graph to show ...'. Knowing the individual needs of learners will help you to recognise where this may be an issue for some.

Helping pupils to select and use appropriate mathematical resources, e.g. individual number lines, measuring instruments, mathematical equipment

In a well-equipped primary classroom there should be plenty of mathematical resources, which are stored tidily and well labelled. However, in secondary schools or colleges, pupils may need to go to a specific resources area or room to get the resources they need. In your role supporting teaching and learning, you should encourage pupils to select those that are the most appropriate and useful for the activity they are carrying out. In some cases – for example, if you are working outside or in a different environment – you may need to prepare and obtain resources for them in advance in order to save time. However, you should ask pupils wherever possible about the kinds of resources that would be most appropriate for the task.

Adapting or differentiating learning materials

For some pupils, you will need to adapt or differentiate learning materials for them to be able to access mathematical activities. Based on your knowledge of pupils, you will usually know who these pupils are and how materials may need to be changed.

For more information relating to this, see AC 2.1 on page 130 of this unit.

Using targeted prompts and feedback to support pupils' use of relevant mathematical knowledge and skills

As with working on activities in English, the kinds of prompts and feedback you give pupils will depend on their learning needs and abilities, but using them will help to develop pupils' independence when using mathematical skills. Targeted prompts may be visual, spoken or written, and will depend on the situation. You should always ensure that you know pupils' targets in mathematics so that you are able to reinforce their learning. For example, a pupil who has moderate learning difficulties may need to work through a list of steps when working on mathematical activities, which you could devise with them.

Explaining and reinforcing the relevant mathematical language, vocabulary and concepts

You should act as a role model and reinforce the use of mathematical language, vocabulary and concepts as often as you can so that pupils become used to using them in the correct context. For example, 'Yes Jenna, we need to use subtraction here. Can you think of any other words that mean the same thing?'

Activity

Look at the following mathematical terms:

- standard units
- number bonds
- rounding
- number sentence
- pentagon
- vertices
- product or sum of
- equivalent
- estimate.

Devise a maths question for a pupil using one of these and ask a friend to solve it. Why might activities such as this be helpful for the development of mathematical vocabulary in children and young people?

AC 3.2 Use opportunities to support the development of learners' maths skills

You will need to be able to use opportunities that arise during learning activities to support the development of learners' maths skills. This covers the knowledge and understanding needed to use and apply mathematics in the following areas.

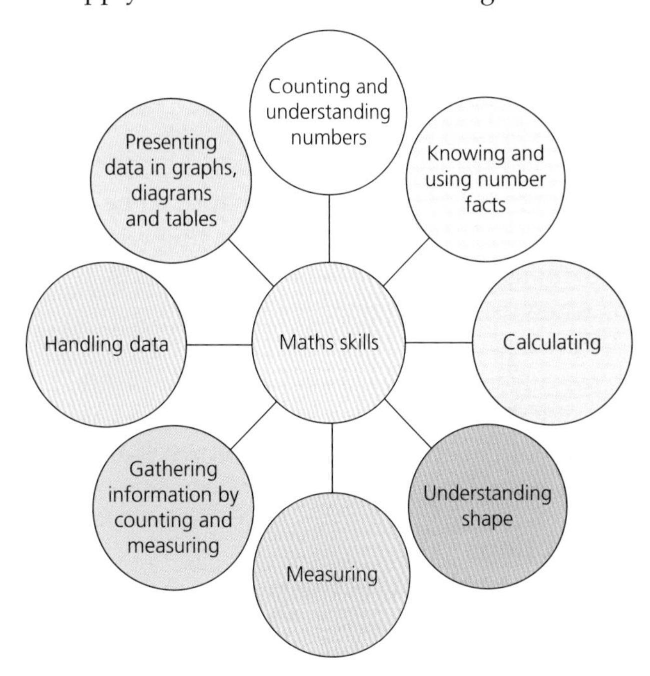

▲ Figure 8.3 Types of maths skills

Counting and understanding numbers

In the early years in particular, you should use as many opportunities as you can to count and use this skill so that you build up their knowledge quickly. This will reinforce children's learning as well as show them one of the uses of maths. For example, when taking the register you could ask younger pupils to tell you how many children are in school today and count how many are having packed lunches. You could then compare this with the day before and ask whether there are more or less. This will also reinforce mathematical vocabulary.

Knowing and using number facts

It is important that pupils have a good grounding in the use of number as it is a basis for much of what they will learn in maths. Number facts such as tables, for example, will provide a useful foundation for many activities.

Calculating

Pupils will use skills of calculation throughout school and college and beyond. They may need to be encouraged to remember different methods they have used so that they can choose the one that is most straightforward for them to support their learning. For example, if they need to add together two large numbers, ask them to think about the numbers themselves so that they can do this in the most straightforward way.

Understanding shape

Pupils' knowledge and use of shape can be used in many ways, for example, predicting whether something will roll in a science investigation or when using shapes to create patterns and pictures in art lessons. If you support the pupil across all subjects, you can question pupils in ways that encourage them to think back to their learning in maths in order to reinforce their learning.

Measuring

Learners are likely to need to use the skills of measuring in other subjects – for example, science or food/design technology. You may need to ask about the units they will need to use, or reinforce their learning by discussing how best to measure a specific item.

Gathering information by counting and measuring

When gathering information for use in different subjects, for example in science lessons, pupils may need to be reminded about ways in which they have done this during maths sessions, so that they can think about the most effective method for a specific activity.

Handling and presenting data in graphs, diagrams and tables

If pupils are asked to gather and present data for any other subject area, they will need to use the skills and knowledge they have developed during maths lessons. You may need to ask and remind them about how they have done it in the past, and about any strategies or methods they have found useful.

Activity

As much as possible of the AC 3.2 headings should be observed, however you can also use them to write about occasions on which you have used opportunities in other subjects to reinforce mathematical learning.

AC 3.3 Use a range of strategies for supporting learners to use and solve mathematical problems

Problem solving is an important aspect of maths as it enables pupils to use and apply what they know in different situations. Although the process is important, learners may be able to find the answer in different ways. Problem-solving activities can be carried out by whole classes, individuals and groups, and may or may not take place in maths lessons.

When you are working with pupils on problem-solving activities in any subject that involves mathematics, you will need to use a variety of teaching and learning strategies. Solving problems requires pupils to use and develop a range of skills, including analysis, planning, organising, reasoning, justifying and representing, and they will need to practise using these skills regularly. They will also need the vocabulary to talk through what they are going to do and, depending on their individual needs and abilities, may need support in working through problems systematically.

For more on supporting children and young people during learning activities, see Unit 7.

Helping learners to interpret and follow instructions

You may need to read through the problem carefully with learners so that they are able to work out exactly what is being asked. This will enable them to work logically through the task and work out a mathematical solution. It may also help to consider the following:

- What am I trying to find out?
- How can I solve it? Have I done anything like it before?

- What steps do I need to take?
- How can I check my work?

Reminding learners of teaching points made by the teacher

Check that learners have taken account of the teaching points that have been made. For example, if the lesson has been about area they may need reminding about the formula for to help them to solve a problem.

Questioning and prompting learners

Remember to use effective questioning as a prompt when you are supporting learners so that you scaffold their learning when needed and encourage them to think of the next steps.

For more on questioning and scaffolding learning, see Unit 7, pages 117–18.

Helping learners to select and use appropriate mathematical resources, e.g. number lines, measuring instruments, games, computer software and learning programs

When working on problem-solving activities, pupils may need to be reminded about the mathematical resources that are available to them and that may enhance their learning.

Explaining and reinforcing correct use of mathematical vocabulary

When working through problems, you may need to prompt and support pupils with their language. This is because problem solving requires them to set out their thoughts and represent them mathematically.

Using praise, commentary and assistance to encourage learners to stay on task

You should ask pupils about what they are doing throughout the process, and encourage them to talk through their reasoning or talk to them about it yourself (this is known as commentary). In this way you will be able to find out whether they need further questioning or assistance to stay on task.

Activity

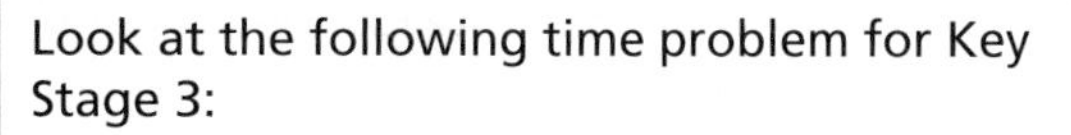

Look at the following time problem for Key Stage 3:

'Which is longer – 2600 hours or 15 weeks? Show your method of working.'

Show how you could change this problem slightly so that pupils can reinforce their learning.

Praise is important, particularly for effort when pupils are trying to work through a problem.

Introducing follow-on tasks to reinforce and extend learning, e.g. problem-solving tasks, mathematical games, puzzles

If you need to provide further learning for pupils following a problem-solving activity, there are several ways to do this. An effective way of consolidating pupils' learning is change one aspect of the problem so that they can repeat the process to find a different outcome. Alternatively, more able pupils may be able to devise their own problems and ask one of their peers to solve them. It can also be helpful to have a list of problem-solving activities available for pupils to move on to if they finish their work.

AC 3.4 Show how to work with children and young people in ways that encourage self-esteem and confidence in relation to maths skills

Maths can be a subject in which many lack confidence in their own ability throughout their lives. This can be for a number of reasons, but if confidence is not developed during pupils' time in school or college, it can be very difficult to acquire in later years. Those who develop a negative mind-set when it comes to maths will be much less likely to try to find ways to solve a problem. You should use opportunities that arise during the teaching of maths to help them to develop a more positive self-concept when talking about mathematical ideas (see Table 8.5 on the next page).

▼ Table 8.5 Ways to develop self-esteem and confidence in children and young people in relation to maths

Strategy	How to use
Show pupils what they already know about maths	Children and young people may not always be aware of how much they know already about maths. As part of your practice, encourage them to think about how they might use it on a day-to-day basis.
Teach pupils that failure and getting things wrong are a part of learning	Many children and young people lack confidence with maths because they are worried about 'getting it wrong'. They mistakenly think that maths is all about the answer rather than the process. Educators need to instil in students the importance of working through a series of steps.
Use of play	It is important to show children and young people that maths is fun. Playing games is an effective way of learning about counting up and down, adding and subtracting, and other aspects of maths such as problem solving. These may be board games, playing cards, internet games, or others.
Encourage problem-solving activities	It is important that pupils learn to develop problem-solving skills, and to know that there is not always a 'right' or 'wrong' way of finding the answer. Working with others on practical activities is a good way of doing this as it is fun and shows them different ways of approaching a task.
Play with numbers, for example finding patterns in times tables or other calculations	Pupils may enjoy finding patterns and looking at different ways in which they can use these to predict outcomes in maths. For example, if I know that $3 \times 3 = 9$, I can predict that $30 \times 30 = 900$.
Relate maths to real life	Any opportunities you can use to put maths in context will benefit pupils, particularly those who are reluctant to take part or who lack confidence. This may be when shopping, gardening or cooking, or many other real-life situations.

Class discussion

Discuss and share as a group some of the most effective support materials you have used when supporting English and maths, and say why they have been useful. These may be anything from physical maths equipment such as dice or number fans, to online resources. You can then create your own list for future use.

Tips for best practice: supporting English and maths

- Be as organised as you can – ask teachers for plans in advance so that you can prepare yourself, as well as gathering resources and materials.
- Make sure you know as much as possible about pupils and their learning needs in each subject.
- Use other opportunities and subjects to back up mathematical ideas and vocabulary.
- Talk to colleagues about strategies that are useful, as well as in teaching assistant support groups and online forums.

Check your understanding

1 Where will you find information about pupils' current levels in English and maths?
2 Give two reasons why it is important that everyone is aware of learning objectives.
3 Give two examples of ways in which you can provide English support to help pupils to access their learning.
4 How can you develop reading skills in children and young people?
5 How do phonics support the process of learning to read?
6 Outline four benefits of reading.
7 Why is it important to know about the individual needs of learners when providing English and maths support?
8 Describe three opportunities you can use to support the development of pupils' maths skills.
9 Why does problem solving develop such a variety of skills in learners?
10 How can you develop confidence and self-esteem in learners when carrying out maths activities?

Assessment preparation

As far as possible, this unit will need to be observed in the workplace by your assessor. You should plan your observations carefully so that as much as possible can be seen, although it will not be possible to cover all of these headings in one observation.

1 For AC 1.1, you can use the 'In practice' activity. You should show your assessor the teaching and learning objectives of the learning activities you are supporting when they come to your workplace, to cover AC 1.2.
2 For AC 2.1, as much as possible should be seen but can be backed up by the activity. For AC 2.2, your assessor should observe you using opportunities to develop pupils' English skills. For AC 2.3 you should use as many of these strategies as you can so that your assessor can observe them, and write the rest up with examples.
3 For AC 3.1, as much as possible should be seen by your assessor in the workplace but you can also write a reflective account for others as shown in the activity for AC 1.2. AC 3.2 should be seen as much as possible, but you may need to use the activity to write about occasions in which you have reinforced learning of maths through other subjects. For AC 3.3, as many of these strategies as possible should be observed and the rest should be written up with examples in order to complete the unit.
4 AC 2.4 and AC 3.4 should be seen by your assessor.

Legislation

There is no legislation for this unit.

Read about it

Reference books

Reithaug, D. (2002) *Orchestrating Success in Reading*, National Right to Read Foundation.

Weblinks

There are many commercial websites and programs available that support the teaching of English and maths, and it is not possible to list them all here. You may be directed towards some by teachers and other colleagues as your setting may use particular programs and interventions that it finds particularly effective.

www.interventionsforliteracy.org.uk Literacy interventions and their use – follow the link for 'What works for children and young people with literacy difficulties?' by Grey Brooks

http://webarchive.nationalarchives.gov.uk/20110203115237/https://nationalstrategies.standards.dcsf.gov.uk/node/84996 Mathematical vocabulary – this is now an archived publication from the DfES but is very useful when supporting primary pupils

www.tes.com The TES website has a wide range of resources and tips that are helpful for teachers and teaching assistants in primary and secondary schools

www.nrichmaths.org This site is for parents, children and teachers, and provides a range of resources and information

https://literacytrust.org.uk/ The Literacy Trust is a charity that supports the development of literacy, providing advice and support for schools, teachers and parents of children of all age

www.thecommunicationtrust.co.uk The Communication Trust – organisation that supports communication with children; provides resources for parents and professionals

9 Support the use of ICT in the learning environment

About this unit

Although the curriculum area itself has the subject name computing, ICT is now being used in all subject areas across the curriculum. Interactive whiteboards are a key teaching tool in most classrooms, and all adults working with children and young people will need to know how to use these as well as other technologies in order to support teaching and learning. You should be aware of the different kinds of resources that are available and how to access any consumables that are needed on a day-to-day basis. Your role may mean that you use ICT in different ways, but you should be able to show how you follow the policy of your setting to enhance learning through ICT in a way that is the most appropriate for the needs and age of the pupils you support.

Learning outcomes

By the end of this unit you will:

LO1 Understand the policy and procedures for the use of ICT for teaching and learning

LO2 Understand how to prepare ICT resources for use in teaching and learning

LO3 Be able to support the use of ICT for teaching and learning

Getting started

Think about all the different ways in which you come into contact with ICT and technology in a day in your setting, from phones, tablets and personal computers (PCs) to interactive whiteboards or more specialist equipment for pupils who have additional needs. What training have you had in how to use them or have you learned on the job? Who is the computing co-ordinator in your setting and who is responsible for technical issues?

LO1 Understand the policy and procedures for the use of ICT for teaching and learning

AC 1.1 Describe the setting's policy for the use of ICT for teaching and learning

Your school or college will have a policy for the use of ICT, which will outline the required procedures when using resources for teaching and learning as well as general health and safety requirements. You will need to be familiar with the guidelines that are provided so that you can ensure you follow correct procedures, particularly around e-safety. Your school or college may ask you to sign it to show that you have read and understand your responsibilities. Depending on the age of the children, they may also be asked to sign the policy or an ICT acceptable use agreement to show that they understand their responsibilities too. Policies and procedures are likely to cover the following areas.

Safety and security of equipment and passwords

You will need to be aware of the importance of ensuring that equipment is stored safely and securely, and that passwords are kept confidential. Data will also need to be stored securely, and only teaching and administrative staff should have access to this information.

Use of the internet

The policy is likely to outline the way in which the school or college guarantees that sites are filtered, while also ensuring that pupils are aware of internet safety and understand their responsibilities.

Use of mobile phones and email

Pupils and staff should use school or college email addresses or phones only when they are communicating with others to carry out their work. Personal mobiles should be locked away during the day and should not be used when on school or college trips. Pupils and staff should ensure that they do not take or pass on personal information or photographs, particularly those of other pupils.

Communication with parents and carers

These days, schools and colleges use websites and email when communicating with parents and carers. All staff will need to ensure that the policy is followed when writing emails to parents. There may also be information evenings and talks on e-safety to raise awareness of what parents can do to help keep their child safe online.

For more information on this, see the 'Read about it' section on page 156 at the end of the unit.

Use and installation of software

Only software that has been approved and installed by the school or college should be used, in line with licensing agreements. If staff and pupils are using memory sticks or other devices for transferring data or information these should be checked before use.

Health and safety

Health and safety requirements, such as the length of time it is safe to spend on computers, as well as correct sitting heights and procedures, should be available or on display in computer rooms and classrooms. All staff and pupils should be aware of the importance of following correct procedures when using ICT equipment.

Role of the ICT co-ordinator

There will be a member of staff responsible for the teaching and learning of ICT within the setting. The policy is likely to outline their role and responsibilities.

▲ Figure 9.1 What do you know about the ICT policy of your school or college?

In practice

Using a copy of the policy of your setting, highlight the parts that describe how staff should support teaching and learning using ICT. Ensure that you include all aspects of your role so that you can use this as evidence.

AC 1.2 Identify the ICT resources used for teaching and learning within the learning environment

Your school or college is likely to use a wide range of ICT resources to support teaching and learning. As technology is an area that is constantly changing, you may need additional training in this area as new resources are introduced or if you are working with a pupil who needs access to specific equipment.

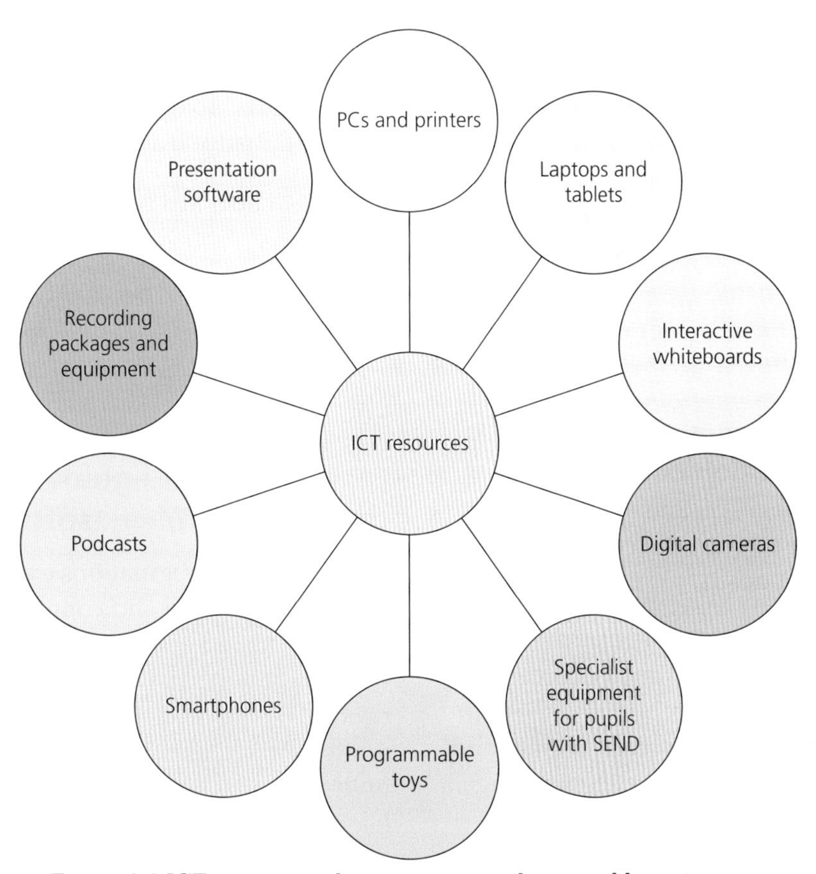

▲ Figure 9.2 ICT resources that support teaching and learning

Research it

Find out about the range of programmable toys available for use in schools and whether you can access these. They will be available on commercial websites.

PCs and printers

Although previously mainly seen in classrooms, there is now likely to be only one per class, to be used by staff and to interact with the whiteboard. PCs tend to be used in staffrooms and communal areas rather than in classrooms, due to space issues.

Laptops and tablets

These are most commonly used by students, particularly if you are working with groups, as they are portable and easy to share between classes.

Interactive whiteboards

Most classrooms will now have interactive whiteboards as teaching aids. These are a useful teaching tool and are used as a way of showing a range of resources, from software to film clips.

Digital cameras

Although used less often, there will still be cameras for use in school or college and on trips outside the setting. They are an easy method of taking and deleting pictures and are good to use with younger pupils.

Specialist resources for pupils with SEND, such as voice recognition equipment

You may be asked to use specialist ICT equipment in order to enhance teaching and learning for pupils with additional needs.

Programmable toys and equipment

These may be used by all age groups in order to learn how to use programming. You may need to ensure that they are charged up ready for use and that you have a supply of batteries when taking groups to work with them.

Smartphones

Staff may be issued with mobiles for school or college use as they should not use their own for taking photographs of pupils.

Stretch and challenge

Find out more about the use of podcasts to support teaching and learning, and whether they are an effective tool. Write down what you think might be their advantages and disadvantages.

Activity

What ICT resources do you use in your school or college? Make a list of all those that are available for teaching and learning, including any of those mentioned here, and outline briefly how they are used. You can then use this as a reflective account to provide evidence for your portfolio.

Podcasts

These can be downloaded by students and used to support teaching and learning. They may have been recorded by teachers or tutors so that older pupils can listen to lectures or classes, or they may be radio programmes where there is a particular relevance to subjects being covered and they are used to enhance learning.

Presentation software and recording packages

These are software packages that are designed to enhance presentations, such as PowerPoint, or those that record pupils' work.

AC 1.3 Outline relevant legislation, regulations and guidance in relation to the use of ICT, e.g. software licensing

Legislation and regulations exist to ensure that information stored and communicated through ICT systems is kept safe, and that pupils and staff use equipment safely. School and college managers need to have policies and procedures in place, while employees need to be aware of legalities and of their responsibilities, as well as how they should keep pupils safe. The main relevant legislation is:

- software licensing agreements
- Computer Misuse Act 1990
- Copyright and Rights in Databases Regulations 1997

Research it

Choose two of the laws or regulations listed here and research how they will impact on the use of ICT in schools and colleges. Do a presentation to your group outlining what you have found out. By making notes on others' presentations, as well as keeping your own notes, you can use this as evidence.

- Health and Safety at Work Act 1974 and EU Health and Safety Directive 87/391
- Data Protection Act 1984 and 1998
- Freedom of Information Act 2000.

AC 1.4 Describe the requirements and procedures for storage and security of ICT resources

If you are supporting the use of ICT, you should be clear in advance on where to find resources and equipment when needed. There may be specific requirements and procedures in place – for example, a signing-out system for laptops or smaller equipment, or passwords that are needed to access programs.

When you have finished using ICT resources, always ensure that they are back in the right place promptly and signed back in if required. Make sure that you have plugged them in to recharge where necessary so that they are ready for the next person to use them, and label any equipment that is faulty or follow your setting's policy for reporting to the appropriate person.

In practice

Check and highlight your setting's ICT policy for the requirements and procedures for storage and security of ICT equipment. You can annotate the policy to show how you follow your setting's procedures when using it.

LO2 Understand how to prepare ICT resources for use in teaching and learning

AC 2.1 Describe the risks associated with ICT resources and how to minimise them

There are a number of regulations for employers around safety when working with computers and other technologies, however, these do not all apply to schools and colleges. Although pupils are not likely to be working at screens for long periods, it is important that staff are aware of the kinds of risks that may occur and that equipment is checked regularly by an electrician.

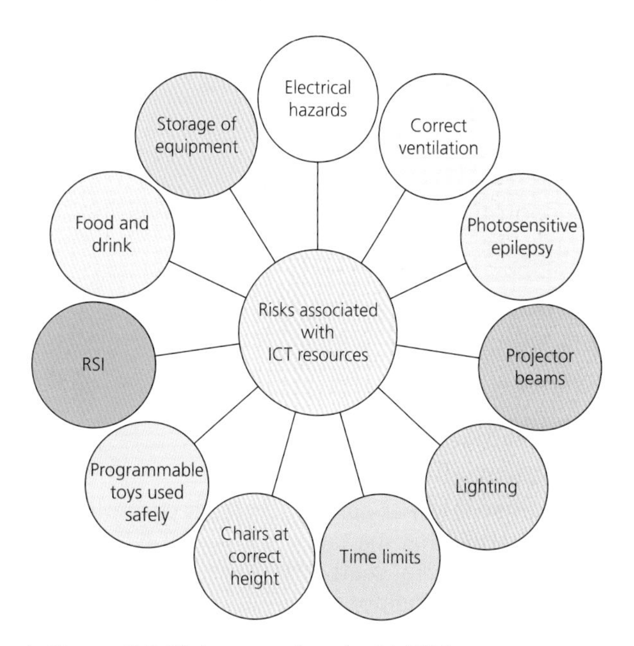

▲ Figure 9.3 Risks associated with ICT resources

Electrical hazards

These can be caused by issues such as overloaded plugs, wires that are left trailing, and equipment that becomes overheated. Always carry out safety checks before using equipment to ensure that any risks are avoided.

Correct ventilation

There should be sufficient ventilation, particularly around PCs and laptops so that they do not overheat. Ensure that pupils do not leave jumpers or other items on top of screens or other places where ventilation occurs.

Triggers to photosensitive epilepsy

You should be aware that flickering screens and flashing lights can be triggers to photosensitive epilepsy. This is also the case when watching anything on a screen, such as TV.

Projector beams

Adults should be aware that these can be dangerous to both staff and pupils if they look directly into the light – for example, when doing presentations or standing in front of the class for any reason. Always ensure that anyone facing the group does not stand in the path of the projector beam.

Lighting

It is important that lighting is appropriate when using computer screens and that there are blinds on windows so that glare is reduced.

Time limits when using equipment

Pupils should not be able to use computer or screen equipment for long periods. If they are given work that requires them to research using the internet, they should have frequent breaks and be encouraged to do other tasks away from the computer.

Chairs/screens at correct height

All computers should be set up so that screens are at the correct height (eyes at the same height as the top of the screen) and chairs are positioned appropriately (adjustable and comfortable, with appropriate support). Although younger pupils are unlikely to be seated at computers for any length of time, older children should be aware of the risks of RSI (repetitive strain injury) or of injury to their fingers, wrists, arms, neck or back, as well the risk of headaches and eye strain.

Programmable toys used safely

If you are using these on the floor in the learning environment, you should ensure that you are well away from other pupils so there is no risk to them of tripping over.

Food and drink

This should not be consumed anywhere near computers in case there are spillages on electrical equipment. Food and drink should not be consumed in classrooms in any case, and equipment should always be put away after use to ensure that it is stored safely.

Case study

Emma in Year 10 has epilepsy, which is controlled by medication that she takes at home. She has not had a fit for several years. The office staff have records of her condition on admission forms but teachers and support staff do not know about it.

You are working with a group including Emma during a lesson in which she has been allocated a computer with a faulty screen that flickers persistently. As there is insufficient working equipment for the group and Emma wants to complete her task, she tells you that she wants to carry on using it. However, after a time, Emma tells her friend that she is starting to feel unwell.

1. What should have happened here?
2. Why is it important to follow correct procedures?
3. Should Emma tell staff and/or her peers about her epilepsy?

▲ Figure 9.4 Where would be a safe place to use programmable toys in the learning environment?

Storage of equipment

All equipment and consumables such as batteries, bulbs and so on should be kept safely and in a cool, dry place so that there are no risks from overheating.

Take a look at Unit 2, which has more information on supporting health and safety in a learning environment

AC 2.2 Identify and obtain accessories, consumables and information needed to use ICT resources

When you are using ICT equipment and resources, you will need to be aware of the kinds of accessories and consumables that are needed. This is because when pupils are working with equipment there are likely to be times when these run out or stop working. You should know where replacements are stored or how to gain access to them quickly if needed. The kinds of accessories and consumables you might need could be batteries, printer inks/toner, paper, specialist resources for pupils who have SEND, websites or software, headphones or earphones, and so on.

You will also need to have all the information you need in order to operate and use resources or software before the start of lessons. Teachers should give you this information in advance or you should have time to work through it so that you are not trying to work out how to use it while also working with pupils. This includes how to use specific software or teaching and learning packages. You should also have to hand any passwords or codes you may need to operate equipment such as printers.

Activity

Write down a list of the kinds of accessories and consumables you need to have for the pupils with whom you work, and outline how you gather the information you need before starting to use the resources. You can then use this as a reflective account for your portfolio.

AC 2.3 Explain the importance of the use of screening devices to prevent access to unsuitable material via the internet

All schools and colleges are required to use screening devices so that pupils are prevented from gaining access to unsuitable material via the internet. These should be automatic and sites will be blocked when pupils try to use them. However, you will also need to be aware that there may be cases in which pupils inadvertently gain access to sites that are not appropriate. For this reason, young pupils in particular should not be given access to computers, laptops or tablets without adult supervision.

In practice

Find out about the kinds of screening devices your school or college has set up in order to prevent access to unsuitable material. Who in your setting is responsible for ensuring that it works?

LO3 Be able to support the use of ICT for teaching and learning

For the first three assessment criteria under this learning outcome, your assessor will need to see you doing them or you should have witness testimonies from those with whom you work in order to show that you can use ICT equipment safely and also support its use by others.

AC 3.1, 3.2 Use ICT resources correctly and safely, when asked to do so and give clear guidance and instructions to others on the use of ICT resources

It is important that you know how to set up and use ICT resources in advance so that you can pass on this information to pupils and can talk through safety guidelines with them. In this way they will become used to following safety procedures themselves as a matter of course. Always make sure that the learning environment is safe before starting your work with pupils.

When supporting others using ICT resources, you need to show that you are able to give them clear guidance and instructions. This may not only be with pupils, but also with staff for training or support purposes. Make sure when you are passing on information that you do not give them too much to take in at once and that you allow others some time to practise using resources themselves before moving on to the next instruction. You may need to work with the following groups of people.

See Unit 3, AC 3.3 for more information on measures to keep children and young people safe when online.

Teachers/other support staff

This may be done through training sessions if you often work with ICT, or on a day-to-day basis if you are asked to help someone who is less experienced. You should plan training sessions carefully and make sure you are clear about what you want others to know by the end of the session. If you are working with individuals, go through what they need to do carefully before asking them to have a go themselves.

Learners

Pupils are likely to be using ICT as part of other areas of the curriculum as well as computing itself, and you need to be able to use a range of different resources so that you can support them effectively. You should make sure that you encourage them to do as much as they can for themselves while providing assistance if they need it.

See also AC 3.3 in this unit and Unit 7, which deals with supporting children and young people during learning activities.

Research it

If you have not done so already, read through the programmes of study for computing in your UK Home Nation. These are available at:

England: www.gov.uk/government/publications/national-curriculum-in-england-computing-programmes-of-study

Northern Ireland: http://laganonline.co/new-computer-science-programme-launched-in-northern-ireland/

Wales: this is currently under development and will be launched in September 2018; for Key Stages 2–3, see http://learning.gov.wales/docs/learningwales/publications/130424-ict-in-the-national-curriculum-for-wales-en-v2.pdf

Scotland: this is currently under development.

Stretch and challenge

If you are a confident user of ICT, ask your line manager if you can carry out a training session with other staff in your school. This may be a small or a large group and can be teachers or support staff; you may be able to use a staff meeting. Choose an area of ICT you know about and that it will be helpful for others to learn more about. You can record this or ask a witness to verify that you have done it so that you can use it as evidence.

AC 3.3 Provide an appropriate level of assistance to enable learners to experience a sense of achievement, maintain self-confidence and encourage self-help skills in the use of ICT

When you are working with pupils you will need to balance the amount of assistance you give them, while allowing them to develop their independence. As in other subject areas, your role is to enable and encourage them in their learning so that they do not become over-dependent on adults. ICT is an area in which some pupils are more confident and able than others, and you will need to give a different amount of assistance to pupils depending on their ability. You will need to be able to support those who have less confidence when using ICT resources through praise and encouragement, while allowing them to work on activities as independently as possible. For those who are more confident, ensure that they have enough to stretch and challenge them so that they are able to experience a sense of achievement.

See also the teaching and learning strategies in Unit 7.

▲ Figure 9.5 How can you ensure that you give pupils an appropriate level of assistance when using ICT resources?

See Unit 7, which deals with supporting children and young people during learning activities.

AC 3.4 Describe the sorts of problems that might occur when supporting learners using ICT and how to deal with these

Sessions using ICT resources seem to be those in which problems arise regularly and you will need to be ready to deal with them when this happens. There are a number of areas in which issues may occur, as listed in Table 9.1.

▼ Table 9.1 Preparing for a session using ICT

Potential problem	Possible resolution
ICT resources • Problems with resources are often basic issues such as equipment that has been left unplugged or not charging, so that there are insufficient laptops or tablets for the amount of pupils, or printers that run out of ink. • Technical issues such as pupils unable to log in.	In this situation you will have to ask pupils to share and make sure that you report any faulty equipment to the appropriate person. Make sure you are aware of the location of consumables such as printer inks and toners so that you can resolve these issues promptly. Make sure you have pupil log-ins before the start of the session, to avoid delays. If technical issues come up during the course of the session it is unlikely that you will have time to resolve them, so send for technical support and use another computer or ask pupils to share.
Teaching and learning • There may be issues if one pupil is more able than another and is trying to take over. • Being unfamiliar with the program you have been asked to use. • Task too easy or too difficult – pupils will lose interest quickly. • Work gets lost.	Encourage pupils to take turns and to allow one another to have their time. Ask more able pupils to instruct less able pupils verbally and to allow them to use the equipment. Always ask for training and support, or ensure you have time beforehand to look through what you need to do. Have extension activities available for those who complete the task. Be ready to modify activities that are too difficult, to keep pupils on task. Get pupils used to saving work regularly.
The learning environment • Classroom too hot or too bright. • High noise levels within the environment.	Check the lighting and ventilation in the environment before you start, particularly if you have a number of computers together, as rooms can become very warm, and always use blinds in order to reduce glare. Use headphones to reduce noise.

Tips for best practice: supporting the use of ICT for teaching and learning

- Make sure all equipment is fit for use before the lesson.
- Follow school or college policies such as safety and security guidelines.
- Check that you know and understand how to use equipment and resources beforehand.
- Check for health and safety hazards.
- Ensure that you give clear guidance to pupils and allow them to use equipment for themselves.
- Identify and address own learning needs in relation to ICT.

Check your understanding

1. Why do schools and colleges need to have a policy for the use of ICT for teaching and learning?
2. What kinds of ICT equipment and resources do pupils have access to within your learning environment and where are they stored?
3. Describe three risks associated with the use of ICT resources and say how you would resolve them.
4. What is the purpose of a screening device when using ICT resources?
5. Name three ways in which you can ensure that you give an appropriate level of assistance to pupils.
6. What kinds of problems might occur when supporting ICT with learners? How might you resolve these?

Assessment preparation

In order to meet the requirements of this unit, you will need to show that you understand your responsibilities for the teaching of ICT and computing.

1. For LO1, you can use the features within the unit as evidence for this. For AC 1.2 and 1.4, use the 'In practice' features as indicated. For AC 1.2 and 1.3, use the activity and 'Research it' features as evidence. For AC 1.1, use the 'In practice' activity.
2. For LO2, AC 2.1, you will need to write a reflective account, have a professional discussion, or describe the risks and how to minimise them, with your assessor. AC 2.2 and 2.3 can be evidenced using the features within the unit.
3. LO3 will mainly need to be assessed in your learning environment by your assessor as you will need to be able to show them how you support the use of ICT for teaching and learning in the learning environment. You can also use the 'Stretch and challenge' activity on page 154 to gather evidence for this.

Legislation

For the legislation relevant to this unit, see AC 1.3 on pages 150–1.

Read about it

Reference books

Bird, J. and Caldwell, H. (2017) *Lessons in Teaching Computing in Primary Schools*, Learning Matters.

Lau, W. (2017) *Teaching Computing in Secondary Schools: A Practical Handbook*, Routledge.

Weblinks

www.gov.uk/government/groups/uk-council-for-child-internet-safety-ukccis
UK Council for Child Internet Safety (UKCCIS)

http://homepages.shu.ac.uk/~edsjlc/ict/becta/information_sheets/parent.pdf and **www.childnet.com** Information for parents on the use of ICT

www.gov.uk/government/publications/national-curriculum-in-england-computing-programmes-of-study National Curriculum for computing statutory guidance

10 Support assessment for learning

About this unit

In order to complete this unit you will need to show that you know, understand and have the skills to support assessment for learning in your school or college. You will need to be able to show that you are competent in using a range of assessment strategies to promote learning and embed this in your work with learners. You will also need to be able to demonstrate how you support learners in being able to review their learning strategies and achievements, and how you work alongside the teacher to review the way in which you monitor the assessment for learning process. You will also learn about how to maintain learner records while ensuring that you follow organisational policy.

Learning outcomes

By the end of this unit you will:

LO1 Understand the purpose and characteristics of assessment for learning

LO2 Be able to use assessment strategies to promote learning

LO3 Be able to support learners in reviewing their learning strategies and achievements

LO4 Be able to contribute to reviewing assessment for learning

LO5 Be able to maintain learner records

Getting started

How are you monitoring your own learning as part of your qualification? Are you looking at and monitoring your progress, and being active in identifying any areas for development? If so, give examples of ways in which you are doing this.

LO1 Understand the purpose and characteristics of assessment for learning

AC 1.1 Analyse the role of the support worker in relation to assessing learner achievement

Teaching and support staff will have responsibilities within the classroom that should complement one another; by the nature of your job description your main role is to support teaching and learning under the direction of a teacher. The teacher will be responsible for teaching and learning while monitoring the progress and assessment of each learner in their class or tutor group; this assessment will be ongoing and will take different forms.

Teachers and tutors will have overall responsibility for the teaching and learning of their pupils. They will plan schemes of work, lessons and learning activities that should challenge and motivate pupils in their learning so that they can progress to the next stage. These activities should also have learning objectives that are clear both to students and to adults within the classroom. In this way pupils will know what they are learning and adults will know the success criteria of the lesson. Teachers' long-term planning may also include formal assessments at the end of topics or schemes of work so that they can look at the way in which pupils are progressing and plan the next stages.

▲ Figure 10.1 How does the role of the teacher compare with your own role?

Teaching assistants should ideally have sight of schemes of work and lessons in advance. They should also have an awareness of what the learning objective will be so that they can enable learners to reach the objectives through a range of teaching and learning strategies. They will work with or observe learners during teaching and learning activities; their role is then to feed back to teachers and pupils about learning so that progress can be assessed.

Both teachers and support staff will also have common aspects to their roles in the ongoing assessment of learners' progress and achievements. They should each encourage pupils by ensuring that they understand objectives and promoting their independent learning skills through the use of **assessment for learning** and embedding this in their practice.

See Unit 7 on supporting children and young people during learning activities.

Key term

Assessment for learning: a method through which information from assessment is used to raise the achievement of learners. Evidence from the ongoing assessment process will support teaching and learning in finding out what students know and what they need to do to improve.

Activity

Create a diagram, table or visual map showing how the roles of the teacher and support assistant overlap and vary when looking at and carrying out an assessment. Highlight those areas that are specifically the role of the support worker. You can then use this as assessment evidence for your portfolio.

AC 1.2 Summarise the difference between formative and summative assessment

Teaching staff will use two main types of assessment when looking at pupil learning; these are known as formative and summative assessment. Assessment for learning is an example of formative assessment. Summative assessment is also sometimes known as assessment of learning.

Formative assessment

This is ongoing, which means that it takes place on a day-to-day basis when teachers are talking to pupils, observing them and listening to the way in which they respond to learning activities. Examples of this might be:

- using observations to check on pupil learning
- questioning pupils to check their understanding
- listening to pupils' reasoning when they are talking about their learning
- asking pupils to review their own or one another's progress (peer reviewing).

Summative assessment

This is used to check on pupil learning so that teachers, schools and colleges can feed back to pupils, parents and other staff at the end of a term, year or stage of the curriculum. It will take place through testing or other more formal or standardised methods of assessment that may give a grade or level to pupil achievement. Examples of this might be end-of-year exams or specific curriculum tests that are carried out at different stages – for example, SATS at the end of a key stage, or GCSEs, T levels or A levels.

Class discussion

Thinking about your own experiences of pupil assessment, what do you use in your school or college? Have you, teachers and pupils found it useful? How does it contribute to the teaching and learning process?

Activity

Consider the differences between formative and summative assessment. You can read about this online and speak to staff in your setting to help you. Which do you think is the more useful way of assessing pupil learning and why do you think this is the case? Back up what you say with evidence and by using your own experience.

AC 1.3 Explain the characteristics of assessment for learning

The key concept of assessment for learning came from the research of two professors based in the UK: Paul Black and Dylan Wiliam. They discovered that pupils who are enabled to learn in a formative way are able to achieve more than those who do not. These results were published in 1998 in a booklet entitled 'Inside the Black Box: Raising Standards through Classroom Assessment'.

Assessment for learning is a type of formative assessment. It is the process by which teachers and tutors enable students to look at their progress and take responsibility for their learning as part of the teaching and learning process. This occurs through supporting them in setting targets and giving them support as they work towards them. Assessment for learning means:

- identifying a student's learning range
- sharing learning objectives with students
- developing students' awareness of their targets
- involving students in the learning process
- giving constructive feedback to students
- enabling reflection for improvement.

Identifying a student's learning range

You will need to know the ability of the student so that you can set targets that are achievable for them. Working with teachers alongside the student will help you to identify targets that will stretch and challenge them without being inaccessible. Learning will follow a natural progression that can be scaffolded so that they can attain the next stage.

Sharing learning objectives with students

This should always happen as a matter of course during teaching and learning activities. In this way they will know what the outcomes should be for each session and whether they have been able to meet them.

Developing learners' awareness of their targets

It is helpful for learners to have targets or learning goals for each term or half term, particularly in key subjects such as English and maths. In this way they will be able to focus on the next stage in their learning and develop their responsibility for keeping on track.

Involving students in the learning process

Talking with learners about the process and what they will need to do to achieve will help them to clarify what they need to do. It will also develop their confidence and understanding of the learning process.

Giving constructive feedback to learners

Talking to students about their progress and giving them constructive feedback will help them to see things in an alternative way and help them to improve.

Reflection for improvement

Assessment for learning also means supporting students in being able to reflect on ways in which they can improve. By asking them to think about their learning and what they found challenging or straightforward you will help them to start to do the same independently so that they can move forward in their learning.

Stretch and challenge

Find out more online about the origins of assessment for learning. You can use the work of Black and Wiliam or other academics to do this. If there is time, have a classroom discussion in which you talk with others about more of the characteristics of the process and give examples of it in your own practice.

LO2 Be able to use assessment strategies to promote learning

AC 2.1 Use clear language and examples to discuss and clarify personalised learning goals and criteria for assessing progress with learners

Pupils are likely to have personalised learning goals or targets as an ongoing part of the assessment process. These will take account of their learning range, mean that they will be based on their current learning needs as well as past achievements, and should be reviewed regularly with their involvement. You should be sure that learners understand what these targets are, so that they know what they are working towards. It is also helpful to have personal targets to hand when you are working with pupils so that you and they can check against them when needed.

Learners should also know what the learning objectives are for the session. It is important that learning objectives and outcomes are clear so that learning and progress can be measured against them. For example, a learning objective that starts 'To understand/to be familiar with/to be aware of ...' is very difficult to measure against as it is too broad. Learning objectives need to clearly state what the learner will be able to do using active verbs such as those in Table 7.1 on page 115.

Case study

Iona and Jamie (Year 1) are working with you on a maths activity in which they need to be able to arrange different shapes according to their properties. The learning objective is 'I can sort shapes'. One of Iona's targets is 'To describe the properties of a square, circle, rectangle and triangle', so it ties in nicely.

1. How could you tie Iona's targets in to the activity so that she can link them?
2. If Iona achieves the learning objective, what could be her next steps for learning?

Activity

Look at the learning objectives below.

- I can convert between different metric measures.
- I can understand the reasons for the Spanish Civil War.
- I am familiar with different methods of editing using Word.
- I can use brackets for parenthesis.
- I am aware of different methods of multiplication.

Are they measureable in each case? Where they are not, can you change them so that they are?

AC 2.2 Use assessment opportunities and strategies to gain information and make judgements about how well learners are participating in activities and the progress they are making

You should make the most of all opportunities you have for checking on pupil learning so that you can ensure that you are assessing their progress effectively. The kinds of assessment opportunities and strategies you might use could be those listed in Table 10.1.

▼ Table 10.1 Suggested assessment opportunities and strategies

Assessment opportunity/strategy	How it may be used
Using open-ended questions	Open-ended questions are those that give us the opportunity to find out more about what learners are thinking. They are also an opportunity to extend pupil learning by moving their ideas forward. A closed question (i.e. one with a yes or no answer) will not do this. For more on open and effective questioning, see Unit 7, pages 117–18.
Observing learners	Observing learners and looking at the way they are working will give us more opportunities for assessment as we will be able to see why they have approached their learning in a particular way. We can also see how much they have relied on others to complete the task.
Listening to how learners describe their work and their reasoning	Asking learners to describe their work and reasoning gives us a clear idea of how and why they have done something.
Checking learners' understanding	You can do this by asking them to talk things through with you as they are working or when they have completed the activity.
Engaging learners in reviewing progress	Ask learners to consider their progress with you by going through the steps they have taken to check whether they are on track.
Encouraging learners to keep in mind their learning goals and to assess their own progress	Make sure learners are mindful of their learning goals and ask them to check these so that they can think about them as they are working.
Encouraging learners to review and comment on their work	When pupils finish a piece of work, encourage them to look it over carefully with the learning objective in mind and to check on their learning. If they can, ask them to comment on what they have done while thinking about the objectives.
Praising learners when they focus their comments on their personalised learning goals	Praising learners for focusing on their targets and learning goals both encourages them and highlights the importance of each.
Encouraging peer assessment	Peer assessment is helpful as it encourages pupils to think about the objective and judge the work of their peers against it. This is another way of practising being able to evaluate their own learning. See also AC 3.3, page 163.

In practice

Observe the teacher or an experienced support assistant when they are working with a group of pupils. How many of these assessment opportunities and strategies do they use? Make note of any you think may be useful for you to use yourself when working with pupils.

LO3 Be able to support learners in reviewing their learning strategies and achievements

AC 3.1 Use information gained from monitoring learner participation and progress to help learners to review their learning strategies, achievements and future learning needs

One of the most important aspects of the assessment for learning process is that pupil progress will be assessed against their own achievements and learning goals. While you are assessing pupils and supporting them in monitoring their progress, you will get to know the way in which they work and how they approach their learning. As a result you will need to be able to discuss this with them so that they can review what they are doing and think about how they have approached their learning. This should take place both during and after learning activities as well as at different stages in their learning journey as it is a continuous process. In this way they will be able to think about how they approach their learning and use this information to move it forwards.

AC 3.2 Demonstrate ways to encourage learners to communicate their needs and ideas for future learning

Learners should be given opportunities throughout the learning process to communicate their needs and ideas, both so that you can support them effectively and to help them to assess their learning needs. You should talk to them at different stages of the process and provide encouragement so that you can enable them to communicate their needs to you. You can do this by encouraging them to reflect on what they are doing, look at their progress and think about how they might identify any areas for improvement. (See also AC 3.4, page 163.)

Effective marking can also help learners to do this as it should include next steps for learning as part of their feedback. At the end there should be a clear comment from a teacher or teaching assistant asking the learner a question that takes their learning forward.

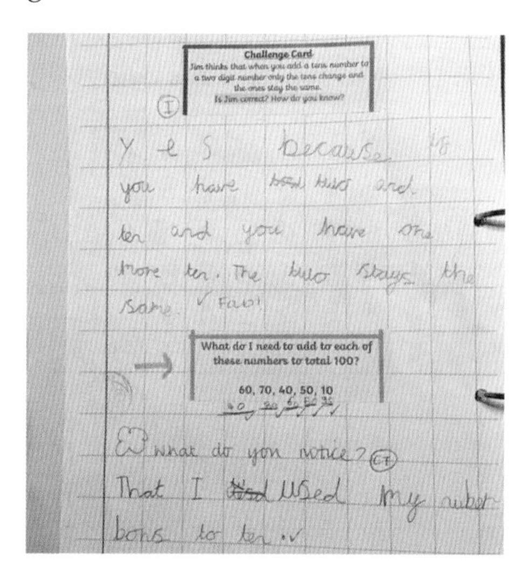

▲ Figure 10.2 How has the teacher extended this child's learning here?

Case study

Look at the following two examples.

Rita is a college student who has a young baby. While she is serious about her course, she has little time to organise her work while she is at home. You have noticed that, although her work is very good, she rarely completes assignments or follow-up work after her college sessions.

Kieran is a Year 3 pupil. You often work with him as you are based in Years 3 and 4. Kieran finds it difficult to organise himself and stay focused when completing learning activities. He often says that he 'can't do it'.

1 How might assessment for learning help in each case?
2 What could you do to support each learner to review their strategies and achievements?

Activity

Look at some previous examples of marking for students you support and comments that have been made regarding next steps. How does this enhance the assessment for learning process?

AC 3.3 Show how to support learners in using peer assessment and self-assessment to evaluate their learning achievements

Peer and self-assessment are helpful tools in enabling pupils to use assessment for learning. When they start to use this process, they should be supported by an adult so that they know what they are looking for and how they should look at a piece of work against the learning objectives and assessment criteria.

A key aspect of evaluating learning is to make sure that learning outcomes and assessment criteria are kept clear and simple so that pupils will be able to identify what to assess the learning against. The use of peer assessment is a good starting point as it is a way of introducing how to do this. For learners, this will always be more straightforward when looking at something that is not their own, particularly if they are younger pupils. It should be remembered that they are not doing it to compare with their own work, but that they are looking at it against the criteria. In this way they will start to look at how teachers measure achievement and assess their learning. Pupils can then move on to using self-assessment to reflect on their own learning and achievement.

▲ Figure 10.3 How does peer assessment also help pupils to reflect on their own learning?

In practice

Using a piece of work you are carrying out with students, ask them to peer and then self-assess their learning against the learning objective. (Check with the teacher or tutor first that they are happy for you to do this.)

- How often do they use the process?
- Ask them whether it helps them to assess their learning and what aspect of the process is the most helpful.

AC 3.4 Show how to support learners to: reflect on their learning; identify the progress they have made; identify their emerging learning needs; identify the strengths and weaknesses of their learning strategies and plan how to improve them

The following learning activities show how you will need to support pupils to think about their learning, identify progress and consider their future needs.

With younger pupils, you will need to use a more simplified approach; there are different strategies for doing this. Your school or college may use its own method, for consistency, and you should be familiar with this if so.

▲ Figure 10.4 Supporting learners to reflect on their learning and identify progress and learning needs

Using smiley or sad faces/traffic light systems

In some classrooms, particularly when working with younger learners, teachers will use a smiley faces or traffic light system to ask pupils how they feel about their learning. These are sometimes used verbally at the end of a session and pupils may have cards that they hold up. Alternatively, if their work is in books or on sheets they may draw their own at the top when they have completed the activity.

▲ Figure 10.5 Does your school or college use a specific system to help pupils review their learning?

Writing down any unclear areas

Thinking about unclear areas can help learners to focus on the things they may not understand so that they can look at them again.

Expressing key points

Asking learners to tell you about key points and express their thoughts will help them to think back on their learning. As they go through the process this will help them to review what they have learned.

Reviewing with partners

Looking with a partner at what they have done can be a useful process as they will be able to talk about and discuss their learning. If you use peer assessment this will also help them to start to think about their own learning.

Using whiteboards to write down what they have learned

This can be helpful as it focuses the learner on their learning. You can also ask them to check against the learning objective.

If you are working with a group of pupils, you can also take your own notes about the way in which they have approached their learning so that you can feed this back to them and help them to review their strategies.

Identifying strengths and weaknesses of their learning strategies and planning how to improve them

As part of this process, pupils will also need the opportunity to identify strengths and weaknesses in their learning strategies. This will help them to think about how they might approach their learning next time. Some pupils may take to this more easily than others and, for those who are more anxious about their learning or not used to the process, it can be a challenge. You may need to discuss the importance of making mistakes as an important part of the learning process. When looking at their strengths, pupils should be able to identify the ways in which they learn best so that they can use these to support their learning. Learners could also be encouraged to keep a learning journal in which they note down any strategies or ideas that may be helpful to them so that they can refer to them along with their personalised targets.

Research it

Why are mistakes important as part of the learning process? What can you find out about the importance of teaching children and young people how they can develop from making mistakes? How can you support learners in finding out how they learn best? Can you use this as part of your practice?

LO4 Be able to contribute to reviewing assessment for learning

AC 4.1 Provide feedback to the teacher on: learner participation and progress in the learning activities; learners' engagement in and response to assessment for learning; learners' progress in taking responsibility for their own learning

Providing feedback on learner participation and progress

You will need to ensure that you work closely with teachers and feed back to them following the activities you have carried out with pupils. It is important to talk to them about how much pupils have participated in the activity and whether they have met the learning objectives. This is because they will need to look at the learners' responses in order to plan for the next stage of learning. This feedback can be verbal or recorded on the lesson plan or a feedback sheet, but should be done as soon as possible following learning activities, while it is fresh in your mind.

Refer to Unit 7, page 125, for more on providing feedback to the teacher.

▲ Figure 10.6 How soon after activities do you feed back to the teacher?

Providing feedback on learners' engagement and response to assessment for learning and taking responsibility for their own learning

Teachers will also need to know how pupils have responded to the assessment for learning process and have taken responsibility for their own learning. It may help you to take notes during the teaching and learning process to help you remember their level of participation as well as any comments they have made during the activity so that you can feed these back to teachers.

Older pupils may also feed back at the end of sessions as a group following peer or self-assessment. They may discuss with one another and with adults the process of assessment for learning. In this way teachers can also observe the way in which learners have responded to the activity.

Tips for best practice: assessment for learning

- Ensure that pupils are aware of learning objectives.
- Be aware of any personalised learning goals that pupils have.
- Use open-ended questions to check on learning.
- Listen carefully to pupil responses to guide your questioning.
- Ensure pupils know how assessment takes place.
- Allow opportunities and time for pupils to peer and self-assess.
- Ensure you feed back to teachers promptly.
- Evaluate your own contribution to the process.

LO5 Be able to maintain learner records

AC 5.1 Collate the information needed to update learner records from valid and reliable sources

In your role supporting teaching and learning you will probably need to maintain learner records; these are likely to need updating regularly as they will be used as working documents. They may exist in different forms and may be stored on computers, or in filing cabinets or cupboards in your workplace. They are likely to include:

- attendance records
- records of progress and achievement/assessment
- special needs or medical information on pupils
- planning and schemes of work
- pupil records of achievement and information from other schools or colleges
- records for extended school or college provision or clubs
- personal information
- records of accidents and illnesses.

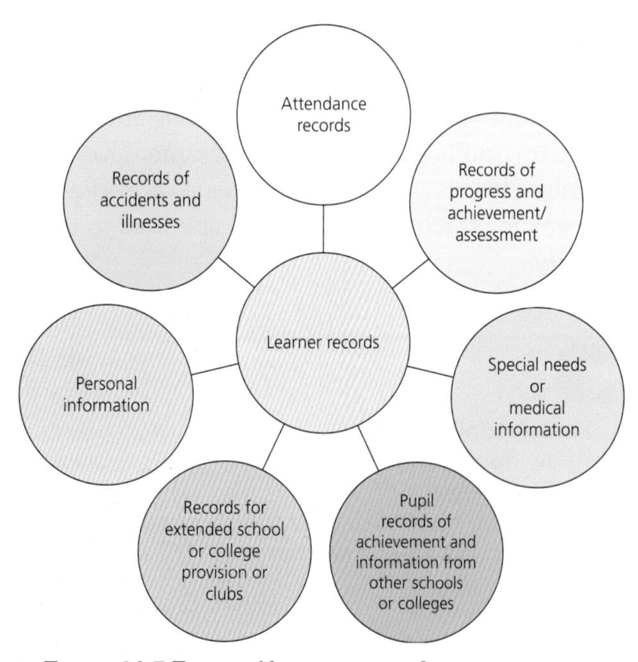

▲ Figure 10.7 Types of learner records

When collating information in order to update records, you will need to make sure that the sources are reliable and that the information is valid and up to date. If information has been given verbally, check that you are sure that this is the case. Be very careful that any records you are responsible for are updated quickly and scrupulously.

> **Research it**
>
> What records have you had to update in your school or college? Find out the location of the different types of records listed above and how they are stored in your setting.

AC 5.2 Show how to raise any concerns about the information with the relevant people

If you have any concerns about information you have been asked to update, you will need to raise them with the relevant people before proceeding.

Concerns may relate to:

- **the validity of information** – whether it should be included in the pupil's records
- **the authenticity of information** – where the information has come from and if it is a trustworthy source
- **the sufficiency of information** – whether there is enough information to include in the pupil records
- **the wider implications of the information (such as attendance patterns, child protection concerns)** – if you notice any patterns or are concerned while updating information, you should always speak to the relevant person in your school or college.

Relevant people may include those listed below.

- **Teachers:** you may need to speak to teachers or tutors if you are unsure about information you have been given regarding pupils and how to update the records.
- **Head of subject/year group:** if you are working on records for a subject or in a particular year group and notice a pattern of some kind or need to speak to a member of staff urgently and teachers are unavailable.

- **SENCo (Special Educational Needs Co-ordinator):** you may need to speak to the SENCo if information is not clear regarding pupils with special educational needs or if you have concerns about information that has been given to you.
- **Programme co-ordinator:** you should speak to the programme co-ordinator if you have concerns about information regarding a student on a college course.
- **Senior management:** senior management may need to be consulted if you are unable to speak to teachers or tutors, particularly if you have concerns about pupil welfare.
- **Designated safeguarding officer:** this person will need to be informed if you have child protection concerns about a pupil when updating their information. The designated safeguarding officer in a school is often the head teacher or SENCo.
- **Education welfare officer:** the EWO would need to be contacted regarding pupil attendance if you have noticed attendance patterns that are a cause for concern – for example, if a pupil is always absent on a Friday or if they take regular holidays or other time away from the setting. The EWO is usually based outside the setting and will visit regularly to check records of attendance.
- **Office or admin staff:** usually, pupil records that are stored centrally will be in the school or college office. If you have concerns about records that are based here, such as pupils' personal information, you should pass these on to office staff.

Case study

Nyko is working in a small village school and is updating some pupil information in the school office. While doing this he comes across records for a pupil in his class who he knows has moved house recently, but he sees that the address and phone number have not been updated.

1. Should Nyko say something? If so, to whom? What should he do first?
2. Give reasons for your answer.

AC 5.3 Review learner records to ensure they are accurate, complete and up to date

You may from time to time be asked to review learner records in order to ensure that they are accurate and up to date. For example, you may be given information about a new pupil or need to update medical records. In this situation you will need to make sure that they are completed quickly. If you notice that any records are incomplete or that you need to add more information you should do this while speaking to the member of staff responsible for them first.

AC 5.4 Show how to maintain confidentiality according to organisational and legal requirements

You must be able to show that you maintain confidentiality. All staff need to be aware that learner records are confidential and come under the Data Protection Act (1998),* which states that information should be shared only with those people who need to see it. Schools and colleges will have a policy and procedures for confidentiality, and staff should be aware of this and pass information on only on a need-to-know basis.

AC 5.5 Use organisational procedures to ensure secure storage of learner records

Your school or college will have its own procedures for ensuring that records are stored securely and safely. However, you should ensure that you are careful when working with or updating any records and replace them as soon as you have finished updating them. This also applies to records that are stored on computer systems: make sure that screens are not left visible to others if you have to leave them for any reason, and that passwords are kept secure and not given to others.

* This will be changing to GDPR (General Data Protection Regulation) in May 2018.

Tips for best practice: maintaining learner records

- Keep records secure and observe confidentiality requirements.
- Report any concerns to the appropriate people as soon as you notice them.
- Store any passwords securely and do not give yours to anyone else to use.
- Ensure that records are updated promptly.

Check your understanding

1. What is your role when supporting the assessment for learning process?
2. Give three features of assessment for learning.
3. What is assessment for learning?
4. What is the purpose of personalised learning goals?
5. Give three methods of using assessment opportunities or strategies to make judgements about pupil progress.
6. How does using peer assessment help learners when starting to think about assessment for learning?
7. Explain the importance of supporting learners when carrying out the assessment for learning process.
8. Why should you reflect on your own contribution to assessment for learning?
9. Name four members of staff you may need to report to when completing learner records.
10. Where are learner records usually stored?

Assessment preparation

This unit will mainly be assessed in the workplace by your assessor. The guidance states that learning outcomes 2–5 must be assessed in a real work environment. However, the first learning objective is about your understanding of the assessment for learning process. If you complete the activity for AC 1.1 you can use this as evidence. For AC 1.2 and 1.3 you can write a reflective account of the characteristics of assessment for learning, and what is meant by formative and summative assessment.

Legislation

Data Protection Act 1998 (this will be changing to General Data Protection Regulation in May 2018, see Unit 4, page 57). Although this is an EU directive it is likely to be converted to British law.

Read about it

Reference books

Black, P. and Wiliam, D. (1998/2006) *Inside the Black Box: Raising Standards through Classroom Assessment*, Granada.

Bosanquet P., Radford, J. and Webster, R. (2016) *The Teaching Assistant's Guide to Effective Interaction – How to Maximise your Practice*, Routledge.

Weblinks

http://ccea.org.uk/sites/default/files/docs/curriculum/assessment/assessment_for_learning/afl_practical_guide.pdf Assessment for Learning: A Practical Guide

www.nwea.org/blog/2012/dylan-wiliam-the-5-formative-assessment-strategies-to-improve-student-learning/#sthash.KRTC7rMK.dpuf 'Dylan Wiliam & The 5 Formative Assessment Strategies to Improve Student Learning'

11 Engage in personal and professional development

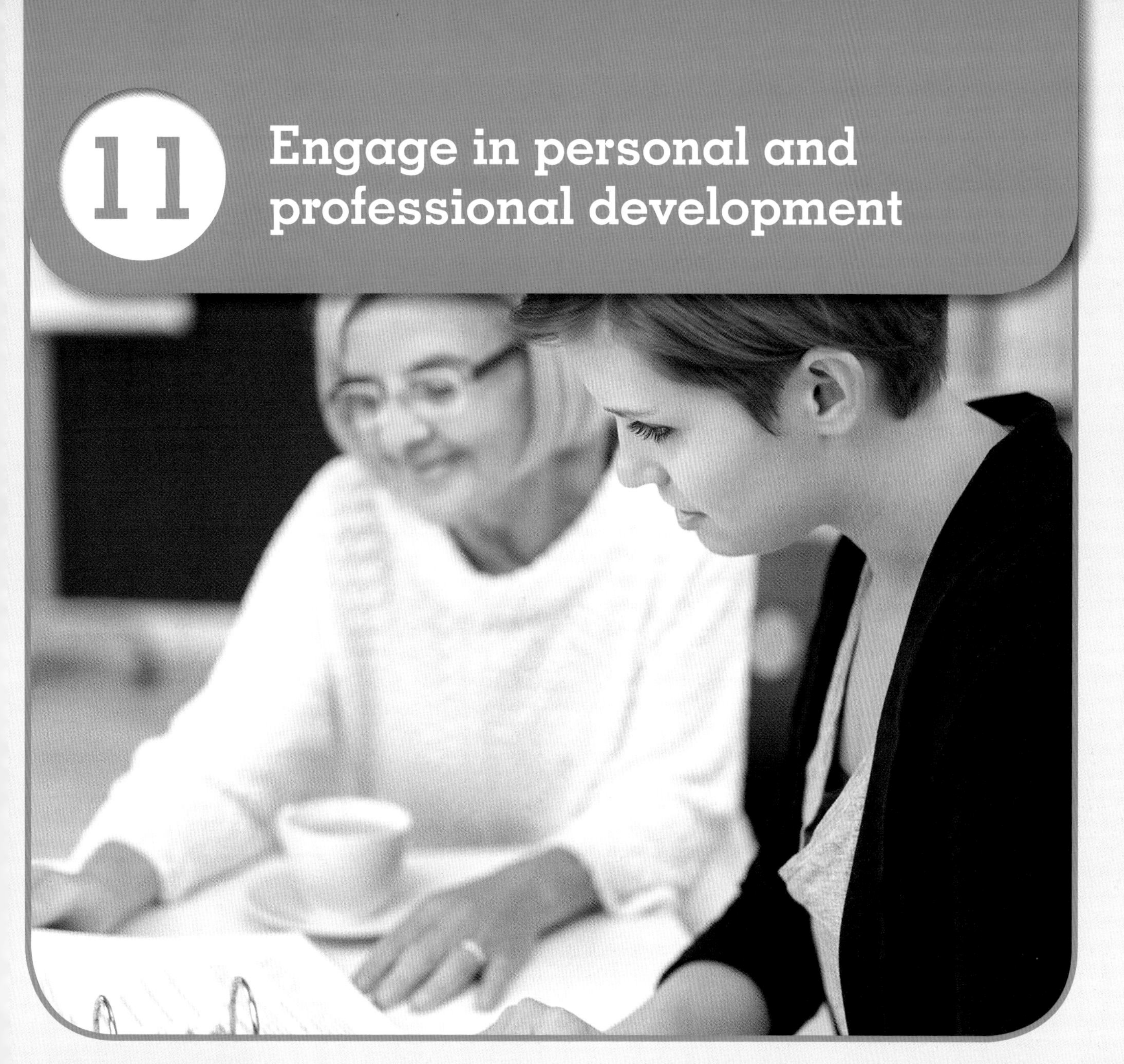

About this unit

Engaging in personal and professional development is about how you consider and reflect on your role in the learning environment. For this unit you will need to think about your practice and evaluate your performance through having an appraisal with your line manager or mentor and setting targets for development. This will then give you a focus that you will be able to use as evidence for your portfolio.

Learning outcomes

By the end of this unit you will:

LO1 Understand what is required for competence in your work role

LO2 Be able to reflect on organisational practice

LO3 Be able to evaluate own performance

LO4 Be able to agree a personal development plan

LO5 Be able to use learning opportunities and reflective practice to contribute to personal development

Getting started

When you are working on this unit, you will need a copy of your job description (or use the one in Figure 11.1) so that you can look at it in relation to your practice. You can also look at Figure 11.1 as a group, or search for an example from your own sector online. How does the job description marry up with what you do? Can you see whether any changes need to be made?

Case study

Jamie has recently started in a school and been given a generic job description for a level 3 teaching assistant. However she has asked other support staff and found that they all have exactly the same job description, despite the fact that their roles are very varied.

1 Should Jamie say something?
2 Why is it important that her job description is relevant and up to date?

LO1 Understand what is required for competence in your work role

AC 1.1 Describe the duties and responsibilities of your work role

In your role in supporting teaching and learning, you will need to be clear from the start as to what you are expected to do and on your own duties and responsibilities within the learning environment. Once employed, you will have a job description that outlines these and, if it is up to date, you will be able to use it for your portfolio. Alternatively, you should be able to talk it through with your line manager and make changes where needed.

The school or college is also likely to have a person specification for the post, which will show the kinds of qualifications and training, skills, experience and personal qualities it will be useful for you to have. These may be listed as essential or desirable requirements. These are used particularly when recruiting new staff so that employers can check against each one. When you are applying for a post, you will need to look carefully at the person specification and make sure you have shown how you meet these criteria in your application.

Activity

Using your own job description or the example in Figure 11.1, describe your main duties and responsibilities. Try not to just list them, but explain what you need to do for each one. You can then use this for AC 1.1 in your portfolio.

Job description

Title: Teaching assistant
Post No: Level 3

Summary of responsibilities and duties:

Support for the pupils

- Establish productive relationships with pupils, acting as a role model
- Provide supervision and support to pupils, responding to their individual needs
- Contribute to the development and implementation of individual education plans (IEPs)
- Promote the inclusion and acceptance of all pupils by encouraging pupils to interact with each other
- Set high expectations in order to promote independence and self-esteem
- Provide feedback to pupils on their progress and achievement under the guidance of the teacher

Support for the teacher

- Prepare and maintain an orderly, supportive learning environment
- Assist the teacher in lesson planning, evaluating and adjusting lessons/work plan as appropriate
- Monitor pupils' progress and achievements, through observation and marking pupils' work, providing objective and accurate feedback to the teacher
- Promote good pupil behaviour, dealing promptly with conflicts in line with the school's behaviour policy
- Establish constructive relationships with parents and carers
- Assist with the preparation of teaching and learning materials and resources
- Administer, invigilate and assess routine tests and exams
- Provide admin support e.g. photocopying, typing, filing, administering coursework etc.

Support for the curriculum

- Participate in planning and evaluating structured and agreed learning programmes for pupils, adjusting them according to individual needs
- Implement literacy and numeracy programmes and be aware of opportunities provided by other learning activities to support the development of literacy and numeracy skills
- Provide specialist support to help pupils access learning activities where necessary
- Support pupils in the use of ICT in learning activities and promote independence in its use
- Prepare and maintain teaching materials and assist pupils in their use

Support for the school

- Comply with policies relating to child protection, health, safety and security, confidentiality and data protection, reporting all concerns to an appropriate person
- Contribute to the overall aims/ethos of the school
- Ensure all pupils have equal access to learning and development opportunities
- Appreciate and support the roles of other professionals
- Attend and participate in meetings as required
- Assist with the supervision of pupils before and after schools and at lunchtimes
- Accompany teaching staff and pupils on out of school visits and trips
- Promote diversity and ensure all pupils have equal access to learning and development opportunities
- Recognise own strengths and areas of expertise and use these to advise and support others

▲ Figure 11.1 Do you have a copy of your job description?

PERSON SPECIFICATION

Teaching assistant level 3 (secondary school)

Qualifications and training

- To have relevant qualifications to at least NVQ or STLS level 3
- To have good levels of literacy and numeracy to GCSE or equivalent
- To have specialism and experience in specific curriculum areas
- To have a willingness to participate in ongoing development and training

Experience

- Relevant experience within a secondary setting (Key Stages 3 and 4)
- Understanding of policies and codes of practice
- Awareness of relevant legislation

Knowledge and skills

- To be able to supervise groups of students effectively
- To be able to maintain records
- To understand the need for confidentiality
- To be able to work effectively with others, including teachers and teaching assistants
- To be able to use ICT to support learning
- To be able to self-reflect and seek opportunities for development
- To have effective oral and written communication skills
- To have good organisational and time-management skills

Personal qualities

- To have an ability to work on own initiative and be adaptable
- To have good interpersonal and communication skills and the ability to build positive relationships with others – colleagues, pupils and parents
- To be able to work calmly and with patience
- To have empathy with pupils who may face barriers to their learning
- To have a commitment to helping young people to achieve to the best of their ability
- To have a sense of humour

▲ Figure 11.2 What personal qualities do you have that are useful for your role?

LO2 Be able to reflect on organisational practice

AC 2.1 Explain how reflection supports improving the quality of the learning environment

All staff in schools and colleges should be able to reflect on what they do rather than repeating same thing every year without thinking about it. If no changes or improvements are made to working practices, organisations become stuck in their ways and individuals start to become resistant to change. Schools and colleges should look regularly at all aspects of their practice, from staffing and organisational planning at a management level to looking at how the learning environment is organised at a teaching and learning level, so that improvements can be made. Teachers, tutors and support staff should think regularly about the following points with regard to the learning environment.

Organisation

The learning environment should be organised so that the best use is made of space and pupils have sufficient room to move around the environment. You will need to think particularly about access for any pupils with disabilities. Resources and materials should be easy to find and storage spaces labelled so that children can start to be independent at taking them out and putting away from an early age.

General tidiness

All equipment and materials will need to be kept tidy so that they are easy to find, and to ensure that there are no health and safety issues, such as coats on the floor or chairs not pushed under tables. Children and young people will need to be reminded of the importance of safety and the need to take pride in their surroundings.

Displays

Displays are an important part of the learning environment as they fulfil a number of different purposes:

- presenting information
- improving the environment
- celebrating achievement and diversity
- providing a learning resource
- showing pupils' work.

Staff should be continually looking at and assessing displays in their own environment to check that they have not become untidy or out of date. You should also be familiar with your school or college's display policy so that you can check whether displays in your own areas meet their requirements. Do not leave the same display up for months at a time – they can be changed, refreshed or reused in another part of the school or college.

Responsibilities

Children and young people should be encouraged to develop a sense of pride and responsibility for their environment. This should start from an early age, when young children first come into school, and they should have ownership and responsibility for their surroundings. Staff can encourage this by allocating jobs to children and young people, and giving them tasks in the learning environment such as keeping a particular area tidy, monitoring resources, or ensuring displays are kept tidy and giving them the opportunity to create their own.

▲ Figure 11.3 Why should displays in the learning environment be reviewed regularly?

Activity

Go for an environment walk in your school or college and look carefully at how the learning environment is organised as well as the use of displays, organisation and general tidiness. Talk to staff about how the environment is maintained; talk to children and young people about their learning environment and what they like about it. Then report back to the group on what you have found out and whether there are any areas of good practice that can be shared.

AC 2.2 Demonstrate the ability to reflect on practice

The role of the teaching assistant has changed greatly in recent years. It has become that of a professional and, as such, you will need to be able to reflect on what you do. Reflection is a tool that you should use as it offers an opportunity to improve and develop your practice – for example, supporting teaching and learning, your professional conduct, your work with colleagues, how you work with teachers, your training needs, and so on. It also means thinking about and evaluating how things are going, what went well or not so well, and how you might change things next time; in other words, learning from your experience. Reflecting on your practice (**reflective practice**) and planning how you will move forward is also empowering, as you take more control over what you do and are part of the process.

One of the ways in which schools and colleges support their staff to reflect on their practice is through **appraisal** or performance management. Although this is not a statutory requirement for support staff, many schools do it anyway as it is good practice and supports their **continuing professional development (CPD)**.

As you will need to demonstrate your ability to reflect on your own practice to complete this unit, it will be helpful for you to ask your line manager to carry out an initial appraisal with you if this does not happen already. This unit will guide you through what you need to do to in order to complete this.

▲ Figure 11.4 Why does reflection help you to improve and develop your practice?

Key terms

Reflective practice: the process of thinking about and analysing what you do so that you can improve your professional practice.

Appraisal: a regular opportunity to reflect on your own progress and discuss it with your line manager.

Continuing professional development (CPD): this is the ongoing process by which individuals keep up to date with what is happening in their professional area.

If you are not used to evaluating your practice, you may like to start the process by carrying out a self-appraisal or self-evaluation; this should involve asking yourself the following types of questions:

- Is my job description still accurate? Are there any changes that need to be made and, if so, what are they?
- What do I think are my greatest strengths and what are the areas that need improvement?
- What areas of my job satisfy me the most?
- Do I have gaps in my knowledge? What skills or training would help me to improve my performance?
- What goals or targets would I like to work towards over the next 12 months?
- What support will I need to achieve these?

Activity

Using these questions complete a self-appraisal so that you are ready for your next review meeting. It will also help you to have a copy of your job description with you.

AC 2.3 Describe how your values, belief systems and experiences may affect working practice

Although you may not be aware of it, your own values, experiences and belief systems will all affect the way in which you relate to and work with others. As you are thinking about and reflecting on your practice, you may find that you are challenged by some of the issues that arise. The process is not an easy one and you will be reflecting not only on your work with children and young people, but also on your own attitudes and beliefs. You may be prompted to consider things that you had not previously thought relevant to what you do as part of your role. However, you will need to be professional in your dealings with others and work with them as much as possible even if your own views are not in line with theirs.

Everyone is moulded by their own experiences and backgrounds, and this will have an effect on the way in which you live and work. The kinds of things that may affect and influence this may be:

- your own family background and social environment
- educational influences
- cultural or religious influences
- moral influences.

Your own family background and social environment

This means the way in which your family is made up and how this has influenced you, for example if you come from a large extended family or are an only child, or if you have been brought up by same sex parents. You may have come from a very disciplined household with many rules or been allowed more choices. Your parents and family may have been very sociable or you may have been at home more often rather than out with others. You may have had your basic needs met or it may have been a struggle on a daily basis for your parents or carers to find enough money to feed and keep the family warm. Your family may be very close both geographically and emotionally, or you may have become separated from them for whatever reason.

Educational influences

You may have come from a school that was single or mixed sex, sent to boarding school or been to school in your local area. Your school may have been one in which you felt nurtured and supported or it may have been one which did not. You may have had a happy time in school or have been bullied, been academic or found school work challenging. You may have stayed on until you were 18 and gone to university, or left as soon as you could.

Cultural or religious influences

Looking back, you may have found that religion played a big part in your early life and this may still be the case. You may attend religious services regularly and this may be a part of your own community and home life. Alternatively, you may reject religion and religious practices and be unable to understand those who do. You may be from the same culture as the majority of those in the school or college or you may not be, and this will affect how you feel.

Moral influences

Your home life and values that have been passed on to you may be important to you, or you may have rejected them. Your parents or carers may have had strong feelings or opinions about topics such as marriage, equality in society, corporal punishment, homosexuality, alcohol or drugs. These kinds of factors will have had some influence on the way in which you view these things.

All of these influences will affect your own values and beliefs whether you are aware of it or not, and it can be difficult to remain objective in certain situations.

Class discussion

Looking at the kinds of influences on the previous page, reflect on your own for a few minutes about how your own values, belief systems and experiences have affected you. Consider the following in particular – marriage, religion, risk taking in children and young people, male/female roles within families and society.

Discuss in smaller or larger groups the ways in which your own personal opinions on these topics may challenge your professional practice.

Case study

Ross is working as a teaching assistant in a small village primary school. He has been asked to work with a group of children in Year 2 to make pizzas and the children are able to choose their own toppings. One of the group says that they are vegetarian so they will not be able to touch or use the meat toppings. Ross is upset as he does not believe that young children should be vegetarians and asks the child if they think it is a good idea for them not to eat meat.

1 What should Ross have done?
2 Should he have said anything to the child about this? Why?

LO3 Be able to evaluate your performance

After you have reflected on the requirements of your role and have started to think about your practice, the next part of your appraisal will be to evaluate your own performance. You can use different sources to help you.

AC 3.1 Evaluate your knowledge, performance and understanding against internal or external benchmarks

When you are thinking about your knowledge and performance, it will help you to have different benchmarks available to refer to. These will also help you to focus on different areas of your practice and give you ideas for development. These may be available within your school or college, or could also be external. The kinds of things you could look at might be:

- codes of practice
- regulations
- minimum standards
- Ofsted report
- staff handbook
- job description.

Codes of practice

The main code of practice you may refer to and that relates to the role of many support staff is the SEND Code of Practice. This is the statutory guidance for schools and colleges and all who work with children and young people up to the age of 25. It has separate sections for those working in schools and further education and how provision may be put in place, and this may help you in relation to your role. (For more on this, see Unit 10 on supporting children and young people with SEND.)

Regulations

The rules and regulations you need to think about are those that relate to schools and colleges. These are available at the government website **www.gov.uk** under 'Running a school or college'. You may also find regulations and guidance regarding support staff and teaching assistants here.

Minimum standards

The Professional Standards for Teaching Assistants are non-mandatory and non-statutory but exist to set out recommendations for their role and deployment. They were published by the NAHT (National Association of Head Teachers), the National Education Trust (NET) and MITA (Maximising the Impact of Teaching Assistants) in June 2016, and were originally drafted by educational experts chosen by the DfE. However the government chose not to publish them and is no longer associated with them.

They have four headings or themes:

1 Personal and professional conduct
2 Knowledge and understanding
3 Teaching and learning
4 Working with others.

It is suggested that they are used by teaching assistants to support their own practice during professional development. They are available through the NET website: **http://nationaleducationtrust.net/wp-content/uploads/2016/06/Professional-Standards-for-Teaching-Assistants.pdf**

Ofsted

It may help you to look at the previous Ofsted inspection of your school or college as this is likely to set out what it needs to work on in terms of improvement. This may have a direct impact on your role if, for example, there is a need to update whole staff training in a particular area.

Staff handbook

Your staff handbook may be a helpful reference as it should contain basic employment information as well as the ethos and values of the organisation. It should be relevant to all staff and is often given out as part of the induction process. If there are aspects of the staff handbook you were not aware of or that are not clear to you, you should talk to your line manager.

In practice

Using the Professional Standards for Teaching Assistants, think about how you could use them to shape professional development and appraisal. You may like to score yourself against them at the start of your course and then re-do this at the end to show progress.

Activity

Check your school or college's most recent Ofsted report if you haven't already. This will give you an insight into strengths and areas for improvement. Take note of any that have direct relevance to you in your role.

Research it

To get the wider picture, find a copy of the School or College Improvement Plan for your setting. This is likely to be on your school or college website and will give you an insight into the way in which school and college management teams plan areas for development several years in advance. It is likely to incorporate Ofsted targets and other recommendations.

Job description

As we have already discussed, your job description will be a useful document to help you when thinking about your day-to-day practice. It may also help to look at it against the Professional Standards for Teaching Assistants mentioned above.

You may decide to use these benchmarks to help you, as well as evaluating your practice against previous targets that have been set by your line manager. It is helpful to have as many places to refer to as possible so that you can be sure you are doing all you can to improve and develop.

AC 3.2 Demonstrate use of feedback to evaluate your performance and inform development

All those who work in education will be given observations and feedback on their performance from time to time. This is designed to be constructive – you should not take it as a criticism but as a way of helping you to develop what you do. It will often be useful to see things from another point of view and you may learn things that you had not considered before. You will need to be able to show that you have used feedback in order to think about and evaluate what you do as part of your role. If your assessor or a mentor observes your practice and gives you written feedback, which you then use to evaluate your development, you should use this to help you and show progress throughout your course. Make sure you show how you have used the feedback to reflect on what you have done and how it will inform your practice going forward.

You should also be given feedback as part of your appraisal meeting and this should be written down so that you have a record of it. This may also be following an observation or it may be more general feedback on your practice overall. Remember to use it to help you to think about what you do, and how you can develop and improve your practice.

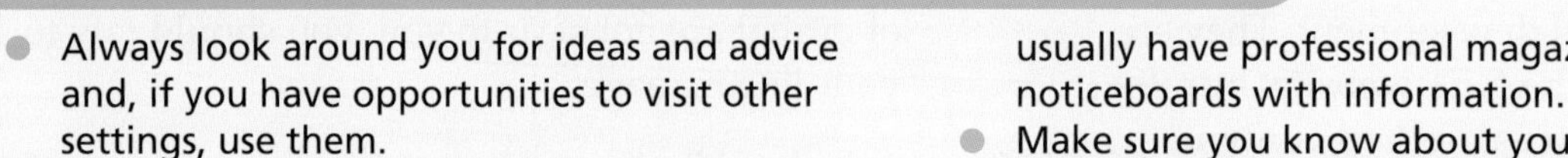

Tips for best practice: evaluating your own performance

- Always look around you for ideas and advice and, if you have opportunities to visit other settings, use them.
- Look for development opportunities and training where you can.
- Keep a record of all the training and additional qualifications you gather during your career, with dates. Remember this may take place within your school as part of a staff meeting.
- Keep up to date with what is happening in education by reading around – staffrooms usually have professional magazines and noticeboards with information.
- Make sure you know about your latest Ofsted report so that you can be up to date with what your school or college needs to do and tie in with this.
- Think about any informal conversations you have with others regarding their practice – these may be a useful source of advice.
- Remember to use feedback constructively, and as a way of moving forward and developing your practice.

Stretch and challenge

After your assessor has been to observe your work with children and young people, and spoken to your colleagues, you will be given feedback and areas for development. Following your feedback, think about these as well as the areas in which you have shown good practice. Answer the following questions as fully as you can:

- Are the points raised different from what you had expected?
- What has been particularly useful about the process?
- How will this feedback inform your development?

LO4 Be able to agree a personal development plan

In order to agree a plan for your own personal development, you will need to work with others in your school or college. There may already be something that is in place for teaching assistants to do this. You should have a formal appraisal or professional development meeting once or twice a year so that you can set out a plan and review targets for development, but there will also be other sources of support to help you.

AC 4.1 Identify sources of support for planning and reviewing your development

To help you to review your practice, you will need to use different sources of support on an ongoing basis. This means that, as well as having your appraisal, you should use other opportunities around you. These may include:

- formal support discussions
- informal support discussions
- one-to-one supervision
- appraisal
- within the organisation
- beyond the organisation.

Formal support

This will be through your college tutor, or through your line manager or mentor in your school or college. Formal support will be given through meetings, either with these individuals or in a larger group, so that you can discuss your practice. This is likely to be recorded in some way so that you have paperwork to refer to.

Informal support

This will be the support you gain from talking to colleagues as well as teaching assistants in your own and other schools or colleges about what they do, and also gathering advice from them about how they might deal with particular issues.

One-to-one supervision

These are meetings that you may have with your mentor or line manager at work if you need to have extra support more regularly. They are a way of discussing any issues that arise at work, as well as personal ones that may have an impact on your practice – for example, relationships within the team, morale within the teaching and learning environment, work issues or any other concerns you may have.

Appraisal

The appraisal process will help you to discuss, evaluate, plan and review your development in a structured way. Remember that appraisal should be an ongoing working cycle rather than just looking at it as an annual meeting.

Within the organisation

Your school or college will have procedures in place for planning and reviewing personal development, and you should be able to speak to others about the process and to gather ideas.

Beyond the organisation

You may have opportunities or networks outside your school or college that can help you to plan and review your development. These may be other teaching assistants you meet as part of your course, or those with whom you share a professional or curriculum area – for example, if you work mainly in a speech and language unit, or have a subject specialism in a secondary school.

> **Activity**
>
> Which of these sources of support will you be using as part of your own appraisal or review of your practice? Outline how you will use them and why you have chosen them.

AC 4.2 Show how to work with others to review and prioritise your learning needs, professional interests and development opportunities

The conversation you have with the person who is supporting you should shape how you review your own learning needs. However, you may also have the opportunity to speak to others about ways in which you can develop.

▲ Figure 11.5 Others may help you to review and prioritise your learning needs

Carers

In your role you may find that you are working closely with parents and carers, particularly if you are supporting a child or young person who has special educational needs or disabilities. They may have ideas or suggestions as to sources of information or training that will be helpful, or link you up with organisations that are specific to the needs of their child. You can then use this information to help you to develop your knowledge and skills.

Advocates

An advocate is someone who works with vulnerable people or those with specific needs or disabilities to defend and safeguard their rights and to make sure their views are heard. Advocates will also help them to explore options that are available to them and access information and services. If you are working with a child or young person who has an advocate, you may be able to link your own development targets to this through the way in which you work together to support them.

Research it

What else can you find out about advocacy? How does it support those in need to make decisions about their lives?

Supervisor/line manager or employer

Your supervisor, line manager or employer will be the person who goes through the appraisal process with you. They are likely to be a member of the senior management team – for example, the deputy head or head of school in a college. They should be able to guide you through the process and help you to prioritise development opportunities, and will be able to tie these in with whole school or college targets.

Other professionals

As part of your role, you may work with other professionals, both within and outside your organisation. This is particularly likely if you support children and young people who have special educational needs and disabilities. Your development targets could link to a specific action you are working on with them as part of an **Education, Health and Care (EHC) plan** or statement of special educational needs.

Key term

Education, Health and Care (EHC) plan: a plan in England and Wales for a child or young person up to the age of 25 who has special educational needs or disabilities. It will take into account their educational, health and welfare needs, and will set out the additional support they will be given. It will be written and reviewed annually through the local authority.

The area of special educational needs and available provision is explored in Unit 14.

In practice

You will need to show how you work with others to prioritise your learning and development needs. Consider your own role: you may work with all or only one or two of the examples discussed. Are there any other individuals with whom you work who will help and support you to prioritise your learning and development needs?

AC 4.3 Show how to work with others to agree a personal development plan and set targets

When setting out your personal development plan and agreeing targets, you will need to work with your line manager or mentor. Ideally, you should try to encompass training and development opportunities that are taking place during the year, or issues you are undertaking as part of your role. For example, the whole school may be undertaking training in behaviour management, or a group of support staff may all be working on their Specialist Teaching and Learning Services (STLS) qualification during the year. In this way, you are not trying to think of additional targets on top of what you are already doing. As a general indicator, many teaching assistants will have one whole school target, one personal target that they would like to achieve and one suggested by their line manager.

When you are setting targets for development, remember that they will need to be SMART. If you look at Table 11.1, it will help you to think about how you should set out what you are going to do and ensure that your targets are achievable in the time available. You should set between three and five targets as any more than this will be difficult to achieve in the time available. These should then be signed by yourself and your line manager or mentor to show that they have been agreed.

▼ Table 11.1 SMART targets

S	**Specific:** you must ensure that your target is clear.
M	**Measureable:** you should be able to measure whether you have been able to achieve your target.
A	**Achievable:** make sure that your target is achievable, and do not be over-ambitious.
R	**Realistic:** check that you will have access to any training or support that is needed.
T	**Time-bound:** there should be a time limit to achieving your target, which is not over-generous to ensure that you will do it!

In practice

You will need to have set your targets early on in your STLS course, and to allow at least six months between this and reviewing them. In this way, you will be able to show how you have progressed and developed over time and include this as part of your portfolio.

Professional development meeting

Name: Sinem Assapardi Date: 28/9/2017

Role: Individual support assistant for Year 9

Record of discussion following self-appraisal:

Sinem has recently started at St Richard's; she previously worked as an ISA in a primary school. Priorities for her include getting to know a different school sector and structure, as well as getting to know MR, the child she is supporting in Year 9. Sinem would like some support with autism training to help her in her new role.

Review of targets:

1) N/A as Sinem has just started at the school, but previous priorities have been to develop her skills in ICT and she has completed a level 2 course.
2)
3)

New targets for development:

1) To complete school induction and orientation as soon as possible
2) To attend monthly meetings with mentor
3) To complete whole school training on e-safety and radicalisation during autumn term
4) To attend autism awareness course
5) To complete STLS level 3 qualification by the end of the academic year

Review date: July 2018

Signed:

TA -

Line manager -

▲ Figure 11.6 Look at this appraisal form. Are all the targets SMART?

LO5 Be able to use learning opportunities and reflective practice to contribute to personal development

AC 5.1 Evaluate how learning opportunities identified in your personal development plan have improved performance

For this section you will need to look at the way in which you have used learning opportunities to improve your own performance. These may have been through targets that you have set as part of your appraisal, as well as other learning opportunities that have been available to you. It is important for your qualification that you evaluate the impact this has had on your practice.

Your appraisal paperwork may do this and it may help you to consider the following:

- **Formal courses such as first aid:** have you been sent on any formal courses that have helped you? If so, how have they done this and what impact has this had on your day-to-day practice?
- **In-house training:** have there been any learning opportunities given to you through meetings or in-house training, such as updating safeguarding, or whole school behaviour management training, that have had an impact on your work?
- **Practical exercises:** you may have undertaken some practical exercises that have helped you professionally, as part of whole school training and development. Have these been useful? Is it easier for you to learn things in this way?
- **Online updating and webinars:** as part of your training, you may have had to complete online updates for your CPD. This may be through watching webinars or doing online courses to support your development. Evaluate how useful these have been, and whether you have completed them in your own time or alongside colleagues for support.
- **Shadowing colleagues:** you may have been able to work with or shadow a more experienced colleague to help you to gather ideas and support reflection on your own practice. Consider how this has helped you to think about what you do in the classroom and why it has been useful as a process.
- **Independent research or reading:** you may have found a particular journal or online article that has been helpful in enabling you to find out more about a subject or the support that you give to children and young people. Evaluate why and how it has helped you.

AC 5.2 Explain how reflection on your practice has led to improved ways of working

You will need to describe how thinking about your practice has led to an improvement in the way you carry out your role. It may help you to think about the sources of your reflection, for example:

- **Talking to colleagues:** has speaking to colleagues or a conversation with a line manager helped you to reflect on your practice? What has been the reason for this? How has it helped you?
- **Training you have had:** a specific course or training has given you a reason to think about and focus on an aspect of your role.
- **Reading around on websites, in magazines:** an article or website has been helpful in sparking your interest in a particular idea and given you a reason to think further about it.
- **Networking with others:** sometimes talking to others from different schools or colleges may make you think about something in a different way, or they may show how different working practices may be better. This may encourage you to try them out in your own setting.

In practice

Write a reflective account that outlines how thinking about and evaluating your practice has led to improving your work. Give as many examples as you can to show how you have reflected on and developed your practice as part of the process.

AC 5.3 Show how to record progress in relation to personal development plan

Make sure your appraisal paperwork is included in your portfolio so that it is clear how going through the process has supported your practice. You will need to include a whole performance cycle – in other words, from your initial interview with your line manager and target setting, to reviewing your targets and looking at your progress. You will then need to write about how the process has helped you personally and enabled you to improve.

Check your understanding

1. What is meant by a job description?
2. Explain why it is important to use reflection in the workplace, and how this may help you in your practice.
3. How might your own belief systems and values conflict with your role?
4. What kinds of benchmarks can you use to help you to evaluate your knowledge, performance and understanding?
5. What is the purpose of a professional appraisal?
6. What sources of support are available to help you to plan and review your professional development?
7. Which of the following are NOT suitable as SMART targets?
   - Completing a Makaton course.
   - Completing maths and English level 2 qualifications.
   - Shadowing an experienced assistant who is working with an individual child.
   - Making sure you give feedback to the teacher after each session.
   - Developing ICT skills.
8. How can other professionals with whom you come into contact help you with your personal development plan?

Assessment preparation

Carrying out the appraisal process in your workplace and showing that you have done this over time will cover many of the criteria you are required to meet for this unit. You must include all of the documents you use as work products (AC 1.1, 2.2, 3.1, 3.2, 4.1, 4.2, 4.3, 5.1, 5.2, 5.3).

For the others, you will need to write a reflective account explaining the following:

1. How reflection supports improving the quality of the learning environment (AC 2.1)
2. How your own values, belief systems and experiences might affect your working practice (AC 2.3).

Legislation

There is no legislation for this unit.

Read about it

Weblinks

www.gov.uk/government/publications/send-code-of-practice-0-to-25 SEND Code of Practice

www.seap.org.uk SEAP – advocacy support; this organisation is an independent service to support the rights of vulnerable people

12 Support children and young people's speech, language and communication

About this unit

This unit is about the importance of children and young people's speech, language and communication, and how these affect their overall development. You will need to know about the speech, language and communication needs that children and young people may have and how they are affected by them. You will also need to know how to contribute to a positive learning environment that best supports the language development of children and young people, both when supporting individuals and in groups. Finally, you should be able to reflect on your own role and consider how you influence the development of the speech, language and communication of the children and young people with whom you work within the learning environment.

Learning outcomes

By the end of this unit you will:

LO1 Understand the importance of speech, language and communication for children and young people's overall development

LO2 Understand the role of support staff when supporting speech, language and communication development in the learning environment

LO3 Be able to provide support for the speech, language and communication development of children and young people in the learning environment

LO4 Be able to contribute to maintaining a positive environment that supports speech, language and communication

Getting started

Think about all the different ways you communicate with others over the course of 24 hours. Include the number of times you use your phone to message people or 'like' posts on social media. You may use speech, language, other communication or a combination. Why do you think it is so important for us as humans to be able to communicate with one another?

LO1 Understand the importance of speech, language and communication for children and young people's overall development

AC 1.1 Explain each of the terms: speech; language; communication; speech, language and communication needs

Speech

Speech is defined in the dictionary as 'the expression or the ability to express thoughts and feelings by articulate sounds'. In order to speak we have to use the air that travels through our mouth and nose to form specific sounds with our mouth, tongue, teeth and lips, as well as using our muscles and vocal chords. This is a complex process, which also involves the sending out of signals from the brain to make the desired sounds.

Language

Language is a form of communication that can be spoken or written, and that uses words and symbols in a structured way. It also refers to the way in which meaning is communicated, including expression, gestures and body language.

Communication

This is the way in which we exchange information, thoughts or feelings through different media. Communication is important because it enables us to understand what others want to tell us, as well as express what we want to say. As humans, we need to be able to communicate our thoughts and needs to others.

Activity

Carry out an activity in which you are not looking at the person you are communicating with. Sit back to back and give them instructions about how to redraw a simple picture that you are looking at, then compare the two pictures.

- Do you think this activity is more difficult because you can't see their facial expressions?
- How much do we rely on gestures and eye contact when talking to others?

All of the methods listed in Figure 12.1 will help us to communicate with others. Depending on our own strengths and abilities, we may use some or all of them, although their use may be dependent on our own understanding of some of the nuances of language, gestures and expression.

Speech, language and communication needs

If a child or young person has difficulties in listening, understanding or communicating with others, they may have speech, language and communication needs, or SLCN. These may be caused by any of the following, or sometimes by a combination.

Speech and language delay

This means that the child or young person's use of speech and language is progressing at a slower rate than others, although it is in the usual order.

Speech and language disorder

This means that the child or young person's use of speech and language is not developing in the expected way or in the usual order. It can affect both their expressive and receptive language.

Expressive language needs

This is the way in which individuals make themselves understood through using words and expression. This may be through speech, signing or written language. Some children and young people with speech and language needs may have a smaller vocabulary than others of the same age, or experience difficulty in remembering words or tenses and using more complex sentence structures.

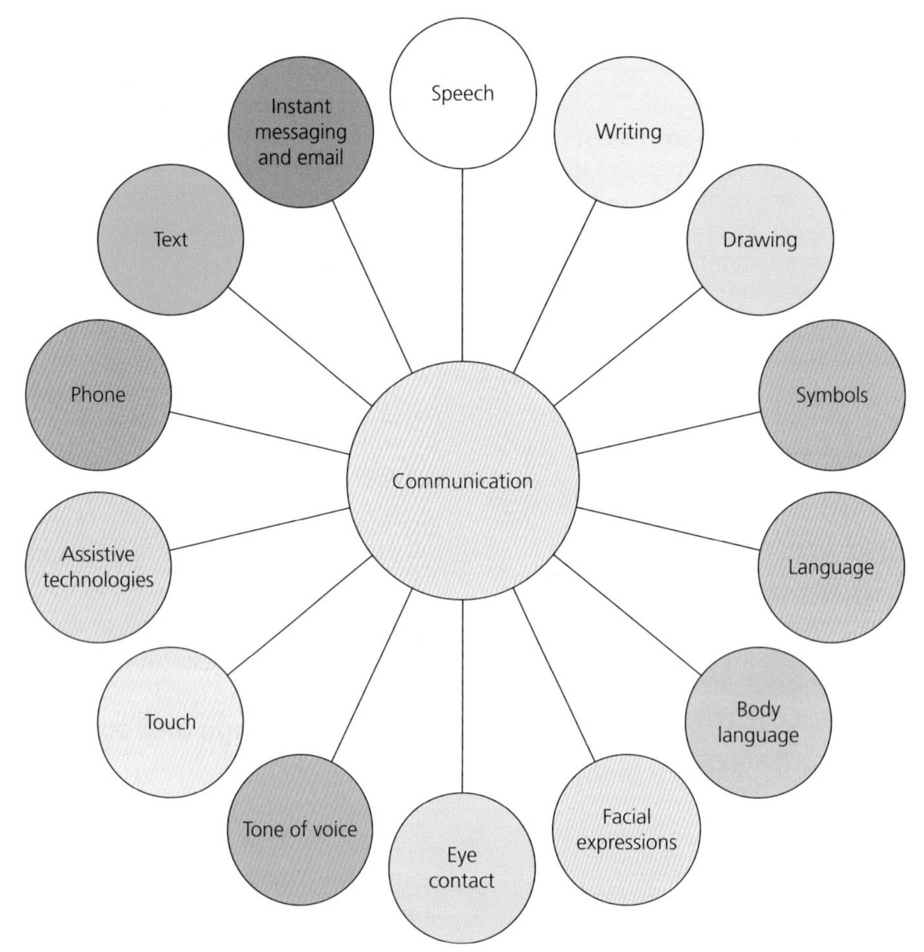

▲ Figure 12.1 Methods of communication

Receptive language needs

This is the way in which individuals understand and process information. Children who have problems with this may find it difficult to understand instructions or pay attention in a group situation.

Selective mutism

This is a complex anxiety-based mental health disorder that affects around 1 in 150 children in the UK and prevents them from speaking in some social situations. Although the term 'selective' implies that the child is choosing not to speak, this is not the case. They will usually be able to speak with familiar people at home but find that they are unable to do so when at school and around different people. Selective mutism is more common in girls and will usually pass over time with support from speech and language therapists. However, it can continue into adulthood.

Autism

Children with autism will often find the process of communication difficult as one of the features of the condition is issues with communication and interaction. In some cases they do not see a need to communicate, so may avoid these kinds of situations and prefer to 'screen out'.

Speech, language and communication needs are often developmental, but they can also be acquired, for example after an injury or a stroke when the part of the brain responsible for language has been affected. Aphasia, for example,

Research it

Selective mutism can be very debilitating for the individual. Find out more about it and the best ways of supporting children and young people who may be affected by the condition.

Case study

Aaron, aged 7, has recently been diagnosed with a speech and language disorder that affects both his receptive and expressive language. He has some difficulties in understanding language unless it is set out in a very straightforward way. He is quite shy and is having difficulties with reading and writing. The class teacher has asked you to work on some speech therapy targets with him.

1. How might other areas of Aaron's development be affected by this?
2. Why is it important to carry out the therapy on a regular basis?

is a brain-based disorder that affects the way in which people use words both for speaking and reading or writing.

Speech, language and communication needs are often hidden and it is not always clear that the child or young person has them. Practitioners will need to work alongside their SENCo and other professionals if they have concerns about the communication needs of a child or young person.

For more on these speech, language and communication needs, and how they may affect other areas of development, see AC 1.3 in this unit.

See Unit 4, AC 1.1, page 54, which discusses why effective communication is beneficial.

AC 1.2 Describe theoretical perspectives in relation to speech, language and communication development

To explore different theoretical perspectives, we are going to consider five well known theorists to find out more about their contribution to language development (see Table 12.1). Their theories are based on the 'nature vs nurture' approach – in other words, while some theorists thought that the way in which children learn language is innate, others believed that it is influenced by their need to communicate with others and the way in which they respond.

Stretch and challenge

What more can you find out about these theories? How do they help us to understand more about the way in which children learn to use language? Do you think that it is through nature, nurture – or both?

AC 1.3 Explain how children and young people's speech, language and communication skills affect other areas of development

Difficulties in the areas of speech, language and communication will affect other areas of children and young people's development as they are interrelated. This is particularly true of social, emotional and cognitive development. It is interesting to note that, of all the areas of special educational need, speech, language and communication difficulties are the most prevalent need of primary school children.

Social and emotional development

This area of development is about how children and young people learn to express and manage their feelings and emotions. It also relates to the way in which they develop relationships with others.

- Speaking, listening and communication develops between parents, carers and their children, and helps in the formation of the child's first secure attachment.
- If children or young people are not talking, or if their speech is unclear, this will affect their self-esteem and confidence as they may see themselves as less able or popular – good communication skills make individuals feel more confident, but poor communication skills can affect children and young people in a negative way.
- Without the necessary language, children and young people may become frustrated as they will not be able to express how they are feeling. They may have problems controlling their behaviour as they will not have the language to express what they want to say.

▼ Table 12.1 The theories of nature vs nurture

Theorist	Theory
Noam Chomsky, 1928 (nature)	Chomsky believed that young children are born with what he called a 'Language Acquisition Device', which helps them to understand the system of language, in other words to make sense of syntax and grammar. They are able to make sense of grammar and apply the rules through this inbuilt mechanism.
Jean Piaget, 1896–1980 (nature)	Piaget had a similar idea to Chomsky in that the language system is inbuilt, however, he puts it down to different stages that the individual must pass through in order to process language. He believed that it could not occur until the individual had the ability to represent symbols and that cognitive development led to the growth of language.
BF Skinner, 1904–1990 (reinforcement)	Skinner's theory is based on the idea of behaviourism. He believed that language development was based on environmental influences, and that children learn through positive reinforcement by repeating language that is met with positive responses. For example, if a child puts her arms out and says 'up', and then the parent picks her up, this is a rewarding outcome, which will boost the child's language development.
Lev Vygotsky, 1896–1934 (nurture)	Vygotsky believed that language development was based on social interaction rather than just reinforcement. In other words, its greatest influence was through the child's surroundings and the extent to which they were able to socialise with others in different social environments. This idea takes into account Skinner's ideas, as the child's language development will be reinforced through positive motivators.
Jerome Bruner, 1915–2016 (nurture)	The next stage in this theory is that of Bruner. He believed that we have a Language Acquisition Support System (LASS), which means that adults support the language development of children through encouraging them in social situations, for example, through asking questions, pointing and using other gestures during speech. This is crucial in helping to acquire language, and children who have not experienced the support of caregivers have problems in their language development.

- Socially, they may find it more difficult to make friends and develop relationships with others. Friendships are very important as they enable children and young people to learn to share and be aware of others' feelings and needs, and develop empathy. Poor communication skills will be a barrier to positive play experiences.
- They may feel left out as they may not pick up on signals given through gestures or vocabulary.
- If children or young people are anxious due to their communication needs, they may develop a stutter or a stammer.

Cognitive development

Children and young people need language in order to learn – the process of teaching and learning is dependent on language and on interacting with others.

- In most children between the ages of 3 and 6, vocabulary will extend from 900 to up to 14,000 words. Being stimulated in this way will support a child's cognitive development.
- Children and young people who have poor language skills are at a disadvantage as they will find it more difficult to listen to others and to put their own ideas forward in the classroom.
- Without a good grasp of language, it will be more difficult for children and young people to order and process their thoughts, which will mean that more abstract ideas will be difficult for them.

▲ Figure 12.2 How does the development of speech and language support other areas of a child or young person's development?

- Having a good memory is vital for the development of knowledge, and also for the development of language, so one will feed the other.
- Research shows that bilingualism supports better cognitive performance, finding that language helps children to master more complex cognitive tasks.
- Communicating with others is a form of stimulation that will positively affect cognitive development as it develops neural pathways in the brain.
- Being able to use language effectively enables children and young people to ask questions, experiment and develop their ideas.

See Unit 5, LO2, page 79, for more about factors affecting children and young people's development.

AC 1.4 Describe the potential impact of speech, language and communication needs on holistic development in the short and long term

As well as affecting overall development, difficulties with speech, language and communication are likely to affect the child or young person in the longer term.

▲ Figure 12.3 Potential impact of speech, language and communication difficulties

Poor literacy skills

Spoken language skills are crucial in supporting early literacy. If a child has early speech, language and communication difficulties, they are extremely likely to struggle with an aspect of reading or writing. According to I CAN, the children's communication charity, there is strong research to show that 50–90 per cent of children who have SLCN go on to have reading difficulties. These can have long-term effects if they are not resolved at an early stage.

Feelings of isolation, low self-esteem

Children and young people who have poor communication skills are likely to suffer feelings of isolation and low self-esteem in the long term. This is because they are less likely to interact with others and find social situations more difficult. This may be self-perpetuating and long term if they are not encouraged to communicate through working one to one or in small groups to develop their confidence.

Mental health issues

Speech, language and communication difficulties will put children and young people at a greater risk of ongoing mental health issues. This is because they will be limited in how much they are able to communicate with others and discuss how they are feeling. This is important for the development of self-esteem and to prevent anxiety. Children and young people who have SLCN are a third more likely to develop mental health problems as they get older.

Research it

Find out more about why speech and language are so important for the development of reading and writing.

Stretch and challenge

The Rose Review into the teaching of reading (published in 2006) outlined the importance of speaking and listening skills for the development of reading. What were its key findings about the relationship between reading and speaking and listening?

Poor behaviour

This is likely to be caused by frustration if children and young people are not able to explain how they are feeling or if they do not understand what others are saying to them. This may then become a cycle as the child or young person develops patterns of behaviour. In some cases, SLCN are undiagnosed and poor behaviour is put down to conduct disorder or behavioural issues. Studies by I CAN show that two-thirds of 7–14 year olds with serious behaviour problems have language impairment, and that at least 60 per cent of young people in young offender institutions have communication difficulties (Bercow, 2008).

Poor social skills

Children and young people who have speech, language and communication needs are more likely to have poor social skills when relating to others. These may include:

- lack of awareness of conversational 'norms' such as taking turns, listening skills, awareness of others' personal space
- difficulty in understanding the emotions of others, such as reading facial expressions and body language, knowing the vocabulary of emotions
- not being able to deal with conflict situations – for example, anger management skills – not being able to ask others for help, not being able to respond in a non-aggressive way
- lack of friendship skills, such as knowing how to choose appropriate friends, being able to deal with peer pressure, understanding the meaning of what others are saying
- difficulty in understanding the importance of being pleasant to be around – for example, by being polite and kind to others, smiling and offering to help.

The long-term effects of this can include isolation and reduced confidence when communicating with others, which can in turn lead to low mood and depression.

Reduced level of employability

The UK Commission for Employment and Skills reported in 2009 that 47 per cent of employers find it difficult to find employees with sufficient levels of oral communication skills, and report that this is now a higher priority than qualifications.

By being aware of these factors so that we can look out for them, and by knowing about the long-term impact of speech, language and communication problems, we can help and support children and young people more effectively.

Vulnerable to being bullied/missing education

Pupils who have speech, language and communication needs may be more vulnerable to bullying in the learning environment, as their needs may isolate them from others. They may also be more likely to miss education as the social aspect of school or college will be more of a challenge. This in turn may make them feel uncomfortable in social situations.

LO2 Understand the role of support staff when supporting speech, language and communication development in the learning environment

AC 2.1 Explain how support staff can effectively support and extend the speech, language and communication development of children and young people through the use of: visual prompts and cues; different types of interaction; developing vocabulary; using different forms of communication; adapting methods of communication to meet the needs and abilities of children and young people

All adults in the setting will be responsible for supporting and extending the speech, language and communication development of the children and young people with whom they work, as they will learn by listening to and interacting with others in different contexts. As a member of support staff this will be a key part of your role.

If you are asked to work with children or young people who have speech, language and communication needs and you should have help from your SENCo to decide on targets for the pupils with whom you work. You should also be given support and training if you are asked to use resources or equipment to support your work with them. There are different kinds of augmentative and alternative communication (AAC) that can be used: no tech, low-tech and high-tech.

Visual prompts and cues

These are often used with young children or with children and young people who have autistic spectrum disorder (ASD). They are helpful as they give another clue to the pupil about what is being said or information that needs to be passed on, which may be difficult for them to understand when presented verbally. Visual prompts and cues will help the child or young person to focus on the important information, rather than being distracted by other things in the learning environment, for example children and young people with ASD will be particularly sensitive to sounds.

Visual prompts are known as *no-tech* forms of communication as they do not need any additional equipment. They are usually gestures such as pointing, nodding, gesturing or touching an object so that the child is drawn to the important information. Cues are usually items such as cards, which show simple symbols that depict what the pupil needs to do. These are known as *low-tech* communication systems. They can be used both to pass information to the pupil and for pupils to pass information to adults. In many early years and primary classrooms, visual timetables or schedules are used as they are helpful to all young children in understanding what will be happening that day. If symbols are used, this should be consistent so that pupils become used to them and understand the meaning of each one.

Some pupils with autism, or those with selective mutism, may have these kinds of cards in their pocket so that they can ask for

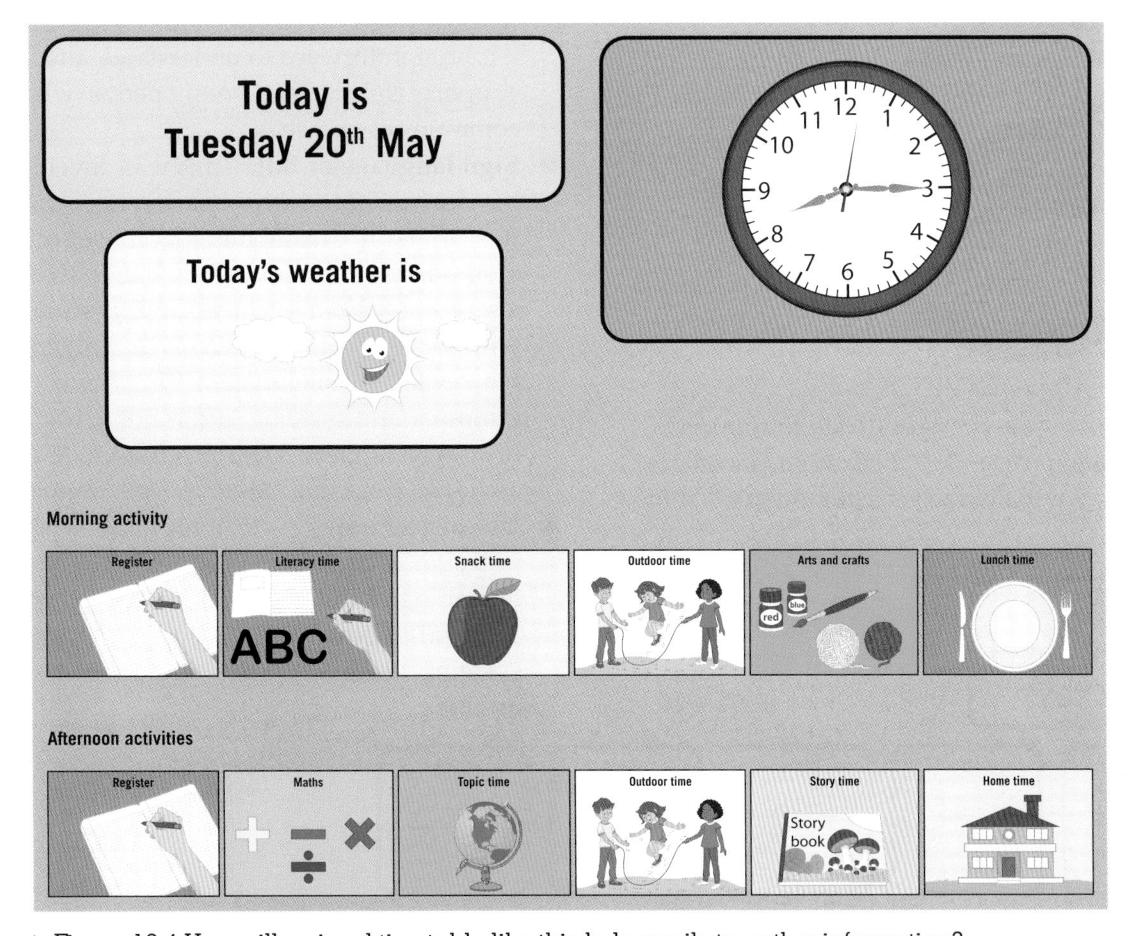

▲ Figure 12.4 How will a visual timetable like this help pupils to gather information?

what they need without pressure, for example, if they need the toilet, their asthma pump or are feeling unwell.

Visual supports can also be used to help with social skills such as understanding the 'rules' of conversation, understanding danger or, for older pupils, supporting independent living skills.

For some pupils it will make sense to show this as a visual prompt through the use of speech bubbles:

This symbol is to demonstrate to pupils that they are not allowed to enter:

Some symbols are designed to support pupils when making requests. For example, 'I want' or 'I need'. They will then select a picture of what this may be:

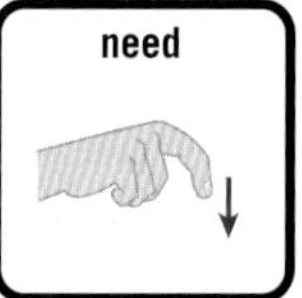

Research it

What kinds of approaches use visual prompts and cues to help pupils? How are they used and why are they effective?

Visual prompts and cues are very effective because, as well as supporting understanding, they help to promote independence and reduce some of the anxiety that children and young people may have around speaking and listening to others.

Different types of interaction

The use of prompts and cues is one type of interaction that may be used with pupils who have these kinds of needs. Other types may include the following.

- **Makaton** – this form of communication is a programme that involves gestures and signs in order to support spoken language. It is often used in schools and colleges as it is straightforward to understand, and supports children and young people who have communication needs.
- **Sign language or BSL** – this was developed for the deaf or those with a hearing impairment. It is similar to Makaton in that it uses other methods to communicate meaning, in this case a series of hand movements and gestures along with body language and facial expressions. However, it is a language with its own grammar and systems, and is not a 'translation' of spoken English. The signs used in Makaton are taken from those used in sign language.
- **Use of technology** – in some cases when individuals are unable to speak, assistive technologies may be used to support them. These are known as *high-tech* communication systems. (See AC 3.2, page 195, for more on this.)

Developing vocabulary

It is also helpful to work on developing different vocabulary with pupils who have speech, language and communication needs as this will also help them with reading skills; knowledge of the meanings of words will help children and young people with decoding. There are specific types of interventions and programmes available that relate to receptive vocabulary and word finding so that children can understand and participate in learning activities more effectively.

Using different forms of communication

The three forms of communication are written, verbal and non-verbal. In written communication, the meaning is read and can be re-read. In verbal communication, the meaning is listened to, and in non-verbal communication it is observed. Children and young people who have SLCN may find it difficult to process information quickly and assimilate the full meaning when they are listening to it; it is therefore helpful to use different methods to back it up, such as Makaton or non-verbal communication. In some cases they may also use technology to support this. (See AC 3.2 on page 195 and also Unit 4, AC 4.1, page 61 for more on this.)

Activity

Find out about the kinds of interventions that are used in your school or college to promote speech, language and communication. How are levels of success measured?

Adapting methods of communication to meet the needs and abilities of children and young people

You may need to adapt the way in which you communicate for different reasons.

- **Due to the age or abilities of the child or young person** – you will need to have knowledge and an awareness of the different levels of ability and attention that children and young people may have when communicating. Depending on their age and level of ability, you will need to model the correct use of language, make allowances for their level of understanding – particularly with vocabulary – and support them when they need to talk things through in different contexts. (See also LO3 on page 194.)
- **Due to the context** – in schools and colleges there may be a number of different contexts in which you speak to children and young people. These will include formal teaching and learning situations, and social situations such as break times. You will need to adapt the kind of language and vocabulary you use in these different contexts so that the level of formality is appropriate, and it is also important to remain the level of formality that is appropriate between pupil and adult.
- **Due to communication differences and special educational needs** – you will need to be sensitive to communication differences if you are working with pupils who have SLCN. For example, if you are working with a pupil who has a speech and language disorder and is

Tips for best practice: supporting speech, language and communication development

- Make sure pupils with SLCN are sitting facing you and away from distractions so that they can see you clearly when you are speaking.
- Take time to listen to children and young people and show that you are interested in what they have to say.
- Ensure that you are aware of their needs and abilities, particularly if they find communication more challenging, and adapt how you communicate if necessary.
- Give children and young people 'think time' if they need it and do not pressure them to speak.
- Find opportunities for pupils to speak in different contexts.
- Ask pupils to repeat things back to you in their own words to check their understanding.
- Find a system that pupils can use to ask for assistance if they cannot understand, such as a help card.
- Use body language, a signing system and/or facial expressions when you are speaking to them, to back up what you are saying.
- Give plenty of praise.

anxious, you should not rush them to speak or put them under pressure to do so. In addition, if you are working with pupils who have additional needs you may need to have specific training to enable you to adapt the way in which you communicate with them.

LO3 Be able to provide support for the speech, language and communication development of children and young people in the learning environment

AC 3.1 Demonstrate how to provide support for speech, language and communication for individuals, children and/or young people taking into account the: age; specific needs; abilities; home language; children and young people's own interests

You will need to show how you provide support for children and young people's speech, language and communication development, while taking the following factors into account.

Age

You should show an awareness of how the age of the children or young people you work with affects the way in which you interact with them. For example, when speaking with very young children you might spend more time on nursery rhymes and songs, or encouraging them to listen to one another to resolve conflicts. As children become older you may involve them in planning activities involving teamwork where they need to collaborate and show respect to their peers so that they can take part. With secondary pupils and older children, involve them in debates or give them the chance to give presentations and develop their confidence. Make sure there are plenty of opportunities for different types of speaking and listening so that children and young people can develop their skills in different ways. (For more about this, see LO2 on page 190 of this unit.)

Specific needs

If pupils have specific needs, you are likely to need additional training so that you can support them effectively. This should come from your SENCo or from a speech and language therapist, and the child or young person may have an **Education, Health and Care (EHC) plan** so that all who are involved will know what is needed. If you work with a pupil who has specific needs, you should know their targets and your role in supporting them.

Abilities

You should be able to use the type of language that is appropriate for the abilities of the children and young people you work with, whatever that may be. Sometimes you may be asked to work with gifted and talented pupils, or those who have a particular interest. You should personalise the kind of language you use where you can, so that you can engage and motivate pupils, as well as ensure that they understand and respond to you.

▲ Figure 12.5 How much do you know about the specific needs and abilities of the pupils you work with?

Key term

Education, Health and Care (EHC) plan: a plan in England and Wales for a child or young person up to the age of 25 who has special educational needs or disabilities. It will take into account their educational, health and welfare needs, and will set out the additional support they will be given. It will be written and reviewed annually through the local authority.

In practice

Thinking about the pupils you work with, gather as much information as you can under the AC 3.1 headings so that you are able to bear these in mind when you are supporting them, and demonstrate them as much as possible to your assessor.

Home language

Make sure you are aware of those pupils in your class, group or tutor group who speak English as an additional language. You should take into account the fact that a child or young person speaks another language at home, even if they appear to have a very good knowledge and command of English. This is because speaking another language may affect their speaking and listening in English, particularly in the early stages. You should also be aware that if their communication skills in English are still developing, their abilities may be ahead of these and they should have opportunities to develop their skills in all areas.

Children and young people's own interests

It will help you to have an idea of the child or young person's own interests so that you can take these into account when working with them. Children and young people are more likely to want to talk about something that affects them directly or that they are interested in. Even if this is just a quick question about what they have done over the weekend or yesterday, it may help them to start talking to you.

AC 3.2 Analyse how the use of technology supports the development of speech, language and communication

Technology has gradually changed the way in which people communicate with one another – although many of us have always communicated by phone, the advent of the internet, email, social media and smartphones has made communication via technology much more commonplace. However, although technology helps communication, it can also prevent face-to-face speaking and listening, as children and young people are more likely to be communicating through their smartphones or other devices. This can mean that, for children and young people, direct communication is less commonplace than it used to be for previous generations and they can even avoid using it altogether. Children and young people should be encouraged to use technology alongside speech so that it does not replace it.

▲ Figure 12.6 How does technology support communication in your school?

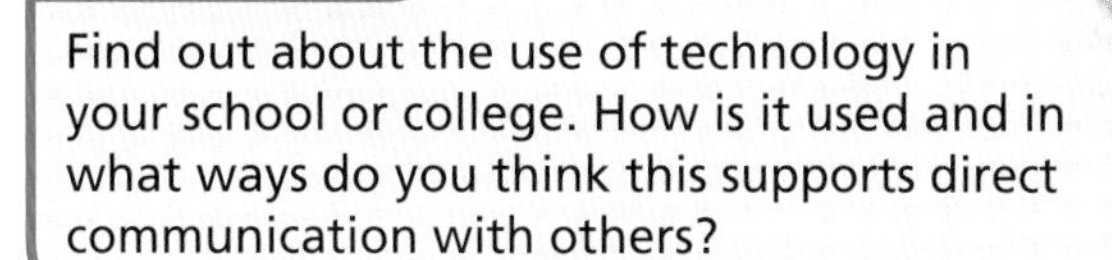

Research it

Find out about the use of technology in your school or college. How is it used and in what ways do you think this supports direct communication with others?

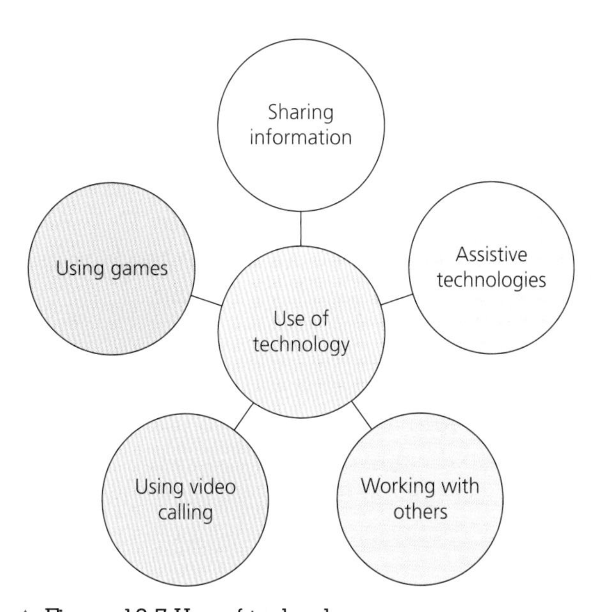

▲ Figure 12.7 Use of technology

Sharing information

For all pupils, technology can be used to support the development of speech, language and communication, if adults and other pupils are able to talk to them about what they are doing. Simply using a camera to record what has happened either at home or in your setting, and sharing photos with others, gives children and young people an opportunity to talk.

Assistive technologies

There are a number of assistive technologies that can support pupils who have speech, language and communication needs. These range from very simple to quite complex technological devices and include the use of different types of communication software as well as eye or other movement-sensitive devices, which help to create messages. Ordinary PC computers can also be helpful for pupils to type out messages or use in other ways to support communication.

High-tech aids may be recommended for some pupils by speech and language therapists. These are controlled by supporting the child or young person in the way that is best suited to their needs. Voice output communication aids (VOCAs) are to help people who are unable to use their own voice at all, and work in a number of different ways, including pre-recorded messages, to produce a synthesised voice. They may be used through devices such as tablets and laptops or through specially designed equipment.

Voice-activated software allows the person's words to come up on the screen. It can be helpful for those with speech, language and communication needs to help them to communicate with others if they are not confident when using their voice.

Activity

Find out what you can about the use of assistive and other technologies to support pupils who have speech, language and communication needs. You can do this in different ways – through research, or interviewing your SENCo or speech and language therapist, or talking to children and young people who use them. You may like to devise a questionnaire or compile their answers in another way so that you can analyse their use more effectively.

Working with others

Using technology to work alongside others gives children and young people opportunities to work collaboratively. They may work on specific projects and use these shared experiences as an opportunity to communicate with one another.

Using video calling

Video calling is a helpful medium as it focuses the child or young person on who they are communicating with. There may be fewer distractions as they know they need to look at the screen and listen only to the person who is speaking to them, and as they are in a different environment they may have to describe what is going on around them.

Using games

The use of PC games, as well as interactive experiences online, can support communication if used carefully. They will encourage children and young people to speak and communicate with one another as well as to take turns.

The Communication Trust has produced a ten-point plan for parents on using technology as an opportunity for communication: **www.thecommunicationtrust.org.uk/media/20750/ten_point_plan_-_making_technology_communication_friendly.pdf**. Some of the following may also be useful for practitioners to use in the learning environment:

- Draw up a list of their top ten games using technology (apps, console games or online). Children and young people can work on their own or in groups but will need to decide on their top ten and say why they have chosen them. They can then extend this by using negotiation and persuasion skills so that others can decide who wins.
- Play 'Name that tune/film/TV programme' by downloading tunes or scenes they will recognise and playing the first few bars. This is good for developing listening skills. Talk about what helped them to guess.
- Use the internet to research what happened in the world on the day they were born. Make comparisons with the day another child/an adult was born, and talk about any similarities and differences.

- Ask them to teach one another or adults something about technology that they may not have known before. What have they found out? What has surprised them?

AC 3.3 Demonstrate how to work with children and young people to develop speech, language and communication in the following situations: on a one-to-one basis; in groups

As a member of staff with responsibility for supporting teaching and learning, you are in a key position as you may have more time than teachers to develop relationships and talking opportunities with pupils. Research projects into the impact of teaching assistants on teaching and learning by the EDTA (Effective Deployment of Teaching Assistants) in 2010/11, however, cited interactions as one of the key areas in which teaching assistants needed to develop their practice. It is particularly helpful when thinking about how you work one to one with pupils. Recommendations on this were published by the EEF (Education Endowment Foundation) in 2015, as follows.

Developing interactions with pupils

Principles of effective classroom talk and effective questioning, and scaffolding pupil learning

We will look at scaffolding pupil learning in Unit 7, on supporting learning activities, however it is important to know about the principles of effective classroom talk. You should be wary of using the following, which is known as the IRF (initiation/response/feedback) model, which was analysed by Sinclair and Coulthard in 1975:

- **Initiation** – the adult asks a question, for example 'What is the capital of Spain?'
- **Response** – the pupil responds 'Madrid'
- **Feedback** – the adult gives feedback to the pupil – 'Yes, that's right. Madrid is the capital of Spain.'

In this model, the pupil only gives the response the teacher wants to hear and there is no opportunity for further talk or to develop the pupil's ideas. It is similar to a 'closed' question, which has only a yes or no answer. It also means that there is very limited interaction between the adult and the pupil, or opportunity to take their learning and the conversation forward. Now look at the following model, known as 'dialogic talk', in which both participants have an equal part to play:

Adult: 'Why do you think it would be good to visit Spain?'

Pupil: 'I would like to go to Spain because I want to see Real Madrid play!'

Adult: 'Yes that would be great. I would like to do that too, and to eat lots of paella in the sunshine!'

As can be seen, this type of talk gives both sides the opportunity to carry on the conversation, and for the adult to find out more about what the pupil knows. Opening questions will usually start with 'why' and 'how' rather than 'what', 'how many' or 'who'. It is helpful both for teaching and learning and for the development of speech, language and communication skills.

For more on dialogic talk and how it supports learning, see Unit 7, page 118.

In groups

Working with groups will be similar in that you will need to be mindful of the way in which you approach questioning and feedback. However, you will also need to think about the group's dynamics and whether pupils are more or less likely to speak and listen due to those who are in the group. Larger groups should be avoided if you are working on speech and communication skills as it may be difficult to involve all pupils.

Stretch and challenge

What more can you find out about dialogic talk and how it was developed? Read Robin Alexander's research project to find out more: www.robinalexander.org.uk/wp-content/uploads/2012/05/wolfealexander.pdf

How can this help at a classroom level?

AC 3.4 Demonstrate ways of supporting children and young people with communication and interaction needs to actively participate in learning tasks and activities

If you are working with a pupil or pupils who have communication and interaction needs, you will need to take your lead from the teacher or tutor and from your SENCo as to how best to support them. As we explored in LO2 on page 190, adults will need to consider different ways of communicating as well as ensure that their own speech and instructions are clear to pupils. It may be worth having a checklist to use when you work with pupils with specific communication needs, to ensure that you remember the points you need to.

See page 120 of Unit 7, which deals with supporting learning activities.

In practice

Complete/amend the table below for pupils with whom you work, showing important points to remember for each pupil, and take this with you to help you when your assessor is observing you working with pupils. You can also use it afterwards to reflect on whether you did this.

	What I need to remember when supporting speech, language and communication
	Sit away from distractions and noise
	Be clear in my expectations: 'I'm looking for good listening and turn taking when you are talking'
	Give praise when your expectations are met
	Allow thinking time/time to answer

LO4 Be able to contribute to maintaining a positive environment that supports speech, language and communication

AC 4.1 Show how to create a positive environment for supporting speech, language and communication development

You should be aware of the importance of a positive learning environment to support the development of speech, language and communication in all pupils and not only those who have SLCN. A positive environment is one that optimises the free flow of communication in the classroom – whether this is verbal, non-verbal or written.

AC 4.2 Reflect on your role in relation to supporting speech, language and communication development

Your role in supporting speech, language and communication development will be to ensure that you make as much of a difference to their communication skills as you can. You will need to reflect on how you do this to ensure that what you are doing is as effective as it can be.

The table in the activity that follows formed part of the Skills for Life strategy booklet. Skills for Life was launched in 2001 to improve adult language and other basic skills for learners aged 16 plus, however, many of the questions raised here are helpful to most learners. It contains a useful reflective log to support practitioners when thinking about ten aspects of speaking and

In practice

Consider the learning environment in which you work and consider whether it contributes positively to the development of pupils' speech and language. Write about or explain this to your assessor so that you can use this as evidence.

listening. You may wish to use this format to help you think about what you do – whether this is through writing it down or talking about it with others.

In addition, these kinds of reflective questions may be helpful to you when thinking about how you approach communication with children and young people.

▼ Table 12.2 Factors affecting communication development

Factor	How it affects communication development
Noise level	It is important to regulate the level of noise that exists in the classroom. While some noise is inevitable and should be encouraged during teaching and learning activities, too much will prevent children and young people from being able to concentrate or to speak and listen to others. Ensure you are aware of the strategies that are used in the room for managing noise levels and gaining pupils' attention so that you can support the teacher and implement them where needed.
Layout	The layout of the learning environment should be such that it supports communication in different contexts, for example, when working as a whole class, in groups or in pairs. If there are pupils with specific needs, such as those with a hearing impairment, these needs should be taken into account during different learning activities and these should be structured accordingly.
Resources	Resources to support speech, language and communication should be readily available and in use for pupils who need them, for example, cue cards or additional technologies. Make sure you know where they are and that they are prepared in advance so that you can use them with pupils.
Displays	These should be labelled clearly and set up to support communication, depending on the ages and abilities of children and young people. Labels and photographs will help younger children to find different areas in the learning environment, and adults should point them out so that learners' attention is drawn to them, particularly if they have recently been put up.
Clear routines	The classroom and wider school or college environment should have clear routines so that pupils know what to expect. These may be displayed for everyone to refer to or simply a part of what happens on a day-to-day basis. For example, a visual timetable will be useful for most children to help them to understand routines and be able to predict what is happening next.
Positive relationships	All adults in the setting should model positive relationships with one another and with children and young people in an environment that enables the flow of communication and opportunities for speaking and listening.

Activity

Using the table below, carry out a professional discussion with others in which you talk about your own roles in supporting speech, language and communication in your learning environment. You may wish to record this so that you can use it as evidence for this assessment criterion.

Aspect of speaking and listening	What you said/did/thought	What worked well	Learning points
Facilitating discussion Consider the amount of pupil talk relative to practitioner talk.			
Asking questions (initial and follow-up) Do you use closed or open questions? Do learners have enough thinking time to answer? Does questioning extend learners' thinking?			

Aspect of speaking and listening	What you said/ did/thought	What worked well	Learning points
Enabling learners to ask questions How do you encourage pupils to ask questions?			
Explaining How do you make sure learners understand the teaching and learning that is taking place? Summarise what you have said to reinforce learning.			
Checking understanding How do you know that the learner has understood what you have said? Do you ask them to repeat back to you what they have understood?			
Listening Do you actively listen to learners? How do you show them that you are listening? How do you help them with their own listening skills?			
Use of non-verbal communication in combination with speaking and listening Do you think about non-verbal communication/use it to enhance your speaking and listening?			
Links between your thinking and your speaking and listening Are you clear in what you communicate to pupils?			
Use of technical/specialist language Think about whether you use any technical or specialist language and, if so, whether pupils have understood your meaning.			
Giving praise and encouragement Consider how often you praise/encourage your learners. Is this verbal or do you give it in other ways?			
Other (Please specify)			

Adapted from *Improving speaking and listening skills – a practical guide for Skills for Life teachers* (DfES, 2007)

Activity

Work through the questions below to help you to think about your own practice when supporting pupils' speech, language and communication.

- How do you explain something that you are teaching in terms that the learner understands?
- How do you ensure that the learner can understand the language you use?
- What tone of voice do you use when you are explaining something?
- How do you make sure that you do not rush an explanation?
- How do you use pauses?
- How do you summarise what you have said?
- How do you emphasise particular points in your explanation?
- How do you incorporate, as appropriate, examples from the learner's everyday life into your explanation?
- How do you use visual aids to reinforce what you have said (such as using a diagram of the National Standards when explaining about them)?
- Do you use any humour to make your explanation more memorable to the learner? If so, how?
- How do you use the learner's body language to judge whether he or she has engaged with what you have said?

Source: *Improving speaking and listening skills – a practical guide for Skills for Life teachers* (DfES, 2007)

Check your understanding

1. Outline what you understand by the term 'communication'.
2. Describe two theories of language development.
3. How do speech, language and communication development affect other areas?
4. Why do children and young people with speech, language and communication difficulties often have problems with literacy skills?
5. Name three ways in which adults can effectively support speech, language and communication development in pupils.
6. Why might poor behaviour be an issue with pupils who have speech, language and communication needs?
7. What factors should you take into account when providing support for speech, language and communication?
8. How does the use of technology support the development of speech, language and communication?
9. What is dialogic language, and why is it important to use it with pupils?
10. How can you contribute to a positive environment for supporting speech, language and communication?

Assessment preparation

This unit will be assessed partially by knowledge as well as through a demonstration of your skills. LO1 and LO2 are knowledge based and you will need to demonstrate your knowledge through the use of reflective accounts, assignments and professional discussions. For LO3, you will need to be able to show how you support pupils to develop their speech, language and communication skills. You will also need to reflect on your own role when doing this and how you use this knowledge to develop your skills.

The 'In practice' in AC 3.1 and 'Activity' in AC 3.2 will help you to gather evidence for this, while for AC 3.3 you will need to demonstrate to your assessor how you work with individuals and groups. AC 3.4 is about showing how you support pupils with communication and interaction needs. It will help you to complete the table provided to show what you should take into account when doing this. The activities for LO4, alongside observation, will enable you to show how you contribute to a positive learning environment that supports speech, language and communication.

Legislation

There is no legislation for this unit.

Read about it

Reference books

Alexander, R. (2004) *Dialogic Talking*, Dialogos.

Alexander, R. (2017) *Rethinking Classroom Talk*, Dialogos.

Alexander, R. (2017) *Towards Dialogic Teaching: rethinking classroom talk* (5th edition), Dialogos.

Alexander, R. (2018) *The Dialogic Teaching Handbook*, Routledge.

Bercow, J. (2008) *The Bercow Report: A Review of Services for Children and Young People (0–19) with Speech, Language and Communication Needs*, DCSF Publications.

Blatchford, P., Bassett, P., Brown, P., Martin, C., Russell, A. and Webster, R. (2009) *The Deployment and Impact of Support Staff Project. Research brief* (online), Institute of Education, University of London. Available at: **http://maximisingtas.co.uk/assets/content/dissressum.pdf**.

Bosanquet, P., Radford, J. and Webster, R. (2016) *The Teaching Assistant's Guide to Effective Interaction*, Routledge.

DfES (2007) *Improving Speaking and Listening Skills: A Practical Guide for Skills for Life Teachers*, Department for Education and Skills. Available at: **http://webarchive.nationalarchives.gov.uk/20130321070106/https://www.education.gov.uk/publications/eOrderingDownload/SandLPACK02.pdf**.

Russell, A., Webster, R. and Blatchford, P. (2016) *Maximising the Impact of Teaching Assistants* (2nd edition), Routledge.

Sharples, J., Webster, R. and Blatchford, P. (2015) *Making Best Use of Teaching Assistants* (online), Education Endowment Foundation. Available at: **https://v1.educationendowmentfoundation.org.uk/uploads/pdf/TA_Guidance_Report_Interactive.pdf**.

Webster, R., Blatchford, P. and Russell, A. (2013) *Challenging and changing how schools use teaching assistants: findings from the Effective Deployment of Teaching Assistants project*, School Leadership and Management, 33(1): 78–96.

Weblinks

www.autism.org.uk National Autistic Society

www.autismeducationtrust.org.uk Autism Education Trust

www.gov.uk/government/publications/exploring-interventions-for-children-and-young-people-with-speech-language-and-communication-needs-a-study-of-practice Exploring interventions for children and young people with SLCN (DfE, 2012)

www.gov.uk/government/publications/speech-language-and-communication-needs-in-the-youth-justice-system Speech, language and communication needs in the youth justice system (guidance) – Youth Justice Board for England and Wales

www.ican.org.uk I CAN – charitable organisation to help children to communicate, and which provides resources and support for schools

www.ispeak.org.uk iSpeak – organisation to help those who have selective mutism

www.makaton.org Makaton charity homepage

www.pecs-unitedkingdom.com Picture Exchange Communication System UK

www.rcslt.org Royal College of Speech and Language Therapists

www.smira.org.uk Selective Mutism Information and Research Association

www.talkingpoint.org.uk Information on speech and language support

www.thecommunicationtrust.co.uk The Communication Trust – organisation that supports communication with children; provides resources for parents and professionals

13 Understand how to support bilingual learners

About this unit

This knowledge-only unit requires you to gain an understanding of the ways in which you can support bilingual learners in the learning environment. You will need to be able to assess their level of fluency in English as well as being able to find out more about their level of competence in their first language and any other languages used. You are likely to need to work with others and share information about bilingual learners. This will also help you to assess their level of understanding. When working with bilingual learners you will also need to consider the kinds of challenges they may be facing and what strategies you will need to use in order to support them effectively.

Learning outcomes

By the end of this unit you will:

LO1 Understand how to contribute to the assessment of bilingual learners

LO2 Understand how to support bilingual learners to access the curriculum

Getting started

Discuss in groups how it might feel to be in a new classroom with only a basic command of the language everyone else is speaking. Think about how this might affect children and young people of different ages socially, emotionally and intellectually. Draw up a three-point starter plan to support the age group you work with.

LO1 Understand how to contribute to the assessment of bilingual learners

AC 1.1 Define the terms: English as an additional language (EAL); bilingual; advanced learner of EAL

If you are supporting bilingual learners, you will need to be clear on what these terms mean and how this affects the pupils you are supporting. For pupils who are new to the school or college, whether this is mainstream or overseas, there may be a greater focus on developing language skills in English, particularly when they first arrive, and especially if they are new to the language.

English as an additional language (EAL)

A pupil who speaks English as an additional language is a learner whose first or home language is not English. In England, the school census showed that in primary schools 20.1 per cent of pupils speak a language other than English at home, in secondary schools this percentage is 15.7 per cent. This figure is steadily increasing due to:

'an increase in the birth rate (rather than direct current immigration) which is driven in turn by an increase in the number of children born to non-UK born women (compared to those born to UK-born women) which more than doubled between 1999 and 2010 (the years in which most children currently in schools were born)'

Source: *Schools, pupils and their characteristics: January 2016*, National Statistics, DfE

Activity

Using the websites of three different schools, one of which should be an international school, look at their policies for speakers of English as an additional language. What do they have in common?

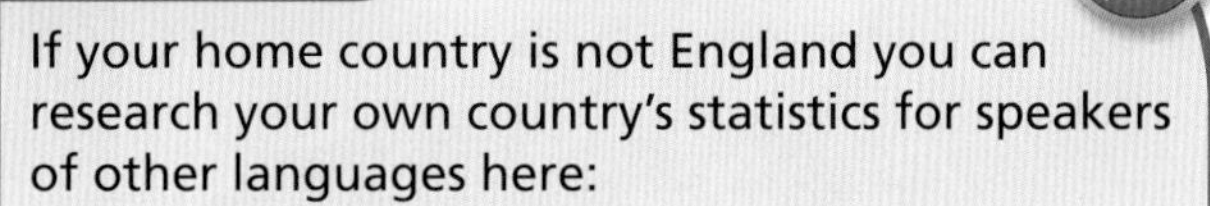

Research it

If your home country is not England you can research your own country's statistics for speakers of other languages here:

Wales – https://statswales.gov.wales/Catalogue/Education-and-Skills or email school.stats@wales.gsi.gov.uk

Scotland – www.gov.scot/Topics/Statistics/Browse/School-Education/Summarystatsforschools or email school.stats@scotland.gsi.gov.uk

Northern Ireland – www.education-ni.gov.uk or email school.stats@deni.gov.uk.

Bilingual

A bilingual learner is someone who is able to speak two languages to communicate. This may happen, for example, if a child has parents who speak different languages so they have learned one from each parent. However, the definition of levels of bilingualism varies and it can mean the child or young person:

- can speak both languages fluently
- is fluent in one language but far less so in the other
- has a minimal level of proficiency in either language.

In addition, bilingual people may be able to speak two languages but be able to read and write in only one, or in neither. Sometimes in schools and colleges, bilingual pupils are listed with those who have special educational needs, although it should not be an assumption that they have these – speaking an additional language and not having fluency in English is not a learning difficulty.

There are further differences between some types of bilingualism:

- **Sequential bilingualism** – if a second language is learned after a first, this is known as sequential bilingualism.

- **Simultaneous bilingualism** – where a person has grown up learning two languages simultaneously, this is known as simultaneous bilingualism.

Advanced learner of EAL

An advanced learner of English as an additional language is a person who has passed the first stages of learning the language and is able to communicate with confidence. However, they may have gaps in their knowledge of the language, or not have the literacy skills that are needed in English. Bilingual pupils are likely to need ongoing support even if they appear fluent in both languages, to ensure that they are able to cope with the demands of the curriculum, particularly at secondary school level.

Case study

Mariam is bilingual, and speaks Arabic and English fluently. She has always managed fairly well with her written work but is now in Year 10 and starting her GCSE coursework. Many of the teaching staff are not aware that Mariam is bilingual because her level of spoken English is so good. Recently, she has started to find the demands of the curriculum difficult as she does not have the level of English needed to answer some of the higher-order questions and has asked you for help.

1. What would you do first?
2. How could you ensure that Mariam gets the help she needs?

AC 1.2 Explain the importance of conducting an initial assessment of bilingual learners

If you are working with bilingual learners it is important that they have an initial assessment so that as much information is gathered about them as possible, and all those who work with them can plan and support their learning effectively. It will need to be done in a way that is not intimidating and they should be put at their ease as much as possible so that they are not made to feel anxious by the experience. All cultures and ethnicities should be valued within the school or college and wider community, and pupils should know that they are valued and supported as they will be affected by the attitudes of others.

An initial assessment should include information about pupils':

- home language and ethnic background
- level of fluency in English
- previous educational experience and achievements
- wider needs, such as their home situation.

▼ Table 13.1 Key information about bilingual learners

Assessment need	Why this is important
Home language and ethnic background	Parents and families should be able to tell the school or college about the pupil's home language and ethnic background. It is important to know what languages are spoken by the pupil and whether others in the setting can support them, particularly in the early stages of learning English. The local authority will also want to know data about first languages that are spoken in the school or college.
Level of fluency in English	This is important so that practitioners are able to set targets and measure language progress for pupils. If you are asked to do an assessment, you should be provided with materials and given support in doing this.
Previous educational experience and achievements	If pupils have come from another school or college, it is helpful to know their previous educational experience and their strengths, and the previous setting should provide information on this. If not, or if this is not available, assessments may be carried out by the school or college to find out what level of English the pupil is currently working at.
Wider needs, such as a learner's home situation	Parents or carers will also be able to tell you about any additional needs the pupil has and what their background has been before starting at the school or college – for example, if they have been asylum seekers or have come from a traumatic situation. Alternatively, they may have always lived in this country but only speak the home language in their community. It is important to know this as you will need to be able to build up a profile of the pupil and get to know their circumstances.

This information helps practitioners to personalise the pupil's learning and set targets for them so that their progress in English can be measured. It may be kept centrally so that it is accessible for all those who work with the child or young person.

In 2000, the Qualifications and Curriculum Authority (QCA) produced a booklet called *A Language in Common – Assessing English as an Additional Language*, to support the assessment of English as an additional language for pupils between the ages of 5 and 16: **www.naldic.org.uk/Resources/NALDIC/Teaching%20and%20Learning/1847210732.pdf**. Although it has now been archived it is still helpful when looking at the assessment of EAL pupils.

International schools may use programmes such as the ISA (International Schools' Assessment), which tests the core skills of pupils whose first language is not English. This is related to international benchmarks and expectations, rather than being specific to one curriculum.

Local authorities may also produce versions of assessment skills tests in order to check language skills. The version as shown in Table 13.2 is taken from the London Borough of Bromley Record of Progress for Bilingual Children in the Early Years Foundation Stage.

In practice

What does your local authority use to assess bilingual pupils? Find out more about the way in which bilingual pupils are initially assessed in your school or college and by whom.

AC 1.3 Identify the types of information relevant people may require, to help them in meeting the learning, language development and well-being needs of the bilingual learner

In your role, when supporting the teaching and learning of bilingual pupils you should know about the different types of information on bilingual learners, which will be needed by those who have a need and right to know. This

▼ Table 13.2 Communication skills for bilingual children in the Early Years Foundation Stage

Skill	Date achieved	Date reviewed	Date reviewed
Makes eye contact with other children (Muslim children may not make direct eye contact)			
Is silent but uses non-verbal gestures to respond to greetings and personal questions, and to indicate meaning			
Watches other children, may repeat words			
Listens and observes adults, echoes words and expressions			
Joins in a repetitive story or songs			
Can name objects (nouns)			
Can use simple verbs, e.g. 'come', 'look', and adverbs such as 'here', 'there'			
Beginning to put words together in phrases, e.g. 'come here', 'me put it'			
Responds to simple instructions			
Can initiate conversations with children in play			

Source: *Record of Progress for Bilingual Children in the Early Years Foundation Stage*, Bromley Council, 2012

information will help them to meet the learning, language development and well-being needs of the bilingual pupil.

Types of information needed may include:

- previous education
- level of understanding
- additional needs
- language used at home/other languages spoken.

Previous education

It is important to find out whether the pupil has had any previous education, either in the UK or their own home country. If in the UK, records should be available so that staff can find out what they can about their previous level of education and whether they have been given support. This will help plan the pupil's learning as well as language development needs.

Level of understanding

An initial assessment will need to be made (see AC 1.2, page 205) to make sure that all staff are aware of the pupil's level of understanding. This information will also need to be passed to the relevant people outside the setting. In some cases where pupils have more specialist language needs, an external assessment may need to be made to check their level of understanding.

Additional needs

This information will be necessary so that staff are able to support the pupil effectively and meet their learning needs. In some cases, and in the first few years of school, it can be unclear if bilingual pupils have additional needs as these may not be apparent straight away.

Language used at home/other languages spoken

Information on pupils' **home language** and other languages used is needed so that staff can take the steps necessary to facilitate pupils' assessment, and also to communicate with them if they do not speak the **target language**. It is also helpful for pupils' well-being needs so that they do not feel isolated, particularly during the first few weeks in the learning environment.

Key terms

Home language: the language or languages that are spoken in the home environment.

Target language: the additional or second language needed by bilingual learners, i.e. English as an additional language.

The relevant people who need to know this information will include:

- family members
- teachers responsible for the learner
- ethnic minority achievement co-ordinator
- bilingual language support teacher
- bilingual teaching assistants
- EAL specialist teacher
- language co-ordinator
- English/Welsh/Gaelic language teacher
- relevant local authority.

Family members

Family members or carers will need the school or college to give them any information it holds on the pupil. This will include information about the level of understanding the pupil has in the target language, or any additional needs they have. If family members do not speak English, you may need to have a translator so that information can be passed between the school or college and home. Family members have a right to know any information about the pupil that is given to the setting, or about assessments that the setting carries out itself.

Teachers responsible for the learner

All teachers who have contact with the pupil should be made aware of the pupil's home language and of any additional needs so that they can plan a programme of learning that will support them in the best way. When a pupil first starts in school or college, the previous school will usually send files and information about their level of development/understanding and academic progress, including any additional needs. If the pupil has come from a school in the UK this is likely to be the case. However, if the pupil has not attended school before, or has come from a situation in which these records cannot be obtained, this may not be possible.

Ethnic minority achievement (EMA) co-ordinator

The school or college will sometimes have an ethnic minority achievement co-ordinator or they may be based at the local authority, although schools are no longer compelled to receive specific funding to support EAL pupils. The EMA co-ordinator will be responsible for monitoring and promoting the teaching and learning of EAL pupils in the school, college or borough. They will need to have as much information about the pupil as possible, including their home language, level of understanding, any additional needs (if known) and previous education.

Bilingual language support teacher/teaching assistant

Bilingual language support teachers and teaching assistants will usually speak the home language of bilingual pupils. They will need information about the pupil's home language and may also be able to assess the level of the pupil's fluency in this. They will also need to know whether any additional languages are spoken, as well as the pupil's level of English. Bilingual teachers give learners the opportunity to use and strengthen their home language, which further supports access to the curriculum, as well as helping them to feel more included. This raises their self-esteem, and so enhances well-being. They are also a valuable link to parents and the wider community.

In practice

Find out what happens in your setting around information sharing in the case of bilingual pupils. Write a reflective account explaining how this takes place and who has access to it.

Research it

Find out what you can about the history of funding for pupils who speak English as an additional language. What are the current levels of funding available to schools and colleges? Is this the same in all areas and countries of the UK?

EAL specialist teacher

EAL specialist teachers and teaching assistants will also work closely with pupils and so will need information about their level of ability in English, previous education and language or languages used at home. They will use this information when planning activities alongside other staff so that they can support pupils by preparing key vocabulary and visual information, modelling language and enabling them when working in groups.

Language co-ordinator

A language co-ordinator will again need all the information possible about EAL pupils in the setting. This is so that they can work with teachers and specialists to monitor pupil progress and ensure that there are sufficient resources available to do this.

English/Welsh/Gaelic language teacher

The person acting in this role will need to work with EAL pupils to support their development of the target language. They will need as much information as possible so that they can support the learning, language development and well-being needs of pupils.

Relevant local authority

The local authority is likely to need information about the number of pupils in your school or college who speak English as an additional

▲ Figure 13.1 How does your local authority assess the language skills of bilingual pupils?

language. They will also need to know the ethnicity and home language of pupils. These data are kept for statistical purposes and are also used to decide whether additional funding is needed for EAL pupils.

AC 1.4 Explain why a specialist assessment may be required

A specialist assessment may be needed if a child or young person has been in school or college for some time but does not appear to be making progress in the target language. Usually, pupils will start to pick up a second language in a relatively short time, even if they have a limited understanding when they start at the setting. However, in some cases a child or young person may not make the progress expected if they have additional needs in addition to their language needs. In this case, a specialist assessment may be carried out by a professional who is internal or external to the setting, and can include one or more of the following:

- level of proficiency in the home language
- any special educational needs
- health assessment
- care assessment.

Level of proficiency in the home language

A check for level of proficiency in the home language will help practitioners to know about the child's ability to process language. This may be carried out by a bilingual teacher who may be external to the school. In some cases an EAL pupil may also have a language delay or disorder and need the support of a speech and language therapist through a block of sessions and follow-up practice.

Any special educational needs

An assessment may be needed to check whether the pupil has any special educational needs as, in some cases, speaking English as an additional language may make this harder to detect. This will usually be carried out by an educational psychologist or a speech and language therapist, who will come into the setting.

Activity

Find out about the following special educational needs:

- speech and language disorder
- childhood apraxia of speech
- social development needs
- a sensory impairment, such as hearing or visual.

How may having one of these affect a pupil who is bilingual? What would you need to do in order to support their learning?

Health assessment

A health assessment may be needed if it is suspected that a child or young person is not making progress due to a health or medical condition. In some cases, for example, pupils may suffer from an undetected hearing or visual impairment that impacts on the development of their language skills.

Care assessment

A care assessment may be needed if the child or young person is in a home situation that is detrimental to their physical or emotional health. They may be living with their own parents or in care, or there may be issues with their housing needs. This in turn may have had an impact on their capabilities in the classroom.

LO2 Understand how to support bilingual learners to access the curriculum

AC 2.1 Explain the importance of using the learners' preferred language to introduce and settle them in to the learning environment

When you are settling bilingual learners into a new environment, if at all possible, it can be helpful to use their preferred language. This is because it will help them to feel that the learning environment is accessible to them and develop their confidence in the new setting. If you are bilingual yourself and speak their home language this is ideal if that is what they wish to use, but you may need to seek help from the child or young person's parents or carers, or others in the school or college who can translate for you. Alternatively, bilingual pupils may prefer to settle in using the target language so that it is easier for them to learn specific vocabulary that they will be using on a day-to-day basis.

As with all new pupils, it will help to talk to bilingual learners about the following things.

- **Their main classroom or department** – specific areas, what they will be doing there, when they are expected to be there, whether they have their own area such as a desk or drawer (younger pupils), where to look for specific information and timetables (older pupils).
- **Rules, timetables and routines** – these will need to be discussed when the pupil is sitting down so that they are not distracted by other things. They will need to be very clear on class and school or college rules and expectations, where they should be at set times, and how to find different areas of the building. It may help them if you allocate a 'buddy' who has the same lessons so that they can be supported in doing this.
- **Toilets, dining rooms, cloakrooms** – pupils should know where to find these areas themselves so that they do not need to ask others. In the case of toilets and cloakrooms or locker rooms, these should be quite close to the classroom.
- **Key staff** – if you are showing bilingual learners around, always introduce them to key staff if you can and make sure that colleagues know that they will be coming. Also, importantly, check that the pupil clarifies their name or what they wish to be known as in class.

Activity

If you can, carry out an interview with a bilingual child or young person who has come to your school or college. Ask them about their settling-in experiences and whether the school or college could have done more to support them at this time. What suggestions do they have for this process and what worked well for them?

AC 2.2 Describe different learning activities and resources that can be used to promote personalised learning including development of learners' language skills

Bilingual learners have two tasks ahead of them – they will have to develop their knowledge of the target language as well as be able to learn in it. After an initial assessment and settling in, school or college staff will need to work together in order to develop a plan that will support the bilingual pupil in the classroom. This is likely to mean sitting down with the SENCo, language co-ordinator or EAL specialist teacher, and class or subject teachers, to discuss targets that will support the development of the child or young person's skills in the target language as well as thinking about how they will be able to access the curriculum effectively. These targets will be personalised according to the needs of the pupil – for example, if they are in the early stages of learning English they may need to have one-to-one support for some of the time. Targets will also need to be reviewed very regularly as the pupil acquires more of the language of the setting and may need a different focus. Teaching staff will need to differentiate learning for bilingual pupils and also discuss the kinds of activities that will support their language development.

All learning activities will be good for the development of language, particularly those that have a high proportion of speaking and listening opportunities. However, in order to give maximum benefit to bilingual pupils, a wide range of different types of activities and resources should be used (see Table 13.3 on the next page).

See also AC 2.4, page 214, for strategies that can be used to support the language development of bilingual learners.

▼ Table 13.3 Learning activities and resources used to promote personalised learning

Activity/resource	Why it is important
Create a positive/inclusive environment for the pupil	Even if you do not have many bilingual resources, you should ensure that the learning environment is a positive one through including linguistic and cultural references and displays for all pupils. Activities should also be inclusive and reflect the different languages spoken, where possible.
Use group work regularly	Collaborative work is a good way of encouraging pupils to speak, as well as giving them more opportunities to hear language being modelled correctly by others. For older pupils, debates, school or college councils or other opportunities to develop different uses of language can be beneficial.
Practise language orally before writing	This develops the pupil's confidence and also enables them to repeat and rehearse what they are going to write.
Using games	Games are a useful and informal way of using language with peers. They are also sociable and encourage the use of more informal language.
Using talk partners	This can be helpful during learning activities as it will develop the use of curriculum-specific language and develop bilingual pupils' confidence in using it.
True-or-false statement activities	These kinds of activities can be fun for pupils to do and also test their understanding. They can also be used with children and young people of any age or level.
Scaffolding activities	This means taking pupils to the next level of learning by building on what they know and extending their learning rather than simplifying it, in order to ensure that they are challenged. For more on scaffolding learning, see Unit 7, page 118.
Describing items/pictures/people	This supports the development of vocabulary and can be used at any time to enhance a pupil's language learning.

Activity

What other activities or resources have you used or can you find that might support the language development or learning of a bilingual pupil? Give reasons for your answer.

See also the 'Read about it' feature at the end of the unit for websites offering activities to support bilingual learners. You may also like to add some of your own.

AC 2.3 Identify the challenges the bilingual learner may face to access learning

Bilingual learners may face a number of challenges when trying to access learning, as well as when taking part in wider aspects of school or college life. You will need to be aware of these so that you can support them if this happens, in order to develop their confidence and help them to feel that they are part of the school or college and wider community.

Racism and prejudice

In schools and colleges it should be clear that any kind of racism and prejudice is not tolerated. This should be part of the school or college charter, and an important and regular focus for discussion as well as forming part of the anti-bullying policy. Racist bullying is also a criminal offence and should be treated as such by staff.

Racism and prejudice can sometimes be subtle or unintentional, if the perpetrator has a set of beliefs that are fixed, or if their knowledge or awareness is limited. For example, they may think that a person who has a name that is not British-sounding is an immigrant and subsequently make comments about where they are from, when they have in fact lived in the UK all their lives. In some cases individuals may feel that a racist comment has been made when the other party has not intended this at all. These situations will need to be managed and talked through carefully.

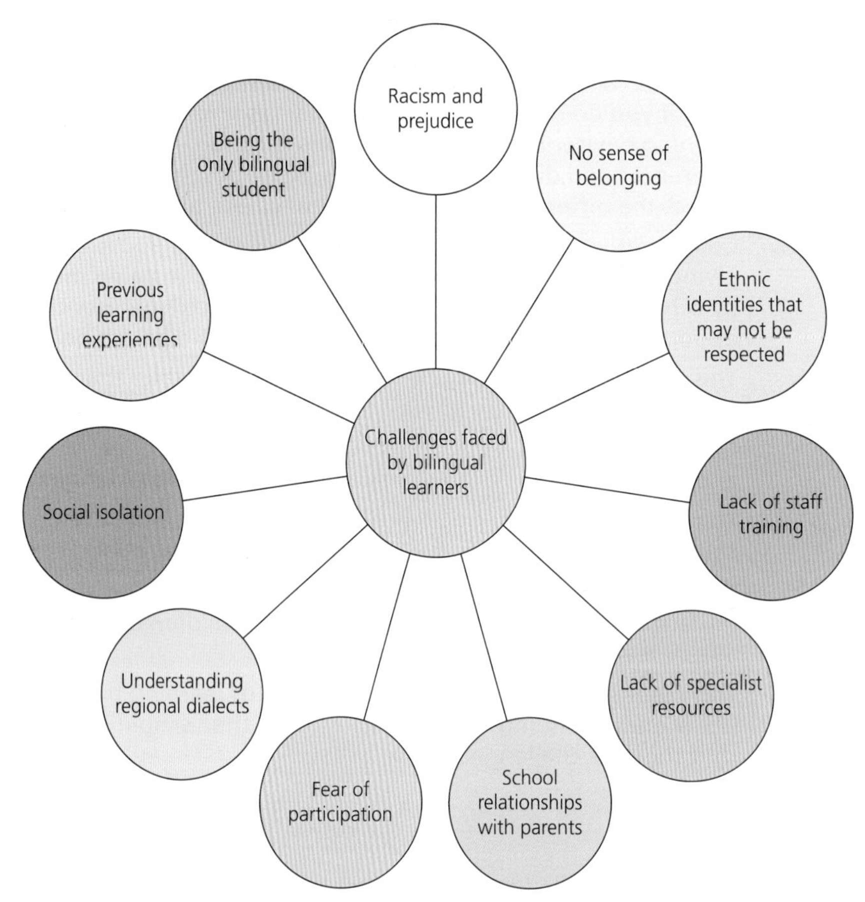

▲ Figure 13.2 How might a bilingual support assistant enhance the teaching and learning of bilingual pupils?

No sense of belonging

Pupils who come from a different culture or community from the majority of others in the school or college may feel that they do not belong in the setting. Each school or college should be a learning environment that is inclusive, and promotes equality and diversity through welcoming all cultures and languages in different ways:

- through the wider curriculum
- through the way in which it treats all pupils
- through the promotion of its equality and diversity policy.

Ethnic identities that may not be respected

The ethnic identities of all pupils should be treated with respect, as all individuals need to be treated fairly and equally. This is true not only on a human level but also under the Equality Act 2010, which aims to promote a fairer society, and equality and diversity.

Stretch and challenge

Using the advice from the Equality and Human Rights Commission, find out about the duties of schools and colleges to prohibit discrimination against pupils.

See *What Equality Law Means for You as an Education Provider: Schools Advice and Guidance* (Equality and Human Rights Commission, 2014). Available from: **www.equalityhumanrights.com/en/publication-download/what-equality-law-means-you-education-provider-schools**.

What does it say specifically about race and religion, and why is it important for schools and colleges to follow this guidance?

Case study

You are an experienced assistant working in a Year 6 class with a newly qualified teacher. During a maths activity, she has asked you to work with a group of six pupils, all of whom are bilingual. Several of them do not need support to complete the activity and you are unsure whether the teacher has put them together only because they speak English as an additional language.

1 Would you say anything and, if so, what?
2 What else can you say about this situation?

Lack of staff training

Staff may lack confidence or not be trained in working with pupils who are bilingual. This can cause issues when they are asked to do so. It is important that all those who are asked to support bilingual pupils have had some training or instruction in how to support their access to the curriculum.

Lack of specialist resources

Some settings may not have access to the kinds of specialist resources that are needed when working with bilingual pupils (see AC 2.2, page 210). If you have been asked to support a pupil without specialist resources you should seek advice from others, such as your language or EAL co-ordinator, about what you should use. In some cases, the school or college may develop its own resources over a period of time, which can be used by all who need them.

School relationships with parents

In some cases, school relationships with parents may be difficult, particularly if they do not speak the home language themselves. This in turn makes it harder for parents to support children and young people at home. There may also be social or cultural differences that will affect the way in which parents or carers view and communicate with staff in the setting, and you should be aware of this. The setting should be inclusive to all parents and families through communicating with them as much as possible and involving them in the life of the school or college through inviting them to different events, or involving them in promoting specific festivals or cultural events. However, parents may be reticent in doing this, particularly if they are not comfortable in this environment and lack confidence in the target language. In some areas, key documents are available in other languages.

Fear of participation

This may occur if a pupil lacks confidence in the target language and is worried about 'getting it wrong'. They may need to have some encouragement in order to participate, or work in a pair or smaller group until they feel ready. Make sure you do not 'over-correct' pupils, as this may diminish their confidence. If you need to make a point about spoken language it is better to repeat back what they have said, modelling the correct language.

Understanding regional dialects

It can be difficult for pupils who are in the early stages of learning English to understand regional accents, particularly if these are very broad. Extra time and care should be taken to ensure that they have understood what is being said.

Social isolation/being the only bilingual student

There can be a danger of social isolation with bilingual pupils, particularly if they are the only speaker of a particular language. Adults will need to find ways of ensuring that they are included in all aspects of the setting and keep a watchful eye on them outside the classroom to ensure that this does not happen. One way of doing this can be to give them a 'buddy' so that they are with another pupil and can get to know another person.

Previous learning experiences

If bilingual pupils do not have previous learning experiences, or their experiences have been very different from those of other pupils, it may take them some time to settle in to a different way of doing things, particularly if they are having problems with language. They are likely to need support and time in order to do this.

In practice

Using a copy of your setting's equality and diversity policy, outline positive steps you could take in order to overcome these challenges and support bilingual pupils to access the curriculum.

Tips for best practice: supporting bilingual pupils

- Make sure you have information about their level of English and proficiency in their home language.
- Ensure you are working towards any targets.
- Ask teachers about any wider needs that pupils may have.
- Use as many resources, activities and strategies as you can to give variety to pupils' use of language.
- Model correct use of English rather than correcting pupils.
- Be aware that pupils may be anxious about speaking English, and try to put them at ease.

AC 2.4 Describe the strategies that support the learning and language development of individual bilingual learners

It is important that home languages are valued and that pupils are encouraged to use them where possible. Research shows that bilingual pupils are able to transfer cognitive and linguistic awareness between languages – in fact, they will also benefit cognitively from learning two languages. They are better equipped at controlling their attention and ignoring information that is not needed. Parents should also be aware that it is very important for them to continue to speak their home language in the home and not attempt to help their child by speaking in the target language. A strong proficiency in their home language can only support the learning and development of the second.

Although you may not be able to use all of these strategies if you do not speak the pupil's first language, you should know about them so that you can use those that you can and also support your colleagues. All situations will be different and each pupil unique, so you will need to use those that are the most appropriate to the child or young person.

Home visit in own language prior to starting school*

This may take place if it is known that the child is bilingual and if there are staff that can assist in speaking to families. This helps the learner as well as their language development, as they will be able to ask questions in their own language and find out more about the setting.

Peer buddy in own language

This can be helpful if it is possible, as their buddy will be able to translate and clarify things for them as they go along; this will both save time and stop things from being missed as there may not always be time to come back to them during the course of the day.

Interpreting oral and written information

Bilingual pupils are likely to need to have support in interpreting information, whether this is oral or written. It will help them to look at any cues that

Case study

Damien is 7 and has just moved to Wales from England. The school to which he has moved teaches pupils only in Welsh. Both he and his parents are quite anxious about Damien having to learn a new language. Although it is the middle of the school year, the head and class teacher, who both speak English, are going to visit Damien at his home before he starts at the school.

1. What will be the advantages of this to Damien and his family?
2. Are there advantages to the school also? What might these be?

are available, whether these are in the learning environment or in the text they are reading. Using open-ended questions can be helpful, as can giving clues to help pupils make connections themselves. You should also teach topic or subject vocabulary discreetly, and clarify and rehearse key words so that bilingual pupils are able to practise using them in context.

Using shared language or appropriate target language to explain information or instructions

Depending on your own language abilities and those of the pupil, you may be able to decide which would be more appropriate in order to explain information or instructions. If possible, you should use whichever language is most comfortable for the pupil. To ensure that they have understood information or instructions, ask them to repeat back what you or the teacher have just told them. This will also support their development of language.

Supporting the use of learners' first languages with peers and bilingual staff*

As already mentioned, developing the learner's first language will support the development of the target language. This strategy will also develop both pupils' understanding and confidence in the setting. It will also encourage more reticent or younger pupils to speak if they are reluctant or unable to speak the target language.

▲ Figure 13.3 What types of resources are available to you when supporting bilingual pupils?

Developing bilingual learning resources such as vocabulary books, and using appropriate bilingual books, dictionaries and materials to support learning

Bilingual resources should be available to pupils who need them, as these will help them to translate vocabulary quickly and independently. Your setting may already have a bank of resources that you can share, or you may need to develop your own as you work with pupils; it would be a good learning activity for you to do this together. Bilingual resources may also be online programmes or apps that can enhance learning.

Selecting culturally relevant resources to increase motivation and involvement

If you can, it will help the pupil if you select resources with which they can identify, such as those that are culturally relevant to them. This will act to involve and motivate them more in their learning.

Monitoring learners' understanding in ways that do not involve the use of the target language only*

If you can speak the pupil's home language you will be in a good position to monitor their understanding and thought processes during learning activities. You should check their understanding regularly through talking about the task with them in their home language, and share this information with teachers or tutors.

Exploiting previously used language to activate prior knowledge and link to learners' experience

If you work with pupils regularly, you should ensure that you remind them at the start of a lesson about vocabulary and language you have used

Class discussion

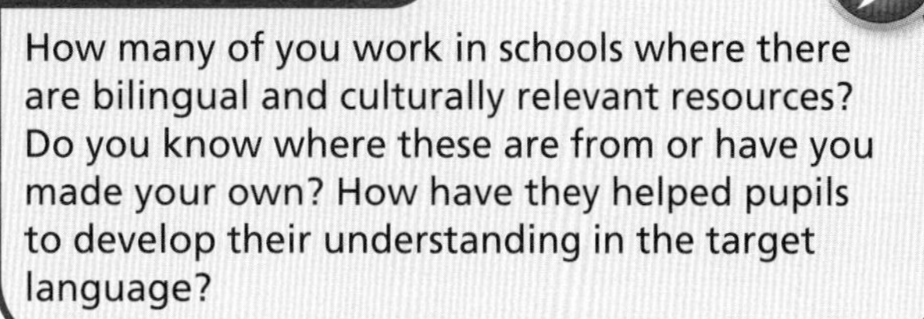

How many of you work in schools where there are bilingual and culturally relevant resources? Do you know where these are from or have you made your own? How have they helped pupils to develop their understanding in the target language?

previously. This may be topic or subject based and will help them to put their learning in context.

Promoting thinking and talking in first languages to support understanding*

Anything that promotes pupils to think and communicate will be positive, particularly in the earliest stages of learning a new language. They will need to develop their confidence and thinking skills, and using their first language will be the way in which they do this.

The following teaching, learning and assessment methods have been added to the guidance as things to think about when supporting bilingual pupils:

- allowing time for learners to adjust and become familiar with the structure and pace of lessons
- ensuring learning objectives are explained clearly through visual supports
- introducing, explaining and illustrating key vocabulary related to subject content
- providing key visuals and displays that illustrate the process of tasks and the steps to take
- scaffolding writing tasks
- scaffolding communication with tasks such as speaking and listening, contributing to discussion/taking discussions further/participating in a debate
- modelling oral and written language to support acquisition
- using ICT programs to support language skills and to reinforce learning
- integrating speaking, listening, reading and writing in the target language
- reinforcing language learning and understanding through repetition, highlighting vocabulary learned, summarising and recording what has been learned and creating opportunities to revisit key concepts through questioning
- encouraging learner responses and promoting interaction using different forms of questioning.

If you are working with a bilingual child, these will be useful for you to consider and use as a reference as you will need to encourage them to use language in a wide variety of contexts.

Check your understanding

1. Explain the term 'bilingual'.
2. How is a bilingual pupil different from an advanced learner of EAL?
3. What is the purpose of an initial assessment and what should it include?
4. What other information should practitioners have about bilingual learners in order to support them effectively?
5. In what situations may a specialist assessment of a bilingual pupil be needed?
6. What types of activities and resources might you use to promote the language skills of bilingual learners?
7. Do you need to be bilingual yourself in order to support bilingual pupils? Give reasons for your answer.
8. What types of activities might be effective when supporting bilingual pupils':
   - language skills
   - teaching and learning?
9. Name three challenges that may be faced by a bilingual pupil.
10. What strategies might you use in order to support a bilingual pupil? Where might you go for support in doing this?

* To use these strategies you will need to be able to speak the pupil's home language.

Assessment preparation

This is a knowledge-only unit so you will need to ensure that you show you know about the different ways in which you can support bilingual pupils.

You will need to use a range of evidence in order to show that you have the knowledge needed. You may gather this through assignments, reflective accounts, or through questioning or professional discussions that are witnessed by your assessor. Alternatively, you can use the questions below to cover some of the assessment criteria. You must make sure that all assessment criteria have been covered by your evidence.

1. Create a leaflet for use at your school, college or academy group for those who work with bilingual pupils. You may like to use advice from your local authority or other local support. You will need to outline:
   - the meaning of the terms EAL, bilingual, and advanced learner of EAL
   - how to conduct an initial assessment
   - why information is needed on bilingual pupils and who needs it
   - cases in which pupils may need a specialist assessment (AC 1.1, 1.2, 1.3, 1.4).
2. Describe different activities, strategies and resources that you have used successfully with bilingual pupils or have seen others use. Note them down in a list similar to that in Table 13.3 on page 211, saying why they have been useful (AC 2.2, 2.4).

Legislation

- Equality Act 2010. This legislation is about our duty to foster equality of opportunity and to protect the rights of all, both in the workplace and in wider society. It merged other legislation to cover discrimination, including:
  - Race Relations Act 1976
  - Sex Discrimination Act 1975
  - Disability Discrimination Act 1995
  - Equality Act 2006/2007.
- Education (Additional Support for Learning) (Scotland) Act 2004. This places a need on schools and colleges to match provision to the needs of each pupil.

Read about it

Reference books

Baker, C. and Wright, W. (2017) *Foundations of Bilingual Education and Bilingualism*, Multilingual Matters.

Ofsted (2003) *More Advanced Learners of English as an Additional Language in Secondary Schools and Colleges*, Ofsted. This NALDIC booklet, published by Ofsted, gives advice to those working with advanced learners of English in secondary schools and colleges. Available from: **www.naldic.org.uk/Resources/NALDIC/Teaching%20and%20Learning/OFSTEDadvanced.pdf**. NALDIC also produces many other publications and offers guidance on a range of subjects around the teaching and learning of EAL pupils.

Weblinks

https://ealresources.bell-foundation.org.uk/teachers/eal-nexus-resources This website provides guidance, and directs teachers and teaching assistants to resources for the teaching of EAL

www.equalityhumanrights.com Equality and Human Rights Commission

www.naldic.org.uk NALDIC – the National Association for Language Development in the Curriculum (UK)

www.teachingenglish.org.uk This site has a wide range of activities to support the language learning of secondary students

www.tes.com Tes – contains resources for bilingual pupils; use the search facility to find these

www.gov.uk Go to this main page and enter 'teaching resources for English as an additional language'; you will find some archived materials, for example, sessions on supporting writing in English as an additional language

14 Understand how to support the learning of children and young people with special educational needs and disabilities

About this unit

Throughout your career in your role supporting teaching and learning you are likely to work with a range of learners who have special educational needs and disabilities. This unit gives you the knowledge and understanding to be able to do this. It requires you to know about the principles of inclusive practice and the rights of disabled children and young people and those who have special educational needs. You will need to know how to obtain information about their individual needs, abilities and interests and about the importance of early intervention. Finally you should know the strategies you can use to support the needs of all pupils more effectively.

Learning outcomes

By the end of this unit you will:

LO1 Understand the principles of inclusive practice and the rights of disabled children and young people and those with special educational needs

LO2 Understand how to obtain information about individual needs, capabilities and interests of disabled children and young people, and those with special educational needs

LO3 Understand the special educational needs of children and young people with cognition and learning needs

LO4 Understand the special educational needs of children and young people with emotional, behavioural and social development needs

LO5 Understand the special educational needs of learners with sensory and/or physical needs

LO6 Understand the kinds of strategies needed to support children and young people with special educational needs and disabilities

Getting started

In 1970, the Education Act made it a legal requirement for children with disabilities to participate in education. Up until that point, many children with disabilities were segregated and classed as being 'unable to be educated'. Look at the following two quotes and discuss, taking into account different aspects of the children's development:

'I was in the hospital for five years and every week my mum used to visit me, but she wasn't allowed in the ward, not once in all that time. She just looked in through the window in the ward door and waved at me like all the other parents. That was really upsetting, much more than if we had had proper visits. She used to leave me presents to have when she'd gone home but of course it wasn't like seeing her properly. All year we would look forward to the garden fete in the summer so then we could be with our mums properly for an hour to two ...'

Jean Hollamby, Tite Street Children's Hospital, 1928–1933 (to be 'treated' for cerebral palsy)

'I went to a school for handicapped children. I could read a bit when I went there but we just had baby lessons at that school. Very basic things like the ABC and adding up two numbers. They treated you like imbeciles. Dressmaking was the main subject, well, needlework. It was all we learnt. We used to just sit for hours stitching.'

Betty Holland, LA School for Crippled Children, 1920s

Source: Both quotes taken from *Out of Sight: Experience of Disability, 1900–50* (Humphries and Gordon, 1992), referenced in *Inclusion in schools: Course book* (Disability Equality in Education, 2002)

LO1 Understand the principles of inclusive practice and the rights of disabled children and young people and those with special educational needs

AC 1.1 Identify the requirements of current legislation in UK Home Nations in relation to inclusive practice

Inclusive education is embedded in legislation in the UK, which requires that all children and young people should have equal access to education without discrimination. This is also a requirement of international human rights law. The requirements of current legislation are incorporated in the following conventions and Acts:

- European Convention on Human Rights (Human Rights Act 1998), Protocol 1, Article 2 – no person shall be denied the right to education
- United Nations Convention on the Rights of the Child (ratified by the UK in 1991)
- United Nations Convention on the Rights of Persons with Disabilities (2009)
- Help Children Achieve More (2010).

Children and Families Act 2014/Special Educational Needs and Disability Regulations 2014

These are tied in to the Special Educational Needs Code of Practice, which came into law at the same time. They streamlined the assessment process for children and young people with special educational needs and disabilities so that it is run jointly by local authorities and health services.

Human Rights Act 1998

This legislation came into force in October 2000. It brought the requirements of the European Convention on Human Rights (ECHR) into law.

Equality Act 2010

This Act of legislation brought together different equality laws in the UK and aims to prevent any kind of discrimination. With regard to inclusive practice, schools and colleges are required to ensure that all pupils are treated equally and given the same access to the curriculum and to all areas of school and college life.

Research it

If you are not in the UK, find out about the requirements of your own UK Home Nation in relation to inclusive practice.

AC 1.2 Summarise the rights of children and young people with special educational needs and disabilities

All children and young people have certain rights, as discussed in Unit 3, and these include the right to an education. Children with SEN and disabilities should be given the opportunity to take part in all areas of the curriculum, and this should be part of your organisation's equality, equal opportunities and inclusion policies. The needs of individual pupils should always be paramount and you will get to know these the more you work with them. However, pupils who have special educational needs and disabilities can be more vulnerable than others. The legislation listed in AC 1.1 outlines the following rights for pupils with special educational needs and disabilities.

- The right to an education; this is stated by:
  - Article 2 of the Human Rights Act
  - Article 28 of the UN Convention on the Rights of the Child
  - Article 24 of the UN Convention on the Rights of Persons with Disabilities.
- The rights of children and young people to participate in decisions and issues that affect them; this is stated by:
  - Article 12 of the UN Convention on the Rights of the Child
  - Article 7 UN Convention on the Rights of Persons with Disabilities.
- The right to special education and care if you have a disability; this is stated by:
  - Article 23 of the UN Convention on the Rights of the Child.
- The right to be treated equally and without discrimination; this is stated by:
  - Equality Act 2010
  - Article 14 of the European Convention on Human Rights.

▲ Figure 14.1 What are the rights of children and young people with special educational needs and disabilities?

Activity

Look up each of the Acts listed and write the details of the rights of children and young people under each one.

See Unit 3 for more on safeguarding and the rights of children and young people.

AC 1.3 Summarise the provision, assessment and intervention frameworks for children and young people with special educational needs and disabilities

When thinking about provision, assessment and intervention for pupils with special educational needs and disabilities, you will need to refer to the SEND Code of Practice (2014). This sets out the statutory guidance for early years providers, schools, colleges and healthcare professionals, as well as youth offending teams for children and young people aged between 0 and 25 years. It starts with an introduction to the guidance and is then divided into the following sections:

Activity

Using the SEND Code of Practice or the Nasen guide, write a brief summary of what is available under the headings 'Provision', 'Assessment' and 'Intervention frameworks'. In this way you will be able to use this as your evidence for this assessment criterion.

1 Principles and legislation
2 Advice and support
3 Working together across education, health and care
4 The local offer
5 Early years providers
6 Schools
7 Further education
8 Preparing for adulthood
9 Education, health and care needs assessments and plans
10 Children and young people in specific circumstances
11 Resolving disagreements

The Code of Practice is available at **www.gov.uk** and you can find a quick guide at **www.nasen.org.uk**.

AC 1.4 Explain the importance of early recognition and intervention for children and young people with special educational needs and disabilities

For pupils who have special educational needs and disabilities, the sooner these are recognised, the sooner interventions and provision can be made to support them. Research on development of the brain has shown that the early learning patterns that are set down will form the basis of all future learning. Pupils with special educational needs and disabilities are at greater risk of falling behind their peers in reaching their potential, so action should be taken as soon as possible to support them through interventions.

The SEND Code of Practice also highlights the importance of early intervention and makes clear the responsibilities of schools in this: 'All schools should have a clear approach to identifying and responding to SEN. The benefits of early identification are widely recognised – identifying need at the earliest point and then making effective provision improve long-term outcomes for the child or young person' (section 6.14). Schools must also publish information to show how they implement their policy for SEND. This has to include 'policies for identifying children and young people with SEN and assessing their needs' (section 6.79).

Case study

Jess is working in Year 2 as a teaching assistant in an international school. Due to the nature of the school, pupils often move on and new children take their place. Jess has noticed that a pupil who has recently started at the school is having some difficulty with her fine motor skills and her whole right side often seems 'lazy' compared to her left.

1 What should Jess do first?
2 What other professionals might be involved in the identification process?

If you are working with a pupil and have concerns about them it is important that you speak to teachers and your SENCo straight away. If this is not possible for any reason, always make a note of any observations you have made so that you can back up what you are saying.

AC 1.5 Identify barriers to participation for children and young people with special educational needs and disabilities

Pupils who have special educational needs and disabilities may face barriers to their participation in activities within the setting and on educational visits. These barriers may relate to anything that prevents them from taking part fully in the activities and experiences that are offered by the school or college. Barriers can be:

- **Organisational** – these are barriers that may be within the organisation. For example, if the school or college is not prepared with an up-to-date SEN or Inclusion policy, or does not ensure that measures are put in place to support them so that they can access the curriculum.

Activity

Using your Equal Opportunities, SEN and/or inclusion policies, note down the different ways in which your school or college supports inclusive practice and aims to prevent barriers to participation for pupils with SEND.

- **Physical/environmental** – these kinds of barriers may relate to access to resources or information, or may occur if the environment has not been adapted or provision is not made for pupils with SEN and disabilities.
- **Attitudes of others** – in some cases, negative opinions and attitudes may still exist when it comes to the abilities of pupils who have special educational needs and disabilities. This means that individuals within the organisation may hold discriminatory views that are not in keeping with those of the setting.

You should ensure that you support the inclusion of all pupils and challenge any discrimination if it occurs in your setting. This may be on the part of governors, parents, colleagues or pupils. Make sure you are fully aware of your inclusion policy and respect the individuality of all in your school or college to ensure equality of access for all.

LO2 Understand how to obtain information about individual needs, capabilities and interests of disabled children and young people, and those with special educational needs

AC 2.1 Outline how to observe and identify the needs, capabilities and interests of children and young people with special educational needs and disabilities

The best way in which you can observe and identify the needs, capabilities and interests of children and young people with SEND is to spend time with and get to know them and their families. By doing this you will gather important information about their background, the impact of their special educational need or disability, and the areas in which they need the most support. You will also find out about their personalities and what interests them both within and outside school or college. If they are new to the school or college, your SENCo is likely to set up a meeting between parents or carers and teachers in order to discuss their needs and how your setting can best support their needs. If you are going to support the pupil, you should either be present at the meeting or given information so that you are clear on their needs and requirements.

Class discussion

How do you find out about the needs, capabilities and interests of children and young people with SEND in your setting? Discuss anything you have found useful and share with others.

You may also be able to gather information from others who have worked with the pupil, including colleagues within the setting, professionals from other schools they have attended, healthcare professionals and others external to your school or college (see AC 2.2). Those who are external to the setting may also send reports or recommendations to help educational professionals in planning to meet the needs of the pupil. However, depending on the age of the pupil and whether they have been in the education system in your country, there may be limited information available to you and others about the nature and extent of their needs. You may need to carry out formal and informal observations alongside teachers so that you can gather information in order to plan for them.

For more on carrying out observations, see Unit 5, page 90.

AC 2.2 Explain the roles and responsibilities of others who contribute to the support of children and young people with special educational needs and disabilities

If you are supporting pupils who have SEND, you will need to be able to work with others, both within and external to your school or college.

Key term

Education, Health and Care (EHC) plan: a plan in England and Wales for a child or young person up to the age of 25 who has special educational needs or disabilities. It will take into account their educational, health and welfare needs, and will set out the additional support they will be given. It will be written and reviewed annually through the local authority.

In practice

If you are working in a school setting, how are midday supervisors and those in extended school provision such as clubs made aware of the needs of pupils who have special educational needs and disabilities? Find out about your school's policy for ensuring that all information is passed on to those who need it.

This is because each of these people will be able to provide information and support so that your school or college is able to meet the needs of the pupils more effectively. They will also give regular recommendations for targets for pupils who have an **Education, Health and Care (EHC) plan**.

Family members

Family members will be able to provide background to the special educational needs or disability of the pupil and should meet regularly with school or college staff to discuss the pupil's progress, both formally and informally. This information sharing should take place on a regular basis so that both sides are kept up to date with any developments.

Teachers/specialist teachers

As a member of support staff, you should work alongside teachers and specialist teachers to enhance the teaching and learning of pupils with SEND. They will devise plans that are differentiated to meet the needs of pupils and if you are providing individual support you may be asked to contribute towards planning. Teachers and specialist teachers will also work with the SENCo to ensure that she or he has up-to-date information about the needs of pupils with SEND.

Other adults in the setting

As well as teachers and specialist teachers, you are likely to work with others in the setting who will also get to know the pupil and work with them. These people will include the SENCo, who is responsible for gathering and co-ordinating information from all those who have contact with the pupil, both internally and externally. Administrative staff, midday supervisors and other members of support staff may also contribute to their support through their job roles, and you may need to liaise with them. In addition, if your school or college runs extended provision, other adults who are supervising or working with pupils will need to be aware of their needs.

Professionals external to the setting

When working with pupils who have special educational needs and disabilities, you are likely to come into contact with a range of professionals who are external to the setting. These may be people such as educational psychologists, physiotherapists, occupational therapists, speech therapists, sensory support professionals and others. Depending on the needs of the pupil, they may be regularly involved in meetings and information-sharing sessions so that the ongoing needs of the pupil can be met. They will also provide reports and recommendations for targets and ongoing teaching and learning needs.

Health professionals

If the pupil has health needs, health professionals such as nurses are likely to provide information to help education professionals to meet these needs. For example, a diabetic or asthmatic pupil may need school staff to ensure they have sufficient medication in school and are monitoring it, particularly if the child is very young. Nurses may also come into the setting to train staff, for example, on how to use an EpiPen for those pupils who have nut allergies. Medical professionals may also need to train school or college staff if pupils need to carry out specific exercises, for example, physiotherapy. Your school or college is also likely to have a policy on supporting pupils with medical conditions and how their needs will be met.

AC 2.3 Evaluate the benefit of working with others to support children and young people with special educational needs and disabilities

There are many benefits of working with others to support children and young people with SEND. Information sharing is of key importance, to enable professionals to effectively co-ordinate provision and meet the needs of the pupil. The views of the pupil themselves should also be sought regarding issues concerning them. Sharing information is also a requirement of section 3 of the SEND Code of Practice. It stipulates that education, health and care professionals should work together in order to improve the outcomes for pupils with SEND. Some of the benefits are described below.

To provide a wider knowledge of the pupil

Adults who work in school may see only that aspect of the pupil. However, each professional will have their own specific knowledge of the pupil and his or her special educational need or disability. Sharing this knowledge will mean that all adults working with the child will have a greater awareness of their needs on a broader scale.

Being able to provide the most effective support for the child or young person

If information is shared regularly between all those who are working with the child or young person, they will each have the best possible understanding of the 'whole' pupil. This will particularly help those in school or college to provide the most effective support and meet their needs.

Sharing professional knowledge

Sharing knowledge between professionals will help to give some background to the child or young person's special educational need or disability. It will also enhance the knowledge of each one regarding the reasons behind different aspects of the child or young person's development.

Providing mutual support

As well as providing more effective support for the pupil, sharing information between those who work with them will be beneficial for the group as a whole. It will also provide a range of ideas and points of view.

> **Activity**
>
> Look at section 3 of the 2014 SEND Code of Practice. What legal obligations do local authorities have to ensure that agencies work together when supporting pupils with special educational needs and disabilities?

When working with pupils who have SEND, information sharing between professionals is very important to ensure that all those working with the pupil have all the information they need. In the same way, parents and families can find it difficult to negotiate the different kinds of support and information that is available to them. Since 2014, alongside the SEND Code of Practice, local authorities have been required to publish a 'local offer' for families that sets out all the information for the local area with regard to special educational needs. This is designed to ensure that information about the support available is all in one place. Each local authority is therefore obliged to provide this to parents and families through a designated website.

▲ Figure 14.2 What is the local offer for pupils with SEND in your local area?

> **Activity**
>
> Go online and find out about the local offer in your area. What information is available to parents and carers?

LO3 Understand the special educational needs of children and young people with cognition and learning needs

AC 3.1 Describe the range of cognitive skills necessary for effective learning

In order to learn effectively, children and young people will need to be able to develop cognitive skills. These are the skills we need to use to process information in different ways. All individuals will develop these skills differently and at different rates, and may be strong in some areas and not in others. However, pupils with special educational needs that are **cognition and learning needs** are likely to need support in several different areas.

Key term

Cognition and learning needs: needs of those learners who demonstrate features of: moderate, severe or profound learning difficulties; specific learning difficulties, e.g. dyslexia, dyspraxia; autistic spectrum disorder.

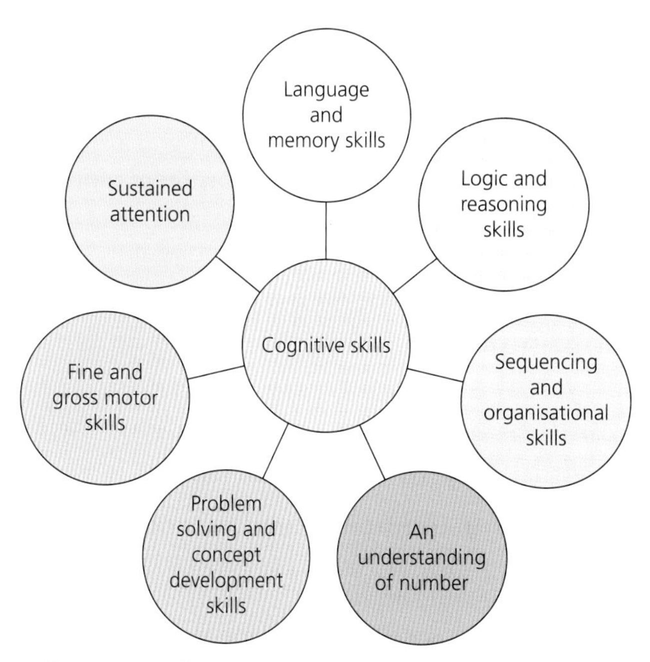

▲ Figure 14.3 Cognitive skills

- **Language and memory skills** – as a child develops their language skills, this will in turn enable them to start to use their thinking skills as they will start to be able to organise information mentally. Memory is very important to learning as children and young people will need to be able to remember and build on what they have learned previously.
- **Logic and reasoning skills** – this is how we organise our thinking in a way that enables us to move forward in our learning.
- **Sequencing and organisational skills** – this is our ability to plan and sequence what is happening in a particular order.
- **An understanding of number** – we need to have a basic understanding of number in order to start to understand more abstract numerical ideas.
- **Problem solving and concept development skills** – this is the ability to think through and solve problems. We often think of this in a mathematical sense, but it can simply be thinking of different ways of approaching a task.
- **Fine and gross motor skills** – this means the ability to move our muscles through using brain signals and 'telling' our bodies to move in different ways.
- **Sustained attention** – children need to be able to develop their concentration so that they can keep their attention on a task over time. While very young children will find this difficult, adults can help them by talking through what is happening with them and asking questions about it.

Activity

What do you know about:

- dyspraxia
- autistic spectrum disorder
- dyscalculia?

How might a difficulty in each of these areas impact on a pupil's learning?

In practice

There are several different cognitive ability tests available free online. Find out what you can about your own cognitive skills and think about how this impacts on your own learning.

AC 3.2 Identify the significant differences between global and specific learning difficulties

While the term 'learning difficulties' may be used to describe some pupils who have special educational needs, it is important to understand the difference between global and specific learning difficulties.

Global learning difficulties

This term is used to describe difficulties in all areas of learning. Individuals may have difficulties in the area of social communication, as well as reading, writing and numeracy and the development of their cognitive skills. They may also need support in developing independence and life skills, and may have limited maturity when compared to their peers.

Specific learning difficulties

This term is used to describe difficulties in a particular aspect of learning. For example, a pupil may have a learning difficulty such as dyslexia or dyscalculia, which only affects their reading/writing or number recognition, respectively. A specific learning difficulty will not affect other aspects of a pupil's cognitive skills but is likely to affect their emotional development if support is not given.

Research it

Find out what you can about different types of specific learning difficulty and how these can be recognised and supported.

AC 3.3 Explain how cognitive difficulties impact upon the development of language and communication and how this might affect learning

Depending on their nature and severity, cognitive difficulties are likely to impact in some way on the development of language and communication. This is because a child will need to have a good developing memory in order to remember language and vocabulary, as well as having the processing skills needed for understanding and using receptive and expressive language and organising their thoughts. The process of learning is also dependent on language and the two skills support each other, so cognitive difficulties will make it harder for these pupils to develop their communication and language skills.

For more on speech, language and communication needs, and how these may affect other areas of development, see Unit 12, AC 1.3, page 187, and Unit 5, AC 2.1, page 80.

LO4 Understand the special educational needs of children and young people with emotional, behavioural and social development needs

Some pupils in your school or college are likely to have behavioural, emotional and social development needs, which means that they will have difficulty in managing their emotions. They are likely to have challenging and disruptive behaviours, specific learning difficulties, such as attention deficit disorder (ADD), lack concentration, be withdrawn or have immature social skills, and others. These kinds of issues can be very challenging to manage, and you will need to know and understand the needs of pupils and the reasons behind them so that you are able to work with others to support them more effectively.

AC 4.1 Explain how aspects of upbringing, home circumstances and physical and emotional health of children and young people can affect their ability to relate to others

Upbringing and home circumstances

For all children and young people, a secure, loving and stable home life is the ideal as this will influence their social and emotional development and their ability to relate to others. They should be able to develop relationships with members of their close family and friends, as well as know the influence of positive role models and have plenty of opportunities for social interaction. The benefits of a secure and stable home life for children and young people are:

- to develop their confidence and learn social skills, which will help them to relate to a range of different people
- to allow them to experience routines and security, which will allow them to feel safe and prevent anxieties
- to experience positive relationships with others and understand how to form them, which will enable them to do the same themselves.

Sadly, in some cases, these positive influences will be disrupted by other factors during a child or young person's early life. They may experience limited adult interaction and attention, living in poverty, having negative role models, an environment of abuse or limited security in their home environment. As a result of any one of these, they are likely to develop emotional or behaviour problems that can be long term. Other factors, such as trauma during childhood, acting as a young carer or inconsistent boundaries for behaviour, may also impact on their ability to relate to others.

Physical and emotional health

The ability of children and young people to interact with others will also be affected by their physical and emotional health. This might include:

- long-term health conditions or chronic illness
- physical or sensory impairments and disabilities
- emotional health issues.

Those who have long-term health conditions, disabilities or chronic illness may find it more difficult to build and sustain friendships; this can be due to being regularly out of classes for treatment or therapy, or because they are unable to physically join in as much as others with some activities.

Those who have physical or sensory impairments, including communication difficulties, may find that interacting with others is more challenging due to the nature of their needs.

Those who have problems with their emotional health will also find relationships and interactions with others more challenging. This is because their self-esteem and ability to initiate interactions with others may be limited. They will be less resistant than their peers to managing different social situations and may find it difficult to build trust with others. They may also find it harder to take into account the needs of others and empathise with them.

To read about the effect of a primary disability on children and young people's development, see AC 5.1, page 230.

AC 4.2 Explain how mental health could impact on a child or young person's life

A child or young person's emotional well-being and mental health is just as important as their physical health. Through having good mental health and a positive outlook, they may be more resilient to challenges in life and more able to solve their own problems when they come up. Mental health issues are likely to have a huge impact on a child or young person's life – if they are not acknowledged and given a voice, the effects can be long lasting. According to MQ: Transforming Mental Health, a charity looking at research into mental illness, 75 per cent of those with a mental health condition start to develop it before the age of 18. The Young Minds organisation, which supports mental health in children and young people, reports that one in three adult mental health conditions relate directly to adverse childhood experiences. If mental health is not treated, and children and young people are not given help, they are at greater risk of suicide, self-harm, eating disorders, and long-term depression and anxiety.

In practice

What does your school or college have in place for developing pupil well-being? Does it offer opportunities for pupils to talk to adults about any concerns they have if they need to?

In order to support children and young people to develop and sustain positive mental health there are also general guidelines that schools and colleges can offer:

- educating pupils as to the importance of keeping healthy, for example, eating healthily and exercising
- adults taking time to listen to pupils, especially those who are more vulnerable
- offering a range of activities and clubs to develop pupils' interests and self-esteem
- developing well-being and recognising pupils' talents and achievements
- being inclusive and giving every pupil a sense of belonging.

See Unit 3, LO5, to find out about signs of mental health concerns and ways in which you can support children and young people to develop resilience and mental well-being.

AC 4.3 Explain how to work with children, young people and others to identify and set behaviour goals and boundaries for children and young people with emotional, behavioural and social development needs

Behaviour, emotional and social development needs may include:

- emotional and behavioural difficulties
- withdrawn, isolated or school-phobic reactions
- disruptive and disturbing behaviours, hyperactivity or lack of concentration
- immature social skills or personality disorders
- challenging behaviours, which may arise from other complex needs.

Key term

Behaviour, emotional and social development needs: these are sometimes referred to as BESD needs. A BESD need is the inability of a child or young person to manage their emotions effectively, to the extent that they will often show inappropriate behaviour when they are in situations that upset them.

For pupils with the types of behaviour, emotional and social development needs listed above, you will need to work with others so that you can develop support strategies and enable them to set goals as well as boundaries. This is likely to involve the input of other professionals such as your SENCo or an educational psychologist. Working with these pupils can be very challenging but they often respond to the stability of the school or college environment and it can be a very rewarding role. Teachers and outside professionals should gather as much background information as they can; in this way they will be able to construct a picture of the 'whole' pupil so that they can find the best ways to help them. They will need to work with the pupil as well as parents and carers, and the pupil themselves will need to want to make a change in their behaviour and take responsibility for doing this.

Setting goals is helpful both to pupils and to adults. For pupils, they should set out simple, manageable steps that they can work on to help them make the right choices. They should be involved in setting goals and understand how these will help them as well as knowing their own responsibilities in the process. Ideally they should be given small steps that are reviewed regularly by pupils, parents or carers and all those who have ongoing contact with them. If your role is to support an individual pupil or you are working in the same class or classes, you should be involved in this process so that you can liaise with others. Depending on the age of the pupil and the type of school or college it is possible that you may have the opportunity to speak to parents regularly and discuss ongoing behaviour at home.

Case study

Look at the following case study.

Maya is 11 and lives with her mum and sister. She has never lived with her father and does not see him as he was violent towards her mother. She moved home several times during her first few years and at one point was taken into foster care with her sister when her mother could not cope. Maya has been back with her mum for two years although they were again new to the area just before she started in secondary school. Maya is now at the end of Year 7 and has been displaying disruptive and inappropriate behaviour with her peers for most of the year. She is working at below average levels in most subjects, although she is a talented artist and enjoys designing clothes, which she sometimes does in her spare time. However, she says 'Secondary school is rubbish.' Her teachers are concerned and several of them have spoken to the SENCo about her. Maya's behaviour is always particularly bad during the lesson immediately after lunch.

John, the SENCo, has a meeting with Maya's mum, Andrea. He finds out that she has problems with Maya at home, and that Maya is argumentative and aggressive with both her mum and her sister. When at home she spends most of her time on the computer talking to her friends, and on social media, although her mum is concerned about this. However, she says she is unable to stop her and says she doesn't know what to do. She has always been a restless child, and Andrea had several meetings at her primary school because they thought she had attention deficit hyperactivity disorder (ADHD) although this was not confirmed.

- Write down individual reasons that you think Maya might be behaving in this way.
- What goals do you think it might be helpful for the SENCo to suggest to support Maya?
- How could the school help Andrea both in the short and long term?

Stretch and challenge

Find out about other ways in which schools and colleges can support pupils who have behaviour, emotional and social development needs. It may help you to speak to your SENCo and look at your school's behaviour policy, as well as looking at what is available locally.

AC 4.4 Reflect on ways of developing self-reliance and self-esteem to support children and young people with emotional, behavioural and social development needs

All pupils will need to be given opportunities to develop independence – this includes the chance to develop self-reliance and self-esteem. From the early years onwards, children should be given opportunities to be independent so that they are able to initiate and work things out for themselves where possible. If adults always do things for them, they will not develop or be able to reach their potential because they will always be looking to others for support. Pupils who have behaviour, emotional and social development needs may find this difficult as they will often lack confidence in their abilities and have a fear of failure.
Pupils who have special educational needs and disabilities because they may need more support and reassurance than others; however you should know when to step back and let them work things out or do them for themselves. It is important for these pupils in particular that they learn to:

- communicate their feelings, needs and ideas
- make their own decisions
- accept responsibility for their actions and the consequences.

Communicate feelings, needs and ideas

It is very important that these pupils can communicate effectively so that they are able to tell others how they are feeling and/or what they need, and are able to put forward their ideas. Sometimes, pupils will have BESD needs due to difficulties in communicating, and therefore experience feelings of frustration that can lead to poor behaviour. Adults who work with these pupils should regularly encourage them to communicate and talk about their feelings and needs. They may need you to give them the tools to do this through developing their vocabulary and talking about what they can do when they feel upset. There are many resources, strategies and group activities that can be used to do this, which you may be able to access online or through your SENCo or teachers, although you should always check with them before using them. Pupils may also find it helpful to express themselves in different ways such as through music, art or drama activities.

Make sure also that you are not always only talking to these pupils about problems or issues that have come up. Get to know them and find out about their interests and ideas so that they can have positive conversations with you and talk about the good things that are happening in their lives.

▲ Figure 14.4 It may help pupils who have BESD needs to express their feelings and ideas in different ways

Make their own decisions

Pupils who have behaviour, emotional and social development needs will need adults to give them the space and time they need to make their own decisions. In this way, they will be able to make a contribution to their learning experiences and enhance their relationships with others. This is because being decisive will help them to form a positive self-image and boost their confidence, as well as show others that they are competent. We may need to support these pupils by making decisions simpler, for example, giving them limited choices rather than asking open questions. By giving them a voice and involving them in issues that concern them, we are also helping them to exert some control over their behaviour as we are developing their sense of responsibility.

Accept responsibility for their actions and the consequences

Children and young people should also know the consequences of the actions they take and may need to have this explained to them. It is important that they are able to make the link between what they have done and the effects. For example, 'Chris, if you carry on teasing Josh and being unkind to him we will have to put you on time out as you are choosing to break one of our class rules.' School or college rules should be clear and all adults consistent in enforcing rules so that pupils know exactly what will happen if they make inappropriate choices. Similarly, if pupils do the right thing, adults should notice and let them know.

For more on supporting children and young people's positive behaviour, see also LO6, page 232, and Unit 6.

LO5 Understand the special educational needs of learners with sensory and/or physical needs

AC 5.1 Explain the effect of a primary disability on children and young people's development

When you are working with a pupil who has **sensory and/or physical needs**, as well as caring for their immediate needs you will need to consider what effect this may have both on their development and their well-being. These may be the effects of:

- the physical disability itself
- long-standing or progressive conditions
- chronic illness, pain and fatigue.

Key term

Sensory and/or physical needs: learners who demonstrate degrees of hearing, visual and/or physical impairment.

The effects of a physical disability

A physical disability will have both physical and psychological effects on an individual. Depending on whether they are born with the disability or not, this may vary, although the impact may be on all areas of their development. It is likely to affect:

- the child or young person's self-esteem and confidence
- motivation – it may produce feelings of helplessness and being unable to do what they want to do
- their ability or inclination to join in with others in some activities, therefore leading them to feel left out
- some aspects of physical development, which are likely to take longer or not be fully possible in some areas, depending on the extent of the disability
- intellectual development, however, this is more likely to be due to lack of motivation or self-esteem rather than the disability itself.

Long-standing or progressive conditions

Progressive or long-standing conditions may affect a child or young person's behaviour as well as making it difficult for them to focus on day-to-day activities. Again, their self-esteem and motivation may be affected, as well as the condition leading to frustration. They may also have feelings of hopelessness or depression, particularly if the condition is progressive.

Chronic illness, pain and fatigue

A chronic illness or condition is one that is ongoing over a period of years, and in many cases is lifelong. It is one that cannot be cured but can be managed and controlled through medication or therapy. It will have a number of physical and emotional effects on the individual, which may feel worse as the illness may not be visible to others. These may be:

- constant feelings of tiredness, which may mean that the pupil finds it difficult to participate in some activities
- side effects of medication, which may also make the pupil more tired or depressed
- constant pain, which may be a feature that can be managed to a greater or lesser degree
- other effects – depending on the condition, there may well be other considerations, for example, the effects on the family, or limited independence.

In addition, these pupils may experience anger, anxiety, frustration and depression due to their condition, and those around them need to be aware of this as it is likely to affect their behaviour and motivation.

See Unit 5 for more on understanding how children and young people develop.

AC 5.2 Describe a range of specialist equipment and technology resources available for children and young people with special educational needs and disabilities and reflect on how they help to overcome or reduce the impact of sensory or physical impairment

Depending on the needs of the pupils with whom you work, you may need to use a range of specialist equipment and resources with them. There are many available, which can make a dramatic difference to the way in which you can enhance the teaching and learning experience of the children and young people that you support, particularly in the area of assistive technologies. Table 14.1 gives a few examples, however there are many more resources available. Your SENCo and any other professionals working with the pupil will be able to give teachers and yourself help and training in their use.

▼ Table 14.1 Resources that can help overcome or reduce the impact of sensory or physical impairment

Area of SEN	Type of equipment or resource
Cognition and learning needs	• Computer software and equipment for specific needs such as dyslexia • Life Skills software
Behaviour, emotional and social development needs	• Social stories software • Puppets to help discuss emotions • Circle time games
Speech and language needs	• Text-to-speech software • Recording devices • Speaking and listening games • Speech amplifiers
Sensory needs	• Hearing aids, microphones, hearing loops • Visualisers, magnifiers, speech software, Braille embossers • Light source and sensory tubes • Sensory bags
Physical needs	• Computer equipment such as adapted mice and keyboards • Programs to aid fine motor skills • Touchscreen technologies

Look at Unit 9, which has more information on supporting the use of ICT in the learning environment.

Activity

Find out more about the different kinds of specialist equipment and technology resources available for pupils with special educational needs and disabilities. It may help you to speak to your SENCo and to think about the needs of some of the pupils in your own school or college. Write a reflective account to show how the equipment and technology helps to reduce the impact of their sensory or physical impairment.

LO6 Understand the kinds of strategies needed to support children and young people with special educational needs and disabilities

AC 6.1 Explain how to work with children and young people using strategies to support their learning and development

Adults working with children and young people should be able to use a range of strategies to support and enable their learning and development. Depending on your experience, you should be able to use these as necessary so that pupils can achieve learning objectives and success criteria. For those who have special educational needs and disabilities, you will need to be mindful of these at all times and should have a good understanding of their abilities and of those aspects of learning that they may find challenging.

You should read this section alongside Unit 7, AC 3.1, page 115.

Providing levels of individual attention when needed

When working with pupils who have special educational needs and disabilities, you may need to provide individual attention more often than with other pupils. They may need more support in order to achieve objectives, or their behaviour or level of attention may require you to intervene more regularly than with others. However, you should ensure that you provide support only when it is needed so that pupils are able to develop their own independence and learning skills, and use questioning techniques or scaffolding rather than providing answers. You are also likely to need to give more attention to these pupils outside the classroom and within the wider school or college community. Others may not be aware of their needs and there may be circumstances in which you need to intervene. Make sure you speak to others where necessary and inform teachers if there have been situations where pupils have needed additional support.

Modifying or adapting learning activities

It is likely that you will need to modify learning activities some of the time so that learners with special educational needs and disabilities are able to fully access the curriculum. In some cases this may be done by the teacher through differentiation, although in others you may need to modify activities for their specific needs, for example large-print hand-outs for those who are visually impaired, or through the use of information technology or other equipment if it is needed to enhance learning. If tasks are too difficult or unsuitable for the pupil, you may need to modify or simplify them by talking through the steps they need to take so that they are able to achieve the learning objective.

Promoting learners' self-esteem, self-confidence and self-help skills

This is particularly important for pupils who have special educational needs and disabilities. You should ensure that you notice their effort and progress through the way in which you respond so that you promote their confidence and self-esteem. This may be through verbal praise, through talking through what they are doing or, for younger pupils, through stickers, charts or house points. Encourage pupils to work things through for themselves as much as they can without asking for adult assistance.

▲ Figure 14.5 How does your setting reward learners who are working hard?

Encouraging learners with special educational needs and disabilities to take responsibility for their own learning and develop their independence

You should make sure that all learners know what to do if they find an activity challenging, and this is true for pupils who have special educational needs and disabilities. There should be regular discussion in class about the steps they should take before asking an adult for help so that they do not develop a tendency to rely on adults.

For more on this, see Unit 7, which deals with supporting children and young people during learning activities.

Listening carefully to learners and encouraging them to communicate their needs as well as ideas for future learning

Always ensure that you take time to listen to pupils and encourage them to put forward their own needs and ideas. You should take particular care with pupils who have communication needs and who may find this more difficult than others. Give them opportunities to stop, and ask them about how they are feeling about the task or activity, particularly if they do not seem to be making progress. If you do not know the pupil well, you may need reminding about aspects of learning they find more challenging.

Supporting learners in reviewing learning strategies and planning how to improve them

When thinking about assessment for learning, pupils with special educational needs and disabilities may need more support. Following learning activities it can be helpful to discuss with them the way in which they have approached the task and whether they may do this differently next time, breaking this down into smaller steps. You may need to annotate learning diaries or books so that they have a reminder for next time.

Take a look at Unit 10 to read more about supporting assessment for learning.

Activity

If you support pupils with SEND, write an account highlighting some of the strategies you have used. Which do you find the most effective and why?

In addition, if you work in a special school or a pupil referral unit you may find that the organisation of the setting itself supports the specific learning needs of pupils who have special educational needs and disabilities.

- The organisation of the setting is such that pupils have a higher adult:pupil ratio and work in smaller groups. This means that staff are more likely to know each individual pupil and are able to meet their needs more effectively.
- Timetabling is such that sessions may be shorter, and lessons are geared more towards pupils with specific needs.
- There are facilities within the setting that make it possible for pupils who need it to have therapies on-site during the school day.
- Each pupil at the school will have an EHC plan, and school staff will work together to co-ordinate their learning and development needs.

Tips for best practice: supporting pupils with special educational needs and disabilities

- Find out as much as you can about pupils you are supporting through talking to parents, colleagues and the pupil themselves.
- If you are working as an individual support assistant, make sure you are up to date through speaking to your SENCo and asking for any paperwork concerning the pupil's EHC plan. Make sure you know about any meetings that are taking place.
- Talk to pupils regularly about their needs and ideas, and ensure that you involve them in any decisions that are made about them.
- Keep parents and carers closely involved and communicate with them regularly.
- Ensure that targets that pupils are working towards are set out in small, achievable steps.
- Work closely with teachers to plan for the needs of pupils and feed back to them after learning activities.

Check your understanding

1. Name two requirements of legislation in your UK Home Nation in relation to inclusive practice.
2. What are the rights of children and young people with special educational needs and disabilities?
3. What kinds of barriers to participation might pupils with SEND face?
4. Give examples of three other professionals who may contribute to the support of a pupil with SEND.
5. Name three different types of special educational needs with which you may come into contact.
6. How might mental health issues impact on a child or young person's life?
7. In what ways can you develop skills of self-reliance and self-esteem in pupils who have social and emotional development needs?
8. How might a primary disability affect a child or young person's development?
9. What is the difference between a sensory and a physical impairment?
10. Name four strategies you might use to support the learning and development of pupils who have special educational needs and disabilities.

Assessment preparation

This knowledge-only unit can be assessed through assignments and reflective accounts, which can be set by your tutor and assessor. However, if you work with pupils who have specific needs you may also be able to use observations, work products and other forms of evidence for this unit. You should speak to your assessor about the best ways in which you can show that you have met the criteria. In addition, you can do the following:

1. Write a reflective account for AC 1.1 and use the activity in AC 1.2 to cover this AC. For AC 1.3 and 1.5, use the Activity on page 221 and 222 as evidence. For AC 1.4, write a reflective account explaining the importance of early recognition and intervention for pupils with special educational needs and disabilities.
2. If you have a transcript of the classroom discussion for AC 2.1 highlighting your input, which is signed by your tutor, this will provide evidence for AC 2.1. For AC 2.2 and 2.3, create a booklet for parents that explains the roles and responsibilities of those who contribute to the support of pupils with SEND. Write an evaluation outlining the benefit of working collaboratively with others in order to meet their needs effectively.
3. For LO3, write an account of the range of cognitive skills necessary for effective learning, and how difficulties in this area might impact on the development of language and communication. Include a description of the difference between global and specific learning difficulties.
4. For LO4, write a reflective account covering AC 4.1 and 4.2. For AC 4.3, use the case study to cover the assessment criteria. For AC 4.4, reflect on two ways of developing self-reliance and self-esteem to support children and young people with behaviour, emotional and social development needs.
5. Explain in your own words the effect of a primary disability on children or young people's development, to cover AC 5.1. Use the activity in section 5.2 to cover AC 5.2.
6. If you support pupils with SEND, use the activity in section LO6.

Legislation

- Human Rights Act, Article 2
- UN Convention on the Rights of the Child
- UN Convention on the Rights of Persons with Disabilities
- Children and Families Act 2014
- Disability Discrimination Act 1995/2005
- Equality Act 2010 – this protects groups of people from discrimination, therefore those with disabilities or special educational needs should not be discriminated against
- SEN and Disability Regulations 2014

Read about it

Weblinks

www.crae.org.uk Children's Rights Alliance for England – children's rights and the law

www.gov.uk/government/publications/send-code-of-practice-0-to-25 SEND Code of Practice: 0 to 25 years

www.gov.uk/government/publications/supporting-pupils-at-school-with-medical-conditions--3 Supporting pupils at school with medical conditions – statutory guidance

www.headstogether.org.uk Heads Together – breaking the stigma of mental health

www.mencap.org.uk Mencap – charity that is the voice of learning disability

www.mqmentalhealth.org MQ – research into mental health

www.nasen.org.uk National Association of Special Educational Needs – a quick guide to the SEND Code of Practice: 0 to 25 years can be downloaded from the Nasen website

www.thelocaloffer.co.uk Information about SEND provision in the local area

www.unicef.org UNICEF – the booklet, *Take Us Seriously! Engaging Children with Disabilities in Decisions Affecting Their Lives*, is available for download here: **www.unicef.org/disabilities/files/Take_Us_Seriously.pdf**

www.youngminds.org.uk Young Minds – support for mental health issues in children and young people

15 Support children and young people during transitions

About this unit

This unit requires you to know about and respond to the different types of transitions that will occur in the lives of children and young people. Transitions are the kinds of changes that will occur in their lives and the impact can affect their ongoing development, both in a positive and a negative way. They will need to be managed sensitively and carefully so that any negative effects on pupils' learning and development are limited where possible. Being able to support transition enables us to manage pupils during periods of change so that they develop skills of resilience that will equip them to deal with adversity in their lives. You will need to have the knowledge, skills and understanding to be able to recognise and work with the signs and effects of transition in children and young people, as well as to support teachers in working through planned events so that you can support pupils through the kinds of challenges they may face.

Learning outcomes

By the end of this unit you will:

LO1 Understand the range and impact of transitions that children and young people may experience

LO2 Be able to recognise and respond to transitions in children and young people's lives

LO3 Be able to support children and young people to manage transitions in their lives

Getting started

What do you understand by the term 'transitions'? Make a list of some of the transitions you have experienced in your life and say how you have been affected by them. Which of these were more difficult for you? Do these transitions have anything in common?

LO1 Understand the range and impact of transitions that children and young people may experience

AC 1.1, 1.2 Explain the different types of transitions that children and young people may experience and how they may affect a child or young person

We will all face a number of **transitions** in our lives; these will vary from life events that happen to all, to those that happen to only a few. Changes can be very difficult for children and young people as they can mean leaving behind familiar faces and routines and starting something new. Different types of transition may affect a child or young person's behaviour as well as their ongoing development, and they might have short- or long-term effects. As adults, we cannot prevent or shield them from the stresses and difficulties that will happen to them, and this would not help them in the long term. It is important that adults support children and young people appropriately so that they will develop resilience and learn how to cope with the changes that will inevitably occur during their lives.

Transitions may be of different types:

- **Emotional** – a change that relates to a child or young person's personal experience, for example, the death of a family member or pet, moving into foster care, abuse, parental separation.
- **Physical** – a change relating to their environment or surroundings, for example, a change in their country, or moving house, school or class.
- **Intellectual** – a change due to reaching the end of a key stage, or changing to a new school or college, or finding their first job or university, due to their age.
- **Physiological** – change due to puberty, being on medication or finding out they have a chronic illness.

In addition, transitions may fall into two categories: those that most children will experience and those that are limited to only a few. Transitions that might happen to all children and young people may be:

- starting at school
- starting with a new childminder/carer or breakfast/after-school club
- moving between classes at the start of the school year
- moving home
- changing between school/college
- puberty.

These types of transition may be short term and easier to anticipate as we know they are coming and can prepare children and young people, for example, preparing Year 6 pupils for secondary transfer. However, any kind of change can

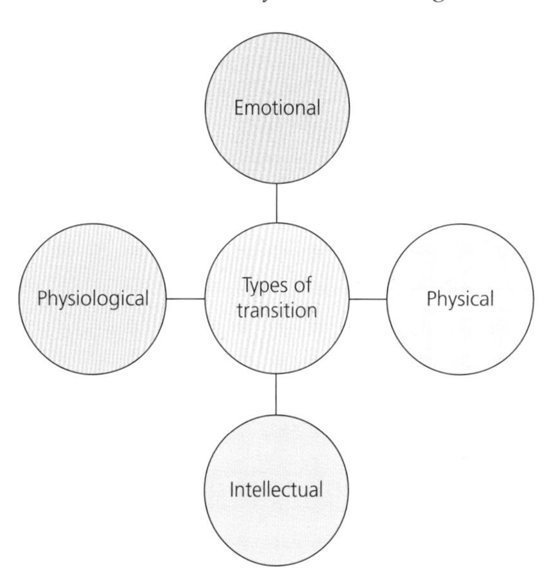

▲ Figure 15.1 Types of transitions experienced by children and young people

Key term

Transition: a significant change or event in a child or young person's life.

cause worry and anxiety, and schools should have routines in place to support both pupils and parents, and provide information about the process. They also need to be prepared for variations in these where the pupil needs more support than others, for example, if they have started in the school or college speaking English as a second language.

Starting at school

This can be easy for some children although much more of a challenge for others. In all cases this will be a big change to their daily routine and can be difficult to manage both socially and emotionally. This can be for different reasons – having greater confidence and a more secure family background may help children to settle more quickly, whereas those with a more anxious personality may find the process very difficult. Starting a new routine and having to be more independent, as well as being apart from their main carer for the day, can make some children tearful and unsettled. This is added to the fact that they are also likely to be very tired, particularly if they also attend a breakfast or after-school club.

Starting with a new childminder/carer or breakfast/after-school club

Again, this may be more difficult for some children than others, depending on the extent of the change and how relaxed they are in their new environment. They may become tearful, clingy or have tantrums or periods of aggression if they are unhappy about what is happening. By visiting the setting and talking through what is going to happen some of this anxiety may be reduced.

Moving between classes at the start of the school year

This can be unsettling, particularly where pupils are moving between key stages, such as from reception to Year 1, or from Year 6 to Year 7. Anxiety about new routines and teaching staff may cause pupils to be withdrawn and reticent about taking part in lessons or unwilling to attend. Staff will need to ensure that they prepare children by talking to them about what will happen, as well as ensuring that they visit classrooms and speak to their new teachers where possible.

Moving home

This can be exciting but will also bring uncertainty, particularly if it also means moving to a different area and changing schools. Children and young people are likely to be anxious about leaving friends and having to make new ones, as well as getting used to new routines and environments. It is important to make sure that children and young people know as much as possible about what is going to happen and are given the opportunity to talk about their new home.

Changing between school/college

This can be a big change for young people as they will find that they have more freedom and independence in a college environment. They will need to take more responsibility for themselves and for managing their learning. This freedom can make it easier for some pupils to miss lessons and to get behind with coursework, and teaching staff will need to ensure that they are aware of the importance of keeping on track.

▲ Figure 15.2 How might starting college affect a young person's ability to stay focused?

Puberty

For information on the effects of puberty see Unit 5, page 85.

Other transitions may be more difficult to manage as they are unexpected, and these will not occur in the lives of all children and young people. They may also have longer-term effects due to their nature, and children and young people will react differently to them depending on their own personalities, backgrounds and stages of development. These types of transitions could be:

- bereavement
- long-term illness of pupil or parent/carer
- divorce of parents
- starting with a new childminder/carer or breakfast/after-school club
- a parent having a new partner
- new sibling/stepbrother or stepsister
- change of carer or foster parent
- trauma such as refugee status, homelessness.

Bereavement

The extent to which the child or young person is affected by this will depend on the closeness of their relationship with the person who has died. Death may be difficult to understand and come to terms with, particularly for very young children. They may be quiet or withdrawn and easily upset for some time afterwards, or lose their appetite. They may also be tired if they are finding it hard to sleep. Children and young people may also be deeply affected by the death of a pet, which can cause similar feelings of loss to those experienced when losing a relative. In some cases where the death of an individual is very unexpected and is close to home or part of the school or college community, the organisation may need to provide emergency support both to pupils and to parents.

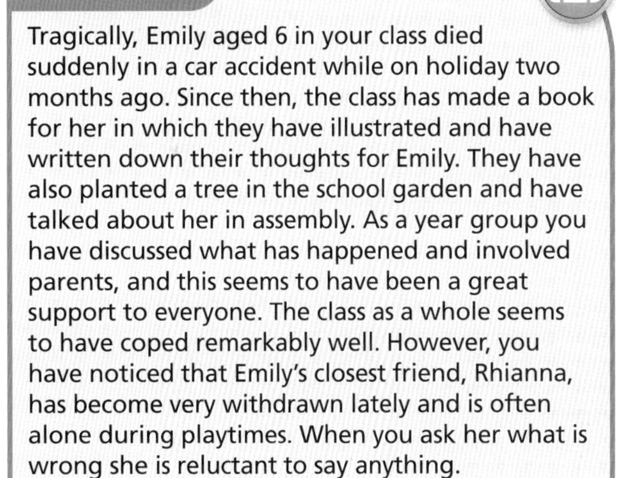

Case study

Tragically, Emily aged 6 in your class died suddenly in a car accident while on holiday two months ago. Since then, the class has made a book for her in which they have illustrated and have written down their thoughts for Emily. They have also planted a tree in the school garden and have talked about her in assembly. As a year group you have discussed what has happened and involved parents, and this seems to have been a great support to everyone. The class as a whole seems to have coped remarkably well. However, you have noticed that Emily's closest friend, Rhianna, has become very withdrawn lately and is often alone during playtimes. When you ask her what is wrong she is reluctant to say anything.

1 What should you do in this situation?
2 Why is it important that this is addressed?

Long-term illness of pupil or parent/carer

This is likely to have a long-term effect due to its nature. If the pupil her- or himself has a chronic illness they may need to miss periods of schooling, which can make them feel anxious about what they have missed. If parents or carers are unwell, children or young people may need to provide long-term care. They may also be on medication, which may have some kinds of side-effects. This may make them tired, unable to socialise with their peers, and have less time for school or coursework.

Divorce of parents

This may affect a child or young person in different ways – they will be affected by a sense of loss, as well as feeling anxious that their life as they know it is likely to change and they will live with only one parent or split their time between the two. They may also blame themselves for their parents splitting up. In this situation, children and young people should be encouraged to talk about their feelings, and it is important to show sensitivity when speaking to them as well as when discussing any issues with their parents.

A parent having a new partner

This can be very challenging for a child or young person to cope with, and will depend on their age and on how they are introduced to the new partner, as well as the amount of contact they have with their other parent. It can have a big impact due to anxiety and uncertainty about what this will mean for them and the fear that the absent parent is being 'replaced' by someone else.

New sibling/stepbrother or stepsister

This may affect younger children more as they will not know what to expect. If this is their first sibling they will have less attention from their parents and in some cases this can cause children to regress in their development, for example, by bedwetting. They may also be more demanding of adults as they will be seeking more attention.

Change of carer or foster parent

For looked after children and young people, a change in carer or foster parent may be a regular occurrence. This will be hard to manage due to feelings of insecurity in the child as well as the upheaval of possible changes in schooling. There may be ongoing issues with behaviour and emotional development, and schools and colleges should communicate regularly with outside agencies as well as meeting with them and the pupil to discuss any issues as they arise.

Trauma such as refugee status, homelessness

If a child or young person arrives in your school or college as a refugee or has experienced a trauma in their home country, it may take them a long time to settle. Their behaviour may be affected and they may be learning English as an additional language, which will make it harder for them to communicate their feelings.

These types of transitions that have longer-term effects can affect the behaviour and development of children and young people in several ways as they will be unsettled. Their emotional development may be the most obviously affected, due to feelings of anxiety or unhappiness, and they may withdraw from others or react in an aggressive way. However, it may also make them unable to concentrate, and therefore they may find that they are unable to take in new information and academic progress may be slowed down over time.

However, although transitions can be very difficult for children and young people, they can also have positive effects in the long term if they are managed effectively. These may be:

- **Emotional resilience** – resilience can be defined as the ability to 'bounce back' from adversity. In some cases, and over time, the child or young person may feel that they have been made more resilient by what has happened to them, even though the event may have been traumatic or stressful for them. They may feel stronger and more motivated as a result and, in some cases, it can make them want to help others who may be in a similar situation.
- **Enhanced self-esteem** – children and young people who are able to develop these feelings of resilience will have enhanced self-esteem as a result. This will in turn help them and they will be more able to cope with other transitions as they occur in their lives.
- **An opportunity for growth** – challenges in their lives can be seen as an opportunity for children and young people to grow and develop rather than something from which they should be shielded.

In some cases schools and colleges are not told about transitions that have happened at home. This can make supporting pupils much more difficult, and staff may need to ask parents and carers directly what might have happened to cause a change in their behaviour (see also LO2, page 243).

Stretch and challenge

Find out more about the effects of resilience in children and young people, and what it means for them. Do you think there is a link between resilience and positive transitions?

In practice

What procedures does your school or college have in place for managing transitions? How are these communicated both to pupils and to parents? Your school or college may have a transitions policy that will help you with your answer.

AC 1.3 Explain how a child or young person's approach to transitions may be affected by their culture, religion, personal beliefs, gender, stage of development or previous experiences

Although all children and young people may approach and view transitions differently, there are many reasons for this. Their age, home background and own personal experiences will all play a part in determining how well they are able to cope with change in their lives and how they are affected by it. In addition, some types of transitions are physical and so may affect them in different ways, for example they will be dependent on their gender or stage of development.

Culture or religion

Our culture or religion may affect our ability to cope with transitions. Research has shown that strong resilience factors in the child or young person's environment include both a supportive extended family and membership of a religious or faith community. This is because there are social support networks within each of these that may make the thought of coping with transitions less unsettling and the individual's sense of self stronger. If the child or young person knows others who have had the same experience or is able to talk about their anxieties, both within and outside their immediate family, they are likely to feel less isolated and vulnerable in relation to this experience.

Personal beliefs

The child or young person's personal beliefs will inevitably affect their approach to transitions. They may feel that they are strong and able to

Research it

Find out in more detail about the effects of puberty on a young person's emotional, physical and intellectual development.

cope with change; on the other hand, they may not feel that they are resilient enough to do this. Their approach will influence the amount of control they feel they have over the situation and whether this is positive or negative.

Gender

Puberty is the main transition that may affect boys and girls differently. Girls are more likely to be affected at an earlier age physically, psychologically and emotionally, as they move into adolescence earlier. Often, girls in Years 5 or 6 may become much taller and start to take on the early signs of puberty, whereas for boys these changes will come later. If girls and boys are in school together, this difference can be more marked for both sexes.

Stage of development

A child or young person's age and stage of development may make a difference to the way in which they are able to cope with transitions. Younger children who have less life experience or knowledge of change may be more anxious simply because they have not needed to think about it before and have remained close to one main attachment. However, if they come from a secure background of strong and positive relationships, this may make change less difficult for them. As children grow older and more experienced, they may be better equipped to cope with the types of transition that occur more often. However, children and young people at all stages of development will find unexpected transitions more challenging.

Previous experiences

Children and young people's previous experiences will influence their ability to manage transitions. If they are able to relate what is happening to something that has happened before, or even if another person close to them has experienced it, this may reduce their anxiety and make them

Activity

Consider the links between a child or young person's ability to cope with transitions and their background and previous experiences. Consider in particular the following groups of pupils:

- traveller pupils
- pupils from international schools
- pupils who have SEND
- pupils who speak English as an additional language.

more able to manage their feelings. For example, a child or young person in an international school may move between schools and even countries several times during their school career, which may make the process less daunting for them than for other children. In addition, experiences that have developed pupil confidence and resilience will also help during times of transition. These may have been within or outside the educational environment, for example, through a hobby they have taken up or activities they have completed independently.

AC 1.4 Explain how transitions may affect children and young people most at risk of exclusion or underachievement

For all children and young people, transitions are likely to be a time of stress and some anxiety. For children and young people to be able to manage transitions well, they will need to feel safe and secure in themselves, in their home, and the wider environment. However, for those who are at risk of exclusion or underachievement, these additional stresses may affect them more deeply as they will be more vulnerable and susceptible to risk. Research shows that the prevalence of strong mental health and resilience will give individuals a greater chance of coping with the anxieties surrounding periods of transition.

Statistically, pupils who are on free school meals are four times more likely to be excluded than those who are not (source: *Permanent and Fixed Period Exclusions in England: 2014 to 2015*), DfE,

In practice

Devise a series of questions and interview your SENCo about pupils in your setting who have reacted to transitions in an adverse way. Have there been any links with those who were at risk of exclusion or underachievement? Without using real names, write a reflective account considering the possible reasons for this.

July 2016). In other words, this means that pupils who come from families on lower incomes or whose parents are on benefits may be more affected by transitions than their peers. Pupils who are in care or have special educational needs and disabilities are also more vulnerable to exclusion and underachievement (see also AC 1.5 below).

AC 1.5 Explain why children and young people with disabilities or special educational needs may need additional support to manage transitions

For more on understanding how to support children and young people with SEND, see Unit 14.

Although transitions can be challenging for all pupils, you should be aware that those who have special educational needs and disabilities may need additional support from adults before, during and after the process. Although this will not always be the case, and will depend on their level of independence, when transitions occur it is important that adults who work with them and know them best are able to discuss whether these pupils will need additional support.

As with all children and young people, planned transitions such as changing classes, moving schools, moving house or changing from school to college will clearly be easier to manage due to the opportunity to plan ahead.

The SEND Code of Practice (2014) (section 6.57) states that 'SEN support should include planning and preparation for the transitions between phases of education and preparation for adult life. To support transition, the school should share information with the school, college or other setting the child or young person is moving to.'

For these kinds of transitions, it is even more important for pupils who have SEND to visit new environments and to meet new staff so that they can prepare. They should start to discuss any changes as soon as they can in order to allow time for changes and for any adaptations to be made. For pupils moving into adulthood, the SEND Code of Practice outlines the provision that should be made when transferring to adult social care or health services. Pupils moving to higher education who will need continuing support who have an EHC plan should have a transition plan that will set out how support for them will be maintained during and after the process.*

Preparing for the physical environment

Pupils with sensory or physical disabilities should visit the new setting if at all possible so that they are able to discuss their needs with the school or college and look at ways of coping with their new environment. They may need to prepare by making changes to the learning environment, or by ensuring that they can sit in a particular place in class to benefit their learning.

Preparing for the social and emotional effects of transition

If pupils have additional needs in the area of social and emotional development, they are likely to need considerable support due to the anxieties that are caused during periods of change. Thinking about things in advance can help when pupils will need to be more independent, for example, when starting secondary school. Adults can help by talking through the differences and listening to any worries pupils may have about the changes that will be happening.

In some cases, the specific needs of the child or young person may make it more difficult for them to cope with change or to talk about how they are feeling. Pupils with autism, for example, may become very stressed at the prospect of change and will benefit from plenty of support so that they can work through what is going to happen. They will need adults to be very clear about what is going to happen, and to provide them with reassurance and support. Similarly, children and young people with learning disabilities may be very concerned about changes and be anxious about having someone to talk to in order to provide them with emotional support.

In addition, both the previous and new teachers, as well as other professionals working with the pupil, should meet with them and their parents to discuss their needs going forward. Teachers will also need to pass on information and talk about the background and needs of the pupil, as well as discussing strategies for their day-to-day learning.

In cases of transitions that are sudden or unexpected, pupils who have SEND will be particularly vulnerable, especially those who have social and emotional needs. This is because they are likely to already have issues around the areas of feeling secure and settled, and find unexpected change very challenging. They may react in ways that are unpredictable and this will in turn affect their behaviour.

Research it

Using the SEND Code of Practice (2014), find out more about the kind of support that should be available during transitions for the pupils in different age groups, from early years to adulthood.

LO2 Be able to recognise and respond to transitions in children and young people's lives

AC 2.1 Explain the signs and indications that a child or young person is experiencing a transition in their life

You may notice different signs or indications that a child or young person is going through a transition in their life. They may range from

* For more on coping with the transition to adult health services and social care, see the SEND Code of Practice (2014), pages 133–138.

▼ Table 15.1 Signs that a child or young person is experiencing a transition in their life

Type of behaviour/sign	Possible cause/transition
Withdrawn or uncharacteristic behaviour; lack of interest in activities, inability to concentrate	This will usually mean that the pupil is anxious or upset about something, or is thinking about it to the extent that it prevents them from focusing on what is going on around them.
Aggression or angry behaviour	This may be caused by frustration or inability to do anything about the situation in which they find themselves.
Tired, emotional or tearful	The child or young person may be overwhelmed by what is happening in their life and unable to control their emotions.
Attention seeking or distracting others, negotiating with adults	This type of behaviour may occur if the child or young person feels that events around them mean that they are not getting as much attention as they would like.

being withdrawn or isolated in some, to having tantrums and being completely overwhelmed by what is happening to them in others. If they are approaching a known transition such as changing schools or moving home, it may be easier to identify this as the cause, however, any a change in behaviour over time should be investigated.

AC 2.2 Provide opportunities for children and young people to explore and discuss significant events and experiences that may impact on them

During times of transition, there should be opportunities either at home or in the school or college environment for pupils to talk about what is happening to them. Depending on the age of the pupil this may be approached in different ways within your setting.

With younger pupils

This may be done through in class through story or circle times, or through role-play activities. Many books are available that deal with transitional subjects such as moving house, going to a new school, bereavement, the birth of a sibling, and so on. These give children the opportunity to relate the text to what is happening in their life, and to be able to talk about it openly. It also gives staff the chance to ask them more questions if children start to talk about their own situation. Props such as puppets can also be very effective with younger children as they may talk about their feelings more openly to a puppet than to an adult.

With older pupils

Assemblies and PSHE (personal, social, health and economic) education lessons can open up the subject of different transitions and encourage pupils to talk about them afterwards in smaller groups. If you have developed good relationships with pupils, this will also help encourage them to talk about their feelings and to share any anxieties with you.

In colleges

There may be support groups that have been set up by the college or by students themselves to help those who are suffering from anxiety or

▲ Figure 15.3 What type of opportunities might you have to discuss transitions with the age group of the pupils you support?

In practice

Find out whether you can join in with or start a support group in your school or college to help pupils who are going through different transitions or life events. This should be run at a particular time each week so that pupils know where to find it if they need to.

who need counselling services. Although these are unlikely to be specifically transition based, they will provide the opportunity for students to discuss any issues that are impacting on them.

AC 2.3 Identify signs of concern or distress in children or young people, which may relate to a transitional experience

There may be other signs of concern that are less obvious in children and young people but that may relate to a transitional experience. In some cases it may be difficult to identify them, for example, if a pupil is usually a quiet personality in any case. There may also be some pupils who you know are going through a difficult time but seem to be able to control their emotions; this does not necessarily mean that all is well on the inside. Moreover, if you know the child or young person well, you may notice signs of concern that may not be apparent to others.

Self-harming

This is a sign of stress and can be a way of coping with strong emotions and difficult situations. Harming themselves can relieve tension and make the child or young person feel that they have some control over what is happening to them. Pupils who self-harm may attempt to conceal what they are doing, but clues may be scars or marks from excessive rubbing, regular cuts, scratches or bruises, and long sleeves or clothing worn to cover up, even when it is warm. These are likely to be on the arms, legs or torso.

Case study

Mirella is in Year 9 and her parents are going through a divorce. She is aware of what is happening and has known for some time that her dad will be moving out in the next few months. She has no siblings and her parents have not sat down and discussed with her what will happen; she has only heard them talking about it. The school have not been told anything about the situation.

In school, Mirella is quiet as usual, and is still concentrating on her work and applying herself. She has stayed focused on what is happening as this helps her to cope with what is going on at home. She has a small circle of friends and there do not appear to be any problems. However, you have noticed some cuts on her arms that have been there for some time. You have not said anything to her but are becoming increasingly concerned.

1. What should be the first thing you do?
2. How could you and the school support Mirella?

Lack of sleep

You may not find out about this unless a pupil confides in you or a parent lets you know, but it is likely that you will notice if a pupil is excessively tired or seems to have less energy than usual.

Not eating/eating too much

If you know a pupil well and spend time with them at mealtimes, you may notice a loss in appetite or see that they are gaining weight. Each of these can be linked to stress or feelings of depression or anxiety, and be a cause for concern.

Regression in development, for example, bedwetting or asking for additional help with everyday tasks

This is something that will happen with younger children and can be a sign of anxiety. You may hear about this through talking to a parent or notice that a pupil is wetting themselves or displaying more 'needy' behaviour in class regularly.

AC 2.4, 2.5 Show how to recognise and take account of any signs of change in the attitude and behaviour of individual children or young people, and use procedures of your work setting to share information or concerns about children or young people with the appropriate person

If you notice any changes in a pupil's attitude or behaviour such as those described in AC 2.1 or 2.3 of this unit, you should always note down and share any information or concerns you may have about them with the appropriate person in your school or college. They are likely to have procedures in place to ensure that staff can share information with others where needed. In the first instance you should speak to the child's class teacher in the case of primary pupils, or the SENCo or safeguarding/pastoral lead for your year group in the case of secondary pupils. In each case, you should make sure that you are aware of the organisation's policy for sharing information.

Activity

Find out about procedures that exist in your setting for recording and reporting any information or concerns about a child or young person. If you have reported a concern, you can use a work product to show how you have done this, or ask for a witness testimony as evidence for these assessment criteria.

LO3 Be able to support children and young people to manage transitions in their lives

AC 3.1 Show ways of supporting children and young people to manage transitions in their lives

Once we have identified and started to respond to the kinds of transitions that will inevitably occur when working with children and young people, we need to be able to support them in working their way through them. The effects of transitions may be short or long term, and the way in which we support them will depend on the children and young people's age and stage of development, as well as their needs. Some of the ways in which we might do this are listed in Figure 15.4.

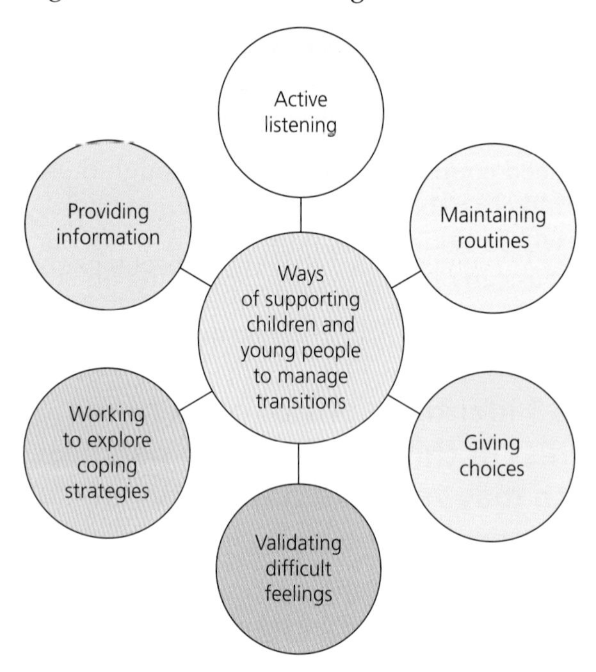

▲ Figure 15.4 Ways of supporting children and young people to manage transitions

Active listening

Listening to the concerns that pupils may have and taking these seriously is crucial, particularly in cases of anxiety and uncertainty. We need to show them that we are listening so that we can reassure them about the concerns that they have. This also shows them that we take their worries seriously and want to help them.

▲ Figure 15.5 How can you show that you are actively listening to pupils when they tell you their concerns?

Maintaining routines

Routines are very important to all children and young people. This is because familiarity and being able to predict what is going to happen each day helps to develop their confidence. In times of transition, when other areas of their lives may bring uncertainty, it is very important for them to be able to maintain routines or develop new ones as soon as possible.

Giving choices

During the transition process, it can help pupils to be given some choices about aspects of what is happening so that they feel they have some control. For example, if they are moving to secondary school, they may want to decide how they are going to get there, or what they will have for lunch. This may also help them to develop confidence and look forward to what is happening.

Validating difficult feelings

It is important that adults who are working with pupils going through transitions can validate the feelings they have. This means telling them that it is OK to feel angry and upset, and that these feelings are normal in some situations. We should not belittle their feelings by telling them not to be upset when they clearly are, but should tell them we will help and support them. When we validate how children and young people are feeling, this helps them to feel understood rather than judged, and helps to avoid resentment towards adults.

Working with children and young people to explore coping strategies

As part of your discussion with children and young people and their peers, it may help them for you to talk about coping strategies to help with periods of transition. These may be suggested by others who have gone through the process, particularly if you are working with older pupils. Exploring coping strategies offers another opportunity to discuss their feelings.

Providing information

As adults, we should provide children and young people who are going through transitions with as much information as we can. In this way they will feel more able to cope as they will know more about what to expect. One of the most difficult aspects of transition for children and young people is the feeling of uncertainty and anxiety about what will happen next.

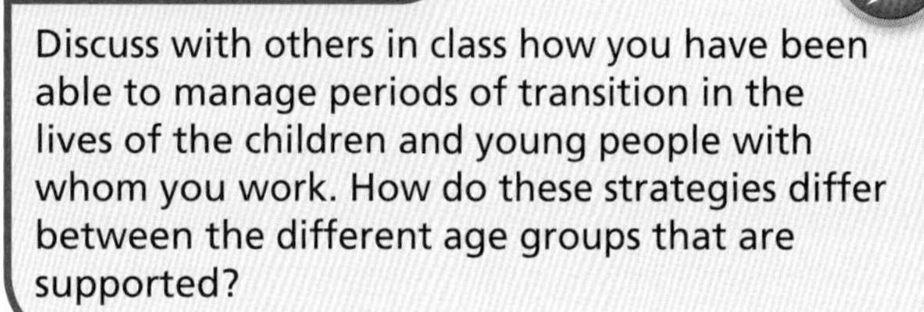

Class discussion

Discuss with others in class how you have been able to manage periods of transition in the lives of the children and young people with whom you work. How do these strategies differ between the different age groups that are supported?

AC 3.2 Provide opportunities for children and young people to discuss the effects and results of transition

Through developing positive and open relationships with the pupils we support, there will be more opportunities available to them to discuss the effects and results of transition. It is important that we give children and young people these opportunities to discuss their concerns as well as how they are feeling. This should be relevant to both their age and stage of development, so that they are able to understand and talk about what is happening as much as possible. Remember also that children and young people may need to discuss how they are feeling with their peers and with their parents, as well as with school or college staff.

- For pupils in primary school, ensure that you make time to actively listen to their concerns when they need to talk or as soon as possible afterwards.
- If the transition relates to moving on to secondary school or college, or to a different year group, one of the best ways of reassuring pupils is to ask those who have experienced it for themselves to come and answer questions that pupils have had the opportunity to prepare in advance.
- If the transition is one that has been unexpected, this strategy can also work if there are other pupils in the setting who have experienced it, for example, in cases where

parents have divorced. It can help to buddy up with other pupils or have a peer mentor so that they can talk about what has happened.

- Encourage parents to talk to children and young people about what is happening and ensure that they are aware of the importance of sharing information and listening to their children's anxieties.

Activity

Create an information booklet for staff that outlines the different ways in which you can provide opportunities for children and young people to discuss the effects and results of transition.

Tips for best practice: managing transitions

- Develop positive relationships and communicate regularly with parents, carers and the pupils themselves so that they are more likely to talk to you and other staff about any issues at home as they arise.
- Plan carefully for those transitions that you can anticipate, particularly for children and young people with SEND.
- Look out for any unusual or uncharacteristic behaviour in the pupils you support.
- Encourage pupils to talk about their feelings, and make time for them to do this or direct them to facilities in your school or college to help them.
- Provide support where you can or speak to teaching staff if you are told about anything you do not feel equipped to help with.
- Give pupils a boost when they manage transitions well – tell them how well they are coping and how this might help them next time. This is very important.
- Provide support and information for parents around transitions where needed.

Check your understanding

1. What are the four types of transitions and what categories might these fall into?
2. In which ways might a child or young person be affected by transitions?
3. How will emotional resilience help children and young people to cope with stressful events in their lives?
4. Why are pupils who are at risk of exclusion or underachievement more vulnerable during times of transition?
5. What kind of additional support should be available before and during transitions for pupils with SEND?
6. What is the difference between transitions that affect all children and young people, and those that are only experienced by a few?
7. What kinds of opportunities might you be able to provide for pupils to discuss events that are significant to them?
8. How can you find out about procedures in your setting for sharing concerns about pupils who may be experiencing a transition?
9. What strategies might you use in order to support pupils who are going through transitions?

Assessment preparation

In order to gather evidence for this unit, you will need to show how you support pupils during different types of transition in their lives. Some of this will need to be seen by your assessor when they visit you in the school or college environment; you may also choose to use some of the suggestions below.

1. For AC 1.1 and 1.2, write a reflective account about the different types of transitions that children and young people may face, and how they may be affected by them. For AC 1.3, explain how their approach to transitions may be influenced by the headings provided. Use the 'In practice' in AC 1.4 as your evidence for this assessment criterion. Write a reflective account to cover AC 1.5.
2. For AC 2.1 and 2.3 write a list of the signs and indications that may suggest that a child or young person is experiencing a transition. Use the activity provided for AC 2.4 and 2.5. For AC 2.2, use the 'In practice' activity.
3. For AC 3.1 and 3.2 use the activity at the end of the unit. Alternatively for LO3, you can talk to your assessor, or provide work products or witness testimonies, to show how you have supported children and young people to manage transition successfully.

Legislation

There is no legislation for this unit.

Read about it

Weblinks

www.autism.org.uk The National Autistic Society – find top tips for helping autistic pupils prepare for change here: **www.autism.org.uk/about/behaviour/preparing-for-change.aspx**

www.barnardos.org.uk Barnardo's – download the report, *Transitions in the Lives of Children and Young People: Resilience Factors*, at: **www.barnardos.org.uk/resources/research_and_publications/interchange-78--transitions-in-the-lives-of-children-and-young-people-resilience-factors/publication-view.jsp?pid=PUB-1400**

www.gov.uk Government website – view the SEND Code of Practice: 0 to 25 years here: **www.gov.uk/government/publications/send-code-of-practice-0-to-25**

www.studentminds.org.uk Student Minds – student mental health charity to support those in college across the UK

16 Support the role of play, leisure and extra-curricular activities for children and young people

About this unit

This is a knowledge-only unit about supporting or supervising the play and leisure activities of children and young people. You will need to know about and understand the benefits of play and leisure, and know the difference between these and adult-led activities. You will also need to be clear on your own role in supporting a range of activities, and on how you can adapt them to ensure that all pupils are able to participate, including those with special educational needs and disabilities. You should also know about the importance of children and young people being able to manage risk and challenge, what this means, and why it is essential for learning and development.

Learning outcomes

By the end of this unit you will:

LO1 Understand the nature and importance of play and leisure

LO2 Understand your role in relation to the requirements of play and leisure activities

LO3 Understand how to balance risk and challenge with the benefits of the play and leisure opportunity

Getting started

What can you remember about your earliest play experiences? How did you feel? What did you enjoy doing?

LO1 Understand the nature and importance of play and leisure

AC 1.1 Describe the benefit of play and leisure and how they contribute to children and young people's development

Play and leisure are important and beneficial for children and young people, and contribute to all areas of learning and development. Through making their own decisions and being able to experiment through play and leisure, children and young people will be developing skills and experience in several areas. Problem solving skills will be developed through play and leisure, as they will have opportunities to work things out for themselves and to try different approaches to problems as they arise.

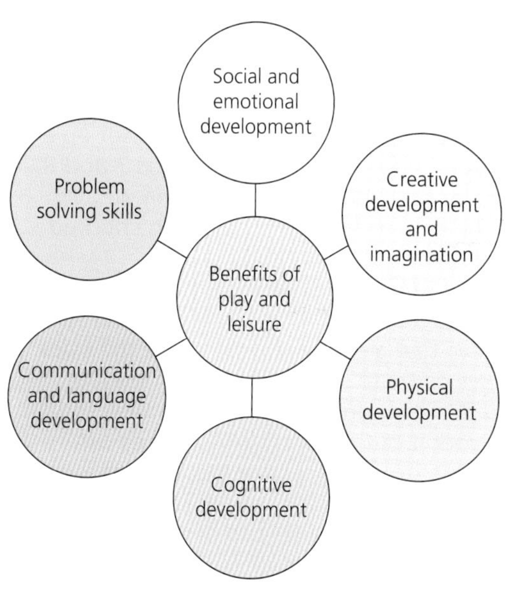

▲ Figure 16.1 How does play and leisure contribute to the development of children and young people?

Supporting social and emotional development

Play and leisure support a child and young person's social and emotional development in several ways:

Social development

Play and leisure enable children and young people to develop their relationships and friendships with one another. They also help to develop their social skills such as sharing, negotiating and taking others' views and ideas into account.

Play and leisure activities enable children to choose what they are going to do, either on their own or with their peers, and to explore their environment in their own way. Sporting activities are good for teens and older children as they are able to 'let off steam' while learning about working as a team and co-operating with one another.

All children and young people will be able to develop their independence through making their own decisions and having control over what they are doing without adults overseeing them. This also encourages them to be able to entertain themselves, and to improvise and use their imaginations and initiative, either on their own or alongside their peers.

Emotional development

Through having the freedom to develop their independence and make their own decisions, children will also develop their confidence and self-esteem. They will also learn to experiment with emotions and explore how different situations may affect other people through pretend play. Sporting and leisure activities help children and young people to learn about and experience winning and losing, an important aspect of growing up. Play can also affect the way in which children deal with trauma and support their mental health; it can be therapeutic as it enables children to share how they feel. It is also an opportunity for children and young people to take risks and to manage any that occur independently.

For more on risk and challenge in play, see LO3, page 257.

Creative development and imagination

Play and leisure activities enable children and young people to develop their own ideas through being free to make and explore imaginative worlds. They will be able to make up their own games and activities, and to engage their creativity through pretend play.

Physical development

Through giving children and young people play and leisure opportunities, we are enabling them to practise, strengthen and develop their physical skills and co-ordination. Engaging in physical activity is also healthy and should be part of an active lifestyle.

Cognitive development

Research shows that the play is beneficial to brain development. Free play encourages children to practise what they see in the world around them, including the development of their learning, as repetition strengthens neural pathways. Through play and leisure, children and young people will also develop problem-solving and decision-making skills.

Communication and language development

Play encourages children and young people to practise their language skills in different imaginative situations. They will copy the language used by those around them and play gives them another opportunity to do this.

▲ Figure 16.2 What areas of development will pupils be strengthening on the playground?

In practice

Consider the different opportunities for play and leisure that exist for pupils in your workplace. Make a list of the benefits and the way in which they support pupil development.

AC 1.2 Distinguish between play and leisure, and adult-led activities

Play and leisure activities are generally those that have been self-chosen by children and young people. This means that they will be able to motivate and self-direct what they are doing in accordance with their own wishes and interests. Usually children and young people are told what to do by adults – they have limited control over what they do and when they do it. Adult-led activities will be those that are dictated by parents or carers, teachers, support staff or volunteers, which means that they will usually have an intended requirement or learning outcome. Adults will therefore be structuring pupil learning and development through their interactions with them, usually via questioning or through a specific end result.

AC 1.3 Outline the requirements of the UN Convention on the Rights of the Child in relation to relaxation and play

The UN Convention on the Rights of the Child was developed internationally in 1990. It is an international human rights treaty that was signed

Activity

Look at the following situations and decide whether they are adult or child directed.

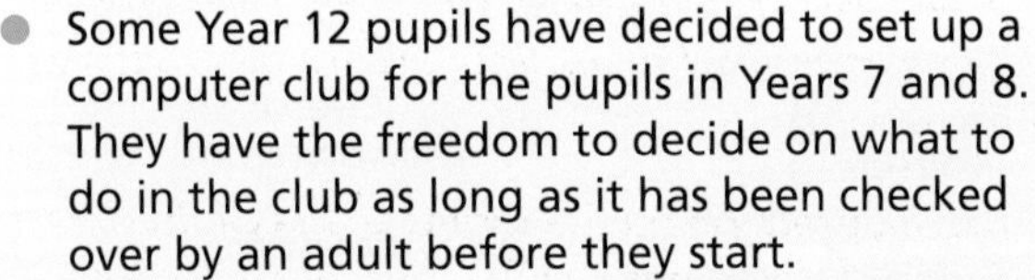

- Some Year 12 pupils have decided to set up a computer club for the pupils in Years 7 and 8. They have the freedom to decide on what to do in the club as long as it has been checked over by an adult before they start.
- Rocco and Sami (Year 2) are on the playground and are playing football in the directed area. They have had a disagreement about the rules and have come to ask an adult what they should do. The adult tells them that they should try to work it out for themselves if they can.
- Three Year 1 pupils are in the book corner in their classroom and have decided to act out 'story time' in which one of them is pretending to be the teacher.
- Two Year 6 pupils are at after-school club and are playing a board game with some younger children.
- A group of Year 9 pupils are taking part in a football match for charity after school, which is refereed by older pupils.

and ratified by all UN member states (196 countries) apart from the United States. It recognises that 'childhood is entitled to special care and assistance', and that 'the child, by reason of his physical and mental immaturity, needs special safeguards and care, including appropriate legal protection'. The Convention acknowledges the rights and freedoms that all children and young people under the age of 18 should have, through a series of 54 articles or entitlements. The nations that have ratified the treaty have to fulfil it by international law. The 54 articles state that children and young people have:

- the right to an education
- the right to equality of opportunity
- the right to develop to their full potential
- the right to be heard
- the right to be with their parents.

As well as these key articles, which affect schools and colleges, under Article 31 children and young people are entitled to a range of play and leisure activities:

1. States Parties recognize the right of the child to rest and leisure, to engage in play and recreational activities appropriate to the age of the child and to participate freely in cultural life and the arts.

2. States Parties shall respect and promote the right of the child to participate fully in cultural and artistic life and shall encourage the provision of appropriate and equal opportunities for cultural, artistic, recreational and leisure activity.

Source: *Convention on the Rights of the Child* (came into force 2 September 1990), Office of the United Nations High Commissioner for Human Rights

Read more about the UN Convention on the Rights of the Child in Unit 3, on page 33.

Research it

Read through the summary of articles that can be found on the UNICEF website at www.unicef.org.uk.

As well as those listed above, what other articles should you know about if you are working in a school or college?

LO2 Understand your role in relation to the requirements of play and leisure activities

AC 2.1 Describe your role in supporting children and young people's play and leisure activities

You will need to know about and be able to describe your own role when supporting play and leisure activities. Although children and young people should be given freedom and the opportunity to develop their skills, adults should provide the environment for them to do this, and may at times need to intervene.

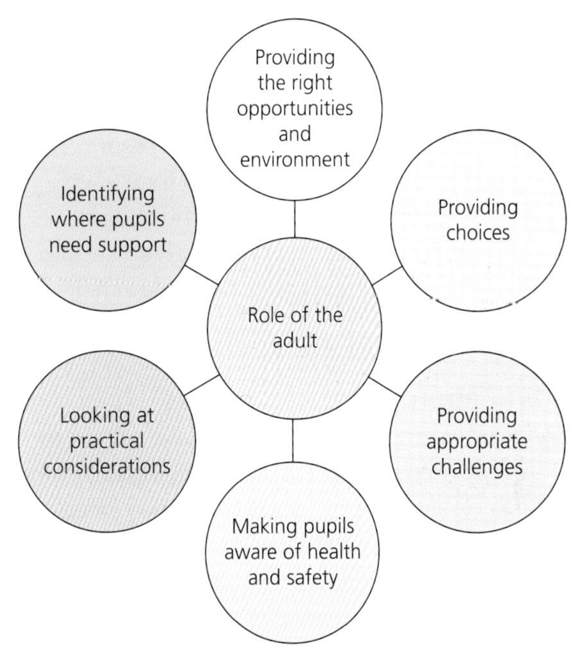

▲ Figure 16.3 What role do you play when supporting play and leisure activities?

Providing the right opportunities and environment

Adults will need to make sure that children and young people are given a range of play and leisure opportunities so that they can choose those that are the most appropriate for their age and their needs.

Providing choices

Older pupils may enjoy being given the opportunity to devise their own activities, or put ideas forward for clubs or games they would like to have available. They should also have a range of indoor and outdoor

▲ Figure 16.4 Pupils should be given access to a range of play and leisure activities

opportunities for play and leisure activities that may take place within or outside the setting. Younger children should be given access to environments that stimulate their imaginations, and allow them to explore and ask questions about their world. They should be able to choose from a range of resources and materials so that they can develop their own ideas for play activities. In each case, the choices which children and young people are given should vary so that they have the chance to change their choice of activity.

Providing appropriate challenges

Children and young people should have access to activities that present them with an age-appropriate level of risk and challenge, and adults may need to give them encouragement. Challenges will enable them to try things that they find difficult, but will also give them a greater sense of achievement.

For more on the value of challenges, see AC 3.1.

Making pupils aware of health and safety

Adults will need to ensure that all play and leisure environments are safe and that children and young people will be able to manage moderate risks as they arise. When they first start a new activity in a new environment, it can sometimes be helpful for adults to check with them so that they are aware of the kinds of hazards to look out for – for example, in an environment such as a sports hall, making sure they have appropriate footwear so that they are less likely to slip. Children and young people should also be taught to put out and tidy away equipment safely so that risks and hazards are minimised. If you work with very young children you should also talk to them about safety, although you will also need to check the environment before use, particularly if it is outdoors – in this way they will start to look for hazards themselves. A quick way of doing this is to use a check form so that you ensure that you do not miss anything.

Case study

You are working in a secondary school and some of the Year 10 pupils have come to you and said that they would like to set up a trampoline club.

1. What would you do first?
2. What else would you need to consider?

Looking at practical considerations

Adults will need to be able to look at the practicalities of play and leisure activities carried out by pupils. Although as much as possible should be done to make sure all pupils can participate, there may be some situations in which this is not possible for practical reasons. This could be due to space, timetables, resources or equipment available at the time, or the level of staffing needed.

Identifying where pupils need support

You may notice that pupils need support during play and leisure activities, for example, if they are unable to find or use a piece of equipment or if they become upset or angry with others (see also AC 2.2). You may also need to support pupils with special educational needs or disabilities if they need it.

In addition, adults can support play and leisure activities by talking about them with children and young people and being interested in their play and leisure choices. This both develops their self-esteem and validates what they are doing.

AC 2.2 Explain the importance of knowing when to leave children and young people to play or relax uninterrupted

You will need to be sensitive to the impact that adult involvement may have on a play or leisure activity.

If the children are very young and are playing outside, for example, adults may need to be very close by, but this does not mean that they should become involved in the activity. If children or young people are playing or carrying out a leisure activity co-operatively, usually adults will have no need to intervene and pupils can carry on uninterrupted. This is the best scenario for all as the pupils will be gaining maximum benefit from the activity. However, there are a few situations in which adults should recognise when they should intervene:

- **If a child or young person is in danger** – you may need to intervene very quickly to prevent injury or harm to pupils.
- **If a child or young person is upset or has had a disagreement** – in this situation they are likely to seek adult support although, depending on their age, they may work through it themselves. However, if not, you may need to support them so that they can continue with the activity.
- **If someone seeks your help** – this may because they are having difficulty using resources or equipment, remembering how to play a particular game, or because another child is hurt. You should stay for the time required and then leave pupils to carry on by telling them that you will be close by if they need you again.
- **If learning can be enhanced by a brief question or comment** – if you are standing close to children and hear a comment that makes you want to become involved, do not always assume that this is the wrong thing to do. Sometimes pupils will need some intervention to support what they are doing or to point out resources.
- **If a child or young person is not being included by others** – if you notice that a child or young person is 'on the edge' of an activity when they would clearly like to participate, it may be appropriate for you to ask others to involve them or talk with them about how they might do so.

Knowing when to leave children and young people to play or relax without interrupting them is important; they should have ownership of what they do during their free time and not feel that it is another area controlled by adults. In this way they will develop independence, confidence, and the ability to use their own initiative and imagination.

In practice

Carry out an observation of pupils on the playground or playing/carrying out a leisure activity in a small group. What do you notice about how they interact and organise themselves? Do they behave differently than when they are with adults? When, if at all, do they seek adult intervention? Do they need it?

AC 2.3 Identify adaptations that can be made to support children and young people with special educational needs and disabilities to participate in the full range of play and leisure opportunities provided

All pupils, including those with special educational needs and disabilities (SEND), should be able to participate in the full range of play and leisure activities offered by the setting. It is a legal requirement under the Equality Act 2010 that all pupils have equal access to provision and that settings make 'reasonable adjustment' to ensure that this is the case. Adults may need to make adaptations to different aspects of the setting to ensure that everyone is able to participate and that they are aware of the needs of all pupils. If you work in a special school you may be familiar with the types of adaptations that can be made.

The environment

Adults will need to ensure that all environments are accessible for pupils who have special educational needs and disabilities, and that there are no barriers to their participation. The Disability Discrimination Act came into effect in 1995 and changed the obligations of all organisations to ensure that they make 'reasonable adjustment' for disabled people and do not discriminate against them. This has had implications for the way in which they provide access to buildings and facilities through the provision of ramps, lifts, handrails and disabled toilets. It has been updated through the Disability Act 2005 and more recently the Equality Act 2010, so that adjustments have to be made to ensure the inclusion of all individuals in the environment. If you are working with pupils who have additional needs you should always check the environment to ensure that they have sufficient access to the activity or potential activity.

Activities

Adults will need to check access to activities to ensure that there are no barriers to the participation of pupils with SEND. As the term covers such a wide range of needs, this can be a challenging prospect. If a pupil who comes to the school or college has a type of special educational need that has not been accommodated before, the SENCo and teachers will need to find out about ways in which they can be supported to access the play and leisure activities, as well as ensuring that they can access the curriculum. The list in Table 16.1 gives some ideas but there will be other resources and forms of adaptation.

Research it

Find out more about the kinds of adaptations that can be made to support pupils in an area of your choice – musical, technological or sport. Share them with others through having a classroom discussion and make notes. You may then be able to use this as evidence for your portfolio.

Case study

Jack, 17, is autistic and finds break times at college difficult. He does not like loud noises or large groups of people so tries to avoid going into communal areas if he can. He finds it difficult to socialise with others and you often see him in the corridor just walking around.

1 What could you do to support Jack?
2 Describe what adaptations could be made by the college so that students with Jack's needs can enjoy their leisure time.

▼ Table 16.1 Adaptions that can be made to support children and young people with SEND

Type of activity	Potential barrier/adaptation required
Music	Adapted musical instruments, both for primary and secondary pupils, are available for pupils with SEND so that reduced mobility or manipulative skills do not prevent them from taking part. Alternatively, ICT software and resources are available to support the inclusion of pupils with different areas of need in both composing and playing music, and there is a wide range of musical technology available.
Technology	Specific equipment or adaptations may be needed to support the pupil's disability if they cannot use the equipment that is provided, for example, large keyboards and magnifiers for those with visual impairments, or specific software programs depending on pupils' needs.
Sport	This can be a challenging area for pupils with additional needs or disabilities, as it is one that is traditionally about competition and strong physical ability. Staff will need to be sensitive as this is an area in which all pupils should have the opportunity to develop their fitness and physical skills as well as their confidence. With some thought and careful planning, sporting activities, equipment and resources can also be adapted for pupils with SEND. The activities themselves may be adapted or changed so that the needs of pupils are met, for example, through changing the way in which a game is played, such as wheelchair cricket or netball with adjustable heights. Always start by thinking about what the pupil can do, so that this can be built on and developed.
Playground	Areas on the playground should be clearly defined and marked, such as those that are designated quiet, sensory or for sport, so that all pupils are aware of them and can be respectful of what others are doing. Some pupils with SEND may also need adult intervention to help them to integrate with others and to involve them in play.
Leisure activities outside the setting	Staff will need to check facilities available at the intended venue prior to the visit and make adaptations if needed. This is likely to include venues such as swimming pools and gyms.

Tips for best practice: understanding own role in relation to play and leisure

- Ensure there is a good mix of potential activities.
- Talk to pupils about health and safety.
- Involve children and young people in decisions about potential activities.
- Intervene only where necessary.
- Adapt activities for pupils who need it, to ensure equal access.
- Never 'take over' what pupils are doing.

Working practice

Staff will need to think about working practices that may potentially discriminate against pupils with SEND. For example, if a computer club is being run at lunchtimes but a pupil in a particular class or tutor group who wants to attend has to go for treatment on that day, the day may need to be changed. Staff will also need to be trained and awareness given in using particular equipment or resources for pupils that need to use them. Working practices may also need to be adapted depending on the pupil's needs – if they have speech, language or communication needs, for example, staff may need to encourage them to use different forms of communication and support others in doing so.

Resources

The type of equipment and materials that are available is also a consideration when working with children and young people who have special educational needs and disabilities. Specialist resources are available, for example, a range of multi-sensory resources exists for those who have sensory impairments.

To find out more, refer to Unit 14, which deals with understanding how to support children and young people with special educational needs and disabilities in the learning environment.

LO3 Understand how to balance risk and challenge with the benefits of the play and leisure opportunity

AC 3.1 Explain the value of risk and challenge in children and young people's play and leisure

Children and young people are naturally adventurous and are drawn to situations in which they can take **risks** and **challenges**. As adults, we are naturally protective of them and are anxious about their safety. However, we also need to step back and consider the value of both risk and challenge to their learning and development.

Remember, as outlined in Unit 2, a **hazard** is something in the environment that could cause harm, and a risk is the chance of someone being harmed by a hazard.

Risks are most valuable to children and young people if they are managed carefully rather than avoided. The idea that we can protect them from every knock and graze is neither practical nor desirable. There are risks everywhere – a toddler who is learning to stand up and walk or manage stairs will automatically fall and hurt themselves; a gymnast who is learning to use a balance beam will inevitably do the same. However, there is a value in taking the risk in order to achieve.

Key terms

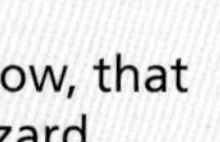

Risk: the chance, whether high or low, that someone could be harmed by a hazard.

Challenge: a challenge is something that requires the individual to undergo effort in order to achieve a goal.

Hazard: something in the environment that could cause harm.

Stretch and challenge

The examples given above are of physical risk. Find out about other types of risk. What is the significance of each? Which might you be most likely to take, and which are you most likely to see in children and young people?

Class discussion

Talk about the kinds of risks you have taken in your own life. These can be physical or to do with work or leisure. What might have happened if you had not taken them?

We have all heard of risk assessments, in which we are asked to consider the kinds of risks that are likely to occur, particularly when on school trips. Although these are valuable, they focus only on the risks and not on the benefits. Risk–benefit assessments (RBAs) have recently been developed that encourage those carrying them out to balance the risks with the benefits of the activity – in other words, how much children and young people would miss out if they did not take part.

Risk–benefit assessment

Location/Activity:		Date:	
Assessor:		Review date:	

Activity	What are the benefits?	What are the risks?	Who is at risk?	Precautions in place to reduce the risk	Overall level of risk
Pond dipping	The decking allows close access to pond contents and is an essential component of exploring this habitat.	Slippery pond decking or edges could lead to: • slips, trips and falls • cuts, grazes and abrasions • drowning.	Young people; adults	• The banks are shallow and planted to prevent accidental entry. • The pond edges are well-defined and clearly visible – free of dense or high foliage. • Dipping platform free of trip hazards, such as nets and trays. • The rules of pond use are clearly displayed and reviewed before each session.	Low
Tree swing	The swing allows users to engage with the natural environment, whilst participating in fun, physical play.	• Swing fitting fails due to wear and/or vandalism. • Damage to branch/ tree, may cause collapse. • Collision with obstacles/other people.	Young people; adults	• Regular inspection of swing for signs of wear. • Chain, cable and fitting of swing made of strong steel. • Pendulum seat discourages more than one user to use the swing at a given time. • The tree has been examined and considered fit for purpose by an expert.	Low

▲ Figure 16.5 Example of a risk–benefit assessment form

Challenges will also occur naturally as part of play and leisure activities. Challenges are valuable for children and young people as they give them the chance to extend their learning and see what they are capable of. Facing challenges will also develop their confidence and self-esteem, and encourage them to aim higher in their ambitions. Children and young people who are anxious about being unable to meet challenges may need encouragement from adults.

▼ Table 16.2 Benefits of challenge

Persistence	Through challenge, children and young people will learn to keep going even when things are difficult.
Resilience	Challenges enable children to develop resilience and to recover more quickly when things do not go as expected.
Thinking critically and developing strategies	Challenges enable individuals to use their ideas and initiative, and find different ways of managing their situation.

Activity

Look at the following and decide whether they are risks, challenges or both:

- allowing an 11 year old to catch a bus on their own
- a 17 year old learning to drive
- Year 1 children taking part in a three-legged race on sports day
- encouraging a Year 9 pupil to go higher on the ropes in the gym
- giving Year 2 pupils glue guns to use in design technology
- allowing a child to ride a bicycle on the road
- taking a group on a school residential trip to an outward bound centre.

AC 3.2 Describe why it is essential for children and young people to manage risk and challenge for themselves

Learning how to manage risk and face challenge is a valuable part of growing up and learning how to manage freedom. Play and leisure activities are a great opportunity for children and young people to develop their awareness of the kinds of risks that may arise spontaneously, and to challenge themselves to achieve greater things. Society has become risk averse in recent years, and children have suffered through being more and more protected against potential risks; this has disadvantaged them as they will not be able to judge risk for themselves.

Class discussion

'In 1971, eight out of ten children aged seven or eight years went to school on their own. By 1990 this figure had dropped to less than one in ten' (Gill, 2007).

- Why do you think this figure has changed so dramatically?
- What impact might this have on children and young people and their ability to manage risk for themselves?

▲ Figure 16.6 How much should adults decide on the kinds of activities that are suitable for children?

As children and young people are likely to be playing away from adults, they will need to learn to manage risk independently. When giving them play and leisure opportunities, you will need to balance the kinds of health and safety risks that may occur with the benefits of the activity, as well as thinking about the age of pupils and whether they will be aware of any risks.

When planning activities and environments for children and young people, however, there are some kinds of risks that adults should not allow children to decide for themselves as they may be placed in direct danger, for example:

- an environment or activity that is too hazardous for the children or young people to assess for themselves
- giving children and young people access to dangerous resources
- adults being unavailable for children and young people to seek support from if needed.

Challenges

Managing and setting challenges for themselves will be an area in which children and young people may need support. They may tend to avoid challenges, particularly if they are afraid of failing. Adults will need to point out the value of challenges and the importance of being able to learn from them so that they are not limited by their own anxieties.

Unit 2, LO3, page 25, has a section on risk and challenge.

Tips for best practice: managing risk and challenge

- Always check the environment first, particularly if it is outdoors or the children are young.
- Talk about safety regularly with pupils so that they develop more awareness of risk.
- Agree ground rules with pupils, depending on the activity, so that they think about them.
- Ensure that there is adequate supervision for the age of the children or young people.
- Set challenges that develop physical and intellectual skills.
- Encourage children and young people to try new things.

Check your understanding

1. Name three benefits of play for children and young people.
2. How do adult-directed activities differ from those that are initiated by children and young people?
3. Why is the UN Convention on the Rights of the Child relevant to play opportunities offered to children and young people?
4. How can adults support children and young people without taking over play and leisure activities?
5. Why is it important that children and young people have autonomy during play and leisure activities?
6. How might working practices need to be altered so that all pupils can participate in play and leisure activities?
7. Why should we encourage children and young people to take a balanced approach to risks?

Assessment preparation

As this is a knowledge-only unit, you will find that most of the evidence can be demonstrated by written work such as reflective accounts, assignments and observed professional discussions. Alternatively, you can use the suggestions below to gather evidence.

1. For LO1, write a play and leisure policy for your school or college. You will need to include an outline of the requirements of the UN Convention on the Rights of the Child. Describe the different play and leisure opportunities available at your setting and outline the benefits of each, saying how they contribute to children and young people's development. Make sure you distinguish between play and leisure and adult-led activities (AC 1.1, 1.2, 1.3).
2. For LO2, write a reflective account of your own role when supporting children and young people's play and leisure activities, and why it is important to know that they should play independently where possible. Include any adaptations you may have had to make to ensure the participation of all, or discuss why these may need to be made. Make sure you cover the environment, the activities, working practice and resources (AC 2.1, 2.2, 2.3).
3. For LO3, write an information sheet about the value of risk and challenge in childhood. Describe ways in which we can support children and young people in learning to manage risk and challenge for themselves, and say why it is important for them that we do this (AC 3.1, 3.2).

Legislation

Disability Discrimination Act 1995/2005 and Equality Act 2010 – these Acts ensure that all workplaces, organisations and educational establishments provide equal access to play and leisure activities for all pupils.

Read about it

Reference book

Gill, T. (2007) *No Fear – Growing Up in a Risk Averse Society*, Calouse Gilbenkian Foundation. Out of print but available online at: **https://timrgill.files.wordpress.com/2010/10/no-fear-19-12-07.pdf**.

Weblinks

A series of booklets were produced by the TDA in 2008/9 for PGCE students; these give examples of ways in which pupils with SEND can be included in different aspects of the curriculum as well as adaptations that can be made. There are separate booklets for primary and secondary pupils, and those relevant to play and leisure include:

Primary and Secondary Physical Education

Primary and Secondary Music

Primary and Secondary ICT

Primary and Secondary Art.

They are available at **http://dera.ioe.ac.uk/** under each subject area.

www.efds.co.uk English Federation of Disability Sport – inclusive sport

www.hse.gov.uk Health and Safety Executive – the booklet, *Children's Play and Leisure – Promoting a Balanced Approach*, is available for download here: **www.hse.gov.uk/entertainment/childrens-play-july-2012.pdf**

www.nasen.org.uk Nasen (National Association for Special Educational Needs)

www.playengland.org.uk and **www.learningaway.org.uk** Play England and Learning Away – risk–benefit assessment forms

www.playworks.org.uk PlayWorks – information about play

www.ukcoaching.org UK Coaching – inclusive sports coaching for pupils with SEND

www.unicef.org.uk UNICEF has a page devoted to the UN Convention on the Rights of the Child

www.youthsportstrust.org Youth Sports Trust

Glossary

Appraisal: a regular opportunity to reflect on your own progress and discuss it with your line manager.
Assessment for learning: a method through which information from assessment is used to raise the achievement of learners. Evidence from the ongoing assessment process will support teaching and learning in finding out what students know and what they need to do to improve.
Balanced approach: taking into account the age, needs and abilities of the child or young person, avoiding excessive risk taking while not being risk averse; recognising the importance of risk and challenge to a child or young person's overall development.
Behaviour that challenges: behaviour that conflicts with the accepted values and beliefs of the setting.
Behaviour, emotional and social development needs: these are sometimes referred to as BESD needs. A BESD need is the inability of a child or young person to manage their emotions effectively, to the extent that they will often show inappropriate behaviour when they are in situations that upset them.
Challenge: a challenge is something that requires the individual to undergo effort in order to achieve a goal.
Cognition and learning needs: needs of those learners who demonstrate features of moderate, severe or profound learning difficulties; specific learning difficulties, e.g. dyslexia, dyspraxia; autistic spectrum disorder.
Confidentiality: the importance of keeping information private.
Continuing professional development (CPD): this is the ongoing process by which individuals keep up to date with what is happening in their professional area.
Data protection: making sure that data is shared only with those who need to know it.
Development: advancement towards maturity.
Dialogic talk: using talk to clarify and explain ideas as part of the teaching and learning process.
Disclosure and Barring Service (DBS): all adults who work with children and young people will need to apply through this service, which will check their background and suitability to work with children.
Education, Health and Care (EHC) plan: a plan in England and Wales for a child or young person up to the age of 25 who has special educational needs or disabilities. It will take into account their educational, health and welfare needs, and will set out the additional support they will be given. It will be written and reviewed annually through the local authority.
English skills: reading, writing, speaking/talking and listening.
Forest School: the provision of learning opportunities in a woodland setting, which enables children and young people to learn through experiences in the natural environment.
Growth: the process of increasing in size.
Hazard: something in the environment that could cause harm.
Holistic: believing that the parts of something are interconnected and looking at the whole as well as the parts.
Home language: the language or languages that are spoken in the home environment.
Inclusion: the right for all children and young people to participate fully in the curriculum.
Long-term planning/schemes of work: this is usually planning for the year or for the duration of a college course.
Maths support: support given to pupils to help them meet the numeracy demands of the wider curriculum.
Medium-term planning: this will be planning for the term or half term and will usually be split into weeks.
Neural pathway: a developed path in the brain that is formed by repeated experiences.
Pattern of development: the sequence (order) and the rate (time frame) in which development occurs.
Policies and procedures: the principles, rules and guidelines agreed and adopted by the organisation.

Reflective practice: the process of thinking about and analysing what you do so that you can improve your professional practice.

Resilience: the ability to recover from difficulties.

Risk assessment: this is a check for potential hazards, which also looks at the risk of them happening so that measures may be put in place to control them.

Risk: the chance, whether high or low, that someone could be harmed by a hazard.

Safeguarding: action taken to promote the welfare of children and protect them from harm (NSPCC).

Sanctions: these set out the consequences of what will happen if the rules are broken.

Sensory and/or physical needs: learners who demonstrate degrees of hearing, visual and/or physical impairment.

Short term-planning: this will be detailed weekly or daily planning, which includes learning objectives and assessment.

Target language: the additional or second language needed by bilingual learners, i.e. English as an additional language.

Transition: a period of significant change or a significant event in a child or young person's life.

Whistleblower: a person who reveals any type of information within an organisation that may be illegal or unethical, or that should not be happening.

Index